D1528629

STUDIES IN COMMONWEALTH POLITICS AND HISTORY

No. 7

General Editors: Professor W. H. MORRIS-JONES
Institute of Commonwealth Studies
University of London

Professor DENNIS AUSTIN
Department of Government
University of Manchester

DECOLONISATION AND AFTER

About the Series

Legatee of a vast empire, the Commonwealth still carries the imprint of its past. And in doing so it may be said to have a collective identity which, in a very varying degree, each of its members exhibits. This, we believe, can sustain a collective inquiry into the political history and institutions of countries which were once governed within the British Empire and we note signs of a revival of interest in this field. In recent years 'area studies' have been encouraged, but there is also a sense in which the Commonwealth is itself a region, bounded not by geography but history, and imperial history in particular. Seen thus the region cannot exclude areas into which empire overspilled as in the Sudan, or areas now outside the Commonwealth such as South Africa and Burma, or the unique case of Ireland. No account of the dilemmas which face the government of Canada or Nigeria or India – or indeed of the United Kingdom – which examines the present in relation to the past can be complete which omits some consideration of this 'imperial dimension'. Without in any sense trying to claim that there is a 'political culture' common to all Commonwealth countries it is certainly the case that some of the institutions, some part of the political life, and a certain element in the political beliefs of many Commonwealth leaders, can be said to derive from the import of institutions, practices and beliefs from Britain into its former colonies.

Nor is the Commonwealth merely a useful category of study. It is also a community of scholars, many of them teaching and writing within the growing number of universities throughout the member countries who share an interest in the consequences of imperial experience and have common traditions of study.

The present series of books is intended to express that interest and those traditions. They are presented not as a guide to the Commonwealth as a corporate entity, but as studies either in the politics and recent history of its member states or of themes which are of common interest to several of the countries concerned. Within the Commonwealth there is great variety – of geographical setting, of cultural context, of economic development and social life: they provide the challenge to comparative study, while the elements of common experience make the task manageable. A cross-nation study of administrative reforms or of legislative behaviour is both facilitated and given added meaning; so also is an examination of the external relations of one or more member states; even a single country study, say on Guyana, is bound to throw light on problems which are echoed in Sri

Lanka and Jamaica. The series will bring together – and, we hope, stimulate – studies of those kinds carried out by both established and younger scholars. In doing so, it can make its distinctive contribution to an understanding of the changing contemporary world.

If it may be said that the Commonwealth is a peculiarly British creation, two qualifications have at once to be added. First, its emergence would scarcely have proved possible had it not been for the contributions of the other member states – initially the 'white Dominions', later the new states of South Asia. Their own stirrings of nationalist feeling coupled with their willingness to retain links pushed London towards a partnership relation in the management of which each had some share. Second, that collective leadership aspect of the Commonwealth assumed overwhelming predominance with the establishment in the 1960s of the Commonwealth Secretariat and the almost simultaneous disappearance in Whitehall of a separate and distinctive Commonwealth Relations Office.

This Commonwealth is the framework within which Britain has conducted both the delicate operation of decolonisation and a large part of her dealings with her former colonial territories. Other ex-imperial powers have found their own somewhat different instruments and frameworks for the same tasks. It should be instructive to place side by side the different experiences of European colonial powers in respect of this process of ending imperial links while still fashioning other ties to sustain ongoing connections. This exercise has not been extensively attempted but it is precisely what this particular book in our series sets out to do with respect to Britain and France.

Even though the papers contained here are not the result of scholars from the two countries actually having worked together, they are at least the outcome of each set seeking to explain their experience to the other. It may well be that the contrasts stand out more sharply than the similarities: the French lacked any equivalent of 'the white Dominions' as forerunners of decolonisation; the British seldom seem to have focussed as sharply as the French on the links of law and language; the French experience is, with the awesome exception of Indo-China, almost entirely African rather than global as with Britain; the process in Britain's case extends over decades, is untidy but mainly peaceful, and is produced by governments of different political parties, whereas in the case of France the stages begin late and in painful blood, only to be completed with despatch under de Gaulle's vision and drive.

Yet such different patterns – and others too when the process is viewed from the position of the ex-colonial peoples – cannot conceal the parallel purposes and character of the enterprise in both cases. No doubt it is too naive and too crude to speak of comparisons enabling each to learn lessons from the experience of the other. On the other hand it would be to claim too little to say merely that one only fully understands one's own experience when one hears about that of another. Probably each reader will find messages for himself somewhere between these maximum and minimum positions.

W. H. MORRIS-JONES
DENNIS AUSTIN

DECOLONISATION
AND AFTER

The British and French Experience

Edited by

W. H. Morris-Jones

Institute of Commonwealth Studies, University of London

and

Georges Fischer

Centre National de la Recherche Scientifique, Paris

FRANK CASS

First published 1980 in Great Britain by
FRANK CASS AND COMPANY LIMITED
Gainsborough House, Gainsborough Road,
London, E11 1RS, England

and in the United States of America by
FRANK CASS AND COMPANY LIMITED
c/o Biblio Distribution Centre
81 Adams Drive, P.O. Box 327, Totowa, N.J. 07511

British Library Cataloguing in Publication Data

Independence and Dependence (*Conference*),
  Paris, 1976
  Decolonisation and after – (Studies in
  Commonwealth politics and history; no. 7).
  1. France – Colonies – Congresses
  2. Great Britain – Colonies – Congresses
  I. Title   II. Morris-Jones, Wyndraeth Humphreys
  III. Fischer, Georges   IV. Series
  909'.09'71244082   JV1818

ISBN 0-7146-3095-0

Typeset by Computacomp (UK) Ltd, Fort William, Scotland

Reproduced from copy supplied
printed and bound in Great Britain
by Billing and Sons Limited
Guildford, London, Oxford, Worcester

Contents

III INSTITUTIONS AND CULTURES

IV INTERNATIONAL RELATIONS

Notes on Contributors

D. G. Austin Professor of Government at the University of Manchester. His recent books include *Malta and the End of Empire* (1971); *Ghana Observed* (1976); *Politics in Africa* (1978).

Anthony Clayton Deputy Head, Political and Social Studies Department, Royal Military Academy, Sandhurst; joint author with Donald Savage of *Government and Labour in Kenya 1895–1963* (1974).

John D. Hargreaves Professor of History in the University of Aberdeen. His most recent books are *West Africa Partitioned* (1974), the first volume of a continuing study, and *The End of Colonial Rule; Essays in Contemporary History*.

Michael Lipton Professorial Fellow in Economics at the Institute of Development Studies, Sussex University. Recent work includes *The Erosion of a Relationship: Measuring Indo-British Relations since 1960* (jointly with John Firn) for the Royal Institute of International Affairs (1975); *Why Poor People Stay Poor: Urban Bias and World Development*, (1977) and a two-volume *Report to the Government of Botswana on Employment, Self-Employment and Labour Use* (1978).

Rita Cruise O'Brien Fellow at the Institute of Development Studies, University of Sussex. Her publications include *White Society in Black Africa: The French of Senegal* (1972). She has edited a special number of *Tarikh* (Nigeria) on 'Whites in Africa' (1979) and *The Political Economy of Underdevelopment: Dependence in Senegal* (1979).

S. K. Panter-Brick Senior Lecturer at London School of Economics specialising in African politics. Editor of *Nigerian Politics and Military Rule* (1971) and *Soldiers & Oil: the Political Transformation of Nigeria* (1978).

R. E. Robinson Beit Professor of History of British Commonwealth, Balliol College, Oxford. Author of

ix

'Imperial Problems in British Politics, 1880–1895' in *Cambridge History of the British Empire*, Vol III, Ch. V. and 'The Partition of Africa' in *New Cambridge Modern History* Vol. XI, Ch. XXII (1962); and, with Jack Gallagher, of 'The Imperialism of Free Trade', *Economic History Review* 2nd ed. Vol. VI, no. 1 (1953) and *Africa and the Victorians* (1961).

G. D. de Bernis Professeur à l'Université de Sciences Sociales de Grenoble, auteur notamment de *Relations économiques internationales* (avec M. Bye), Paris, 1977.

Guy Caire Professeur de sciences économiques à L'Université de Paris X Nanterre, auteur notamment des ouvrages *Les syndicats ouvriers*, Paris, 1971, *La grève ouvrière*, Paris, 1978.

J.-L. Miège Professeur à l'Université de Provence (Aix-en-Provence), Directeur de l'Institut d'Histoire des pays d'Outre-mer, de l'Institut de Recherches méditerranéennes, membre de l'Académie des Sciences d'Outre-mer. Ouvrages sur le *Maroc et l'Europe*, 4 vol. Paris 1961–1963; *Expansion européenne et décolonisation, de 1870 à nos jours*, 1973.

Jean Poirier Professeur à l'Université de Nice, membre de l'Académie des Sciences d'Outre-Mer, auteur de l'*Ethnologie générale* (1968) et de l'*Ethnologie régionale* (1972, 1978), Encyclopédie de la Pléiade, Paris.

Jean Touscoz Professeur à l'Université de Nice et président de cette Université, auteur notamment de *La Coopération scientifique internationale*, Paris, 1973.

Eugène Schaeffer Ancien professeur à la Faculté de Droit de Dakar, professeur à l'Université René Descartes de Paris, directeur de l'Institut des Sciences juridiques du développement, auteur notamment de 'Réflexions sur le droit du développement', *Recueil Penant*, 1974, no. 745.

Christine Souriau Centre de Recherches et d'Etudes sur les Sociétés méditerranéennes, Aix-en-Provence. Chargée de recherche au Centre national de la Recherche Scientifique.

Auteur de *La Presse Maghrébine*, Libye, Tunisie, Maroc, Algérie. Paris, CNRS, 1969 et 1975.

Marie-Claude Smouts Maître de conférences à l'Institut d'Etudes Politiques de Paris, chargée de recherche au Centre national de la Recherche Scientifique et au Centre d'études et de recherches internationales (Fondation nationale des sciences politiques), auteur de *Le Secrétaire général des Nations Unies*, Paris, 1971.

J.-C. Vatin Centre de Recherches et d'Etudes sur les Sociétés Méditerranéennes, Aix-en-Provence. Chargé de recherche au Centre national de la Recherche Scientifique. Auteur de *L'Algérie politique. Histoire et Société*, Paris, 1974.

The French papers were translated by Catherine Cook and W. H. Morris-Jones.

Introduction

This book is the first product of bringing together British and French scholars for the purpose of comparing their countries' experiences in the processes of decolonisation and continuing relations with their former colonial territories.

The idea of organising a colloquium to open up this field of comparative study was first put forward in January 1973 at a meeting held to set up an Association for Franco-British Political Studies. Following discussions between the present editors, it was agreed that the field was one which eminently lent itself to comparative study and that much benefit could come from a joint discussion in which information and ideas about the two experiences could be exchanged. Each editor was responsible for organising a team of some twenty scholars from his own country and the bilingual colloquium took place in Paris from 6–8 May 1976. We are happy to acknowledge that the venture was made possible by financial assistance from the Social Science Research Council and the Centre National de la Recherche Scientifique and by administrative support from the Institute of Commonwealth Studies, University of London, and the Centre d'Etudes et de Recherches Internationales of the Fondation Nationale des Sciences Politiques.

The colloquium was given the title 'Independence and Dependence' and the aspirations of the organisers can be indicated by a few passages from the preparatory notes addressed to participants:

1. The central focus of the colloquium will be on the relations since the transfer of power between Britain and France on the one hand and their former imperial/colonial territories on the other. The task to be undertaken is the description and analysis of the elements of dependence and independence in this post-colonial situation. But the focus on post-independence does not entail the exclusion of historical perspective, nor even its relegation to the background. On the contrary, all papers may usefully ask how far present relations derive from features of the terminal stages of

xiii

colonial rule and of the transfer of power and some papers may be devoted to these features.

2. The primary purpose of the colloquium is to begin a process of systematic comparison of the two experiences. The colloquium itself will serve to familiarise selected scholars with each others' concerns and attitudes, as well as with the nature of work in progress, and by means of publication this knowledge will be made available to a wider audience. But it is an integral part of this purpose that we should seek deliberately to identify areas on which joint or at least parallel Anglo-French research is called for. Participants should therefore be invited to give thought to this aspect and a session should be set aside during the colloquium for explicit discussion of possible work plans for the future.

3 Papers should address themselves to themes but it is recognised that illustrative material will tend to be drawn from particular areas. It is hoped that no important regions will be omitted from consideration and that comparisons between areas will be encouraged. Our discussions will also be inter-disciplinary and contributions will be provided by historians, economists, political scientists, lawyers and sociologists. While papers from each country will mostly be concerned with that country's experience, all papers will, where possible, suggest points of comparison.

4. Papers should avoid excessive emphasis on accounts of formal constitutional mechanisms, our interest being in the exploration of all relations of power and influence. No doctrinal uniformity is sought; indeed an effort will be made to secure the representation among both British and French of a reasonably wide range of different standpoints. Papers should present either fresh research findings (wherever we are able to tap recently completed or on-going inquiries) or fresh re-appraisal surveys of a more general kind. Some papers may successfully combine both, as specific research suggests general views or as general surveys may be centred on particular case-studies.

5. The following list may serve as a tentative guide to the subjects which should be treated in our discussions:
   (a) the nature of colonial relations and the relevance of these to post-independence relations;
   (b) the transfer (whether deliberate or accidental, desired or endured) of metropolitan models over the whole range of institutions and practices — social, political, administrative, educational, cultural — as well as the local response;

(c) the ideas of metropolitan political organisations on the proper relations with former colonies and their own relations with political bodies in the new states;

(d) economic and financial relations including questions of trade, investment, aid, monetary zones, migration;

(e) relations within the groups of the former empires – Commonwealth and Union Française/Communauté/ Francophonie – and the influence on such relations of international groupings such as EEC, UN and Third World countries.

6. One may also indicate the intended scope of our discussions by suggesting in relation to these subjects the kinds of problems and questions to which we should give our attention:

(a) *Assumptions, Expectations and Plans*

How did the colonial power and the local successor elites conceive of future relations? How far were there assessments, plans and preparations among politicians, officials, business and other interests? How did these change through the phases of decolonisation? What sentiments and which calculations were operative? How did they vary from one territory to another according to the particular histories of colonial rule and the circumstances of power transfer?

(b) *Deposits, Links and Networks*

What strands of wire make up the 'cables' which now connect former power and former colonial territory? Which way does the 'current' run? Where have the initiatives come from? What trends – erosion, reinforcement, rejection, etc. – are evident? Which sections of the two sides are the chief beneficiaries? How far have the connections aided or hindered the ex-imperial country's readjustments? How far are the connections helpful, damaging or merely irrelevant to the development of the new states? Which are the decisive strands – trade, aid, migration, education, armed forces, bureaucracies, professions, etc? What factors – ideology, power and size (of the new state), local interests, etc. – most influence the connections?

(c) *Institutions of Linkage*

What is the nature and relative importance of bilateral arrangements and generalised Commonwealth-style frameworks? How do these affect each other? Also how do inter-governmental connections relate to the connections of private enterprise and of non-official associations and 'fraternities'?

(d) *The International Context*

How do all these connections fit into the totality of external relations of both ex-imperial country and new state? How important are the connections as compared with regional or international organisations including both the UN and multinational corporations?

The colloquium was in our view a success in that both teams learnt a great deal from each other as to the main concerns, approaches and methods of work in this field. The quality of the papers presented was remarkably high and their authors deserve our thanks. Unfortunately, in their entirety they would fill two or more volumes; we have accordingly had to undertake the unenviable task of making a selection. We believe that we have been able to include the papers whose topics and treatments suggest the more interesting comparisons and whose publication may therefore stimulate parallel or even collaborative research.

While there are several ways of categorising the papers, it is obvious that they can be so grouped as to reflect some of the basic divisions of the field which were originally envisaged. One group contains those (Austin, Hargreaves, Miège, Robinson) which deal with the late colonial period leading up to the actual achievement of independence and bring out some of the features of relations between imperial rulers and emerging local elites which need to be grasped if post-independence connections are to be understood. Another group examines some of the whole range of bilateral relations after independence. This entails looking at sectional interests in new states (O'Brien compares two cases), examining changes in economic (de Bernis, Lipton) and military (Clayton) connections, the interactions in the field of ideology (Caire, Poirier-Touscoz), of language and culture (Souriau and, in part, Panter-Brick) and of institutional development (Schaeffer, Vatin). A third group focuses on some of the international relations settings in which the links of ex-colonialism take on new forms (Panter-Brick, Smouts).

The picture which emerges from these papers – and perhaps even more from the total set of papers presented and the discussions which took place – prompts a variety of observations on each country's preoccupations, the extent to which there is common ground but contrasting experience and thus different emphases. Only in two papers presented here (Panter-Brick and

O'Brien) do scholars of one country study the experience of the
other; this is no adequate indication of the scope that exists for
learning from comparative work. The task which has been
opened up by the colloquium is one which deserves to be
continued – probably by more focused studies on particular topics
and by smaller groups of participants from both sides. At the
same time such studies might usefully be in another sense
broadened – to include other metropolitan countries and, perhaps
above all, to include scholars from the relevant new states
themselves. In that way we may hope, as former metropoles and
ex-colonies alike, to understand better our places in the changed
and changing world, to furnish an answer to the question posed
by John Ruskin on hearing of the inauguration of the telegraph
link between Britain and India: 'Yes, but what is the message?'

W. H. MORRIS-JONES
GEORGES FISCHER

I

TRANSFER OF POWER

1

The Transfer of Power: Why and How

Dennis Austin

Part A Theory

A preliminary caution:

> 'Contemporary history embarrasses a writer not only because he knows too much, but also because what he knows is too undigested, too unconnected, too atomic. It is only after close and prolonged reflection that we begin to see what was essential and what was important, to see why things happened as they did, and to write history instead of newspapers.'[1]

The question I propose to raise is:
Was the transfer of power from Britain to its dependent territories idiosyncratic in relation to the end of other European empires?

There are two clusters of argument which can be set out by way of contrast.

I FIRST HYPOTHESIS

'That the United Kingdom *was* politically distinct both in its view of empire and in the mode of its withdrawal from colonial rule.' (1) The British gave unusual emphasis to the local autonomy of the colonial unit.[2] The British Empire was non-integrative: hence the perversity very often of its nomenclature, as in the description – a 'self-governing Colony'. Such exceptions as may be found

3

tend to prove the point: the British could never, for example, make up their minds whether Ireland was a colony and should be 'given self-government' (like, say, Newfoundland) or part of the United Kingdom home territory and, therefore, to be represented at Westminster. The very brief excursion into schemes of integration between Britain and Malta in 1955 was quickly abandoned: there was to be no *L'Angleterre d'Outre-mer.*

(2) From an early point in the 20th century the British had always to reckon with the effect (however delayed) which Dominion self-government had on the articulation of demands for reform in the non-European territories, most notably in India, and therefore in the colonial empire.

(3) The British were distinct in their efforts to convince themselves that decolonisation was a *lawful* pursuit, and distinct in their attempt to persuade colonial-nationalist leaders that such a goal (however distant) could be attained peacefully by institutional reforms: primarily by changing the balance of representation on the legislative and executive councils, by extending the franchise and by 'localising' the public service.[3]

(4) The process of decolonisation was also unusual in having as its avowed end the continuation of the imperial relationship by other means, through membership of the Commonwealth. Moreover, the prize of Dominion status was not only held out by Britain; it was invariably part of the 'demand for self-government' formulated by nationalist leaders. One must also recall that the growth of the Commonwealth preceded and paralleled the demise of empire: it was not cobbled together to meet the exigencies of independence, but had an evolution of its own, prior to the main era of decolonisation in the 'third world'.

(5) The devolution of power within one British colony after another has therefore to be traced over a much longer time span than is generally acknowledged, certainly much longer than its European counterpart. For example, the introduction of a form of cabinet government in the Gold Coast in 1950 looks back to the grant of responsible government in Ceylon in 1931, and to earlier reforms in the 1920s. Similarly, the preamble to the Defence and External Affairs Agreements between Ceylon and the United Kingdom echoed earlier phrases concerning the 'white Dominions':

> Whereas Ceylon has reached the stage in constitutional development at which she is ready to assume the status of a fully responsible member of the British Commonwealth of Nations, in no way subordinate in any aspect of domestic or external affairs, freely associated and united by a common allegiance to the Crown ...

It was, remarked Lord Addison, 'the first occasion in which a colony developing this system of self-government of its own accord, has deliberately sought to become a Dominion state in our Commonwealth ... but we hope and expect that it will not be the last.'[4] Indeed it is hardly possible to find a time when the slow process of devolution involving 'some measure of advance towards self-government' was not at work *somewhere* in the old settled colonies of Canada and Australia, or in Asia, Africa, the Mediterranean, the Pacific and Caribbean. There were times (admittedly) when the process was reversed (e.g. in Malta in 1903, 1933 and 1958, in British Guiana in 1953, even in Newfoundland in 1931) but the general movement was towards self-government. (6) Such phrases as 'a measure of advance towards self-government' or 'investing [the unofficial members of the legislature] with a substantial measure of responsibility' were very illustrative.[5] They were cautious, singular, and hedged about. There were no colonial-wide reforms: no *loi cadre*, no 'imperial referendum'. Even the little islands of the Caribbean moved uneasily each at its own pace into independence.[6] Even the linked territories of East Africa attained self-government at different times. Nevertheless, the overall direction, however uneven the pace in particular colonies, was unmistakable.
(7) Throughout the process of decolonisation, control was maintained. Only in the traumatic but relatively minor instances of Palestine and Aden did the 'transfer of power' become a precipitate retreat: a 'finale with chaos'.[7] Even in India, accumulative measures of devolution accompanied the rise in agitation: the story of the emergence of the two new Dominions in 1947 is quite unlike that told by Professor Baudet in his account of 'The Dutch Retreat from Empire'.[8]

II ANTITHESIS

Whatever the theory, for which these general observations may have some validity, it was so heavily curtailed by practice (as one might suspect it would be in a British context) as to remove much of the distinction. Like their European counterparts, it can be argued, the British quite underestimated the cumulative force of nationalist sentiment in the colonial world. They also set limits, of time and description, to the translation into effect of the 'progress towards self-government' as very often to nullify the process. For example:

(1) Certain colonies were excluded, until events forced a change, from the possibility of independence. They were (a) the 'fortress colonies' for which defence requirements of an imperial kind made self-government unreal. As late as 1958, Lennox Boyd dismissed the possibility of full independence for Malta as 'quite unrealistic', recalling Churchill's phrase that the introduction of political reform for the islands was like 'trying to devise a constitution for a battleship'. In July 1954 Henry Hopkinson had declared that Cyprus would 'never' become a sovereign state.[9] Yet Cyprus was independent in August 1960, Malta in 1964. (b) Other colonies were held to be too small or too poor or too vulnerable to move beyond the stage of some limited measure of internal self-rule as in the grant of semi-responsible government in Jamaica in 1944 and the extension of the suffrage in Barbados in 1946. 'In the case of the smaller territories there can, a priori, be no question of journey towards sovereign government,'[10] if only because in the dangerous 1930s world of the dictators, and of economic depression, there seemed little place for the small and would-be sovereign state. (c) A few colonies had (and still have today?) to be seen as continuing to remain dependent by force of circumstance: Hong Kong, Gibraltar, British Honduras, Falklands. (d) Plural societies of white settlers and divided African communities were held, understandably, to be very difficult. 'I am unable to envisage a time', Mr. Lennox Boyd announced in the House of Commons, 'when it will be possible for any British Government to surrender their ultimate responsibilities for the destinies and well being of Kenya',[11] a view noted by the Monckton Commission the following year: 'Conditions in West Africa were thought to have little relevance for the multi-racial countries of the Eastern and Central portions of the continent'.[12]

(2) Assessment of the time available for the movement towards self-government even for colonies which might be thought candidates for independence within the Commonwealth was

often grotesquely unreal, as in the general declaration by Malcolm Macdonald in the House of Commons in 1939:[13]

The great purpose of the British Empire is the gradual spread of freedom among all His Majesty's subjects in whatever part of the world they live. That spread of freedom is a slow, evolutionary process. In some countries, it is more rapid than others. In some parts of the Empire, in the Dominions, that evolutionary process has been completed, it is finished. In some colonies like Ceylon the gaining of freedom has gone very far. In others it is necessarily a much slower process. It may take generations, or even centuries, for the peoples in some parts of the Colonial Empire to achieve self-government. But it is a major part of our policy, even among the backward peoples of Africa, to teach them and encourage them always to be able to stand a little more on their own feet.

(3) It is not easy, therefore, to find the notional colony as the exemplar of a perceptive view of decolonisation in general. The usual answer given is that of Ceylon. But against the range of examples of the transfer of power in other colonies, Sri Lanka begins to stand out as more special than general. That, of course, there were local reforms to ease the position of the Governor, or to assuage the temper of protonational groups, is undeniable, and such measures often gathered momentum, *suo proprio motu*, to feed the appetite they encouraged. But in this respect was 'British decolonisation' as it reached the point of independence very different from the enforced reaction to a pattern of demands which characterised the 'third world' as a whole, whether under British or French or Belgian or Dutch rule?

(4) And here surely is the critical aspect of the retreat of Europe from the colonial world. 'Enforced' is surely the right word – enforced by pressure from the two new powers (both hostile to European colonialism, each in its own way), enforced by the coercive costs of attempts to combat Asian or African or local nationalisms of one kind and another, enforced above all and most simply by a turning away from the classic form of colonialism both on the part of the metropolitan country and its subject territories. And there may be more fundamental reasons still. Imperialism is order. Yet by the end of the first world war much of the world had grown weary of an imposed order. Can we not say that, even at the height of the British empire, at its fullest extent in the aftermath of that war, there was doubt at the

centre about the validity of a traditional order, a doubt most visible (as is always the case) in painting, in music and in literature? There was no 20th century poet, no novelist, no artist inspired by the heroic, or the glory of empire. On the contrary: there was the attack on established forms by Cézanne, Picasso, Eliot, Joyce, Anton Berg and the extremes of Surrealism, Dada and Expressionism. Certainly in England there was an intellectual anti-imperialism, despite the paternalism of the early Fabians, which boded ill for any upholding of empire. We may also add that, despite all the protestations of mutual esteem at numerous independence celebrations, there were the beginnings of a strong undercurrent of cultural and racist resentment on the side of the colonised in respect of the history of the colonial past.

III SYNTHESIS?

Taking heed of our preliminary warning, it is clear that there is unlikely to be any conceptual finality about explanations of the disappearance of so large a phenomenon as the British (and other) empires. If Gibbon, writing fourteen centuries after the event, was unable to find a single explanation of the fall of Rome, much lesser historians, writing so close the end of British rule, are unlikely to be successful in advancing a wholly satisfactory answer to why it should have occurred.

Both sets of arguments were simply hypotheses advanced to satisfy the question raised initially, although one further observation is perhaps worth making, that although the exercise of colonial rule in each British colony was peculiarly self-contained, the reaction to colonial rule was very often far from that. British colonial governments may have thought, and may have been right to think, that they were dealing with singular and particular problems of control, but the growth of an anti-colonial reaction to European rule was very much an inter-related movement.[14]

But can we produce some kind of 'synthesis of explanations' why it was that British rule over its colonial territories came to an end? The simplest resolution would be to take refuge under the general observation by Gibbon that 'the stupendous fabric yielded to the pressure of its own weight', and there is surely a good deal of truth in it in relation to the British Empire: that, in the end, it was simply too complicated and onerous to sustain. But to that we can add:

(1) If the British were overtaken by events, or swept along by those events, they were usually compelled forward while travelling in the same direction. The effect was to push them more quickly along, and in some instances much farther than they had contemplated going. By the early 1960s the pace of decolonisation had increased quite beyond earlier expectations and in a manner wholly unthinkable in the pre-1939 context of Ceylon or the immediate post-war years in West Africa when even indirect rule was still not fully out of vogue. There are many key phrases we can use to illustrate the point. One may suffice. 'If', said Lennox Boyd in November 1958, 'we had a hundred years of steady progress in which to bring all our colonial territories to maturity their independence would cause no misgiving but we are now working in terms of a decade or so.'[15] That quickening of pace brought the United Kingdom into line with their European contemporaries who had quite abruptly changed direction in order to act precipitately. The most remarkable example was the reversal of policy in the Belgian Congo, Ruanda and Burundi. More difficult is to assess the several changes in French attitudes. The first resolution of the conference at Brazzaville in 1944, at which there were no African representatives, noted that:

> The aims of the civilising labours of France in the colonies exclude all possibilities of development outside of the French imperial system; the eventual formation even in the distant future of 'self-governments' in the colonies must be dismissed.[16]

The empire was to be conducted 'in the Roman not the Anglo-Saxon sense'.[17] Defeated in Indo-China in 1954, the French hesitated after 1956 in their application of the *loi cadre* of June that year, and took decisive steps towards independence for Algeria, and *l'Afrique noire* and Madagascar, only after the referendum of 1958 and the Evian agreements of 1962. So at least we are told by de Gaulle.[18]

(2) Some of the assertions in the second hypothesis need to be treated cautiously. There is a neat assumption, often popularly made, that 'the decline of British power' was politically demonstrated by the Suez failure in 1956, and that its consequences may causally be linked with the withdrawal from

colonial rule. Reinforcing factors are added, back to 1942 and the fall of Singapore, forward to the decision to pull back from 'east of Suez' in 1967. It *is* a neat assumption. The empire is ruled by the sword which has to remain sheathed since, once drawn, the weight becomes too heavy for the sword bearer: he grows weary of it. It is the theme of de Gaulle's explanation of the French withdrawal:

> The relative weakening of England and France, the defeat of Italy and the subordination of Holland and Belgium to the designs of the United States; the effect produced on the Asians and Africans by the battles fought on their soil for which the colonisers had needed their support; the dissemination of doctrines which, whether liberal or socialist, equally demanded the emancipation of races and of individuals; and the wave of envious longing aroused among these deprived masses by the spectacle of the modern economy – as a result of all these factors the world was faced with an upheaval as profound, though in the opposite direction, as that which has unleashed the discoveries and conquests of the powers of old Europe.[19]

Yet there is something both old-fashioned and unreal about such an argument. If it is simply saying that once the costs of coercion became too high, no British government, under the scrutiny of Parliament and the Treasury, was prepared to go on paying the cost, then the argument is irrefutable, although very often the 'cost' was calculated in moral as much as in financial terms. But that is a story as old as the Boer war, and it is perhaps implicit in the notion of a trading empire. But one can also be surprised how long successive British governments, Labour and Conservative alike, went on bearing the financial cost of defence bases overseas, or of local engagements such as the defence of Malaysia in the mid-'60s, as well as of the earlier suppression of a communist insurgency in Malaya itself. The belief that British had global responsibilities as a Great Power died very hard and very late. It could be heard for example, still boldly proclaimed, as late as 1964 in Mr. Wilson's first speech as prime minister.[20]

(3) One must also treat cautiously arguments which, in a sense, interpret history in reverse. Since, it is sometimes said, nothing was of great interest in the acquisition of empire when compared with the glittering prize of India, the transfer of power to India also opened the way to a total abandonment. 'August 1947 demonstrated that British governments of whatever political

complexion could dispose of the remaining imperial possessions as soon as they wished. The politicians were not slow to dismantle the "imperial museum".'[21] Well, perhaps: the effect of India's independence must certainly be there; but it would not, I suspect, be easy to trace in Colonial Office thinking or the attitudes of Governors in the immediate post-war years unless, indeed, it was to tighten security and strengthen the authority of the local governments.

Perhaps, therefore, we may tentatively bring together both hypotheses by concluding that it *was* a peculiar and distinctive feature of British colonial rule to have always contemplated its end: the colonial governments went (we might romantically say) consentingly to their fate, but they had also to be pushed in that direction and they were pushed primarily (as I shall try to show) by local events within the colonial territories which obliged the Colonial Office and local colonial governments alike to introduce reforms at a pace which, in the post-war years, began to quicken beyond all earlier calculations. It was as if the British began to walk in a certain direction (having already undertaken the journey in respect of their former self-governing colonies), and constantly announced their intention of continuing to do so, but had then to be prodded forward until the final stages, when at last the attractions of the final destination became overwhelming. Then they ran to that distant wicket gate of self-government, divesting themselves as they went of almost the last rock and atoll.[22]

Part B How was it done?

Woven into such arguments is a constant thread of a different kind, more fact perhaps than fiction, namely not the 'why' of decolonisation but the 'how'. 'How' became very important, since to be assured of how to move forward towards independence often disposed the Governor of a colony and the Secretary of State in London to move confidently in that direction: practice not only shaped decisions by precedent but brought the practice into consciousness as deliberate policy.

In what follows, I have omitted direct consideration of the nationalist side to the story – of protests, riots, hartals, boycotts, assassinations, guerilla action – all of which have to be held in mind as the background (and sometimes the foreground) of action taken by the British.

1. *The redistribution of diarchical power*

In theory, as we have seen, colonies were expected to develop through institutions of a representative nature – 'We are pledged to guide the colonial peoples along the road to self-government within the framework of the British Empire', as the Secretary of State for the Colonies observed in the House of Commons in 1942.[23] Colony was to follow colony 'through the traditional gateway of responsible parliamentary government'.[24] The instrument of political institutionalisation (if we may use such a phrase) was to be the local colonial legislative council and its changing balance of power not only between colonial officials and local 'unofficials' (at first nominated and then selected) but between the colony and the United Kingdom. It was a theory very much of the inter-war years, and it beguiled many observers. 'The whole process of constitutional development', wrote Martin Wight, 'from the fullest double subordination up to responsible government and independent status is by now, after a hundred years of experiment, fairly well defined ... Every dependency, with insignificant exceptions, is in one or other of the stages; and it has become the modern theory of the Empire that in course of time every dependency will have passed through every stage and arrived at self-government'.[25] The examples were legion, carefully plotted by Martin Wight, and I cannot think of any colony, other perhaps than Hong Kong, which did not experience such changes. Very often it had unexpected results, as in the Gold Coast where the coincidence of an extension of the suffrage and an enlargement of the legislative council brought into office a quite novel group of nationalist leaders. But such devices could also be extraordinarily complicated as, say, in Kenya or Northern Rhodesia when weighted franchises, two-tiered electorates, communal electorates and Specially Elected Members were used to try and bridge the gap between a colonial-dominated and a nationalist-party assembly. In theory again, such notions of preparation envisaged an organic growth; in practice, and in the eyes of distrustful nationalists, they appeared as tactics of delay. Sadly, too, one must note that the great 'gateway of parliamentary responsible government' was very often simply the triumphal arch put up for the independence celebrations. Nevertheless, the tilting of power and responsibility within a legislative framework of control provided a useful semblance of an orderly transfer of power, democratically achieved through the ballot box, which contented colonial and nationalist rulers alike.

2. 'Governor's initiative'

At first sight, one might think the phrase signified a degree of self deception since very often a colonial Governor who 'seized the initiative' found that he had become caught in a net of his own devising. In the 1940s and '50s however, the phenomenon had grown familiar. The Governor was by then very often the man in the middle of a see-saw which was becoming unbalanced between imperial interests, which he was told by London to defend, and local interests which he was under signed instructions to advance. Meanwhile, there was pressure for reform from nationalist, or proto-nationalist, groups within the colony. 'Seizing the initiative' was therefore a hopeful way of adjusting the balance of these competing interests, although the adjustment invariably set in motion the demand and need for further reforms.

> The most important thing is to take and to hold the initiative. That is another way of saying the timing is all important. Not to allow frustration to set. Not to allow opposition to bank up. ...

Such, said Hugh Foot, was 'the essence of my experience whether in Asia or Africa or the West Indies'.[26] Examples abound in various colonial territories whereby the Governor was urged forward by a Commission of Inquiry, or because he thought he had to escape from a critically exposed position, or from a perceptive view of the nationalist pressures which were building up. It was true in a most urgent fashion of Mountbatten's rule in Delhi, and of Sir Hubert Rance's final months in Burma. The effect can also be seen at an earlier stage in Sir Andrew Caldecott's famous reforms despatch of 1938 from Ceylon, and on Sir Charles Arden Clarke's governorship in the Gold Coast in 1950:

> There is no doubt that there is a powerful body of opinion in the

highest quarters here [in London] who think that I am going too far
and too fast but as no-one has been able to put forward an alternative
working policy that has the remotest prospect of working I am being
allowed to have my own way.[27]

Again, there is Hugh Foot's later comment, showing not only
the attempt by a colonial government to retain control but to
ward off the misfortune of a riot or agitation, or the very
unpleasant consequences of a 'question in parliament', and a
visiting Commission of Inquiry:

> Not long after [Sir John Macpherson's] arrival we had a vital
> conference in Government House. The Richards constitution had then
> been in full effect for little more than a year and it had been stipulated
> that it must remain in force unchanged for nine years. We reviewed
> the whole political situation; we took into account the disorders and
> changes which had recently taken place in what was then the Gold
> Coast. We came to the conclusion that we must at once take a new
> initiative.[28]

3. *Conference Therapy*

A conspicuous feature of the 1960s when a note of urgency began
to be sounded in proclamations by colonial governments and in
demands by nationalist leaders of the need to arrive at a peaceful
transfer of power. But of course the conference as a brokerage
mechanism between colonial and imperial interests has a long
ancestry which is by no means of British origins. Still, the British
have been addicted to committees and conferences: colonial
conferences from 1887 onwards, special conferences and
committees to argue out Commonwealth problems in 1926 and
1930, Round Table conferences for India, colonial Governors'
conferences in London, regular meetings of Governors in West
Africa under a war-time Resident Minister and in East Africa
under the chairmanship of the Governor of Kenya, conferences to
examine schemes of closer regional union as at Montego Bay in
Jamaica, and the series of conferences in Marlborough House and
Lancaster House in London which brought agreement on the
distribution of power and the allocation of revenues for Nigeria,
Uganda, Nyasaland, Northern Rhodesia, Kenya and others. If it is
not too unfair, one might draw a distinction between the Dutch
and British experience of such meetings:

Generally speaking, the Netherlands encountered their opponent in the full armour of Dutch national peculiarity – paternalism, faith in discussion, constitutionalism, perfectionism, a juridical way of thinking probably characteristic of a nation of traders. The Indonesians countered this with ease. Moreover, as time went on, it became clearer and clearer that the failure of negotiations was more to their advantage than success. In May 1951 Sjahrir stated to Mr. Mitchener of the *New York Herald Tribune*: 'I would have accomplished little if the Dutch had not sent some of the most stupid, aloof and arrogant men I have ever known. We kept our mouths shut and let the Dutch talk. They argued themselves to death.'[29]

That is not the impression one has of the gatherings chaired by Butler or Macleod of whom it might be said that they let the nationalists do the talking. 'Mr. Butler is believed to have inferred [opening the Victoria Falls Conference in June 1963] that while discussion should range widely, rules for debate will include keeping to the point.'[30]

It is worth noting that the interests directly represented at these latter day conferences were almost wholly political and constitutional. They were attended by politicians, civil servants, academics, lawyers and constitutional advisers, not by business men or financiers – only, at best, economists. Whatever may have been the consequences of the independence which derived from such conferences, in the form of a continuation of capitalist links between the former colony and the former metropolitan country, the details of such relationships did not form part of the agenda. It may be asserted that the 'international bourgeoisie' of white, brown and black capitalists conducted their affairs more clandestinely. The point remains that the matters discussed at these conferences were concerned with constitutional devices, minority safeguards (or what passed for safeguards), electoral procedures, party relations, and the distribution of regional powers – the stuff of lawyers' chambers and party headquarters, not the board room.

4. *Elections*

An almost indispensable part of British decolonisation, not least because the greatest transfer of all was carried through with the final determining election of 1946 which preceded the handing over of responsibility to acceptable successors. By 1947 of course it was clear even beyond the need of the ballot box that Congress, and the Moslem League, were the only successor governments able to command obedience. Twenty years later, however, the election formula was actually to acquire a soubriquet: *NIBMAR*, the ballot box being the easiest way (it was assumed) to find the majority. Elections were to become rituals almost of affliction after independence, but they were held in an astonishing variety of circumstances during the whole period of decolonisation, either in the hope of securing a more representative legislature, or to elicit a governing majority, or to try and produce agreement across communal or racial divisions, by a mixture of fancy franchises, weighted voting and cross voting. A mildly interesting aspect was the ingenious devising of different techniques of 'casting a ballot', including the use (I think) of marbles and a bicycle bell in the candidate's box in the Gambia, and of 'queuing openly' behind the favoured candidate during early contests in the more remote areas of a colony under the supervision of the local District Commissioner.

Vox populi vox imperii? No. The ballot box was the great enemy of any prolongation of imperial rule since the move towards adult suffrage within the individual territories of a decentralised empire raised inescapably the problem of legitimacy: who was now the master? There was no room for empire under the conditions of adult suffrage and mass electorates. Elections obliged the colonial elite, however *elitiste*, and however attached many of its members might be to the metropolitan country, to seek support locally and to 'bid for sovereignty'. The ballot box came to resemble Bulwer Lytton's description of democracy: it is 'like the grave — it perpetually cries, "give, give", and like the grave it never returns what it has once taken.' It certainly dug the grave of the colonial power, although it is also true that there were occasions when the Imperial government (or, more usually, the Commission of Inquiry appointed by London to 'make recommendations for reform') was rather more in favour of adult suffrage than the existing local politicians: understandably so, since the Pandora's box of universal franchise released quite unknown plagues and demons.[31] The general theory, however, was that such elections would contain nationalist agitation within the adjusted institutions of colonial rule, and indeed an extension of the suffrage did work that way for a time. (Of course elections to a broadly based parliament are still held in many Commonwealth countries, though not quite as originally introduced, in East Africa, Malta, Fiji, a number of Caribbean islands, Sri Lanka, Malaysia, Malta, India(?)).

5. *Acquiring collaborators*

If elections were to secure consent to a transitional government between the end of colonial and the beginning of independent rule, the successful contestants (it was nervously expected) would also collaborate with what was left of the colonial government during the period of transmutation. Professor Ronald Robinson has suggested ingeniously that the successful nationalists were those who obliged the British to recognise that, having 'run out of collaborators', they were thereby obliged to leave the field. Since (he writes) imperialism was 'as much a function of the victim's collaboration or non-collaboration – of their indigenous politics – as it was of European expansion', so too one might say of the end of the process that: 'Nationalists had to contrive a situation in which their rulers ran out of collaborators. They had to realign against imperialism the same political elements which, hitherto, had been arrayed on the imperial side.'[32] No less ingenious theories have been employed to argue that the collaboration never stopped, or rather that independence was really the end of one kind of collaboration and the start of new forms of collusion: between colonial elites and international companies, and between successor regimes and the former metropolitan power or new patrons of a more powerful disposition. I am not concerned in this paper with the transfer of power in its economic or financial setting, but it is certainly the case, on a much narrower ground of argument, that part of the success of British governments in transferring political power lay in the belief in continuity. Independence would be granted, but it would be within the Commonwealth with all its accompanying linkages including (with exceptions) the Sterling Area, preferential arrangements, aid flows, trade channels and development corporations, all held together by convention and mutual advantage – a concert of convenience which rested on still more insubstantial beliefs in a common political culture for which I suppose the shorthand was 'the export of Westminster' although much else was implied by that. Thus the 'free world' was to be enlarged, and many millions brought within its orbit. How antique such hopes seem today! But they were real enough in the 1950s when it was quite widely stated that a dependent empire was being converted into a free Commonwealth.

Such were the sentiments of that time, echoed not only by the former imperial power but by the newly independent leaders in support of a freely entered upon association.[33] Nor were conditions laid down prior to independence. For India and Pakistan, as for Burma, it was 'without strings of any sort'.[34] Agreements, it is true, were signed with Ceylon which covered defence, external affairs and the public service. There was a short-lived Anglo-Nigerian Defence Agreement. There is still a rather tattered Defence Agreement with Malta, and there are the sovereign bases in Cyprus. But the general rule was unfettered independence in conditions of mutual trust, not least because many colonial governments (though not always under the same Governor) had been quick to adjust to local shifts of political fortune. The once unmentionable – Kenyatta, Banda, Makarios – became cordially spoken of both locally and in London, and when the unexpected happened, as in Ghana in 1950, and quite new leaders were elected, the prison graduates became ministers. There developed a 'close, friendly and if I may say so, not unfruitful partnership',[35] for example, between Arden Clarke and Nkrumah. The days of Amin, of Geary and Sheik Karume were still to dawn.

6. *Commissions of Inquiry*

There being no collective study of the scope and effect of the large number of colonial Commissions of Inquiry during the colonial period, it would be imprudent to try and assess their significance in any particular way. They were certainly many and varied. Some were appointed by the local Governor, as the Watson Commission was in the Gold Coast in 1948. Some were brought together by H.M.G. and despatched to a troubled area as much for internal British-political reasons as for overseas colonial purposes. So at least we are told by Butler as being the justification of the Monckton Commission which inquired into the working of the Central African Federation:

> I never supported the Monckton Commission's appointment. The arguments which persuaded the government were couched largely in terms of our own domestic politics: that is to say, it was held to be for the good of the Federation if Church and middle-of-the-road opinion at home could be reassured by a dispassionate and wide based inquiry and if the Labour Party could be dissuaded meanwhile from any firm commitment to back it up.[36]

The effect of the great majority of the Commissions was (as commented on earlier) to push reform farther along the road to self government, as indeed was the case in the Gold Coast, although I would not now place so large an emphasis as I once did on the dramatic nature of the changes recommended by the Watson Commission. Nevertheless, Commissions became quite powerful instruments of change, though the recommendations they made were not always welcome at home. The Donoughmore Commission succeeded in having its committee form of government introduced into Ceylon, to the dismay of the Governor. The *Report* of the Moyne Commission on the West Indies on the eve of the second world war was suppressed. Lennox Boyd, as Secretary of State for the Colonies, publicly rejected the conclusions of the Devlin Report which included the unusual phrase 'temporarily – a police state' when describing the effect of the riots on the colonial administration in Nyasaland early in 1959.[37] The sequence of recommendations, modifications, further reforms, elections and independence were a familiar aspect of the dismantling of the empire, and it was very often the Commission of Inquiry which began the process.

7. *Aggregations*

If 'divide and rule' has been a principle of empire, 'unite and quit' might no less vulgarly be said to be true of the way in which the British tried to dispossess themselves of residual territories in which the number of the inhabitants, or the availability of revenue, was felt to be insufficient to carry alone the full weight of independence. 'Putting together' became an early hope of reformers:

On the one hand, self-governing institutions in individual Colonies have been advanced through constitutional changes, extended franchise, and the fuller association of the people themselves in local and central affairs. On the other hand, new associations of Colonial territories to assist in their political evolution and social development have been formed.[38]

And the *Report* adds, very characteristically: 'The progress made in these two directions naturally varies with the widely differing circumstances and needs of the individual territories and with the stage of constitutional development already attained. ...' Great trust was put in the notional economies of scale, without much consideration for the politics of the economics involved in these transactional relations. Schemes of closer union, from joint ventures in common services to full federations, were placed before conferences and commissions for the West Indies, East Africa, Central Africa and South East Asia. It was easy (from London) to point to the advantages: Malays and Chinese would be better balanced against each other if Singapore could be added to Sabah and Sarawak in a federation with Malaya. 'Partnership' between black and white might develop in conditions of widening prosperity in Central Africa against the excesses both of apartheid and a black nationalism. The little islands of the Caribbean could join with the larger islands, to give meaning to 'something more than the formal relinquishment by H.M.G. in the United Kingdom of constitutional powers of control'. It was a time (in the mid-1950s) when independence still meant 'paying one's way'.[39] Few of these attempted associations succeeded. By 1975 the United Kingdom too was failing to 'pay its way', and sovereignty began to be bestowed on very small clusters of islands indeed until one might almost say that self-government had arrived for Robinson Crusoe and Alexander Selkirk.

8. *Naming the Day*

Once fully under way, the great enemy of decolonisation was not delay, which could be bought with promises, but 'deadlock' through the clash of local parties or communities. The transfer of power is often thought of as nationalists putting a pistol to the head of the colonial government but there were times when, at the last, the rôle was reversed. As the certainty of independence drew near, one side or other of the nationalist movement often hesitated and even tried to stop the process. Then it was that the local colonial Governor, or the Secretary of State in London, forced the issue. It was not quite like that in India since Jinnah, knowing very much what he wanted, moved in the direction he wanted to travel to the dismay of Congress; but the 'naming of the day' to bring the Congress leaders to the point of resolution for the sub-continent was paralleled in lesser circumstances in a number of colonies in order to force independence through on an agreed basis. Sometimes it was simply a strong declaration of intent, sometimes the precise announcement of a date: e.g. Duncan Sandys (1) 'We in Britain have no desire to hustle Malta into independence or lay down our responsibilities so long as you need us' at the July 1963 London Conference, when despite the protests of Mintoff's Labour Party a precise day – 31 May 1964 – was fixed for independence. A year later, when the date had passed, Duncan Sandys somewhat petulantly told the House of Commons: 'I really think we have got to the point where we have to take it that we have decided that Malta is to be independent' and the ceremony took place in September.[40] Similarly for Uganda, for which a Constitutional Conference opened in London in September 1960 under Macleod. There were angry arguments among the participants, long negotiations, a walk-out by Kiwanuka, an insistence by Macleod on new elections, and then the announcement by the Secretary of State that independence was to be fixed a year hence: 4 October 1962. As Nigel Fisher commented:

> Although, traditionally, Kiwanuka had demanded independence, he had certainly not expected to get it so soon. Indeed, the time-table was unreasonably tight for the Colonial Office lawyers and officials. It involved the preparation of the internal self-government constitution, the enactment of the Uganda Independence Act, and the drafting of the Independence Order in Council, which was only completed a week before the independence date. Further negotiations with four kingdoms had to be concluded, and the general election in Uganda had to be held. It was an exacting schedule.[41]

9. *Intervention by Westminster and Whitehall*

The list of local devices, institutions, procedures and offices by which the transfer of power was effected, would be quite incomplete if it omitted what might be placed first in such a catalogue by inquirers into the end of other European empires, namely intervention by the Colonial Office and the Imperial Parliament. However decentralised the quasi-autonomous colonial territories might be, the line of final authority still led to Whitehall and Westminster. The pressures exerted there by a variety of interests – companies, church groups, Fabian societies, Bow groups, defence interests – have never been explored adequately despite the excellent study by Mr. Lee.[42] I am inclined to believe that still the dominant aspect of the whole field of decolonisation, certainly the one which stands out in sharp relief, is that of the series of local crises and events which placed the colonial government of a particular territory in such a position as to oblige the Colonial Office and the Secretary of State to intervene. But admittedly and quite understandably that has not always been the view of the principal actors at the London end who have been inclined to take an altogether grander view of their powers. Moreover, in at least two particular instances the influence of the Secretary of State was very considerable, that of R. A. Butler in carrying through the dissolution of the Central African Federation in 1962–3, and that of Iain Macleod (at the Colonial Office between October 1959 and October 1962) in moving power away from a European minority to an African majority in Kenya and Northern Rhodesia. Macleod was quite prepared (it is said) to oppose the Governor, Sir Patrick Renison, over the freeing of Kenyatta in the summer of 1961, as he had been to go against the advice of all four governments in Central Africa in the release of Banda from detention at the beginning of April 1960. The January 1960 London conference on Kenya was the first to move the Colony back from the 1952 Emergency to an orderly path of constitutional reform. 'We intend', said Macleod in his opening Address, 'to lead Kenya to full self-government or, if I may use a plainer word, to independence'.[43] Similarly, the summer conference of that year reached agreement under Macleod's chairmanship on a new constitution for Nyasaland, under which Banda became the 'Chief Executive' after the elections in August the following year. It was perhaps the first clear indication that the 1953 Federation was dissolving.

Part C Parenthesis: a comment on chronology

At this point it may be useful to move from themes to chronology. It is a familiar observation that the British withdrawal from empire was 'speeded up' in the early 1960s. We have Macleod's word for it, and Macmillan's phrase: the 'wind of change'. Macleod was quite explicit:

> It has been said that after I became Colonial Secretary there was a deliberate speeding up of the movement towards independence. I agree, there was. And in my view any other policy would have led to terrible bloodshed in Africa. This is the heart of the agreement.[44]

The chain of reasoning is quite straightforward. Macmillan's election victory in 1959 – the third Tory Party success in a row – gave him (it is said) an unusual mastery of his party. His visit to Africa the following year convinced him of the force of African nationalist demands. The shock of the Hola Camp murders in Kenya and of the Nyasaland riots, against the background of the long emergency in Kenya, and the prospect of comparable horrors in Central Africa, were the dark side of the dangers which threatened. On the other hand, the peaceful progress to independence of Nigeria in 1960, of Sierra Leone and Tanzania in 1961, and of Uganda the following year, were held to be bright achievements of an expanding Commonwealth which had avoided the dangers of 'going too slow'. Even in Cyprus, 1959 was 'a year of sheer happiness' for Hugh Foot[45] after the London Agreement was signed. Everyone was let out of detention camps, Makarios was brought back from exile, and elections were held prior to the independence which (after a long argument over the sovereignty of the defence bases) came in August 1962. Moreover, the Belgians had abruptly severed their rule in the Congo, and the French had quickly granted independence to AEF/AOF and Madagascar. Having been the first to move away from colonial control, the British were now in danger of being the last, with Portugal, to have to endure its misfortunes. Such was the gist of Macleod's comment to Michael Blundell recorded in the latter's biography.[46] The critical years therefore, it is argued, were those which saw the reversal of policy in the Central African Federation and the transfer of power to an African majority in Kenya.

Is it right to be so categorical? Lord Butler is more circumspect about reaching too precise a conclusion on the process of 'speeding up'. Certainly at the beginning of changes in the attitude of HMG towards the Central African Federation 'all was darkness and doubt'. There were many pressures exerted: four colonial governments in Africa (one of them 'self-governing' within Southern Rhodesia), the Commonwealth Relations Office and the Colonial Office at loggerheads in London, powerful mining and commercial interests, and both black and white party leaders opposed to each other and to London. Butler observed that 'the nationalist tide was coming in'. He was advised that it was coming in strongly by Sir Glyn Jones, who was now in Zomba and Sir Evelyn Home in Lusaka. And having set up his new Central African Office at Gwyddyr House in Whitehall, he could call on the expertise, not only of Mark Tennant and Duncan Watson, but of his 'small posse' of advisers who travelled through Central Africa during July 1962. But still, as late as the last week of August, he was able to write to Alport in Salisbury: 'What I am not prepared to do at present is to make up my mind as to future action'.[47] Something still, he believed, could be salvaged, and it was not until late in March 1963, after 'some of the most laborious and painful [days] of my career' that the decisions was finally taken to put an end to 'the Federation which had been built up with such hopes since 1953'. The formal end came at the Victoria Falls conference at which Southern Rhodesia, too, asked for but was refused independence since (says Lord Butler) 'the same facts stared me in the face then as confronted the Labour Government later: to give independence to an administration unprepared to open multiracial paths to government is contrary both to British tradition and to Commonwealth unity'.[48]

It is sensible to be cautious, therefore, about 'speeding up'. Over the full and wide range of the transfer of power, the Kenya-Central Africa problems of the mid-'50s and '60s, although of bitter intensity, were still only a small part of the whole story when placed alongside South Asia and Malaysia, the Mediterranean, the Caribbean and Pacific islands, and of much earlier achievements in the old Dominions. Even within the African context, by far the most important British colony, Nigeria, had peacefully attained independence in 1960 (though it was not to remain peaceful very long). The process had stretched back at least to the beginning of the previous decade when, like its smaller West African neighbours, Nigeria moved through various changes in the composition of the local legislative and executive councils, the Africanisation of its public service, initiatives by successive Governors, inter-party disputes, elections, London conferences and the presiding influence of Oliver Lyttleton and Lennox Boyd as Secretaries of State until the final ceremony of transfer when compliments were honourably exchanged. Even the 'speeding up' of decolonisation in 1960–61, in East and Central Africa, seems to me to have been primarily dictated, as elsewhere, by *events* to which Macleod and Butler and local colonial governments had to react, the principal 'event' being the transfer of a radical nationalist sentiment from west to east and central Africa. There is no strong evidence for schemes of reform in the sense of a prescient, pre-emptive policy in London.

Nor were the bitterness and difficulties in extricating the United Kingdom from Kenya and the Rhodesias altogether new. It is a melancholy reflection on the history of the transfer of power from the United Kingdom that the worst conflicts have been where there were communities of European origin. Throughout the 1960s self-government arrived peacefully in southern Africa in respect of the former High Commission Territories, peacefully in the Caribbean and in the Pacific. It stumbled badly, having to be rescued from disaster by direct intervention from London, primarily in Cyprus, Kenya and the Rhodesias, to which one might add Ireland, Palestine and, at the turn of the century, South Africa. It is not an undifferentiated truth, since the failure of British rule in Aden and the South Arabian Federation was also bloody. But still it is the case that the movement towards self-government was particularly difficult where British rule had either evoked the deeply opposed sentiment of an Irish-Celtic, or Hellenic, or Boer nationalism; or where settlers from Britain itself, despite their minority position, believed that they too could follow the path of earlier Dominion self-government.

Part D Concluding Reflections

At its widest extent, the British empire was very large. If it was not Roman in its practice, it was certainly Roman in extent, with

26   DECOLONISATION AND AFTER

influence and power felt well beyond its formal frontiers; an empire of colonies, protectorates, settlements, condominiums, mandates, treaty states and dependencies. It is the closest parallel in our time of that other ancient empire, a parallel which could be drawn of London as its capital:

> The Prince had always liked his London, when it had come to him; he was one of the modern Romans who find by the Thames a more convincing image of the truth of the ancient state than any they have left by the Tiber. Brought up on the legend of the City to which the world paid tribute, he recognised in the present London much more than in contemporary Rome the real dimension of such a case. If it was a question of an *Imperium*, he said to himself, and if one wished, as a Roman, to recover a little the sense of that, the place to do so was on London Bridge, or even, on a fine afternoon in May, at Hyde Park Corner.[49]

The passage of time constantly altered the extent and power of British rule to the point where it has become customary to argue that the notion of self-government in the 19th century was very unlike the fact of independence by the middle of the 20th century. The evolution of responsible government in the old Dominions (it is said) took place within an established imperial order, focused on a metropole which had immense attractive powers as a trading and financial centre, and possessed of a dominant political culture under very distinct liberal parliamentary institutions, whereas both the power and the attraction were much diminished during the present century, the label 'independence' for India in 1947 being very indicative of the notion of separation.[50] I am sure that is so. Nevertheless, the continuation of habits and beliefs (shaped by Oxford and Cambridge or the Inns of Court and, later, by L.S.E.) was still strong enough in the 1920s and '30s to enable many of the formative leaders of India and Ceylon to demand Dominion status after the model of responsible government granted earlier to Canada, Australia and New Zealand. The notion of continuity had a mesmeric effect on the British themselves, as in Attlee's comment to Sir Stafford Cripps before the latter left for Delhi in 1942: 'There is precedent for such an action. Lord Durham saved Canada for the British Empire. We need a man to do in India what Durham did in Canada'.[51] The persistence of a British or Commonwealth political culture, or at least the survival of a belief in its existence, was still able to carry the African, Caribbean and other colonies through to 'independence within the Commonwealth' under a structural imitation of 'Westminster' as late as the 1950s and '60s. I have no wish to extol or mock the view which the British had of themselves, and which they were able to impart to others (although it is difficult not to think that some of the more extravagant manifestations of such beliefs were ill-based) but – to return to where we began – it is surely right to observe that not only the handling of Britain's imperial problems but the political setting in which they occurred was quite unlike that of their European contemporaries, and that the differences sprang from the particularities of British history and its political culture, the formal expression of which was carried over into a large number of British possessions. Indeed, it would be surprising if it were not so.

Still there is that central question which is unanswered. Why was it that the British should have been able to contemplate, and eventually to reach, that ultimate goal of 'colonial self-government' whether in its more powerful 19th century setting or its more precise contemporary form? There is of course an answer, noted earlier. Was it simply the notion, now given a global context by Marxist writers, that the new Commonwealth would be the old empire continued by other means, that what really took place at 'independence' in so many different capitals, from Delhi to Kuala Lumpur to Georgetown, Suva and Gaberones, was only a false decolonisation? It is certainly true that there was often a deliberate effort by many colonial governments to bring the territories for which they were responsible more fully into the world economy. They needed revenue, and they hoped for prosperity. Many also believed in the encouragement of a middle class (and of a general social differentiation in economic terms) if only to try to diminish the intensity of communal conflict through the supposed solvent of class. It was the avowed hope both of the Donoughmore constitution in Ceylon in the 1930s, and of the *Report of the East African Royal Commission* in 1955 which argued that political stability and economic success depended on 'the integration of African rural production into the world economy'.[52] To that intention could be added numerous statements by successive Labour and Conservative governments which implied that the

Commonwealth would remain an area of British influence, reflecting the world stature of the United Kingdom. It was to be one of three inter-locking circles of British interest: the Commonwealth, the United States and western Europe, often in that order. It was perhaps the ultimate fallacy of hope. For whatever the end of empire may look like from the former colonial capital in relation to its continued dependence on the outside world, a good deal has certainly happened to transform its relationship with Great Britain, particularly in its economic setting. I give only one humdrum example. When I lived in Ghana prior to independence the commonest motor car to be seen was made in and exported from Britain: whatever it is today it is certainly not that. From a British standpoint, whatever may have been the intention and the expectations, a very considerable transfer of trade and influence has taken place, despite the ease with which independence was often obtained and the steady expansion in Commonwealth membership.

Nor do I believe that a belief (however mistaken) in the continuation of empire by Commonwealth means fully explains the willingness of the British to surrender formal control. It is too *simpliste* a reason. I would suggest – and it is gathering together points made earlier – that a large part of the explanation lies much deeper, in the long parliamentary history of the United Kingdom which, extended by settlement in distant colonies and transformed there into adapted copies of Westminster and Whitehall, became the model for demands by nationalist elites in non-British-settled colonies. Such demands, though invariably resisted by local colonial Governors in relation to immediate policies, were none the less held to be legitimate in principle, not only because of the earlier history of Dominion self-government (or because of a residual memory of the American revolt) but because it was held to be 'natural' that the liberal principle of self-government should be a desired end. Hence remarks such as that by Adderly in 1869 that 'the normal current of colonial history is the perpetual assertion of the right of self-government'. The application of such beliefs (it is true) encountered formidable obstacles of race and temperament, and it was translated in a very stumbling sort of way, pushed forward by local crises, as I have tried to explain. But that is also perhaps the British mode. 'It is', writes Professor Mackintosh, 'typically British to imagine that it is possible to reform ... without first being clear about its purpose, without settling the value judgements and working out the objectives of the reformed institutions. It is assumed that by looking at the particular machine, by taking evidence about how the present arrangements work, inconsistencies will emerge, obvious changes will suggest themselves and the problem will be solved.'[53] It is a good description of a great deal of colonial government although there was usually, in respect of distant principles, at least the avowed objective of self-government. Unlike their mainland neighbours, the British (it may be readily admitted) are addicted to half-measures, and it was no less a characteristic of British rule abroad. Powerful as a colonial Governor often appeared to be, and almost oriental in his splendour as the Viceroy undoubtedly was, half-measures were always preferred to no measures when the necessity for action was forced upon them. Not for them was the poet's exaltation of power and revolution. 'Beautiful in the splendour of his power is the oriental king Asarhaddon, and beautiful is the ocean of a people's wrath beating to pieces a tottering throne. But hateful — aesthetically displeasing that is — are half measures'.[54] Perhaps. But many colonial Governors (unlike the Romanovs) survived amidst the people's wrath and, by half-measures, helped thereby the United Kingdom itself to escape the turmoil. Nor has such pragmatism been without eloquent defenders. Very cogent arguments have illustrated its use:

> All we can do, and all that human wisdom can do, is to provide that the change shall proceed by insensible degrees. This has all the benefits which may be in change, without any of the inconveniences of mutation. The model will, on the one hand, prevent the unfixing old interests at once: a thing which is apt to breed a black and sullen discontent ... This gradual course, on the other hand, will prevent men, long under depression, from being intoxicated with a large draught of new power, which they always abuse with a licentious insolence.[55]

Many colonial governments tried gropingly to move along such a path, until the slow pace of change became impossible in the last decades of decolonisation, and who would not say that the rush to independence has not led to 'intoxication with a large draught of new power' in many of the territories formerly dependent?

There is one last point to make, and it lies at the very heart of the argument: namely, that the British have always been, or have been until recently, an exclusive race. The empire was always kept therefore at arm's length, away from the delicate balance of British politics with its conventions and procedures. Hence the peculiar horror for the United Kingdom of the Irish experience which was always drawn towards the centre of domestic politics. Imperial problems were very rarely allowed to do that. The United Kingdom did not have to search for an imperial policy within Britain itself between the opposition of irreconcilables. As Philip Williams has observed: 'France was the only country which [under the Fourth Republic] had both a great empire and a strong Communist party. Without the Communists the shrivelled democratic Left and progressive Centre could not muster a majority for decolonisation; but with Communist support came fears for domestic stability and international tranquillity which alienated Centre votes and in turn made it impossible to find a majority'.[56] There were (to be sure) differences also in the United Kingdom, sometimes bitterly expressed between the rival parties and between successive governments over the emphasis and timing of policy on colonial issues – they have been very competently surveyed by Dr. Goldsworthy – but the area of agreement in principle was always much larger than the differences over details of particular events. Of course, luck too played its part. It was fortunate that the Conservatives were in office in the 1950s and early '60s when having to deal with emotive problems of settler interests, since the necessity of a policy which went against those interests was more easily carried through from the right with the willing assent of the left. But that does not affect the overriding principle which I believe to have been at the core of the imperial experience looked at from Britain: that, however sharp or dangerous the colonial crisis might be, it was kept at a distance from the main areas of domestic politics. May we not conclude therefore by asserting that both the possession and the loss of empire were extraneous to the strong sense of national unity, and that the manner in which the British conducted the transformation of their colonial possessions into self-governing states reflected not only, and very creditably, a British acceptance of the right of people to govern themselves but a prudent concern to maintain (it would not be too much to say, to keep inviolate) the autonomy of their own self-rule?

Postscript

Quite different accounts of the transfer of power might need to be given in relation to such particular aspects as the transfer of economic power, or military control, or administrative authority, or cultural interests. But re-reading the general arguments set out in the paper, I am also struck by what might properly be seen as a persistance – indeed the marked inveteracy – of a view which is best described perhaps as a Whig interpretation of history. It is present, I am sure, not only in the *data* (that is, in the evidence from the material used) but in the actual presentation of the arguments (the standpoint, that is, of the writer). It is most readily expressed as a belief in political action, in its broadest sense, as being able to reconcile competing interests through institutional arrangements and an appeal to 'reasonableness'. Politics is seen not as a succession of conflicts between opposed and irreconcilable forces but as the art of what is always possible: amelioration. A quite different view could easily be described, of decolonisation as the enforced retreat of the imperial powers from successive waves of opposition from those they governed. Its history would be the recording and interpretation of various crises – of riots and repression – which forced the 'sea of the people's wrath' to higher and higher vantage points at each successive wave of rebellion, from the early *élitiste* ripple to the engulfing tide of popular revolt. History as revolution certainly has a place in the history of decolonisation, and no doubt it will not come to a stop in the post-imperial account of the ex-colonial states. But history – a substantial component, at least, of English history – is also, in so far as it can be described satisfactorily, the long years of patient and persevering endeavour to reconcile the opposition of ruler and governed, and there is ample evidence (it is the main burden of the arguments used earlier) of *that* in the terminal history of British rule overseas.

NOTES

1. R. G. Collingwood, *Speculum Mentis* 1924, p. 82.
2. Expressed administratively by the Treasury in 1951. 'So far as internal affairs are concerned each administrative unit is in form self-governing and has a complete organisation ... for running itself. Each territory has its own

body of laws and its own set of constitutional instruments ... and *each should maintain financial stability*.' One can add, too, statements by particular governors about the autonomy of their own colony, as by the Governor of Barbados in 1929 to the Local Assembly in respect of early schemes of Caribbean federation: 'The time was past when fears need be entertained that such things meant necessarily abandonment of our independence and sacrifice of our right to individual management of our own affairs.' One must remember, however, that the Assembly in 1929 was already nearly 300 years old.

3. It would be possible to cover *very many* pages of references to such beliefs as far back as the early 20th century to the reforms of the 1930s and the war years. The stress during the 1940s on 'the need to promote the advancement of the Colonies to full self-government within the Commonwealth' probably owed something to the additional need to appear benign to the Americans before and after they were forced into the war, and to convince Roosevelt that the British were not like the French. (See Louis Halle, *The Cold War as History* (1967)).

    See, too, Martin Wight's taxonomy in *British Colonial Constitutions 1947* (1952). The notion of a changing balance of representation in a legislature is of course as old almost as parliamentary government itself in Britain, Upper and Lower Canada in the 1840s, Provincial Legislatures in India after 1905, the Sudan in 1947, etc. etc.

4. *Cmd. 3131*, p. 29 and *Parl. Deb. 4 December 1947, Vol. 152*.

5. Phrases which occur constantly in most reports of visiting commissions of inquiry to India, Ceylon, West Africa, Malaya, the Caribbean etc. etc. They were famously expressed of course in 1917 for India: 'The policy of H.M. Government with which the Government of India is in complete accord, is that of increasing association in every branch of administration and the gradual development of self-governing institutions with a view to the progressive realisation of responsible government in India as an integral part of the British Empire.' Britain was to judge the degree of 'gradualism' and to Congress Leaders such declarations began to look like tactics not of advance but delay. Yet at least the British were prepared to face and even move towards the prospect of independence. And of no other European empire could that be said in 1917 – not until a quarter of a century, and another world war, later: in the Dutch East Indies.

6. 'Post-war history carried the island forward from colonial rule which in 1946 seemed likely to endure for a very long time to independence in 1966. It was not a simple unilinear movement but one which wavered between different possibilities of advance until almost the end. ...' R. L. Cheltenham, *Constitutional History of Barbados* (1970).

7. Christopher Sykes's heading to Ch. 13, *Cross Roads to Israel* (1965).

8. Henry Baudet, 'The Dutch Retreat from Empire', in which decolonisation is seen (very likely as it had to be seen from Holland), as 'a new revolution ... which was substantially finished in Indochina when most of the others were still to begin'. See, too, Arend Lijphart, *The Trauma of Decolonisation*, 1966.

9. *Parl. Deb.* 10 July, 1954.

10. See the argument in Hilary Blood's *The Smaller Territories*, as late as February 1958 (C.P.C. Commonwealth Series No. 4).
11. *Parl. Deb.* Vol. 604, April 1959.
12. Cmnd. 1148, 1960, Para. 31.
13. *Parl. Deb.* 7 Dec. 1938.
14. E.g. through the early pan-African meetings in London and West Africa. It would also be interesting to look at relations between Indian and Burmese leaders, and Dublin, during the inter-war years. See Mansergh, *Commonwealth of Nations* (1948) p. 178.
15. *Parl. Deb.* 13 Nov. 1958.
16 *La Conférence Africaine Française, Brazzaville, Commissariat aux Colonies*, Alger (1944). p. 35.
17. *Ibid.*, p. 71.
18. *Memoirs of Hope*, (1970), p. 83, *seq.*
19. *Ibid.* p. 11–12.
20. *Parl. Deb.* 16 December, 1964.
21. Hugh Tinker, *Experiment with Freedom* (1967) p. 164.
22. Only to experience a different transfer of power to Brussels.
23. And again in *Parl. Deb.* 13 July 1943. See too, *The Colonial Empire 1939–47.* Cmnd. 7167, p. 32.
24. Nicholas Mansergh *et. al.*, *Commonwealth Perspectives* (1958) p. 34.
25. *British Colonial Constitutions 1947*, p. 17–18.
26. *A Start in Freedom*, p. 106.
27. Richard Rathbone, *Transfer of Power in Ghana*, London (1968).
28. Foot, p. 103–4.
29. Baudet, p. 6.
30. *Rhodesia Herald*, 29 June, 1963.
31. As in Mauritius in 1958.
32. In R. Owen & B. Sutcliffe. *Studies in the Theory of Imperialism.*
33. See *inter alia*, *My Life, Autobiography of Sir Ahmadu Bello* (1962).
34. Tinker, p. 144. In contrast (he says) with the U.S., France and the Netherlands.
35. Arden Clarke, *African Affairs, Jan. 1958.*
36. Butler, p. 210.
37. Cmnd. 814 (1959) and Cmnd. 815 (1959).
38. Cmnd. 7167 (1947) p. 32.
39. *Report by the Conference on British Caribbean Federation Feb. 1956. Cmnd. 9733, para. 8. See, too, Cmnd. 8575 British Dependencies in the Caribbean and World Atlantic 1939–52 (1952); Cmnd. 8837.; Report by the Conference on West Indian Federation 1953; and Cmnd. 9618 Plan for British Caribbean Federation, Report of the Fiscal Commissioner, Cmnd. 9619 Report of the Civil Service Commissioner and Cmnd. 9620 report of the Federal Commissioner.*
40. Austin, *Malta and the End of Empire*, London, Frank Cass, p. 102.
41. *Iain Macleod* (1973) p. 179–80.
42. *Colonial Development and Good Government* (1967).
43. *Cmnd. 960*, 1960.
44. *Spectator*, 20 March 1964, and 23 April, 1965.

45. p. 181.
46. Blundell, *So Rough a Wind*, p. 270.
47. Butler, p. 219.
48. *Ibid.*,p. 227.
49. Henry James, *The Golden Bowl*.
50. The 'revisionist literature' on what was implied by 'Durham and responsible government' in the 19th Century is now very large. See *inter alia*, John W. Cell, *British Colonial Administration in the Mid-Nineteenth Century: the Policy-making Process*, Yale University Press, 1970; D. J. Murray, *The West Indies and the Development of Colonial Government 1801–1834*, Oxford 1965; Peter Burroughs, *The Canadian Crisis and British Colonial Policy, 1828–1841*, Edward Arnold, 1972; Helen Taft Manning, *The Revolt of French Canada 1800–1835*, London 1962, and her article 'Who ran the British Empire – 1830–1850', *Journal of British Studies, Vol. V.* (1965) p. 41–61. See too, T. M. Ward, 'The New Empire' in *Historical Studies of Australia and New Zealand, Vol. XIV* Oct.–April 1971 ... 'Bell's view of Empire is mercifully free from what ought to be known as the great Durham illusion'; and R. S. Neale's article 'Roebuck's Constitution and the Durham Proposals', *Historical Studies of Australia & New Zealand, Vol. XIV Oct.–April, 1971*.
51. Mansergh, *India, Transfer of Power 1942–7*, Vol. I, 1970.
52. Cmnd. 9475, p. 181.
53. Quoted in Stankiewicz, *British Government in an Era of Reform* (1976).
54. The Russian poet Bryusov (1905), letter to Alexander Blok.
55. Edmund Burke, *Works, VIII* (Bohn's edition 1873).
56. *The French Parliament* (1968), p. 17.

2

The Colonial Past in the Present

J.-L. Miège

1

An examination of the way in which colonial relations have influenced the post-colonial period presents the historian with a number of problems of definition, of method and of interpretation. Although he is by his training drawn towards the analysis of the particular and concrete and often distrustful of ready-made theoretical frameworks, nevertheless he is anxious to bring out both the individual instances as well as general tendencies. In this subject he is bound to be struck by the range and number of factors to be considered and by the varied ways in which in different countries they can be seen to act upon each other.

The very notion of a 'colonial past' may be most misleading. It leads one to imagine a clear distinction between the 'before' of colonialism and the 'after' of independence, seen as two sharply contrasted periods separated by the moment of decolonisation. But the fact is that often both colonisation and decolonisation took place gradually and by different stages in different countries. The colonisation stages varied according to the degrees and forms of resistance encountered and of adjustments arrived at. (Consider, for instance, Morocco's different periods: 1907–1912/1912–1924/1924–1926/1926–1934.) Nor must it be imagined that colonisation always meant a complete break with the pre-colonial period; on the contrary, traditional features were often reinforced – as in the Protectorate's 'invention' and codification of local custom in Morocco.[1] Likewise decolonisation was on occasion brought about in phases – as with Egypt after 1912 or black Africa from the introduction of the *loi cadre* of 1956 – and in ways which while causing some features of the colonial period to vanish allowed others to survive. Moreover, it is clear that political decolonisation and independence so far from causing a break in cultural or economic relations have often strengthened them.

When looking at the development from the pre-colonial era through to that of independence it is essential to distinguish the influence of imperialism – that is the general domination of the Western economy – from that of colonisation – the political and administrative control of a given territory by a colonial power – and, finally, from modernisation – the general Westernisation of the world which affects countries regardless of their domestic policies or external dependence.[2] Clearly these three elements are closely linked. Sometimes colonisation has encouraged the other two, at other times it has inhibited them. In this context, we should mention attempts to sustain traditional crafts, to preserve ancient towns in Morocco or to defend old customs and institutions (e.g., the Berber *dahir*), albeit on occasion for political motives. After independence some effects of the previous era have persisted but these may well be the results of imperialism or modernisation (and of technical aid) rather than of the colonial past itself.

Certain aspects of the past, which at first seem very similar, are found on closer analysis to be quite distinct and to have different effects. Consider for example the economic crisis of 1930–1934. Research in progress underlines the complex interlocking of several crises affecting each territory differently: the international economic crisis and the gold crisis (imperialism); local political crises (colonial crisis); and crises due to the pre-colonial heritage. C. Fourniau demonstrates in his work the relative independence of the economic (1930–1934) and the political (1935–1936) crises in Indochina and the role which the latter played in strengthening national communism.[3] On the other hand F. Fuglestad underlines the importance in Nigeria of local factors such as food scarcity and famine and their political effects,[4] whilst Maestri shows that in the Ivory Coast the crisis strengthened the links with the colonial power and favoured those classes who supported colonisation.[5]

The forces of colonialism were by no means unified and capable of acting in concert. Co-operation, such as that achieved by the famous 'triangle' in the Belgian Congo which united administration, business and clergy, is found less often than strong differences and even internal conflict. Religious missions and the colonial administrators have often been in conflict. Numerous examples include Kenya in 1930 as described by Lonsdale,[6] or Central Africa in 1915 as portrayed by Phipps.[7] Use was often made of technical improvements to keep the colonists satisfied but as Pascon says of Morocco, 'the type of society designed by the administrative class was not entirely compatible with that which the colonists wanted' and he adds 'the image of the administration of the Protectorate as the instrument of colonisation or of colonisation as the implementation of an imperial plan laid down from on high is no more than a misleading caricature'.[8]

The policy of Paris, that of the local powers, the action of local administration and indeed the interests of French companies and of the colonists are therefore much more than slight variations on some grand common theme; this fact stands out clearly, particularly in Morocco, Indochina and Kenya. Nor can any clear distinction be made between the French style of colonial rule with its direct administration, and the English type of indirect rule which allowed the traditional institutions to survive. This has been demonstrated in recent studies which have compared French and British territories and have closely examined the actual working of administration in particular cases.[9] Again, D. K. Fieldhouse, in his comparative analysis of French and British monetary, fiscal and customs policies in Africa, has shown that even if Lugard and de Sarraut had opposing ideas in 1922 and 1923, developments after 1929 and particularly after 1932 brought attitudes and practices much closer together.[10]

Nor can the past be considered merely as a fixed segment of time, its nature settled once and for all. It is a living reality, changing continually and itself an element in development, affected both by the more distant past and by future prospects. Thus the colonial past is present in various forms according as to whether it is in the context of a revival of pre-colonial ways or the ups and downs of decolonisation or the choices facing the newly independent states.

The difficulty in extracting a typology or even general principles regarding post-colonial developments arises in part because of the complex nature of the pre-colonial heritage which survived the colonial past. The position varies a great deal between those countries which before colonisation had a long history of independence with central political organisations, a specialised administration and a trading economy providing a framework for the pre-colonial nation, and those areas with a tribal system and a subsistence economy. Independent countries, whose colonial past seems fairly similar in the way of administration, stages of development and so on, have made quite dissimilar use of the past, depending on whether they form part of a wide cultural background distinct from that of their coloniser, such as Islam or Buddhism, or whether their cultural background is more limited, in particular without any written language.[11]

Even within just one colony, regional and ethnic differences may cause different reactions to colonisation; in that sense one apparently common past becomes in fact a set of different pasts precisely because it is thus perceived. Economic and political systems are reflected in the geographical history of countries and in relations between regions. Colonialism everywhere tended by its priorities to impose a certain type of geographical organisation; it increased the importance, for example, of coastal areas, of communication routes and of areas supplying the most important export produce which would be the backbone of the colonial economy. But this pattern was often modified for political and strategic reasons, sometimes because some regions were less 'accommodating' than others. In Gabon, for example, the different tribes (the Miene, Fanf, Pounon and Mbede) reacted in different ways to missionary influence and education.[12] There are other examples in the Atlas region of Morocco, in Indochina, and so on.

These comments lead to a major question: whether the study of the relation of the colonial past to independence does not also involve a general consideration of 'acculturation' in the true meaning of the word.[13] What are the deposits left behind by colonial rule according to whether it was just received or adapted or rejected during that period? What materials went into the 'sieve' of the decolonisation crisis, and what was sifted through, depending on whether the process was violent or peaceful? Finally, what did the colonial past contribute to the setting up of the new state and to the working of its institutions?

There are two possible lines of research in the analysis of this complicated process. The first gives priority to the phenomenon of the confrontation of the two cultures – the imported and the local – with emphasis on their disparate elements. This approach sees the outside influence as bringing profound changes, creating a dual society with its two sides coexisting and developing. Benissad emphasises this view in the case of Algeria.[14] The second line – that of 'acculturation' in its true sense – emphasises the coming into being of a new culture which includes not just the new elements but those of the past which have almost imperceptibly been drawn into a new relationship and have thus been basically altered. Numerous studies which subscribe to this view have underlined the artificiality of the supposed conflict between tradition and modernity which, in spite of their apparent opposition, are in fact formed by reciprocal influences and dialectically related.[15]

This is an area of much debate[16] which raises the question of whether evolution is a universal or a specific phenomenon. Some studies insist on the fundamental originality of non-European cultures and therefore on those traditional institutions and cultural features which survived the colonial past.[17] The idea of 'negritude' for instance is partly based on an appreciation of the particular qualities of the 'black soul' as opposed to European ways of thinking.[18] Along this line colonialism is made one of the numerous experiences of history which have been absorbed by the indomitable character of local cultures.

Whilst Vellut emphasises the universal nature of the development of societies, the development of colonial society being no different from that of Europe in the nineteenth century and the study of the latter as relevant to the former,[19] Thomas believes in the coexistence both of a uniform African way of thinking throughout the black continent and of a basic originality in relation to European concepts.[20]

If we take the specific case of urbanisation, we find that expert opinions differ – and this in spite of the fact that this important element of the colonial period played an essential role in social and cultural changes, and might well be thought to offer the best example of the general effects of modernity and the individual characteristics of each colony. Some experts emphasise a perfect analogy between the colonial process of urbanisation and that of Europe and America in the nineteenth century. Thus Hodgkin insists that 'the resemblances between the contemporary new towns in Africa and new towns in England at the beginning of the nineteenth century are neither superficial nor fortuitous',[21] and Paluch in the same vein says that 'the essential features of urbanisation are common to all the countries in question (in colonial Africa) and, in their overall form, to the process of urbanisation everywhere in the world'.[22] However, other experts stress specific features of African urbanisation, relating these either to the different imperial power,[23] or to features belonging to local societies.[24]

Obviously this indication of preliminary questions could be considerably longer. The subject of the colonial past and independence raises the general question of relations between Western Europe and the areas it has dominated over the last fifty years.[25] All the points raised give considerable scope for debate.

II

There are two possible areas of analysis for the relations between the colonial past and the independent state. The subject can be dealt with at the factual level, examining institutions, political life, the economy, society, education and culture, collective behaviour. This entails drawing up a balance sheet, judging what remains from the past, what has been rejected, and what has been transformed by the post-colonial state, and how the process of rejection, adoption or adaptation has played a part in moulding the personality of the new state. Such an attempt comprises a systematic comparative analysis of 'before' and 'after'. On the other hand, the problem can be viewed not by making an inventory of facts, not by comparing 'before' and 'after', but by analysing what the colonial past now represents for the new state, asking what sort of a historical and political myth it constitutes, and then by evaluating the importance of this myth for current behaviour, that is, viewing its formation, development and influence as a real causal factor determining attitudes and choices after independence.

Independence always creates a barrier for historical research; decolonisation brings about a 'remoulding of history'.[26] One of the complaints made against the colonial culture was its ignorance and suspicion of the past of its colonies; one of the strongest desires of independence was for the nation to regain power over its own destiny, 'to turn at last the pages of its own history'.[27] Everywhere national historical journals were founded and multiplied in the course of this great voyage of re-discovery.[28] The re-reading of history − and in particular that of the colonial past by the ex-colony − was a means of self-discovery, of fulfilling the pressing need to find their national identity. In this way, cultural identity too was changed. This at the same time provides an opportunity for the creation of stereotypes or for justifying certain desired courses of action. Thus the interpretation of the history of colonialism has several functions, which explains the selective emphasis on particular episodes or persons, the emotive distortions of the past, also the omissions.

A systematic comparative study of these new discussions of history and their relationship to politics would be of considerable interest, but space permits only the briefest comment. References to the colonial past abound. Some are stereotyped − the anti-colonial struggle, colonial oppression, resistance, colonial exploitation and the end of colonialism − and they serve to wipe out a whole area of past reality and to create pictures of the present and the future painted in moral colours of black and white. Others refer more closely to actual events but still provide the new state with the necessary heroes, real or mythical, even against their own evidence. An extreme example of this recreation of the past is the case of the reinterment of the father of J. B. Bokassa, a martyr of colonialism. Again, it was no accident that the Moroccan opposition suddenly rediscovered the character and activities of Abd el Krim who, while certainly an independence hero, became of far greater importance as the founder of a new socio-political system.[29] Contrasts in the uses to which history can be put underline the way views of the colonial past as a political myth are constantly altering, thus showing that history indeed is not a finished thing but consists of changing interpretations which depend on present conditions and in particular on ideas about the future.

The dialectical relationship between colonialism and independence depends on three factors in particular. First, there is the length of time since the gaining of independence for this affects political roles of different age-groups in the ex-colony. Three generations can be distinguished: one was formed under colonial rule and lived through its triumphs as well as through the traumas of decolonisation; the second grew up during the colonial crisis and the struggle for decolonisation and became the 'freedom fighters' who never forget; the third is the generation of independence. The relations between these generations is changing, mainly due to the decline in the first category and the growth of the last one. Their attitude to the colonial past, real and reconstrued, is not the same. The new generation is increasingly inclined to criticise imperialism as an international system rather than colonialism as a local experience. They criticise not just the coloniser but also, sometimes more harshly, those who they believe to have been collaborators in the colonial system, even if they subsequently took part in the process of decolonisation. The charge of neo-colonialism is therefore levelled more at their own leaders rather than at the ex-colonial power. The point was made early on in the opposition of the urban youth in Brazzaville to the Fulbert Youlou regime and their active participation in the revolution of August 1963.[30] It has been stressed by the Malagasy youth and its role in Tananarive in May 1972 as well as in current movements both in the Maghreb (Tunisia or Morocco) and in black Africa, for example the Ivory Coast.[31]

Secondly, changes in the new state's internal politics − for example coups d'état − or in its foreign policy can also rapidly change the collective view of the colonial past. Hoskins showed this clearly with regard to Tanzania in the three periods, 1961−64, 1964−66 and since 1967.[32] There are many other such examples. Each change affects the interpretation of history but also threatens some of the actual legacies of the past. An excellent book on Madagascar emphasised in 1965 what a fine example this country was of the integration of the colonial past with national development.[33] The same statement could not have been made four or five years later. Similarly an unfortunate parallel could be drawn between the views in 1967 of the relation of past and independence in Libya and the facts of that country in 1972 or 1976.

Thirdly, the development of particular political philosophies (such as Khadafisme) or historico-philosophical ideas on the special nature of national culture and its authenticity can also cause new reassessments of the colonial past. Views of that past are, finally, constantly subject to the influence of the relations between ex-colony and ex-coloniser. These relations are, by their very nature, different from others, being subject to periods of both great storm and calm, during which different historical arguments are used as weapons. Analyses of the press are very revealing on this point.[34] They reveal the complex game of using historical stereotypes to serve political attitudes. Sometimes in fact the discussion of history increases in violence as it attempts to exorcise − or to hide − the permanent effects of the past.

It is possible to analyse some of the concrete aspects of the role of the colonial past in the independent states on the basis of different approaches. One possibility would be to tackle the subject by focusing on particular sectors such as constitution, administration, the economy, social classes, education and culture, external relations. Such a thematic approach will not be attempted here since it is followed in fact by other contributions to this volume. Instead, we shall indicate briefly how one might try to assess the relation between colonial past and independent present by comparative study of the different kinds of colonial rule, the different decolonisation experiences and the various kinds of regime in the new states.

Comparative study is not facilitated by the fact that really good studies of colonial regimes are few in number, unevenly devoted to different territories and based on different principles and methods. However, it would seem that in every country there was in the pre-colonial period a crisis brought about by economic pressures stemming from Europe; this crisis, itself a prelude to colonial intervention, is also the period during which a national bourgeoisie is formed. During the last ten years this 'pre-colonial crisis' has been the subject of important analyses, which have all, in spite of local variations, revealed the same process: the emergence of a social class of traders who invested in land, thus increasing agrarian individualism, and exerted an influence on the administrative machine. The Morocco findings of Miège on this subject[35] have been recently confirmed for Tunisia by Pascon,[36] for Algeria by Valensi,[37] while a first-class summary regarding the controversies over the pre-colonial mode of production is supplied by Djeghioul.[38]

During colonial rule this class increased its powers and its influence. The development of an agricultural economy based on exports is always advantageous for both a specific region and a specific social group; the regions may be those of production (Ashanti in Ghana, Yoruba in Nigeria, Buganda in Uganda, Baoule in the Ivory Coast) or those of the related commerce (market towns inland and in particular the coastal ports). This class, which had often supported colonial rule in order to extend its activities which had been limited under the traditional order, called for its end — at least politically — so as to achieve a new outlet for its ambitions. Once this independence was obtained (and this class was its main beneficiary), the close links between its interests, both economic and cultural, and those of the ex-colonial power remained.

So, wherever this class was, and remained, at the head of its country during the process of decolonisation and the formation of an independent state, important elements of colonialism remained in place. The close links have sometimes even been strengthened in spite of changes in appearance or name, and in spite of political debate and argument.

Hence the special importance of the way in which independence was reached. If decolonisation was peaceful and parliamentary, the middle classes played a key role in the process. Personal contacts between the business world in the metropolitan country and its local partners and also between the politicians on both sides were maintained and sometimes even strengthened in the new relationship. But when decolonisation was violent, and as a result usually long drawn out, the chances of a break in relations were greater. Moderate middle-class politicians were gradually eliminated in favour of new leaders. The state of war itself made it difficult to keep up contacts. The result was therefore radicalised, monolithic regimes which chose to turn their backs on their colonial past.

This interpretation, which was fairly widespread round about 1966, was developed in particular to explain the survival of political pluralism or the advent of the one-party system.[39] It needs to be modified by at least taking into account the variable of length of time since independence. The increasing number of coups d'état after 1968 and the setting up of numerous military regimes perhaps expose the limits of the general theory. (It may be worth remarking that it seems arbitrary to make a systematic distinction between British decolonisation, which supposedly took place by stages and where conciliation was the order of the day, and French decolonisation, which was more difficult and full of conflicts.[40])

Turning to the types of post-independence regimes, it is to be noted that regimes of a similar kind (at least by Western definitions) have imposed themselves on countries which have quite different histories, colonial pasts and socio-economic structures; for example, military regimes are to be found in Uganda, Ethiopia, Somalia and the Central African Republic. But such political upheavals apart, the influence of the colonial past is most clearly transmitted through established elite corps. For these are the most awkward to challenge, because of a certain technicality and complexity in their workings. In this regard one would wish to examine first the army, very different in its recruitment and end product as between British and French colonies, next the universities, perhaps the best maintained examples of the colonial past, and finally the administration.

It would be particularly interesting to compare the development of these bodies in countries where the process of decolonisation has been very different – peaceful or violent, by treaties or by special plans (Libya, Somalia). One would also wish to see how changes in these corps have been affected in countries which, like ex-mandate territories, have undergone several successive colonisations.

The geo-political situation of the independent states must also play a part. One has only to consider border conflicts between neighbours due to the tremendous problems of inherited colonial frontiers; or the strategic significance of areas of international confrontation such as the Indian Ocean; or the special nature of certain territories such as islands or archipelagos where historical influences seem, as it were, to be 'trapped'.[41]

Finally, in any deep and thorough search for the continuing presence of the colonial past, the historian would be bound to try and enter realms of even greater subtlety and uncertainty. The colonial past definitely has most effect on newly independent nations in the area of psychology, of feeling and of behaviour. Analyses are perhaps too often undertaken at the level of the state rather than of the nation, and do not take sufficient account of these imponderables which are hard to pinpoint and even harder to quantify.[42]

The influence of education in this connection is not open to doubt but it has hardly been fully assessed, and the same is true of the mass-media. But we ought to look around much more widely – at habits in food and dress, even at the way in which bits of the folklore of the metropole persist. What are the various forms in which Christmas continues from Algeria to Madagascar? What have the ex-colonies of the British made of the tea-drinking habit and ritual of their former masters?

These are the very influences, perpetuated by cooperation and technical assistance, which the ex-colonial powers are most anxious to retain. Francophonie and the Commonwealth, both with political aims, play on these 'intimacies' like clubs where people recognise each other not just because they speak the same language, but because they behave in the same way. The difference between an old French colony and a British one can be felt simply by travelling from one to the other. It is obvious, though hard to analyse, consisting as it does of atmosphere and background effects. Today, some twenty years after decolonisation, these kinds of difference can still be felt on crossing the old Spanish zone of influence or visiting Tangiers.

Indeed, it is probably here, in this area of the 'exploration of the inexpressible' that we may find the clearest, fullest picture of the deep influence of the colonial past. And of course it is here that literature offers us a way of penetrating these difficult areas, a way too much neglected by both political scientists and historians.[43] The considerable differences between the works of French- and English-speaking writers of ex-colonies derive less from local ethnic values and regional traditions than from the distinctive features of the French and British colonial systems and in particular their cultural and educational systems. Differences in the use of language, in ways of thinking and feeling, are revealed indirectly. Each creative area provides us with evidence: for example, are we not able to see the difference between francophone and anglophone research studies in history, politics or sociology – regardless of their school of thought or ideology – simply by noting their different styles of writing and argument? These closely woven threads of culture, of intellectual attitudes, of feelings and of behaviour all play their part, even if subconsciously, in the choice of leaders at the 'moment of decision'. In the dialectical relations which exist between action and the totality of knowledge, the colonial past is constantly present.

As Berque has argued, the study – whether historical or sociological – of decolonisation inevitably opens up some of the most general and profound problems of history and sociology.[44] The question of the bearing of the colonial past on today's new states raises the largest issues: the argument between the general and the particular; the relation between tradition and modernity; the nature of the colonial enterprise and of the experience of colonial rule, the varieties of both; the ambivalence of attitudes, as well as the variations in practice, towards both the colonial past and its remoter pre-colonial period.

NOTES

1. P. Pascon and A. Bouderbala, 'Le droit et le fait dans la Société Composite, essai d'introduction au système politique marocain,' in *Bul. Econ. Soc. Maroc.*, XXXII, 117, 1972, p. 1–17.
2. Described by Berque as 'mondialisation'.
3. C. Fourniau, *La crise en Indochine 1930–1936*, Aix, I.H.P.O.M. 1976.
4. F. Fugelstad, 'La grande famine de 1931 dans l'Ouest Nigérien. Réflexions autour d'une catastrophe naturelle', in *Revue Française Histoire Outre Mer*, 222, 1., 1974, p. 20 sq.
5. E. Maestri, 'Le Chemin de fer de Côte d'Ivoire, Historique, influences économiques, sociales, culturelles et politiques', thesis, Aix, 1976.
6. J. N. Lonsdale, 'European attitudes and African pressures: missions and government in Kenya between the wars', *Race*, 10 (2) October 1968, p. 141 sq.
7. W. E. Phipps, in *International review of missions*, 1968, p. 230.
8. P. Pascon, 'L'histoire sociale et les structures agraires de la région du Haouz de Marrakech', (Paris, doctoral thesis, 1975), p. 180.
9. O. Ikime, 'Reconsidering indirect rule: the Nigerian example', in *Journ. Histor. Soc. Nigeria*, 4 (3) December 1968, 421–38.
10. D. K. Fieldhouse, The Economics of Africa: Some British and French Comparisons, in P. Gifford & W. R. R. Louis, eds., *France and Britain in Africa. Imperial rivalry and colonial rule*, London, 1971, p. 593 sq.
11. See A. A. Mazrui, 'Islam, political leadership and economic radicalism in

Africa', in *Comparative studies in society and history*, 9 (3), April 1967, 275 seq. for this aspect and especially for the influence of Islam on the uses made of the colonial past.

12. M. Ewendge, *Missions, Enseignement, Société au Gabon*, Mémoire de maîtrise, Aix, 1976.

13. J. L. Miège, 'Probleme Kultureller Einflussnahme im Maghreb der vorkolonialen Zeit', in *Zeitschrift für kulturaustausch*, 1975, 4, p. 7 sq.

14. E. Benissad, 'La formation économique de l'Algérie et le dualisme', in *Mondes en Développement*, 10, 1975, 243–71.

15. E. Hermassi, *Etat et Société au Maghreb, Etude comparative*, Paris, 1975. D. N. Levine, 'The flexibility of traditional culture', in *Journal of Social Issues*, 24, 4, October 1968, p. 129.

16. See the comparative report and extensive bibliography by Samon Kimbara: 'Traditions and innovations in Asia and Africa', 81 pages, paper at the Congrès International d'Histoire, San Francisco, 22–29 August 1975.

17. J. F. A. Ajayi, 'La continuité des institutions africaines sous le colonialisme', in *Perspectives nouvelles sur l'Histoire africaine*, Paris, 1971, p. 192–204.

18. H. Kamphausen, 'Bemerkungen zur geistigen Situation africanischer Eliten aus der Akkulturations – und Heilswartungsproblematik' in *Kölner Z. f. Soziol. u. Sozialpsychol.*, 13 December 1963, 93, 121.

19. J. L. Vellut, 'Pour une histoire sociale de l'Afrique centrale', in *Culture et dév.*, Louvain, VI, 1, 1974, p. 62.

20. V. Thomas, in *Notes Africaines*, 118, 4, 1968, p. 42.

21. G. H. Hodgkin, in *Nationalism in colonial Africa*, London, 1956, p. 82.

22. A. Paluch, 'Changement social et urbanisation en Afrique au Sud du Sahara', in *Africana Bulletin*, Varsovie (16) 1972, p. 9–42.

23. P. C. W. Gutkind, 'African urban studies', in *Canadian journal of African studies*, 2 (1), 1968, p. 63 sq.

24. J. S. Coleman, 'The Politics of Sub-Saharan Africa', in *The Politics of the Developing Areas*, Princeton, 1960, p. 272.

25. Some of the many works are J. L. Miège, *Expansion coloniale et décolonisation de 1870 à nos jours*, Paris, PUF, 1973; C. Giglio, *Colonizzazione e decolonizzazione*, Crémone, 1964 etc.

26. See J. Berque, 'Décolonisation, Intérieur et Nature seconde', in *Etudes de Sociologie tunisienne*, 1.1, 1968, p. 11 sq.

27. N. Assorodobraj, 'Le rôle de l'Histoire dans la prise de conscience nationale en Afrique occidentale', in *Africana Bulletin*, 7, 1967, 9–47.

28. *Afrika Zamani*, Yaoundé, 1974; *Tankara*, Madagascar, 1974; *Godo*, Abidjan, 1975; *L'informateur du Rwanda*, 1967; *Revue d'Histoire Maghrébine*, Tunis, 1974, etc.

29. *Abd el Krim et la République du Rif*, Acte du Colloque International des 18–20 janvier 1973, Paris, 1976.

30. P. Bonafe, 'Une classe d'âge politique: la G.M.N.R. de la République du Congo Brazzaville', in *Cah. Etudes Africaines*, 2.3 (31), 1968, 327–168.

31. J. L. Miège, 'Acculturation, Histoire et classes d'âges', in *Bull. I.H.P.O.M.*, no 10, 1976.

32. C. Hoskyns, 'Africa's foreign relations: the case of Tanzania', in *Internation. Aff.* 44 (3) July 1968.
33. R. Pascal, *La République Malgache*, Paris, 1965.
34. D. Ingram, 'La Grande Bretagne et l'indépendance de l'Afrique' in *Rev. fr. Et. Polit. Afr.*, 35, 11, 1968.
35. For Morocco see Miège, *Le Maroc et l'Europe*, Paris, 4 Vol., 1961, 1963.
36. P. Pascon, 'L'Histoire sociale et les structures agraires de la région du Haouz de Marrakech' (Paris, doctoral thesis, 1975).
37. L. Valensi, *Fellahs tunisiens. L'économie rurale et la vie des campagnes aux XVIIIe et XIXe siècles*, thesis, Paris, 1975.
38. A. Djeghloul, 'La formation sociale algérienne à la veille de la colonisation', in *La Pensée*, 2. 1976.
39. O. Debbash, 'La formation des partis uniques africains', in *Revue de l'Occident Musulman*, 2. 1966, p. 51–95.
40. D. Ingram, 'La Grande Bretagne et l'Indépendance de l'Afrique' in *Rev. fr. Et. Polit. afr.*, 35, 11, 1968.
41. Supon, *Revue de psychologie des peuples*, devenue *Revue d'ethnopsychologie* et aussi les recherches concernant la psycho-pathologie transculturelle v. *Transcultural Psychiatric Review and News*.
42. *Ibid.*
43. S. O. Anozie, *Sociologie du roman africain*, Paris, 1970.
44. J. Berque, Vers une sociologie des passages, in *Etudes de Sociologie tunisienne*, 1.1, 1968, p. 29 sq.

3

Andrew Cohen and the Transfer of Power in Tropical Africa, 1940–1951

Ronald Robinson

Any analysis of the rise and fall of the British empire in tropical Africa leads us into a central paradox. It was acquired at the end of the last century to exclude foreign powers from these territories, but without positive intentions of developing them economically as imperial estates. For the next half century, as a result, the English pro-consuls could do comparatively little to develop their colonies. During the interwar years of 'Indirect rule'[2] they made a virtue of preserving indigenous institutions for which they had brought no substitute, and so looked not unlike curators watching over an ethnological museum. Not until after 1945 when the economic recovery of the United Kingdom from war required it, did the empire begin to invest large capitals in the *mise en valeur* of its African colonies. Yet, at precisely that moment the strategists of Whitehall planned to dismantle their colonial system on the assumption that independence was inevitable within the next two decades. Paradoxically an empire acquired when it was not wanted was to be given up when needed most. Had British planners decided that nationalism was the continuation of imperialism by other and more efficient means? Perhaps. Had African nationalists grown strong enough to send their district commissioners packing? Probably not. Or had anti-imperial sentiment in Britain and the United States cracked the will to empire at last? May be.

Answers to such intriguing questions may be studied in the

calculations and miscalculations of the Colonial Office planners of the day. The question for them however was not one of explaining the fall of an empire, but of judging how much power should be shared with Africans in order to retain colonial control. That depended on the relative bargaining power of rulers and ruled. To put it simply, the rulers came to the table with the idea of keeping authority up to the brink of a situation in which they might have to shoot or get out; subjects came with the idea of enlarging their share of power up to the point of getting shot or backing down. But neither side relished the last resort except perhaps as a market indicator, so that normally the empire found plenty of African collaborators[3] without resigning in essentials. These games of Russian roulette were tests of nerve, gambles on the state of morale on the other side.

In search of these imponderables we examine in this chapter the changing bargains of collaboration which the Colonial Office believed necessary to retain control over the African dependencies at various times in the nineteen forties. It is suggested that, in the minds of the planners at least, the door to colonial self-government had been unlocked as early as 1947, before nationalists in Africa had gathered the strength to force it open; that a rapid advance to self-government was planned, partly because economic and social development seemed impracticable without bringing the nationalists into co-operation, partly to appease British and American anti-colonialism; that the very existence of this long-term plan inclined the makers of policy in London to mistake events in Africa for their expectations and to concede authority before the contingencies planned for actually came to pass; that the initial democratisation of colonial government which had been designed as the first stage of the plan largely created African nationalism as a popular movement; that the British then over-reacted to its manifestations which their own constitution-mongering had brought forth and yielded power more swiftly than they had intended. They were to be disenchanted with the outcome of their planned blunders a few years later when a series of military coups and civil wars exposed the fragility of national movements that had once appeared so constructive.

Assessments of Black Nationalism, 1941–1947

Whatever persuaded the British empire in 1947 to plan its own
demise in tropical Africa, it was not fear of black African freedom
fighters. The threat to colonial control from them seemed derisory
to the Colonial Office from 1939 to 1948, when the Accra riots in
the Gold Coast gave it some substance at last. Such was the
complacency on this score that the Department during the years
between the world wars had reserved the question of self-
government for black Africa for consideration 'in the next
century and possibly the next'.[4] In 1940 the septuagenarian, ex-
Indian governor and African surveyor, Lord Hailey, who became
mayor of the palace of African post-war planning, was sent round
British Africa to assess the situation. Nationalists, he reported,
were nowhere to be found except 'among a few sections of the
Gold Coast and possibly in the coastal areas of Nigeria';[5] and
even there the chiefs had them firmly by the throat. The
assessment was as complacent in 1943 and 1945: 'In West Africa
so far the political elements are a small proportion of the
population'.[6]

A few urban 'agitators' stood little chance of raising a mass
following among the peasantry it seemed, so long as colonial
governments kept the loyalty of local chiefs and notables. That
had always been the political strategy of indirect rule.[7] It was the
collaborative bargains with the chiefs that were crucial. As they
were contributing manpower and production to the war effort
without requital in imports, their loyalty was being bought with
pledges of better living standards and constitutional advances
when the peace was won. For the purpose of honouring these
pledges Hailey prescribed a policy of conservative political
advance on indirect rule principles: build up African
representation in central government through chiefs elected
indirectly from provincial councils and native authorities, to the
exclusion of all but a few urban, educated Africans.[8] His formula
was for continuing the pre-war strategy of backing the traditional
leaders of ethnic groups as bulwarks against nationalist agitation
and rewarding them with limited concessions at the centre.This
formula was repeated in post-war plans up to 1946: 'go
cautiously at the centre ... concentrate on local institutions to
train Africans in managing their own affairs ... social and

economic development may help slow down political demands. There will of course be vocal elements who will want to quicken the tempo. We must expect a certain amount of agitation before things settle down after the war. It is idle to think we are going to satisfy political aspirations entirely by schemes of social welfare'.[9] It was Hailey's backward-looking formula that inspired the reformed constitutions which Sir Alan Burns introduced into the Gold Coast in 1946 and Sir Arthur Richards (later Lord Milverton) set up in Nigeria in 1947. More seats for chiefs on executive and legislative councils apparently would see the empire happily back to the *status quo ante*. Along this cautious road the African dependencies might be expected to come within sight of self-government after some sixty to eighty years. The heroic disasters of 1940 plainly had led to no heroic re-shuffling of the cards of African colonial collaboration. Under the blitz in Whitehall the old players were taking the old tricks unruffled. Events elsewhere nevertheless were making them bite their nails. It was not the black, but the white freedom fighters in Kenya and Rhodesia, in England and the United States that were jolting their assurance in the years 1941 to 1947.

The Great American 'Scare', 1941–1944

During the years 1941 to 1944 the prospect of the Americans making a Boston tea-party of the entire British empire pre-occupied the war cabinet in London. The official mind, indeed, never quite got over the shock, as it was realised that not only the empire but also the metropolis now hung militarily and financially on the whim of the ex-colonial ally across the Atlantic. While it seemed vital to the British to obtain an agreement from the Americans 'that would include defence of the colonial areas without impairing our right to administer them',[10] it seemed right to the Americans that colonial empires should be liquidated as soon as possible under international supervision.[11] Whitehall countered with proposals for a set of regional, consultative commissions in colonial areas designed 'to bring in America in defence and in economic matters'[12] and also to satisfy 'Clem Attlee and the Left in Britain [with an] element of internationalism'.[13] Eventually there came more reassuring news from Washington. After the Pentagon had reminded the State department of its own strategic need of colonial bases in the Pacific,[14] the Americans agreed that the 'Colonial problem should not [after all] be approached from the point of view of the rate at which we should grant political independence, but ... from the angle of Freedom from Want and Freedom from Fear'.[15] Whitehall found this message 'eminently satisfactory, so far as it goes'.[16]

It went no further than this: the immediate, official threat from the United States might be over; official pressure for colonial independence under international supervision might be off; but the slightest agitation of profoundly anti-colonial American opinion might force the administration in Washington to turn it on again at any moment. A fitful and most uncomfortable sleeping partner had joined the imperial board of directors. It was no accident that from 1943 the British began to liberalise their arrangements in order to appease American anti-colonialism. The American 'scare' contributed much to that sense of approaching Nemesis in Africa which a Colonial Office official expressed in 1942:

Nineteenth century conceptions of empire are dead. Forces released by the war are gathering great velocity ... after the war this Island will be exhausted ... immigrant and indigenous populations in Africa will seek ... a wider measure of control over their own affairs. To surmount this danger will require statesmanship, or we shall lose the African continent as we did the American in the eighteenth century.[17]

Dependence on the United States jolted imperial complacency and strengthened the demands of British liberals, humanitarians and socialists for getting rid of skeletons in imperial cupboards and giving loyal colonial subjects a better deal, at first in the field of colonial economic development and social welfare; and, eventually, from 1947 onwards, in the field of political and constitutional advance. American influence in favour of progress toward self-government worked insidiously, unofficially but none the less effectively. The colonial reformers in Whitehall and Westminster could now argue that a transfer of power to colonial subjects would help secure the vital American alliance.

The White African 'Scare', 1942–1944

Unlike the white freedom fighters across the Atlantic, those in Africa were not on the side of progress for black Africans. They had defied the theories of multi-racial equality and paramountcy of native interests with which the Colonial Office had morally re-armed itself since 1923, and rivetted *de facto* white supremacy on the Indian minority and African majority in Kenya and Northern Rhodesia. For the past twenty years the imperial trustees had been impotent to scrap the colour bars or promote native interests in these territories, in the face of threats of settler rebellion with support from Southern Rhodesia and South Africa.[18] It was only with the greatest difficulty that the Colonial Office retained a semblance of authority there. Coercion of the settlers since 1923 had always been ruled out of the question;[19] the British voter whose ancient folk prejudices were on the side of his kith and kin, would not tolerate it;[20] no more would white South Africans. To send troops and enforce official policy, it seemed, would be to risk losing a large part of the white African Commonwealth; not to do so would set the Indian and black West African empires at risk; so the empire had sat still and done nothing amid a prolonged crisis of conscience that divided its interests, races and officials against each other, that sapped its confidence and moral credibility. It seemed as if the world-wide foundations of imperial interests were already grinding against each other in the penultimate upheaval before the fall.

This pervasive moral crisis centred on East Africa was driven into a further cycle of inconclusiveness by the disasters that fell on Britain in 1940. For the next four years the east and central African dependencies seemed to be escaping from the imperial grasp. General Smuts and the South African government had had to take over their defence in 1940 and he was determined 'to have his say over the future of the greater part of Africa',[21] it seemed, before handing them back. The Colonial Office was also frightened, mistakenly as it turned out, that the settlers with South African approval were seizing their independence 'under the guise of machinery set up ostensibly to aid the war effort'.[22] In 1942 Cranborne, then Colonial Minister, proposed to concede responsible government to the settlers over the white highlands of Kenya, but his traditionally negrophile officials united in defence

of trusteeship on behalf of native interests. Cranborne argued:
'we shall be unable to coerce the settlers even if we wish to do so.
If ... we reach a deadlock we shall be beaten as we have always
been beaten in the past'.[23] This was the measure of imperial
confidence lost through appesing the colonists since 1922. One
way of removing the moral canker which was spreading
throughout the empire was to give them what they wanted and
resign the responsibility before British, Indians, and Americans
began tearing the empire apart in order to remove it. Like Amery
in the nineteen twenties, Cranborne chose this way out: his
officials on the other hand argued that, more likely, Indians and
Americans would tear the empire apart to prevent the handing
over of the Indian and African population to a white minority
government: 'the government of India and the Indian nationalists
would ... object as usual';[24] 'opinion in West Africa, in the
Labour party and elsewhere in this country would be equally
critical';[25] 'the spread of South African ideas in East Africa would
conflict with the advancement of Africans envisaged by HMG
and by influential quarters in America'.[26] The officials won their
case. Early in 1944 Cranborne's successor, Oliver Stanley,
shelved the plan for settler self-government; his reason was that
'the front against white settlement has hardened considerably
during the past year'.[27] A bargain with white Africa was not to be
found which would not break the much more important bargains
necessary elsewhere, particularly in the United States, India and
West Africa. But the cancer remained; the official mind continued
to be troubled about white rebels and the advance of South
African influence into east and central Africa. In the early 'fifties,
as we shall see, these traumas were to inspire the setting up of the
ill-fated central African federation.

Signs of Mea Culpa, 1943–44

Now that not only Indian nationalists and British social
democrats but also American anti-imperialists were denouncing
the empire, a sense of guilt made Whitehall more conscientious. It
was true of the British as of other empires that morality improved
as power declined; from 1943 onward the Colonial Office began
to carry out the moral pretentions which it had raised in official

statements of policy since the native paramountcy declaration of 1923.[28]

Ethics have always been the first refuge of the British imperialists, and one should not be too cynical about their continual breast-beatings. If the men of the empire made a habit of moralising their mundane purposes, it is reasonable to suppose that this was because theology was as vital to the imperial process as surplus capital or high velocity guns.

Since the eighteenth century the theology of the British pro-consuls had been defined in terms of 'Trusteeship'.[29] In effect that doctrine equipped them with a Gladstone bag of ethics which could pack almost any principle without bulging. The content was changed from age to age in response to changing ideas in Britain of the proper scope of governmental action and definitions of the good society and how to achieve it; and also to meet changing political pressures in colonial capitals and at Westminster. Kept up to date in this way the doctrine of trusteeship served many purposes: it kept the imperial services abroad in line with opinion at home; it insulated them from the velvet lure of going native; above all, it served to justify the empire at its most vulnerable point. The theology kept the hurly burly of English party politics from playing on the inherent inconsistency involved in a democracy holding an empire in thrall. If it had not done, the will to empire might have frayed at the centre. What is more, the doctrine was adjusted from time to time so that it turned the blade of anti-imperialist critics and stole their weapons for the empire. Their criticisms were met, their utopian ideals were incorporated into the theory of trusteeship as aims of colonial rule. Such changes of moral front had been remarkably effective. They had dissuaded Gladstones and Hobsons, MacDonalds and Bevins to cease decrying the wickedness of empire past and exalt the better empire yet to come. So, alterations in the morality of trusteeship had converted the anti-imperialists of one generation into the imperialists of the next.

Changes in the ethics of trusteeship therefore may be no bad indicator of shifts in the spirit and confidence of British imperialism. One sign of the change of heart which began in 1943 was a new label for the imperial ethic: the word 'Trusteeship' seemed too paternal, too unprogressive for American consumption; it was over-printed with the title of 'Partnership'. Other signs of a transformation of ethical theory were less superficial. In 1943 ministers no less than Colonial Office officials began to confess past imperial sins and think of atonement; even to ask the British taxpayer to make restitution. Surely this was the mark of moral reformation? In that year Harold Macmillan dared as a junior minister to suggest that the Treasury should buy out the Kenya settlers lock, stock and barrel and repatriate them. It seemed the only method of getting them out of the way and getting on with the job of developing the native population; it would be expensive, Macmillan admitted, but it would be cheaper than a race war.[30] Mau Mau was already casting its menacing shadow before. In that year also the colonial minister, Oliver Stanley, asked the Treasury to dispose of another skeleton 'equally scandalous', as he put it 'to modern ideas of trusteeship'.[31] From the beginning of colonial rule the empire had granted the mineral rights in Northern Rhodesia and Nigeria to be the private property of British companies; as a result large mining profits went to shareholders in London instead of going to local colonial exchequers. Stanley pressed the Chancellor to buy the companies out in order to give British colonialism a better image at home and abroad.[32] But the thin lips of the Treasury lords did not smile on the idea of paying for all the past sins of imperialism in Africa; if they began to do so, there would be no end.[33] Nevertheless 1943 was to be *annus mirabilis* in the history of the tropical African empire. To gild a more acceptable reputation in the eyes of British and American public opinion, one hundred and twenty millions was squeezed out of the Chancellor of the Exchequer for post-war colonial development and welfare. It was on this ground rather than on that of the economic need of the United Kingdom that the case for the money was put and won.[34]

If the Colonial Development and Welfare Act was an exercise in public relations, it also announced the advent of a more socialistic ideal of colonial empire. A new generation of politicians and officials had arrived, whom nationalist and economic critiques of imperialism had made somewhat ashamed of the *ancien* colonial *regime*, who were resolved to carry into effect the pledges to its subjects which had been left so long unhonoured. For the first time they were assured of large public capitals with which to do so. As the implications of the rise of

Labour at home and dependence on the United States abroad were realised, these new men were to re-shape the ethics and perspectives of African empire drastically no less from conviction than expediency.

Andrew Cohen

At first it was the Colonial Office's post-war economic and social plans that were transformed by the new wave, but in 1947 it swept over into the political field of the transfer of colonial power. Among the new men who rode it, Andrew Cohen[35] represented the improved ethic and the new course in extreme form. As *alter ego* of his minister, Arthur Creech Jones, from 1946 to 1950, he did more, wittingly or unwittingly, to bring about the dismantling of British colonial rule and the rise of nationalism in tropical Africa than most African politicians.

Of giant stature and energy though boyish in enthusiasms, Cohen was a Jew by birth, a classic Greek by education and outlook. He was born in 1909, on his father's side into the conservative *haute juiverie* of England; on his mother's, into the radical, Unitarian tradition of the Cobbs. At Cambridge his studies in the ancient classics taught him little of modern Africa, but qualified him to join the other classical scholars who monitored the dependent empire at the Colonial Office in 1933. Africa had become his life by chance, and he learned about it from the official historiography in the dusty files. When he first visited the field in 1937 he was so shocked by what the imperial trustees had omitted to do for Africans in Northern Rhodesia, that he began the campaign for nationalising the British South Africa Company's copper royalties which Stanley took up in 1943.[36] He was soon frustrated enough with the remote and ineffective nature of Colonial Office rule to propose that he and his colleagues of the Home Civil Service should hand over their jobs to Colonial Service officers who knew Africa at first hand.[37] A year spent studying the Negro problem in the United States gave him a huge liking for Americans and an abiding loathing of colour bars. But it was as controller of supplies and acting lieutenant governor at the siege of Malta from 1940 to 1943 that he first tasted the power for which he was voracious. The experience left him with a towering contempt for bureaucracy and the strong suspicion that, for purposes of serious work on indigenous society, colonial government of any kind might well prove to be a broken reed. He returned to the Colonial Office in 1943 to share in the frenzy of post-war planning which had begun there.

Cohen indeed was cut out to be a master planner in the style of a Platonic philosopher king: Cambridge had made him insufferably arrogant intellectually, though he was no intellectual in the usual sense of being devoted to a fixed system of ideas. His private passion was rather for lyric and romantic poetry. Ideas, if they were to engage his mind, had to be both practicable and relevant largely for the future; for he was obsessed with a heroic ideal of himself as idea in action. On the other hand Malta had taught him that action required cold appraisals and brutal pragmatism to be effective; and so, he combined a common sense genius for getting things done with a passionately speculative vision of ends to be realised at almost any cost. His self-image and ambition for distinction in the public service drove him relentlessly to define the idea of a better future and drag it bodily into the present. As the Labour party intellectuals seemed the only people with any new ideas of this kind, he became a Fabian socialist of the elitist sort; he believed in the duty of the state to set up a new moral order of society; and he upheld the right of the cognoscenti to define it. Inevitably he aspired to export the socially-democratic, welfare state, already blue-printed for the British Isles, to Africa.

When Attlee's Labour government came to power in 1945 and a year later Creech Jones became colonial minister, it fell to Cohen as head of the African division in the Colonial Office to turn the party's colonial shibboleths into terms of African reality. Their rapport grew naturally: both men were connected with the Fabian colonial bureau which championed the cause of the African intelligentsia in Britain; on socialist principles, both regarded indirect rule as an obsolete relic of reactionary imperialism. Cohen's own vision of the colonial future in tropical Africa was by this time sharply defined. Privately, if not officially, he believed that the age of empires was over; it was and ought to be ended constructively; he also believed on the other hand, that the longer colonial rule could be prolonged the more creative its ending would be. It seemed to him that colonial rule was no longer justifiable in principle, except as scaffolding for building independent nation states. To scrap it before the construction was finished would be folly; at the same time the scaffolding must not be allowed to become an end in itself and get in the way of the building. He felt that the empire had proved too feeble an instrument for engineering the advance of Africa into modern society; its final duty was to create nation states better able to carry out the task. Cohen's vision was essentially moral and peculiar to the man; though his colleagues in the Colonial Office shared much of his thought, none of them shared his frenetic sense of urgency in preparing tropical Africa for self-government. Nevertheless the so-called 'intellectual dreamer of Whitehall'[38] hammered these beliefs into post-war political plans. A colleague who had once been Churchill's private secretary wrote of Cohen's influence at this time: 'He seemed to make the history which we lived in and so affected all our work. He was a giant who towered above all of us of his generation at the colonial office'.[39]

The Cohen Report, May 1947

Toward the end of 1946 Creech Jones set up a committee of officials under Cohen and Caine (the head of the economic department) to 'chart a new approach' to Africa.[40] It was to consider not only ways of speeding up economic advance, but also means of political progress, including the transfer of power.[41] The given reasons why a new course was necessary repeated a formula which had become customary since 1941 for the justification of radical colonial reform: 'the internal situation in the territories themselves, the state of international opinion [not to mention the public relations of the Labour party] demand a new approach to policy in Africa'.[42] There is no specific evidence at present to show that any of these problems had become more acute, except that the dollar crisis had made the economic development of the African empire even more urgent; Labour ministers no less than the rank and file of the party grew prouder of it the more they talked of advancing its welfare;[43] the fires of American anti-colonialism were dying down in the beginnings of the Cold War. Until the cabinet papers for the period are opened, we cannot be sure, but it may well be that the new course was required by nothing more substantial than the prevailing spirit of post-war utopianism and the expectations of the Labour faithful that a Labour ministry ought to do something distinctively different in the colonial field.

Whatever the motive, Cohen's departmental committee certainly succeeded in inventing a striking new departure. Submitted in May 1947, its report attempted to look ten and twenty years ahead and match economic needs to political requirements; the Colonial Office had never done that before. For the first time also it was taking the initiative in policy-making away from the colonial governors and laying down a single set of charts for all the different African territories to follow. Cohen's report which thus began with a comprehensive slaughter of the precedents ended by implying a revolution in African policy similar to that which the Durham report had produced in policy toward the colonies of settlement exactly a century earlier. Durham had recommended self-government for Canada; Cohen planned on the assumption that 'within a generation ... the principal African territories will have attained ... full responsible government'[44] which meant in effect independence within the Commonwealth. It was already foreseen that the Gold Coast would lead the van.[45] At a stroke of the pen the official perspective on the longevity of African empire had been cut from a century to a mere twenty-five years.

Cohen's revolutionary manifesto for the transfer of power was inspired by the belief that if the dependencies were to be developed economically, their administration would have to be democratised and nationalised. The traditional kings and chiefs who had always been the mainstay of British colonial rule were useless as agents of economic growth and national unification; these modern tasks required the co-operation of the hitherto excluded modern, educated elite; their collaboration was not to be had except at the price of an accelerating transfer of power. As Cohen saw it, there was no alternative. Economic investment was bound to quicken the pace of social change and raise up popular discontents; it would be foolish to leave African politicians out in the cold to exploit them, frustrating development and creating anarchy. Without the transfer of power to educated elites, Cohen argued, it would soon become impossible for control over the colonies to be retained. It seemed in any event wiser to err on the side of conceding too much power too early than too little too late. Magnanimity, it was supposed, would put the brake on demand and make for moderately reasonable, rather than revolutionary successors who would continue the British connection.[46] Cohen summed up the implication of these arguments in two characteristic slogans: 'The fallacy of plenty of time ahead' in which to prepare the colonies for self-government; and 'Self-government [however amateurish or corrupt] is better than good colonial government'.[47]

According to his prophetic recommendations power was to be transferred in four stages as circumstances in each territory required it. In the first of these indirectly-elected Africans would be granted a majority of seats on colonial legislative councils, one or two of them being brought also on to the executive councils. Meanwhile, popularly selected councillors would be gaining executive experience in democratised local government authorities, and local electorates would be learning the arts of controlling them. University and training colleges would be multiplying educated cadres capable of filling the higher posts in the colonial services. In the second stage African legislative councillors were to be made responsible to the governor as executive heads of domestic branches of central government. Cohen took it for granted that the more these first two stages were prolonged, the firmer the foundations of self-government would be laid. Ideally therefore, universal franchises and directly elected majorities in legislative assemblies were to be withheld until the third stage had been reached, when African 'members' who enjoyed their confidence should be made responsible for all branches of government, except finance, security and external affairs. Finally in the last stage African ministers representing the majority party would modulate into a cabinet with collective responsibility to the legislature for the entire government on the Westminster model.[48]

It may seem strange for an empire to plan its own demise politically at precisely the moment when as a dollar earner and contributor to the home fat ration its economic value was at its height, but so it was. In 1947 Cohen and Creech Jones swung the aim of policy from one of jealously conserving imperial power in alliance with African kings and chiefs to one of building up independent nations hand in hand with modern elites.

Nevertheless, in Cohen's blue-print each step forward to African self-government was also justified as a step backwards towards prolonging colonial rule. The first three stages of reform designed to win the collaboration of the educated African, for example, were also intended to handicap his race for power at the centre with the dead-weight of the uneducated, communalistic, rural majority. Democratisation so-called aimed 'to bring together literates and illiterates in balanced and studied proportions', so that 'the professional African politician's selfish ambition' would be curbed for the commonweal.[49] Nor was power to be conceded stage by stage until those with pretentions to national leadership proved that they had united enough popular support behind them to insist upon it. To do otherwise would not be to transfer authority in the colonies but to see it dribble away.[50]

But policy issues not on paper but in action. In February 1947 Creech Jones issued the famous local government despatch which Cohen drafted for him.[51] It announced to the African governors that the old household gods of indirect rule had been cast out of the Colonial Office and directed them to do likewise. The very name and title of indirect rule was abolished; its covenants by which neo-traditional native authorities enjoyed a monopoly of administrative privilege and political representation were to be scrapped; they were incapable, the despatch declared, of managing the local economic projects and social services required for rapid modernisation. For this purpose the rejected, educated elites were to be brought in to provide the necessary leadership. 'The modern conception of colonial administration', the Colonial Office insisted, required a 'democratic system of local government on English lines'.[52] How this was to be achieved in the field in technical detail was to be worked out under Cohen's chairmanship at a Cambridge conference by a cross-section of experienced Colonial Service officials. Their report[53] was submitted to a conference of African governors at Church House, Westminster, in November.[54] Old guard indirect rulers at these conferences protested bitterly that Africa was not ready for democracy; democratisation would merely drive the loyal majority into the arms of the disloyal nationalist minority and undermine imperial authority. There were also rumblings among British colonial officials against the Africanisation of higher posts in government. A ringing directive from Creech Jones reminded them of their duty to train Africans to govern themselves. British officials must now prepare them to take over their jobs and retire to an advisory role. Die-hards who objected to doing so should resign, the directive went on; 'There was no prospect of the policy being changed except in the direction of still faster progress'.[55] No sooner had the Cohen committee reported than the first two stages were being carried urgently into effect.

By 1947 evidently, in the mind of the Colonial Office at least, the door to independence had already been unlocked for African nationalists to push open as soon as they became able. It had been unlocked, not in response to, but in anticipation of nationalist pressure, by British economic need and moral utopianism. Though by this time Dr Azikiwe had formed his National Council of Nigeria and the Cameroons, it was not yet a popular movement; in 1947 he was holding meetings in London seeking British support for his delegation's petition for Nigerian self-government. Nkrumah had not yet returned to the Gold Coast from the United States via Manchester. In October 1947 a missionary friend of his wrote to Cohen to inform him that Nkrumah was going out 'to start some kind of nationalist movement' and asked him to see that the young man was treated gently so as not to embitter him.[56] Dr Hastings Banda was still practising medicine in London; Kenyatta up to a few months previously had been working on a newspaper in London. These famous men may have had more support for radical nationalism in their own countries than the British gave them credit for; but by the time that Creech Jones and Cohen opened the gate of independence for them, they had not yet begun to organise elite and people into a popular party. It was the constitution-mongering inspired by the Cohen plan that gave west African politicians the opportunity and incentive to organise mass nationalist movements.

The Premature Implementation of the Plan, 1948–1951

More than all the preaching of the new doctrine from Whitehall however, the scare of the Accra riots of 1948[57] in the Gold Coast and the Colonial Office's reaction sped west Africa on the new course. Creech Jones and Cohen felt that they were racing against time to lay foundations of stability for the self-governing states to come; they were on the look-out for, indeed eager to welcome the emergence of progressive national movements to energise development and unify ethnic mosaics into national societies; and therefore they were prepared to exaggerate the significance of the first signs of nationalism and concede power even more quickly than they had intended. The Accra riots fulfilled their expectation that in the Gold Coast colony at least, colonial control was already breaking down, and they decided to regain it by granting large constitutional advances to strengthen the hand of the moderate chiefs and intelligentsia against the extremists. In 1951 direct elections and a quasi-ministerial system were introduced for this purpose. Four years after the Cohen report the Gold Coast as a result had advanced to stage three of the plan. What was more, the new constitution which had been designed to give electoral victory to the moderate leaders of the United Gold Coast Convention, as the result of a psephological blunder, handed it instead to Nkrumah's new party which wanted independence at once. He had to be let out of gaol and made leader of government business in the legislative assembly. Inevitably this spectacular stroke of luck turned his following into a dynamic mass movement which was to finish the course to independence a mere six years later. What had been given to the Gold Coast soon could not be denied to Nigeria and Sierra Leone, and so the domino effect of vision and miscalculation spread throughout British West Africa. It was Cohen who planned these crucial, initial transfers of power in the Gold Coast and Nigeria; indeed he was soon to claim as personal declarations of faith in Africa's national destiny the government white papers which granted the constitutional concessions recommended first in the Watson and then in the Coussey Commission reports as solutions to the Gold Coast's problems;[58] it was his constitution-mongering that awoke the slumbering genius of nationalism in West Africa. The ballot box, directly elected assemblies and African ministers − institutions which according to the Cohen plan of 1947 should have been withheld until national movements had become powerful − were now yielded prematurely and contributed largely to their manufacture. He had hoped to educate the nationalists more gradually into their responsibilities; but the rising expectations which easy bargains had unleashed were overtaking him. In this sense his plans, however utopian and remote from African realities, predetermined the shape of things to come, even when they were misconceived and misapplied. By 1951 nevertheless Cohen was delighted with the outcome. On his way to virtual exile from Whitehall to Government House, Entebbe, where a governor's boots were supposed to cool his radical heels, he congratulated himself that West Africa had been set on course for self-government beyond recall.

His planned transfer of power in central Africa from 1948 to 1951 proved less fortunate. It is said that he was naive enough to believe that better constitutions could improve human nature, a belief to which socialists are especially prone. If there is some truth in this accusation, it is found in the bargains which his scheme for federating the two Rhodesias and Nyasaland offered the leaders of the white settler minorities there. By yielding them a considerable degree of self-government subject to imperial safeguards for African interests, he hoped at best to persuade them to share their power with the black majority in a multi-racial state; at worst, to stop the spread of *apartheid* from South Africa northward into the British dependencies. It seemed to him better to make sure of half a loaf of political rights for Africans now than to wait for the settlers' repeatedly threatened unilateral declaration of independence which would leave the Africans with none at all. Cohen converted the Labour ministers, Griffith and Gordon Walker, to this plan,[59] but it was left to the succeeding Conservative government to carry out its principles in the British Central African Federation of 1953. However, the anger of the African majority at the imposition of the new structure was such that Kenneth Kaunda and Hastings Banda were able to organise national parties strong enough to break the association and win independence for Malawi and Zambia ten years later.[60] Thus in central Africa as in the Gold Coast and Nigeria, Cohen's constitution-mongering had done much to politicise the grass roots and make the nationalist cause popular.

As governor of Uganda from 1952 to 1957 Cohen practised strenuously in the field what he had preached from the palace of planning in the Colonial Office. He hastened the democratisation of his government from above and below to encourage the formation of political parties and national consciousness. No governor ever tried harder than he to manufacture a nationalist movement strong enough to integrate the dominant Baganda with the other ethnic communities of the protectorate. Impatiently in 1953 he deported the Kabaka of Buganda in order to remove the major obstacle to united self-rule, only to provoke a neo-traditional reaction in favour of Baganda particularism which defeated his object. Wittingly or unwittingly he had succeeded in inducing national movements of considerable power in every territory of British tropical Africa, except his own.[61]

Cohen left Uganda in 1957 to represent the United Kingdom on the United Nations Trusteeship Council in New York. Returning to Whitehall in 1961 he became permanent head of a new department of government from which until his death in 1968, he directed the flow of British aid to independent Africa and other parts of the third world. In so far as any one man provided the vision, Cohen's was the master-mind behind the British transfer of power in tropical Africa. There were many at the time who wished to turn the African colonies into welfare states; there were some who foresaw that the colonial age was expiring; but Cohen was one of the few who grasped the full implications. Not only did he realise that colonial administration would have to be nationalised, but also that it would be a race against time to lay sufficient foundations of stability for self-government. As the realist in him discerned the imperial era was over, the moralist hurried to end it constructively. Few African politicians had done as much as he to build up nationalities under the scaffolding of a falling empire. With Creech Jones and Cohen the African empire came deliberately to the end of the beginning and the beginning of the end where the rise toppled over into decline and fall.

NOTES

1. omitted.
2. Lugard defined 'Indirect Rule' in the *Dual Mandate* as 'Rule by native chiefs, unfettered in their control of their people, yet subordinated to the control of the Protecting Power in certain well-defined directions'. It implied a conservative, non-interventionist philosophy of colonial government which waited on indigenous society to adapt itself instinctively to changing conditions. As a political strategy it required the exclusion of the African intelligentsia to preserve the authority of chiefs on whose alliance the system was based. See A. H. M. Kirk-Greene, *Principles of Native Administration in Nigeria: Selected Documents*, Oxford, 1965, Introduction.

3. On the role of collaborative bargains in colonial rule, see R. Robinson, 'Non-European Foundations of European Imperialism: Sketch for a Theory of Collaboration' in R. Owen and B. Sutcliffe, *Studies in the Theory of Imperialism*, London, 1972, pp. 118–42; also in W. R. Louis, *Imperialism: the Robinson and Gallagher Controversy*, New York, 1976, pp. 128–48.

4. Bottomley, minute, 23 August 1929, C.O. 25334/29.

5. 'Note of Discussion with Lord Hailey, 18 March 1941', C.O. 47100/1/41.

6. Dawe, minute, 9 February 1943, on memo. by O. G. R. Williams (undated), C.O. 33718/43.

7. 'The position given to the Chiefs in this way will be jealously guarded by them and their people against the assaults which may in the course of time be made against it by the Europeanised natives seeking to obtain political control of the country ... we are ... building up a bulwark against political agitators'. Sir D. Cameron, Speech to Tanganyika Legislative Council, December 1927: C.O. C.P. African 1111, p. 7; see also D. Cameron, *Principles of Native Administration*, Lagos, 1934, p. 6.

8. 'Note of Discussion with Lord Hailey, 18 March 1941', *op. cit.*

9. Sir A. Dawe, minute, 9 February 1943: O. Stanley (Colonial Secretary) minuted enthusiastically; 'This is excellent. Please proceed with draft plan', 19 February 1943, C.O. 33718/43.

10. Draft Cabinet Paper, enclosed in Eden to Attlee, 25 October 1942, C.O./323/1858/9057/B/14.

11. Notes of meeting, Eden, Attlee, Cranborne, 3 May 1943; *ibid*/74.

12. Emrys-Evans to Cranborne, 14 October 1942, C.O. 232/1858/9057/B/3807.

13. Cranborne to Emrys-Evans, 9 October 1942, C.O. 323/1858/9057/B.

14. See W. R. Louis, *Imperialism at Bay: The United States and the Decolonisation of the British Empire, 1941–45*, Oxford, 1977.

15. R. Law to Oliver Stanley, 11 April 1944, C.O. 323/1877/9057/B./11.

16. *Ibid.*

17. Dawe, secret memo. 'A Federal Solution for East Africa', July 1942, C.O. 822/111, pt 3/46709.

18. On details see R. E. Robinson, 'The Trust in British East and Central Africa, 1889–1939' (Ph.D. thesis, 1951, University of Cambridge); also R. G. Gregory, *India and East Africa: A History of Race Relations within the British Empire, 1890–1939*, Oxford, 1971, *passim*.

19. 'It is admittedly not easy to understand why the British Parliament should find difficulty in imposing its will upon a small community of British settlers ... [but] Magna Carta year for [them] was 1923 [when] they delivered a blow at the prestige of the British Government in Kenya from which it has never recovered ... With the lesson of 1923 in mind ... the home authorities ... have avoided any head-on clash with the settlers ... the doctrine of the paramountcy of native interests enunciated by the Duke of Devonshire in 1923 ... has in Kenya become an unreal figment'. (Sir A. Dawe, memo. 'A Federal Solution for East Africa', July 1942, C.O. 822/111 pt. 3/46709.)

20. Faced with a threatened rebellion of Kenya settlers in 1923 Devonshire

confessed to the cabinet: neither native nor European troops could be used against them without results 'fatal to British prestige throughout Africa ... further, it may be taken as certain that such action would be bitterly condemned in Parliament.' ('Indians in Kenya', memo. by Secretary of State for Colonies, 14 February 1923; Cabinet Paper (S).99, (23), C.O. 25473/30/1A).

21. Moore to Moyne, telegraphic, 21 November 1940, C.O. 847/23/47173/1: A. Cohen, 'Note on Pan-African Conference', 24 August 1943, C.O. 847/23/47181/29.
22. Cranborne to Attlee, 22 July 1943, C.O. 847/23/47181/21.
23. Ibid.
24. Sir A. Dawe, minute, 19 January 1940, C.O. 822/103/46523.
25. A. Cohen, 'Note on Pan-African Conference', 24 August 1943, C.O. 847/23/47181/29.
26. 'Reasons for urgency in dealing with the East African problem', enclosure 2, in Sir H. Moore to Stanley, 20 April 1943, C.O. 822/108/46523/43.
27. 'Note of Meeting in Secretary of State's room, 4 June 1943'; C.O. 822/108/46523/43/19: 'Note of Discussion between Attlee, Stanley and Cranborne, 5 August 1943', ibid./29
28. 'The interests of the African natives must be paramount and if those interests and the interests of the immigrant races should conflict, the [native] should prevail.' (Cmd. 1922 (1923) 9–10); this principle was defined in 1929 to mean 'the creation ... of a field for the full development of native life [is] a first charge on any territory; having created this field the government has the duty to devote all available resources to assisting the natives to develop it'. (Report of the Hilton Young Commission, Cmd., 3234(1929),40.)
29. On the history of the doctrine see R. E. Robinson, op. cit.; G. V. Mellor, British Imperial Trusteeship, 1783–1850, London, 1951.
30. Macmillan, minute, 15 August 1942, on Sir A. Dawe's memo., 'A Federal Solution for East Africa', C.O. 967/57/42.
31. Stanley to Sir J. Anderson, 25 August 1944, C.O. 583/270/29; (the negotiations on this issue between the Colonial Office and the Treasury began at the official level in 1943).
32. Ibid.
33. Anderson to Stanley, 14 October 1944, ibid/30.
34. 'I make no pretence ... that this is going to be a profitable transaction on a purely financial calculation. The over-riding reason why I feel that these proposals are essential is the necessity to justify our position as a Colonial Power.' (Stanley to Anderson, 21 September 1944, C.O. 852/588/19275.) Here again the negotiations had begun at the official level in the previous year.
35. This chapter is one of several sketches for a biography of Sir Andrew Cohen which a generous grant from the Ford Foundation has enabled the author to undertake. He is indebted to Lady Helen Cohen and Miss Ruth Cohen also for access to Sir Andrew's private papers and for much other information about him.
The author knew him personally and worked under him, first as research

officer, African Studies Branch, Colonial Office, 1947–1950, and then as chairman of the Cambridge conferences on problems of development, 1961–69.

36. Minute, 29 March 1938, on Young's despatch of 19 March 1938; C.O. 795/99/45105/7570.
37. Memo. 'Merging of the Colonial Office into the Colonial Service', 15 September 1943, C.O. 850/194/20807.
38. Lord Milverton, then Governor of Nigeria, branded Cohen with this title at the African Governors' Conference at Church House, Westminster, in November 1947. See also Milverton to Cohen, 4 October 1951 and Cohen's tart reply of 10 October 1951; *Cohen Papers*.
39. Sir J. Martin to Lady Cohen, June 1968, *Cohen Papers*.
40. Ivor Thomas, minute, November 1946, note of in *Cohen Papers*.
41. Report of Committee (departmental), 22 May 1947, *ibid.*
42. Ivor Thomas, minute, *op. cit.*
43. See P. Gupta, *Imperialism and the British Labour Movement, 1914–1964*, London, 1975, caps. 9–10. However there was Fabian pressure for a new course in 1946 as there had been in 1929–1930; see Hinden to Creech Jones, 21 October 1946, *Cohen Papers*.
44. Report of departmental committee, 22 May 1947, *op. cit.*
45. *Ibid.*
46. *Ibid.*
47. Cohen coined these phrases in debate with conservative indirect rulers at the Cambridge summer conference on local government in Africa, August 1947, of which he was chairman. 'The principle on which I stand is this. Our policy is African advancement; our only justification for being in Africa is to guide the Africans towards self-government.' (Cohen to A. Gaitskell, 31 August 1955, *Cohen Papers*.)
48. Report of departmental committee, 22 May 1947, *op. cit.*
49. Minutes by F. Pedler and G. B. Cartland, May 1947; *Cohen Papers*.
50. The details of the Cohen plan were naturally kept secret, but the broad implications were revealed in two articles in a semi-official journal: A. Creech Jones, 'The Place of African Local Administration in Colonial Policy', *Journal of African Administration*, 1, January 1949: Lord Listowel, 'The Modern Conception of Government in British Africa', *ibid.* 1, September, 1949.
51. Circular despatch to African governors, 25 February 1947, C. 60539.
52. *Ibid.*
53. *African Local Government*, report of the Cambridge Summer Conference, 1947, C.O. African, 1173.
54. 'Local Government in Africa', A.G.C.12, enclosed in circular despatch, 13 January 1948.
55. Burns to Lloyd, 11 February 1947; minutes, *Cohen Papers*.
56. Rev. H. M. Grace to Cohen, 22 October 1947, *Cohen Papers*.
57. See D. Austin, *Politics in Ghana, 1946–1960*, Oxford, 1964.
58. Colonial No. 232(1948) and 250(1949); Cohen to A. Gaitskell, 31 August 1955, *Cohen Papers*.
59. Cohen to P. C. Gordon-Walker, 11 January 1952, *Cohen Papers*.

60. See R. I. Rotberg, *The Rise of Nationalism in Central Africa, 1873–1964*, London, 1966; D. C. Mulford, *Zambia, the Politics of Independence, 1957–1964*, London, 1967; P. Mason, *The Year of Decision: Rhodesia and Nyasaland in 1960* London, 1961; J. Barber, *Rhodesia, the Road to Rebellion*, London, 1967.
61. For accounts of his governorship of Uganda, see C. Gertzel, 'Kingdoms, Districts and the Unitary State: Uganda, 1945–1962', in D. A. Low and A. Smith (eds.) *History of East Africa*, 3, Oxford 1967, pp. 65–108; D. A. Low, *Buganda in Modern History*, London, 1971.

4

Assumptions, Expectations, and Plans: Approaches to Decolonisation in Sierra Leone

John D. Hargreaves

1. Perspective Views

To understand the past involves two very different operations, and to synthesize them is a severe test of historical scholarship. On the one hand historians study change over an extended period of time, and try to discern in what underlying direction the twisting course of events was leading; at the same time they must immerse themselves in the detailed evidence for those events, seeking to do justice to the thoughts and purposes of men whose own conceptions of what they were doing, and where they were going, may now seem to have been ironically mistaken. Both operations present peculiar difficulties in studying events so near in time, and so contentious, as the termination of colonial rule in Africa.

In the long perspective of history, the period when Europeans exercised direct political control over West African peoples was brief: except in a few special areas closely involved in the conduct of oceanic trade, it nowhere exceeded the life-time of an old man. But were these years of revolutionary importance? Jacob Ajayi regards the colonial period as 'just another episode ... in the continuous flow of African history'[1]: Africans who successfully practised the 'politics of survival' were able eventually to recover their sovereignty with their essential identities intact, having acquired new institutions, techniques and problems without suffering fundamental social or cultural upheaval. He could find unwanted support among those old imperialists who, shaking their heads over the latest news from Uganda or Angola, conclude that Africans are reverting to their unregenerate past; being colonized has done them no good at all.

Equally unnatural allies believe the colonial interlude to have been crucially important; apologists of empire join hands with radical theorists of neo-colonialism in their belief that the purpose and effect of colonial rule was to change the structures and the values of the colonized society into shapes more congruent with those of the imperial power. Both see colonial empire as something which was historically destined to wither away, once it had completed the 'double mission' which Marx had foreseen for British rule in India: 'the annihilation of old Asiatic society, and the laying of the material foundations of Western Society'. Nowadays historians often describe the early nineteenth century as a period of 'informal empire', when Britain in particular enjoyed many of the perquisites of power in Africa without the responsibilities of rule, hoping that acceptable forms of civilization would develop through moral suasion in church, school and market place. After the partition military force reinforced this suasion, and other forms of power, based upon science and technology, were incorporated into colonial structures. But (so a speculative hypothesis might continue) this superiority of power could not be expected to last for ever. Might not far-sighted colonial masters then seek to encourage a new 'collaborating class', trained to use the weapons of the modern state as well as the sword of the spirit? If power was transferred into the right hands, could their successors not hope once more to enjoy the perquisites without the responsibilities?

Publicly proclaimed purposes of both French and British colonial empires do appear to support the view that these were destined ultimately to be self-liquidating, though in different ways. In French official theory, the end of empire would come, not with restoration of self-government, but with its transformation into a sort of cosmopolitan super-state, through the gradual entry of individuals who had undergone a thorough cultural conversion into full political equality. Behind this astonishing vision lay assumptions so large that they may seem to rest on either naive innocence or conscious hypocrisy.

Psychologically, assimilation implies conditioning individuals so completely that their own cultural inheritance becomes irrelevant – a possibility which enthusiasts found easier to assume for Black Africans than for Vietnamese or Arabs. Politically, the theory assumed the willingness of native Frenchmen to share power in the bureaucracy, the church, the teaching profession, as well as in the Assembly, with foreigners who would eventually greatly outnumber them. And economically, it assumed an absence of fundamental conflict between rulers and subjects – a projection of the famous 'harmony of interests'. Even those who could accept such assumptions could hardly envisage a realisation of the assimilationist ideal in their own lifetimes. Token gestures in this direction were the most that could be expected; until the second world war at least assimilation was as irrelevant to the everyday concerns of the French administrator in Africa as was self-government to his British colleagues. Even the Brazzaville manifesto of 1944, when Republican colonial administrators committed themselves to reforms first propounded under the Popular Front, envisaged no early liquidation of empire; but it provided sufficient evidence of good intentions to win the collaboration of authentic African leaders in its programme. This collaboration was in general maintained when the international pressures of the 1950s obliged France sharply to reverse her tactics, accepting African independence within a general framework of unequal power.

For the British, the post-war crises of empire entailed no such revolution of principles. Statements of intent to involve the peoples of the Empire, at appropriately different speeds, in a majestic 'progress towards self-government' were frequently made by twentieth century publicists and historians, and, less frequently, imprecisely endorsed by official statements, like one by Malcolm MacDonald on 7 December 1938. But as far as Black Africa was concerned, what Kenneth Robinson calls 'the tranquil assumption of the long-term character of colonial rule' was still almost universally accepted. This was true, not only of officials in Whitehall and Africa, but of that somewhat wider circle of politicians, academics, merchants, and missionaries which constituted the 'policy-making elite' of the 1930s and 1940s, and embraced even contemporary radical critics of imperialism.[2] When during the second world war Americans and other foreigners began to interest themselves in these matters, it emerged that the statements of intent had made little impact upon what administrators actually did. Churchill's declaration of September 1941 that unambiguous commitments already guaranteed 'the progressive evolution of self-governing institutions' in each colony could not be substantiated from the record.[3]

By this time the assumptions of British colonial policy were changing; just as wartime vicissitudes led the French to re-assess their policies at Brazzaville, so Churchill's statement reflected growing acceptance of eventual political decolonisation. But though the impact of the war on colonial thinking will be indicated below, the new policies still assumed close co-operation with chosen 'collaborators'; the dramatic changes clearly came later, beginning in 1948. Following a brief attempt to sketch the early stages of this evolution, this paper will illustrate some changing assumptions and expectations by reference to the wartime experience of Sierra Leone. The aim will be to discover whether any of the authors or executors of British policy were indeed seeking to identify and assist potential 'communicators' or 'collaborators' in some new type of 'informal empire' so early as the period of the second world war.

II Towards a West African Policy

During the inter-war period British colonial policy, in West Africa and elsewhere, was subjected to growing external pressures. American-led advocates of international supervision of colonial territories achieved an institutional bridge-head with the foundation of the League of Nations; the anti-colonialism of the Comintern threatened to join hands with the growing international consciousness of Negro protest movements inside and outside Africa; in the 1930s German and Italian demands for a repartition of Africa compelled France and Britain to review some of their own colonial practices. But perhaps the strongest pressures of the 1930s derived, as Dr. Tony Hopkins emphasizes so well, from the international economic depression. On the one hand, this shook imperial complacency by reversing the generally expansionist tendency of the commercial sector of West African economies, which besides sustaining colonial budgets, had created limited opportunities for Africans as well as Europeans to prosper; at the same time it stimulated African movements of protest.[4]

British reformers (like the authors of the French Popular Front programme of 1936) therefore looked mainly to new economic and social policies, for which financial foundations were provided by the Colonial Development and Welfare Act of 1940. Early perceptions of the significance of the proletariat emerging in capitals, ports and mining locations were reflected in the appointment of Major G.St.J. Orde-Browne as Labour Adviser to the Colonial Office in 1938; but political and constitutional reforms still seemed largely irrelevant, if not downright dangerous. In 1938, only such an exceptionally percipient and sympathetic observer as Margery Perham could see that 'groups of educated Africans are showing the first symptoms of nationalism in the face of foreign rule' and consequently that 'we shall increasingly need in Africa men and women who can interpret us to their own people as well as vice versa'. The action she proposed – more visits by selected Africans to U.K., and the encouragement of reading rooms and cultural centres for inter-racial contact in African cities – was hardly revolutionary; but neither the British Council nor colonial officials in West Africa seem to have taken this plea to encourage African 'communicators' very seriously.[5]

After the outbreak of war, British African policy moved slowly towards a new phase, in which prevailing methods of 'Native Administration' became linked to longer views of 'Political Development'. Later in 1939 Lord Hailey, his formidable Indian reputation enhanced by the publication of the *African Survey*, was asked to visit the African territories and advise the Colonial Office on how, in the context of long-term policy, such reforms as increased African representation in central legislatures might be harmonized with 'the policy followed in regard to local native authorities'.[6] His report, eventually printed for official use in 1942, seems in many ways ambivalent. The 'tranquil assumption' of many administrators must have been greatly shaken by Hailey's assertion that, in relation to Asian experience, 'the outstanding impression of Africa must be one of rapid change, and of greater changes pending', and his consequent conclusion – that policies of social and economic development should be regarded as 'an essential part of the policy, to which we stand committed, of fitting them to achieve a self-governing status.'[7] Yet despite his percipient warning of political ferment to come, Hailey's detailed suggestions as to how native administrations in the different colonies might be adapted to 'the more advanced requirements of modern rule' were not free of a certain tranquillity, derived perhaps from the cautious outlook of local administrators.

In April 1941 Hailey chaired a Colonial Office Committee of four Assistant Under-Secretaries, with the wide remit of considering 'Post-War Reconstruction in the Colonies'. An agenda of over fifty items was drawn up, which became the basis for stimulating enquiries and formulations of view within most branches of the Office. But priority was still being given, firstly to economic problems likely to arise in the direct aftermath of war, secondly to improving the capacity of the colonial service to handle longer-term programmes of social and economic development. Item No. 20 on this vast agenda was 'Constitutional Advances in the Colonies, demands for which may be hastened by the war', and No. 46, 'Ultimate Constitutional Objectives'; others posed such broad philosophical issues as 'General Objectives of Social Policy; towards Western Civilization or cultures of their own?'[8] But this committee clearly regarded any transfer of power at the centres of colonial government as a very long-term aspiration, which would remain under their close control.

Greater priority was given to the question of constitutional reform from 1942. In part this was a response (reluctant for many individuals) to growing American pressure to apply the rhetoric of the Atlantic Charter to 'dark races', and introduce international supervision into the post-war colonial settlement;[9] in part, to the traumatic shock of the collapse of British authority in Malaya. But there was also pressure from African capitals, where military attack from Vichy-held territories came to seem a danger at a time when the growing labour force was suffering from increased costs of living. In January 1942 Sir Alan Burns, formerly one of the Under-Secretaries on Hailey's committee, but now Governor of the Gold Coast, proposed to appoint two or three Africans to his Executive Council. 'I believe', he wrote, that the rising tide of anti-British resentment, and the disturbances which in recent years have been symptoms of this resentment, are due to the policy of deferring constitutional concessions until it is too late for them to be appreciated by the people. The Negro peoples, both in the West Indies and in West Africa, are learning that the colonial administrations take no notice of popular feeling until this feeling is manifested in disturbances.

Perceiving 'a growing feeling of antipathy to Europeans and an undercurrent of discontent which affords a fertile field for the subversive activities of enemy agents', Burns, backed by Bourdillon from Nigeria, persisted against objections raised by Hailey and other Colonial Office pundits, and in September Lord Cranborne, the Secretary of State, was persuaded to authorize such appointments in both colonies.[10]

Within the Colonial Office, an important step towards a common constitutional policy for West Africa was taken in the summer of 1943 when the new Secretary of State, Oliver Stanley, preparing for a tour of West Africa, presided over a discussion of a paper by O. G. R. Williams. Basing itself upon Hailey's confidential report this paper argued that, while political advance ought to remain dependent upon programmes of social and economic development designed to narrow the 'enormous gulf' between educated urban Africans and the rural masses, it was nevertheless important to give the educated elite clear pledges that political progress in West Africa would not be retarded by reference to conditions in East Africa. Williams's 'tentative plan for constitutional development' envisaged five stages. In the first of these the emphasis would be largely on local government, the 'gradual modernization' of Native Authorities being accompanied by increased African representation on Municipal Councils, and by the formation of advisory Regional Councils based on the N.As.; but there would also be increased representation of African interests, by elected and nominated members, on Legislative Councils. Rather surprisingly, Hailey himself proposed to extend this phase by appointing Africans as heads of departments with seats in the Executive Council, though without Ministerial powers; he justified this as 'education in responsibility', and a means of preventing educated Africans adopting the role of 'chartered opposition'. Williams's second and third stages were to consist largely of extending the functions of the Regional Councils, together with measures to make both municipalities and Legislative Councils more directly representative. The fourth stage might see African unofficial majorities in the Legislative Councils; but Williams and others were clearly uneasy about this, and thought it might be desirable to move directly to stage 5, somewhat tentatively entitled 'towards self-government'.[11]

Beyond the first stage, this was not really a 'plan' at all, even a tentative one, but a well-guarded declaration of intent. Williams's paper was wholly imprecise about stage 5, suggesting only that it would have to be preceded by a lot of consultation with African interests, and it seems to have been generally accepted that it would require 'a good many generations for its evolution'.[12] Decolonisation would come about only as the culmination of a series of economic, social, educational and political measures, designed to further the 'modernization' of West African societies in forms which had never been clearly defined; the Elliot Commission on Higher Education, appointed about this same time and within the same climate of thought, concerned itself with the training of leaders for a new African State to be born 'within a century, within half a century'.[13] In the process of operating this comprehensive programme, it was expected that a new African leadership would emerge, prepared to collaborate with their rulers in the slow work of nation-building; Hailey's talk of 'education in responsibility' reflected a general desire to encourage them; but until they had served their apprenticeships there could be no question of a transfer of power.

These policies of the wartime coalition, variously described as based on 'trusteeship' or on 'partnership',[14] assumed that colonial government could retain the initiative until wholly acceptable partners had been trained up to carry on. The Labour Government of 1945, some of whose members had helped to evolve this essentially Fabian approach, did not radically depart from it. Only in 1948 did their assumptions, expectations and plans have to be drastically revised, when growing international pressures upon the political and economic basis of Britain's Imperial role were reinforced by African resistance, most effectively mobilized by Nkrumah in the Gold Coast, and threatened to wrest the initiative from British hands. After the Accra riots there were still tardy attempts to establish community of outlook and interest with men like Nkrumah ('*he* is being educated by *us*', one hopeful Fabian wrote in 1953[15]); but in southern Ghana and Nigeria at least colonial policy had become a question of achieving collaboration with available African leaders, rather than of preparing Africans to co-operate in prescribed roles.

But in Sierra Leone (still a colony of potential strategic value) internal African pressures were less insistent and independence was less clearly an inevitable, or indeed an attainable, goal. 'It would be obviously absurd to think of all the existing Colonial units as being equally fit for self-government', wrote O. G. Williams in 1943;[16] no doubt the exiguous territorial, economic and demographic resources of The Gambia were uppermost in his mind, but Sierra Leone, with a population of under two million and a far from impressive economy, was until many years after this frequently spoken of as a marginal case from the point of view of the elusive and rarely defined quality of 'viability'. This uncertainty was increased by the doubts which many Britons felt about an established elite which comprised the oldest group of 'collaborators' in British West Africa – the Creoles. Though a less crucial case than Nigeria or the Gold Coast, Sierra Leone may thus offer good opportunities for studying the contradictions and hesitancies of British policy during this period of change.

III The Sierra Leone Experience. The Rejection of the Creoles

During much of the nineteenth century the Colony of Sierra Leone (that is, Freetown and its satellite settlements) became the home of an African population profoundly influenced by those modernizing and westernizing forces which Victorians summarized as 'Christianity, civilization and commerce'. Although these settlers and recaptives proved less culturally malleable than some expected, fusing African and European elements into a distinctive Creole synthesis,[17] their political spokesmen assumed that the new African nation which they aspired to lead would be decisively influenced by Anglo-Saxon attitudes of church, school and market-place, and would freely collaborate with the British empire.[18] They saw themselves, and were seen by others, as heirs-apparent of the British.

Unfortunately, even before the imperialist impulse of the 1890s brought the expansion of British control over the Protectorate, British officials had abandoned these optimistic assumptions. Racially-minded authoritarians and benevolent paternalists shared low expectations of Creole capacity, and no longer contemplated that transfer of administration which a Parliamentary Committee had envisaged in 1865. The initial successes of Sierra Leoneans in expanding the commercial frontiers of British capitalism were not sustained; African churches ceased to seem relevant to self-government; the schools of the missionaries were reshaped on lines more consistent with scientific imperialism. Although institutions like Fourah Bay College continued to provide colonial West Africa with an indispensable supply of public servants, these worthy men were no longer regarded as political heirs. The immediately permissible limit of self-government was indicated by the emasculated Freetown Municipality created in 1893; conceived less as a seed-bed of liberty than as a method of devolving financial responsibility, this body never inspired much confidence among Africans or Europeans. When it was suspended in 1926 under the shadow of financial irregularities, there was no strong call to replace it. Victorian Britain's model African colony had broken down.

But had the British genuinely sought to prepare a 'collaborating class' to carry on the work of empire in West Africa by other means, the Creoles, with their strong attachment to British political, constitutional and legal values, would still have had much to commend them. It is true that the generation represented by the National Congress of British West Africa, still strident with resentment at their rejection by the new imperialism, did not look very promising as *interlocuteurs valables* for a Sierra Leonean nation;[19] H. C. Bankole Bright, the leading elected member of the Legislative Council from 1924 to 1939, was noted chiefly for an oratorical style as ostentatiously out-dated and inappropriate as his Edwardian businessman's costume. Yet myopic Governors did not use their powers of patronage to encourage alternative leaders; Governor Douglas Jardine, re-nominating the worthy barrister C. E. Wright for a fourth term on the Council, claimed that no other suitable candidates were available.[20] Many of Wright's most distinguished contemporaries were of course in government service, but Jardine's own successor thought this ought not to be incompatible with membership of the Legislative Council; in any case it is by no means clear that the decline of civic virtue among the Creoles was so complete as their critics claimed. Certainly their leaders still coloured their concern to revive and liberalize this stagnant dependency with fervent Empire loyalism. As the weekly *West Africa* was to say at the end of the war:

> To a London official headquarters endowed with a little imagination, it might occur to develop this feeling, as a precious link with Britain, and an advertisement of recent loudly-proclaimed intentions to develop every form of local government in the dependencies.[21]

Yet nobody loved the Creoles. The young Graham Greene reacted to his first sight of Freetown by a blistering satire, which he later admitted was misdirected.[32] Jardine, in a curious phrase, confessed almost shame-facedly to a 'sneaking regard' for this community, yet regarded their political claims as 'rooted in sentiment rather than reason.'[23] Arthur Dawe, responsible for West African affairs as Assistant Under-Secretary in the Colonial Office from 1938 to 1945, who had been Secretary to the 1926 enquiry into the Freetown municipality, regarded Creoles as 'a specially inflammable breed', to whom only restricted liberties could be permitted.[24] Such attitudes seem to reflect an instinctive rejection of black men who might appear to parody attitudes and ideologies of Englishmen; but underlying them was an appreciation of social and cultural differences between Creoles and the indigenous peoples of the Protectorate. For even in the twentieth century the Creoles remained a favoured community – not only enjoying superior (though strictly circumscribed) opportunities for subordinate office, honour and emolument within colonial society, but absorbing a proportionately high share of government expenditure on schools, medical services and economic infrastructure. British administrators perpetuated these distinctions even as they deplored them, hesitating to disturb the tranquil stagnation of the provinces so long as peace could be maintained.[25] During the 1930s islands of social change had begun to appear in the Protectorate, largely as a result of mining developments; internal and external movements of people were intensified and Colony and Protectorate gradually drawn into closer relationships.[26] But in Sierra Leone as elsewhere, the

Colonial Office hoped to control the new problems by the paternal sponsorship of new social and economic policies; politically, they maintained the policy introduced in 1936, of trying to apply the classical principles of indirect rule to the 216 small chiefdoms of the Protectorate. When in 1938 a new Creole-based political movement began to challenge this approach, official hostility intensified.

The Rise of the Youth League

The West African Youth League, a political movement which has recently attracted scholarly attention, was largely the creation of I. T. A. Wallace-Johnson, a critic of colonialism who remains difficult to evaluate.[27] He was clearly eloquent, courageous, and very ingenious in exploiting the circumscribed freedom permitted by British colonial rule; yet in retrospect his career seems lacking in consistency and integrity of purpose. Although 'liberty or Death' was a fine slogan – and Wallace-Johnson suffered severely in the cause of extending freedom of speech and publication – it was never very clear what *use* Africans were to make of their liberty; as Dr Kaniki observes, the Youth League never demanded independence, and the thrust of its radicalism remained indiscriminate and diffuse. The writer's recollection of Wallace-Johnson in his late fifties is of a self-indulgent opportunist, yoked with the most conservative of his former opponents; both opportunism and self-indulgence seem to be foreshadowed in the charismatic hero of 1938–9.

Wallace-Johnson returned to Sierra Leone as a known associate of Communists, and no doubt it was this which led Customs officers to publicize his arrival in April 1938 by seizing copies of the *African Sentinel*. But it is doubtful whether he remained in any sense a Communist;[28] his basic philosophy was a somewhat diffusely radical pan-Africanism similar to that of his mentor George Padmore – whom Johnson used to address in the name of 'my sainted grandfather, Jaja of Opobo'.[29] His reputation did not prevent the intelligent Colonial Secretary, Hilary Blood, from expressing the opinion (later abandoned) that 'the way to neutralize his effect was to appoint him to the Legislative Council';[30] the intense official hostility which soon developed seems to have been due less to the Youth League's specific ideas or programme than to its fiercely independent attitude, and its apparent success in exploiting forces of racial antagonism which Jardine perceived latent within the frustrated constitutionalism of the Creoles.[31]

More dangerous still to the policy of controlled paternalism: the Youth League's cosmopolitan approach to the problems of Sierra Leone not only won enthusiastic support among Creoles (who repeatedly packed meetings at the Wilberforce Hall through 1938, and patronized the *frondeur* journalism of Wallace-Johnson's *African Standard*) but threatened to affect the Protectorate-born proletariat, both in Freetown and in the mining locations. After Wallace-Johnson made a provincial tour in July 1938 (not including the gold and diamond areas) the League claimed branches in Bo, Moyamba, Bonthe, Mano, Lunsar and Pepel. These may have consisted largely of Creoles, and Dr Kaniki is inclined to qualify, for the provinces, W. M. Macmillan's contemporary conclusion that 'the ventilation of constitutional or labour grievances has begun to bridge the deep cleavage between the Creoles and the peoples of the Protectorate';[32] but the provincial administration was embarrassed by the emergence of an organisation capable of observing and politicizing the errors and excesses of its agents. Thus the League took up the claims of residents in Bonthe, whose houses had been irregularly demolished by officials over-zealous for the cause of sanitation;[33] more alarmingly, their investigations of irregularities and cruelties during the collection of House Tax stimulated Parliamentary Questions and press publicity in Britain which provided material for Nazi propaganda. The colonial government, stirred to make its own enquiries, discovered that there had indeed been 'acts of gross brutality' by Court Messengers, and that one reluctant tax-payer had been flogged to death.[34]

Jardine was quick to apprehend that Wallace-Johnson might succeed in mobilizing the growing proletariat to threaten colonial authority; 'in the event of a strike at one of the mines he would be a potential danger to the peace and good order of the country', he wrote on 30 June 1938.[35] Events during the next year increased these fears. Some, like Jardine's abortive attempt to prosecute the Youth League for a breach of official secrecy,[36] enabled Johnson to score points against the government within the recognized

rules of colonial constitutionality; others, like the strikes of
labourers in Freetown in January 1939 and of iron-miners at
Marampa in May, held more alarming implications. Real
grievances over wages and working conditions underlay these
strikes, and the Provincial Commissioner rejected the temptation
to blame the trouble at Marampa on 'external agitators';[37] but it
was Wallace-Johnson who had provided the impetus for the
formation of trade unions, and for a pitiful little 'strike' by Army
recruits in January 1939.[38]

Colonial officials thus reacted with almost visceral hostility to
the political pretensions of the Youth League, even when they
recognized that the conditions it was denouncing required
reform; Jardine had to be discreetly warned by the Colonial Office
'to get off his high horse and to remember that you can't do the
"Sanders of the River" stuff in Freetown'.[39] Even Blood
abandoned hope of collaborating with Johnson, and contemplated
his deportation.[40] He remained, he said:

> anxious ... to get the Youth League on the side of Government or at
> any rate to recognize it as an organisation whom we can meet and
> with whom we can treat, but I see no chance of doing this so long as
> Johnson is Organizing Secretary'.[41]

Jardine's wilder suggestions of abridging the right of election
were ruled out by the Colonial Office, but widespread Creole
hostility was still aroused by four Ordinances designed to control
the activities of the Youth League, and safeguard the security of
Freetown as a defended port, which he was allowed to enact in
June 1939; these provided for the more expeditious trial and
punishment of persons accused of sedition, or of inciting troops to
disobedience; for the tighter control of imported publications;
and for the preventive detention of 'undesirable British
subjects'.[42]

This fortification of colonial authority was however
accompanied by attempts to redress social grievances. The same
session of the Legislative Council passed other Ordinances which
legalized registered Trade Unions, authorized peaceful picketing,
provided for government-sponsored processes of arbitration and
enquiry, and introduced the principle of Workman's
Compensation; and when a newly-appointed Labour Secretary
took up his duties in July he soon began to secure co-operation

from the eight rudimentary unions which Wallace-Johnson had brought into existence.[43] With the outbreak of war jobs became plentiful in Freetown, on defence works and in providing supplies and services to ships assembling in the harbour; and although this activity was clearly generating social problems for the future,[44] the political thrust of the Youth League was blunted when Wallace-Johnson was interned under wartime emergency powers. The war brought out the Empire loyalism of the Creole bourgeoisie, and the continuing sniping of the *African Standard* does not seem to have struck very deeply.

The Aborting of 'Stage One'

With the threat from the Youth League apparently overcome, Hailey's Report on political development provided little stimulus to prepare for decolonisation in Sierra Leone. A short visit to Freetown in March 1940 led Hailey to embrace the official wisdom concerning the essential irresponsibility of the Creole community. 'Their attachment to European institutions is unfortunately not supported by their economic situation and their apparent capacity for improving it', his report asserted; the success of the Youth League showed how easily Creoles could be 'swept away by movements led by persons with low standards of responsibility and lacking in any sense of political restraint'.[45] Even in Freetown, formerly regarded as their 'sphere of civic usefulness',[46] Hailey judged it impossible to restore the powers of the Municipality, given the Creole record and the continuing growth of the non-Creole population.[47] It followed that the 'political development' of Sierra Leone would have to be regulated by change in the protectorate.

Such a view virtually excluded for generations any dilution of the powers of the Governor; for though Hailey's report on the recently-introduced system of native administration was framed in encouraging tones, it revealed only the most rudimentary capacity to administer the affairs of a modern state.[48] By 1941 73 out of 216 chiefdoms had been reorganized; but with an average population of under 10,000 and correspondingly low taxable capacity, they had little opportunity to demonstrate their political responsibility. With the fruits of re-organization visible chiefly in the form of personal emoluments for individuals, of reconstructed

prisons and courthouses, the new system was unlikely to inspire
popular enthusiasm, or to inspire 'the young men element' to play
the civic roles for which Hailey hoped. Nor were administrators
anxious to encourage such possibly troublesome elements. Blood
hoped that eventually the Government would 'be able to point to
the success of the NAs as what can be done by people who are
regarded by the intelligentsia of Freetown as still being in the
same almost savage state,'[49] and many Protectorate men were
indeed already capable of political leadership; but most of them
were employed by the Government, which did nothing to permit
their participation, and envisaged only the admission to the NAs
of 'progressive elements of those groups which by custom have
the right to be represented.'[50] This patronizing approach to the
reform of local institutions from the grass-roots up never inspired
sustained enthusiasm from 'progressive elements' in any African
country; it certainly could not do so in Sierra Leone. Even if the
NAs did make progress with road-building, with providing
dispensaries and schools, such local initiatives could make little
impact upon the total problems of poverty, disease and illiteracy
unless accompanied by increased provision of services and skilled
personnel by the central government.

   The Colonial Development and Welfare Act of 1940 offered
some possibility of financial support for accelerating these
essential preparations for self-government – for example, the
expansion of western education, without which many Native
Authorities would be quite incapable of supervising even the
limited programmes envisaged.[51] Yet in Sierra Leone the
resources provided by the Act were not effectively deployed to
support any clear political strategy. Harassed officials responded
to the new opportunities offered by Whitehall in dilatory and
piecemeal ways. Their reluctance to undertake constructive long-
term planning was reflected in alarm when the Colonial Office
suggested using the war as an opportunity to introduce income-
tax. Jardine resisted this on three grounds; that it was not fiscally
necessary, that it would weaken African systems of providing for
the sick and poor through family structures and voluntary
associations, and that – given the long history of Creole resistance
to direct taxation – it would incite opposition and fortify the
Youth League in demanding constitutional reform. But the
Colonial Office persisted, thinking that Jardine took 'too

conservative a view of the trend of social and economic progress in West Africa',[52] but insisting above all that the *principle* of direct taxation should be established during the war as a necessary administrative and financial foundation for post-war expansion. Eventually Cranborne over-ruled the objections of the Governors of Sierra Leone and the Gold Coast (where the record of political opposition was equally strong);[53] income-tax was introduced in 1943 and, as foreseen, became a leading political issue.

In addition to this general conservatism, there was a special difficulty in reconciling the Colonial Office 'development policy' with the political assumptions of the Sierra Leone administration. Initially, at least, grants to provide more efficiently specialized services might well accentuate the country's lop-sided social and educational structures, for some at least of these would be spent in reinforcing the privileged position of the Creoles. In 1937 60 per cent of all educational expenditure had been committed to the Colony;[54] the structures it provided, inadequate though they might be, would have to form the base of future development. When in December 1941 the Director of Education was invited to 'prepare a programme of educational development' with Colonial Development and Welfare Act funds, his hard-pressed Department took two years to produce a mere patchwork of requests for assistance 'to ensure more rapid development on existing lines'.[55] As the Colonial Office Advisory Committee commented, it was 'solely a memorandum put forward for the improvement and development of the Education Department; but something more than this appears to be needed in Sierra Leone'.[56] Its first three items provided for rebuilding of Colony schools, scholarships for advanced study overseas (which inevitably went largely to well-qualified Creoles),[57] and the appointment of a Classics Tutor to Fourah Bay College.

Fourah Bay, that precarious symbol of past Creole eminence, exemplified this particular dilemma; to abandon it would be contrary to the whole new development policy, to expand it would in the short run reinforce the old foundations of Creole privilege. In 1938 an inspecting Commission had found the College making the best of an essentially unsatisfactory situation. Out of 32 students (20 from Sierra Leone) only twelve were taking degree courses; a small staff had to make 'hand-to-mouth' arrangements to meet very diverse commitments, a tiny library was 'like the curriculum, examination ridden'.[58] In 1942 the College, further depleted in numbers, was displaced from its Freetown site by defence needs and rehoused in unsuitable quarters at Mabang; it seemed hardly relevant to the Elliot Commission's bold design of training cadres for independent African states. Yet even Elliot and his advisers could not contemplate completely abandoning an institution which had done so much to educate earlier West African elites; under Creole and missionary leadership the College retained a steadily growing place in successive educational plans and eventually (almost despite the planners) grew into the national University of Sierra Leone.

The fruits of the Development and Welfare Act were thus accepted in Sierra Leone almost incidentally, and not related to the Colonial Office's emerging ideas of political change. Though those who benefited would within twenty years hold political, administrative and judicial offices in independent Sierra Leone, few local officials seem to have been conscious of engaging in the first stage of a programme of constitutional development. The gap between assumptions and expectations − between the perception of officials like Williams that changing world conditions made it necessary to 'get down to formulating our constitutional policy for West Africa and also be planning a programme for carrying it out',[59] and their lack of confidence that much could be achieved with the human and material resources available in Sierra Leone − inhibited reform. Jardine's successor, Sir Hubert Stevenson, strongly resisted Burns's initiative in appointing Africans to the Executive Council, delayed following suit until March 1943 on somewhat specious grounds of military security, and made it clear to the Colonial Office that he regarded his ultimate compliance as a gesture of little positive value to Sierra Leone.[60]

During the autumn of 1943 Oliver Stanley, the new Secretary of State, toured West Africa, and in Nigeria and the Gold Coast held concrete discussions about constitutional changes. But as regards Sierra Leone Stanley seems to have set out with low expectations, and returned with them lower still. During preliminary discussions Stevenson had insisted that the gap between Creoles and protectorate peoples precluded any rapid progress at the centre, and that the reconstitution of the Freetown City Council was 'the most expedient step in the direction of self-government.'[61] He had already appointed a Committee on this subject under A. C. C. Swayne, official president of the existing Council; its Report of 1944 formed the basis of a draft Bill prepared early in 1945.[62] Firstly the powers of the Council, recently extended to the provision of schools, were enlarged to include municipal housing, sanitation, and transport; the Report however emphasized that this ought not to involve any greater increase of rates than from the existing 2/4 to 3/-. Secondly, the Council was to have an elected majority: a Mayor, three Aldermen and nine Councillors, as against seven nominated members. Three of these were intended to represent 'Labour interests'; this attempt to prevent a Creole monopoly in a city which during the war had acquired an increased majority of illiterate Protectorate immigrants was based on an enlightened concern to avoid fostering ethnic consciousness, by writing in separate representation for the different 'Tribal Headmen'.[63] 'The ideal to which we look forward', Swayne's Committee declared,

> is a Freetown of intelligent and independent citizens, not an agglomeration or even a federation of tribal detachments. The aim should be to instil a Civic sense into the individual and to avoid any course which might perpetuate tribal consciousness ... The Tribal Administrations of Freetown, we feel, may have their places as friendly societies and nurseries of sentiment alongside the Caledonian Societies, and Liverpool-Irish battalions, but not as an integral part of the local Government.

Other nominated members however were to represent government departments; their presence, together with provision for the colonial government to disallow appointments made by the Council, to supervise its finances, and if necessary take over its functions altogether, reflected the British concern 'that in view of the important Imperial interest in the functioning of the port of Freetown, there should be adequate safeguards for efficient administration.'[64] Moreover the Colonial Office, anxious to universalise the principle of multi-racialism, seem to have believed that even in the long run Europeans should have a role in the government of Freetown; their aim was not Africanization but 'harmony of the black and white keys', with 'black and white pulling together in a single team on a single job.'[65]

Although the activities of European sailors and servicemen in

wartime Freetown had inevitably produced inter-racial conflicts
and friction, disturbing Jardine's vision of stable paternalist
relations between rulers and ruled,[66] few Creoles rejected the
principle of co-operation with Europeans; but they did expect a
greater measure of control over their historic 'province of
freedom' than these proposals envisaged, and municipal reform
thus became the focus for a new consolidation of Creole political
consciousness under the leadership of old Youth League militants.
At first indeed the proposals were quite well received. The Notes
of Dissent submitted by J. Fowell Boston, a Creole member of
Swayne's Committee, centred on a proposal that civil servants
should be eligible for election to the new Council; justified as a
means of enlarging the pool of ability before the electorate, this
seemed a possible channel for continuing indirect government
control – and it was certainly notable that no such proposal was
ever entertained for the protectorate, where a far larger
proportion of educated men were in government employment.
But soon other reservations crept into public comment: some
were based on the misapprehension that the Aldermen would not
need to secure election to the Council in the first place, some
doubted the government's willingness to train Africans to serve as
Town Clerk and Engineer, others suspected that the nominated
'labour members' would be used by the government to curb
Creole aspirations. Despite some concessions by the Government,
opposition to the Bill mounted; by January 1945 Boston was
claiming the new Council would be 'in effect a sub-department of
government.'[67]

   The Government's olive-branch to the Creoles now became a
provocation, with criticism increasingly centring on the reserve
powers to be retained by the Governor. When Arthur Creech-
Jones became Under-Secretary in July 1945 he cited
constitutional authorities like W. A. Robson to show that the Bill
followed impeccable British precedents – always an important
argument with the Creole Empire loyalists.[68] To this Thomas
Decker replied that in the U.K. reserve powers were exercised by
a government ultimately responsible to the electorate; Municipal
reform therefore should not precede reform of the Legislative
Council but accompany it.[69] During 1945 the critics mobilized
support for a boycott of the new Council; in August 1945 only
160 applied to register as electors (compared to 3000 qualified

under the old Ordinance) and it became clearly impossible to hold elections.[70]

Attempts to implement in Sierra Leone the first stage of the Colonial Office's 'tentative plan for constitutional development' were thus aborted. While the proposal municipal reform failed to satisfy Creole expectations, development in the Protectorate was proceeding slowly, and on lines which only confirmed their apprehension that the 'backward' condition of the majority would be deliberately used to control the advance of the elite. In response to the thinking of London, plans were indeed made to establish advisory Councils in the twelve Districts, with a Protectorate Assembly largely elected through them; but these bodies would be composed almost exclusively of Chiefs and representatives of Tribal Authorities who could be expected to act under the discreet direction of British officials. The most significant responsibility envisaged for the Protectorate Assembly in the immediate future was the election of twelve members to the Legislative Council.[71] The Colonial Government, under pressure to concede an elected majority in a body which the Colonial Office agreed could not be allowed to fall under Creole control,[72] clearly regarded this as a method of supplying black legislators who could (like the three nominated Chiefs on the existing Council) be depended upon to vote under official direction.

Such transparent expedients were rejected not only by the Creoles but by educated leaders of Protectorate opinion, who now sought to combat the 'conventional wisdom' that an unbridgeable gulf between the two sections of Sierra Leone would continue to preclude real progress towards self-government. The main lines of subsequent development are well-known.[73] The Sierra Leone Organisation Society, which held its first Annual General Meeting at Moyamba in June 1946, attracted support from a 'growing body of literate natives of the Protectorate'[74] who were worried by government policy; in 1951 its alliance with some younger forward-looking Creoles and some Chiefs brought into being the Sierra Leone Peoples' Party, which ten years later would become heirs to the Colonial Government. This however was not because it had developed a mass organization capable of wresting the initiative from the British, but because the British timetable had been overthrown by the multiple crises of the post-war Commonwealth, and the consequent need to accept accelerated decolonisation in the Gold Coast and Nigeria. Once more the assumptions which changed British West African policy over-rode the pessimistic expectations of local officials; if Sierra Leone fell too far out of step with new policies elsewhere in West Africa it would become a political embarrassment – and perhaps a financial liability. When elections were eventually held to a reconstituted Legislative Council in 1951, Governor Beresford-Stooke turned to the Sierra Leone Peoples' Party to co-operate in the first steps towards a transfer of power, not as the trained and designated successors of the Empire, but (given the intransigently particularist line of Bankole Bright and the Creole 'old guard') as the only credible collaborators in sight.

The First Decolonisers

Yet during the 1940s the need to prepare for decolonisation had not been forgotten by all British officials in Sierra Leone, and some SLPP leaders at least had been coached for their new roles. Lord Caradon has spoken of the concern of members of the colonial service to ensure for their African subjects a 'start in freedom'; though he may in his own generation have been more exceptional in this than memory suggests, such concern was certainly present among the post-war intake.[75] Still more was such a concern shared by some of the specialist professional workers brought to Africa to inaugurate new programmes under the Development and Welfare Acts. Educationalists are perhaps the prime example; many who worked in the new Colleges (above all in their extra-mural Departments) had a very clear commitment to the goal of preparation for self-government, and in the teaching of groups and individuals might be explicitly envisaging their future roles within, say, a parliamentary democracy of socialist inclination. Social scientists whose visits to Africa were now sponsored by the Colonial Research Committee might also assist in the political education of those whom they saw as potential inheritors; in Sierra Leone, the correspondence of Dr Kenneth Little with his colleagues in the Fabian Colonial Bureau could provide illustration of this. But perhaps the most striking and most successful example of a new decoloniser was provided by Edgar Parry, a former official of the Municipal and

General Workers Union, who in the early summer of 1942 arrived in Freetown as Assistant Labour Officer.

Colonial Office recognition of the need to pay special attention to labour problems had been reflected in the appointments of Orde-Browne as Labour Adviser in 1938, and of H. A. Nisbet as Labour Secretary in Sierra Leone in July 1939. Both men were former administrative officers, and the broad assumption was that labour policy was essentially a matter of enforcing minimum standards of welfare in such matters as diet, housing, and health; and also the enactment and enforcement of rudimentary legislation covering workmen's compensation and the machinery of industrial bargaining. Though the encouragement of trade unions along British lines was part of their responsibility – and Nisbet, anxious not to leave the initiative to the Youth League, did take this seriously – this was not a direction in which the pre-war Colonial Service was well-prepared to lead.[76] With the entry of the Labour Party into the Coalition Government, however, the Colonial Office was led to accept that the British Trade Union movement itself might have a specific contribution to make to the development of African societies and the preparation of new elites to lead them. Early in 1941 the Colonial Office revealed that it was considering a few 'experimental appointments of Trade Unionists to posts in selected colonies' – hoping thus to offset 'irresponsible and misguided leadership' and to 'assist and encourage the adoption of collective bargaining in preference to the strike weapon.' Freetown was somewhat reluctantly persuaded to adopt this approach, and this provided the opportunity for Parry's appointment.[77]

Dr H. E. Conway has noted Parry's success in promoting a system of industrial relations, based upon British experience, which gave Sierra Leone some twenty years of industrial harmony.[78] The emphasis of the Labour Department's work shifted from the wide-ranging responsibility for social welfare favoured by Orde-Browne towards encouraging the organisation of trade unions, and providing them with opportunities for constructive achievement through Wages Boards and Joint Industrial Councils. This new attitude was exemplified as early as 1943, when the Colonial Office was surprised to find Parry evaluating the policies of the iron-mining Development Company (which administrators had repeatedly criticised for inadequate

concern for workers' welfare but which had now come round to
encourage the formation of trade unions) more highly than those
of the Selection Trust (which provided better housing and rations
but exercised firm authoritarian control over their diamond
concession).[79] By 1946 Parry, though still suffering 'a
considerable amount of social ostracism' from local officials,[80]
enjoyed a high reputation in the Colonial Office, and succeeded to
the senior post of Commissioner of Labour; in 1948 he returned
to London as Assistant, and later Deputy, Labour Adviser to the
Secretary of State.

Parry did not work to encourage trade unionism merely as a
means of securing harmonious industrial relations, but as one
important condition for the growth of social democracy in Africa.
An enthusiastic correspondent of Rita Hinden and the Fabian
Colonial Bureau, Parry's wider aims included promotion of
Labour Parties in West Africa — a cause which in 1946 he
attempted to urge on Dennis Healey in Transport House.[81] He
fulminated against the ignorance and indifference of his European
colleagues towards wider political issues, urging on his Fabian
friends the need for 'the application of a long term policy'.[82] As
far as his immediate responsibilities were concerned this meant
taking the initiative in trade union matters out of the hands of
voluble demagogues like Wallace-Johnson — 'the most
objectionable and unscrupulous person I have met in political
life'[83] — and encouraging labour leaders who could combine
talents for honest and efficient organisation with realistic visions
of a democratic future for Sierra Leone.

Surveying the scene at the end of the war, Parry had been
pessimistic about such a future. 'The general impression held by
many people at home of masses of colonial peoples stirring
against colonial domination is certainly not true of this place', he
wrote; while the Protectorate remained 'contented in a bovine
sort of way', Creole opposition to the Municipality Ordinance
seemed 'peevish' and 'vituperative'. But Parry saw promise
among younger trade unionists, especially in a full-time official
'of my own making'.[84] Three months later Rita Hinden learned
the name of Parry's 'principal discovery': Siaka Stevens, a former
worker for the Development Company, whom Parry had
encouraged first to organise the labour force at Marampa and
Pepel and had now moved to Freetown as General Secretary of

the United Mineworkers Union. 'He has a lot to learn but he knows it and shows an insatiable appetite for the knowledge he stands in need of', wrote Parry, suggesting that he might receive 'sympathetic guidance and encouragement' through officials of the West African Council.[85] At a meeting in Nigeria Stevens had already been elected secretary of a West African Federation of Trade Unions (apparently a premature and abortive attempt to follow up the W.F.T.U. conference of 1945); early in 1946 he duly became first secretary of the Sierra Leone Trade Union Congress.[86]

A basic reason for the rise of Stevens and the consequent eclipse of Wallace-Johnson was the former's skill in obtaining benefits for his members through the industrial machinery which Parry had promoted. By 1946 the Wages Board system was working well; not only were the workers apparently well-satisfied with the increases negotiated there, but the employers were anxious to buttress the system by deducting trade union dues from wages. 'In fact they want to go as far towards the closed shop as they can. I had nothing to do with this. It's this man Stevens. He seems to have fascinated the mine owners.'[87] In 1947 Joint Industrial Councils were established, with similar euphoria.[88] But Parry saw Stevens and his colleagues as partners or collaborators in social-democratic decolonisation; his immediate ambition was 'a trade union and Labour movement ... with its hooks well into both sides of Transport House and not tied up with some fake African nationalist party.'[89]

Siaka Stevens' response to Parry's social democratic idealism was encouraging. In 1947–8, he visited Britain on a government scholarship, dividing his time between studies at Ruskin College and attachment to the headquarters of the British T.U.C. During this period he established friendly relations with Rita Hinden and other leaders of the Fabians, corresponding regularly and fluently; an article he contributed to their journal *Empire* testifies to the 'inestimable value' of 'Labour Advisers ... of the right type'. It is true there were notes of increasing criticism of British policy; in particular he complained that officials were still using chiefs and other traditional authorities to dominate the new Councils in the Protectorate, ignoring 'the general awakening among common men and women all over the world.'[90] 'As far as the repairing of the old Imperial edifice is concerned the Labour

Government has done very well indeed', he wrote. 'But what is
needed is a totally new structure.'[91] These criticisms became
sharper after the Accra riots, and Stevens's own return to Sierra
Leone in October 1948; how, he now asked, could Fabians
reconcile 'all this talk about free grants to the Colonies from
British taxpayers' money while at the same time we can see huge
sums being taken out of the colonies in the form of profits'?[92] Yet
this was frank talk among comrades, whose support was still
desired and highly valued.

> 'On the Wages Boards', Stevens wrote, in terms which might have
> surprised Parry, 'I used to be so full of anger against the bosses that I
> would feel like turning cannibal on them. I feel differently now. I
> realize now that the employers exploit us not because they are white
> men but because they are human beings, having in them all the
> frailties that man is heir to.'[93]

When Siaka Stevens entered the Executive Council and assumed
ministerial responsibility for Lands Mines and Labour after the
elections of 1951 he seemed to have been well prepared for the
role of collaborator in a social democratic programme of
decolonisation; and forward-looking Europeans placed high
hopes upon such an able and robust collaborator. His future
career would indeed be distinguished; but it was not to run
smoothly along the lines envisaged by these decolonisers.

The evidence surveyed here does not suggest that, in Sierra
Leone, there was any long-laid plan to revert to a system of
informal empire, or to transfer power to some neo-colonial
collaborating elite. During the middle years of the war the
Colonial Office began to urge local officials, usually against their
judgment and inclination, to apply their 'tentative plan for
constitutional development'; but administrators showed little
enthusiasm in preparing the bases for an autonomous state, and
scepticism as to whether so small an African country could *ever*
become fully independent long persisted. The dream of
channelling political development through native authorities
necessarily implied postponing self-government to so distant a
date that planning was neither practical nor necessary; any
alternative programme involved heavy dependence on Creoles, in
administrative cadres and in politics, and they had been written
off as possible inheritors of empire.

Once official policy had become reluctantly committed to political change, those who took the commitment to self-government most seriously were indeed anxious to communicate democratic and socialist values to their collaborators – just as in France the post-war years saw the apotheosis of the principled assimilationists. It might be said of both empires that idealists with a vision of continuing Afro-European partnership now proved the most dedicated neo-colonialists. Given time they might have achieved a more thorough preparation; but in Sierra Leone as in much of French Africa the pace of change was set by external pressures, beyond their power to control. Although men like Parry may have laid some durable 'cables' which will affect relationships, the societies which they have helped to create are by no means those which they intended.

NOTES

1. J. F. Ade Ajayi, 'The Continuity of African Institutions under Colonialism' in T. O. Ranger (ed.), *Emerging Themes of African History* (1968), p. 194.
2. K. E. Robinson, *The Dilemmas of Trusteeship* (1965) p. 7.
3. See W. Roger Louis, *Imperialism at Bay; The United States and the Decolonization of the British Empire* (1977). Professor Louis kindly allowed me to consult this work in manuscript while writing this paper.
4. A. G. Hopkins, *An Economic History of West Africa* (1973) Chap. 7.
5. Lothian Papers: Scottish Record Office, GD40/17/365, Perham to Lothian, 15 May 1938, enclosing Memo on 'Cultural Relations between Britain and the African Dependencies.'
6. Native Administration and Political Development in British Tropical Africa. Report by Lord Hailey, 1940–42. Confidential, 1942, p. 1.
7. *Ibid.* pp. 2–5.
8. This agenda, and records of four early meetings of this Committee, are in CO 967/13.
9. Cf. W. R. Louis, *op. cit.*
10. The episode is documented in CO 554/131/33701/42; quotations from Burns to Cranborne, Secret, 30 June 1942. Cf. A. Burns, *Colonial Civil Servant* (1949) pp. 194–6.
11. CO 554/132/33727, Note by Williams on 'Constitutional Development in West Africa'; Note of meeting in Secretary of State's room, 20 July 1943.
12. *Ibid.* Minute by Williams, 4 September 1943; cf. Grantham to Stanley, 11 October 1943.
13. P.P. 1944–45, Vol. V, Cmd. 6655, p. 18.
14. W. R. Louis, *op. cit.* discusses the international background to this semantic discussion.
15. Fabian Colonial Bureau Papers, Rhodes House, Oxford. Mss. British

Empire, S 365. (Henceforth cited as F.C.B.) Box 81, File 2, ff. 83–8, Hyde-Clarke to Nicolson, 17 November 1953.

16. CO 554/132/33727, Note on 'Constitutional Development in West Africa'.

17. On Creole history generally, see John Peterson, *Province of Freetown* (1961); L. Spitzer, *The Creoles of Sierra Leone* (Madison, 1974); A. T. Porter, *Creoledom* (1963). All these important studies derive initially from the fundamental work of Christopher Fyfe.

18. cf H. S. Wilson, *West African Nationalism* (1969); cf. E. A. Ayandele, *The Educated Elite in the Nigerian Society* (Ibadan, 1974).

19. See J. A. Langley, *Pan-Africanism and Nationalism in West Africa, 1900–1945* (Oxford 1973), pp. 153–63.

20. CO 267/667/32010/1, Jardine to MacDonald, Confidential, 12 September 1939.

21. *West Africa*, 20 October 1945, enclosed in CO 267/688/32348, Pt. II.

22. See the introduction to the second edition of *Journey without Maps*.

23. CO 267/670/32210/2 Jardine to Dawe, 1 June 1939.

24. CO 267/682/32303 Minute on Fenton to Lloyd, Secret, 29 January 1941; CO 267/676/32216 Minute on Jardine to MacDonald, Secret, 25 April 1940.

25. M. McCall, 'Kai Londo's Luawa and British Rule' (D.Phil. thesis, University of York 1974) emphasizes the limited impact of colonial rule upon one area.

26. M. H. Y. Kaniki, 'The Economic and Social History of Sierra Leone, 1929–1939' (Ph.D. thesis, University of Birmingham, 1972).

27. Kaniki, *op. cit.* Chapter VIII: Leo Spitzer, *The Creoles of Sierra Leone* (Madison 1974), Chap. VI. His career is being studied by Miss La Ray Denzer of Birmingham and Roosevelt Universities.

28. For references to his Communist associations, see E. T. Wilson, *Russia and Black Africa before World War II* (N.Y. 1974), especially pp. 243–53. Wilson relies heavily on references to Intelligence reports about alleged Communist contacts; until the evidence on which these were based is directly available it seems advisable to treat them with reserve.

29. F.C.B. Box 86, File 2, ff. 1–3, Wallace-Johnson to Padmore, 27 December 1939. CO 267/682/32303/42. Wallace-Johnson to Padmore, 25 May 1942, encl. in Stevenson to Cranborne, Secret, 12 March 1943. CO 267/683/32303/43, Wallace-Johnson to Brockway 16 February 1943 (in Beetham to Stanley, Secret, 12 March 1943).

30. CO 267/666/32215, Note by Williams, 1 September 1938.

31. CO 267/671/32245, Jardine-Dawe conversation, 17 January 1939. Communism is not mentioned in the Attorney-General's memorandum justifying Wallace-Johnson's detention on the outbreak of war – enclosed in CO 267/670/32210/2 Part II. Jardine to MacDonald, Secret, 23 September 1939. Also see CO 267/673/3254/8/39 – Note by Williams, November 1939; Spitzer, *op. cit.* pp. 200–01.

32. C. K. Meek, W. M. Macmillan & E. R. J. Hussey, *Europe and West Africa* (1940), pp. 76–7; Kaniki, *op. cit.* pp. 328–9, 334, 352–3.

33. CO 267/667/32032, Sherbro Judicial District Legislation.

34. CO 267/672/32248, Native Taxation. The phrase quoted is from Jardine's

address to the 1939–40 session of the Legislative Council.

35. CO 267/665/32208, Jardine to MacDonald, Secret, 30 June 1938.
36. Spitzer, *op. cit.* 190–91; the episode is documented in CO 267/665/32210.
37. CO 267/670/32199, Blood to MacDonald, Conf., 14 June 1939, encl. Stocks, 9 June.
38. For Youth League activity during this period, Spitzer, *op. cit.* Chap. 6. For conditions at Marampa, Kaniki, *op. cit.*, Chap. 5.
39. CO 267/667/32032/39. Minutes by Williams, Bushe, January 1939; Dawe-Jardine conversation 17 January.
40. CO 267/670/32210/2 (Part 1). Blood to MacDonald, Secret, 8 February, 1939.
41. CO 267/670/32210 (Part 2) Blood to Dawe, 15 March, 1939.
42. CO 267/670/32210/2 (Part 1) Jardine to Dawe, 1 June 1939. Correspondence regarding the Ordinances, and texts of Legislative Council debates, are in CO 267/672–3/32254 and related files.
43. CO 267/673/32275, Blood to MacDonald, Conf., 22 August, 1939; CO 267/671/32220; CO 167/673/32254/8, Brief by Williams, November 1939. On labour policy generally see H. E. Conway, 'Industrial Relations in Sierra Leone with Special Reference to the Development and Functioning of Bargaining Machinery since 1945' (Ph.D. thesis, University of London, 1968).
44. See P.P. 1940–1, IV, Cmd 6277, *Labour Conditions in West Africa: Report by Major Orde-Browne.*
45. *Native Administration and Political Development in Tropical Africa.* Report by Lord Hailey, 1940–42, pp. 12, 63–4, 81–2.
46. cf. F. D. Lugard, *The Dual Mandate* (1929 ed.) pp. 85–6.
47. Hailey, *loc. cit.* pp. 64–8.
48. This account is based on Hailey, *loc. cit.* pp. 69–83 and on CO 267/679/32097, Blood to Moyne, 110, 30 April, 1941.
49. CO 267/679/32097, Blood to Dawe, 1 May 1941.
50. *ibid.* Stevenson to Cranborne, 75, 23 March 1942.
51. CO 267/679/32097, Minute by Cox, 29 November 1941.
52. CO 267/675/32120/2, Minute by Webber on Jardine to Lloyd, Conf. 24 June 1940.
53. CO 554/131/33696/42, Cranborne to Burns & Stevenson, Tel., 6 December 1942.
54. CO 267/674/32036, Jardine to MacDonald, 752, 11 December 1939 and encls.
55. CO 267/678/32203, Moyne to Stevenson, 256, 23 December 1941; CO 267/678/32036/2, Ramage to Stanley, 226, 8 October 1943.
56. CO 267/684/32036/2, Memo by Advisory Committee, 25 May 1944.
57. CO 267/678/32036/1, Education Department Scholarship Scheme. A list of holders is in CO 267/687/32303/2.
58. CO 267/667/32035 contains a copy of the Commission's Report (Colonial No. 169).
59. CO 267/683/32354, Minute by Williams, 25 July, on Stevenson to Cranborne, 152, 27 June 1942; cf. his Minute of 24 July in CO 554/131/33702/42.

60. CO 554/131/33702/42, Stevenson to Cranborne, Tel., 27 October 1942; 25 March 1943.
61. CO 267/683/32375, Notes of talks with Sir H. Stevenson, 16 July, 12 August, 1943.
62. CO 267/688/32348, Part 1. Sessional Paper No. 4, 1944, *Reconstitution of the Freetown City Council*; Stevenson to Stanley, Conf., 28 February, 1945, enclosing draft Bill.
63. For background to this question, M. P. Banton, *West African City* (1957), Part One.
64. CO 267/688/3248 Part 1, Minute by Williams, 17 March 1945.
65. CO 267/688/32348, Part II, Minute by Varwill, 22 November, 1945.
66. For early signs of such tension, and Jardine's response, see CO 267/673/32285, Jardine to Dawe, Personal and Secret,. 15 October 1939; CO 267/677/32319, Jardine to Williams, 9 October 1940, Note by Williams, 7 November; CO 267/682/32303, Minute by Williams, 1 February 1941.
67. For the growing opposition, and samples of press comment, CO 267/688/32348, Part I; also CO 267/690/32397/1, Memo by Mayhew 5 January 1945.
68. CO 267/688/32348, Part I, Minutes by Creech-Jones, 28 August, 5 September, 1945.
69. *Daily Guardian*, 19 February 1946, enclosed in CO 267/688/32348, Part II, Stevenson to Gater, Secret, 5 March 1946, cf. Wallace-Johnson to CO, 2 November, 27 December, 1945, *ibid.*
70. CO 267/688/32348, Part I, Ramage to Hall, Conf. 29 August 1945.
71. CO 267/684/32009, Ramage to Stanley, Secret, 16 June, 1945.
72. CO 267/684/32010, Stevenson, Tel. 7 November 1944, Minute by Williams, 10 November.
73. J. R. Cartwright, *Politics in Sierra Leone 1917–1967* (Toronto, 1970); M. Kilson, *Political Change in an African State: A Study of the Modernisation Process in Sierra Leone* (Cambridge, Mass. 1966).
74. *F.C.B.*, Box 86, File 1A, R. B. Kowa to K. Little, 17 January 1948.
75. H. Foot, *A Start in Freedom* (1964) p. 15 – a theme which Lord Caradon developed in his unpublished Callander lectures in the University of Aberdeen in 1975.
76. On the general direction of policy, see P.P. 1940–41, IV. Cmd. 6277, Labour Conditions in West Africa: Report by Major Orde-Browne. For references on Nisbet's appointment, cf. above n. 43.
77. CO 267/681/32220 (Labour Department) includes a copy of CO Circular Telegram, 7 February 1941.
78. H. E. Conway, 'Industrial Relations in Sierra Leone ...' (Ph.D. thesis, London 1968).
79. CO 267/680/32199/2/43, Ramage to Stanley, Tel. 15 September, 1943; minute by Orde-Browne, 30 August, quoting Stevenson.
80. F.C.B. Box 86, File 2, fo. 118–9, Parry to Hinden, 29 December 1945.
81. *ibid.* fo. 125–7, Parry to Hinden, 24 November 1946; fo. 128, Hinden to Parry, 24 December.
82. *ibid.* fo. 130–1, Parry to Hinden, 9 February 1947.

83. *ibid*. fo. 113–6, Parry to Hinden, 23 September 1945.
84. *ibid*.
85. *ibid*. fo. 118–9, Parry to Hinden, 24 December 1945.
86. F.C.B. Box 86, File 1A, item 7, S.L.T.U.C. *Statement on the Present situation in the Congress*; File 1B, fo. 111–4, Stevens to Nicholson, 15 May 1948. The WAFTU meeting is not discussed in the standard works on trade unionism in West Africa; for an attempt to follow it by a meeting in Dakar, which Stevens also attended, see W. Ananaba, *The Trade Union Movement in Nigeria* (1969), pp. 43, 91; I. Davies, *African Trade Unionism* (Harmondsworth, 1966) p. 190.
87. F.C.B. Box 86, File 2, fo. 125–7, Parry to Hinden, 24 November 1946.
88. *ibid*. fo. 134–5, Parry to Hinden 16 March 1947; fo. 136–7, Parry to Hinden, 18 May, 1947.
89. *ibid*. fo. 125–7, Parry to Hinden, 24 November 1946.
90. *ibid*. fo. 203–4, Stevens to Hinden, 23 November 1950; cf. Box 87, File 2, fo. 8–11, Stevens to Hinden, 13 March 1952; also correspondence with Hinden and Nicholson in FCB 6/6, fo 184ff. Siaka Stevens, 'Trade Unionism in Sierra Leone', *Empire*, Vol. 11, No. 3, September 1948, p. 5.
91. F.C.B. Box 86, File 1B, fo. 111–14, Stevens to Nicholson, 15 May 1948.
92. F.C.B. Box 86, File 2, fo. 194–7, Stevens to Hinden, 3 December 1949.
93. *ibid*. fo. 199–201, Stevens to Hinden, 4 July 1950.

II

ECONOMIC
AND
MILITARY RELATIONS

5

Some Aspects of the Economic Relationship between France and its Ex-colonies

Gérard Destanne de Bernis

The question of economic dependence has been right at the heart of economic thinking for more than a decade, illustrating that theory finds it hard to avoid dealing with problems which arise from the heart of reality. The study of relations between the two great traditional colonial powers and their ex-colonies should prove particularly rewarding. We shall confine ourselves to certain aspects of the relations between France and its ex-colonies, but this still raises questions of general interest.

When André Gunder Frank talks of internal-external domination, he is referring to the dual dynamics of relations of dominance: that is, of relations between nations and those internal to the dominated nation, and the multiplicity and complexity of the connections between the two.

Colonialism did not appear out of the blue, a mere result of the whim of governments. It was a part of the natural attempt in the 19th century by France and England to make use of foreign markets to regulate their internal economy and secure their own capital accumulation. At a time when this control was based more on the export of capital than on that of goods – also the time when the German and American economies were threatening the dominant position of the British and French in the rest of the world – the 'colonial avatar' (N. Coquery-Visdrovitch) was called for and England felt the need to exchange its universal domination for formal dominion over part of the world

(Hobsbawm): hence the Treaty of Berlin. In the same way the process of political and legal independence after World War II was also an integral part of a world-wide movement based on the massive expansion and internationalisation of capital; France and Britain were involved but they were not the main actors. Just as situations of dependence have never been limited to areas of formal colonial rule, and just as colonial reserves never kept out international capital, so the idea of independence cannot be confined to situations of transfer of power and national liberation.

On the other hand, colonial rule cannot be interpreted as external domination pure and simple. Colonial powers have always tried to lean on particular classes within the colony, and have thereby influenced internal social structures. The changed structures remain after formal independence, and the classes established by the colonial power usually look for external support to maintain their own position within their own society. So, the main aim of international capital, which is to increase its dominance, corresponds to the domestic aim of these dominant social groups who, having taken over at independence, seek to create a domestic situation which will allow them to maintain or increase their power.

This is the context in which we have to examine the economic independence of former colonies. There are four sets of questions to be considered:

—is there any necessary correspondence between independence/dependence and ex-colonial power/ex-colonies?

—what types of independence process have been put into operation by the ex-colonies?

—can the attempts of the ex-colonial power to maintain its dominant position be separated from its preoccupation with its own independence?[1]

—finally, what degree of contradiction is involved in the desire to build independence whilst still remaining in an extremely dependent position?

I

Is the ex-colonial power itself completely independent? There may be doubts about the theory of a hierarchy of national systems of production among the highly industrialised economies, but certainly French undertakings have been pushed out by those of West Germany and the United States from a whole series of contracts with Third World countries in fields of advanced technology. Such constraints have the effect that the ex-colonies have acquired a certain independence with regard to their ex-metropolitan power, though without gaining any extra economic independence from industrialised countries as a whole.

Thus formal independence starts a new 'game' with three sets of players: the ex-colonies, who will wish to convert their new status into more real terms; the ex-colonial powers, which try to retain their position by new methods including the cultivation of language ties; and thirdly, the non-colonial powers, such as West Germany or the United States with great industrial capacity and desire for fresh markets.[2]

If the pairs dependence/independence and metropolitan power/ex-colony have to be interpreted in the context of the internationalisation process which characterises capitalism today, we are forced to ask what the nation really is in economic terms. Easy answers may have been possible in the 1950s but in the case of France, for example, the position has become complex and confused as a result of great changes between the 4th and 7th Plans. An increasingly large share of the French industrial sector was 'colonised' by foreign firms who took over for themselves the 'rights' of the old French firms abroad. Can the overseas country be considered dependent on France when it is really dependent on the French subsidiary of a foreign company? At the other end, is the nation any more than a wish if it is divided into sectors, each occupied by different firms working solely for the profit of foreign capital? Cameroun as a colony was dependent on France; this at least was clear. But now, if we speak of the Cameroun economy, what can be meant? Where is its centre? Where are its decisions taken? For whose benefit? Does it make sense to describe it as dependent on a French economy when, in reality, local industries in the Cameroun are directed from decision-making centres which are only nominally 'French' and which drain away the surplus from the Cameroun for the profit of capital which is neither French nor Cameroun but international?[3]

II

What are the processes set in motion by the ex-colonies to attain their much-discussed objective of economic independence? Their first priority must be to have the least unfavourable economic relationship with the ex-metropolitan power and also with international capital. At the same time they will recognise that *industrialisation* and independence are each necessary supports to the other.

Without in any way considering Algeria as a perfect example of industrialisation, it must be said that it is one of the few countries in the Third World which is attempting an effective policy in this area. It has arrived at the progressive increase of capital within its territory and the establishment of new industries within a system of state companies, thus reducing the use of foreign capital except in providing services in the oil sector where the state still only has a minority holding. Secondly, it has undertaken the systematic investment of the surplus from mining in the setting up of an industrial system aimed both at producing goods to improve agriculture (tractors, motors, pumps, fertiliser, plastics) and at building up the industrial sector (plant, chemicals). Third, Algeria has used foreign trade to acquire capital goods with minimum capital expenditure (gas-liquefaction plants are financed by special credits from gas purchasers) and it has pressed for the collective control of markets by the producing countries, notably through its role within OAPEC (organisation of Arab countries exporting oil). Next, complete state control of the monetary and financial sector has been secured. Fifth, agrarian reform is aimed at a complete reorganisation of agriculture and a considerable change in social status for the peasant. Finally, by developing its own engineering units it has avoided dependence on foreign companies who have often secured control through their engineering services.

None of this has been achieved without mistakes and, while not the cause of all problems, these errors must be identified and analysed so that they do not endanger the whole process. For example, there have been internal social conflicts which have caused a great deal of delay and disequilibrium. Property owners and others have stood in the way of rural development and slowed down agrarian reform. As a result, too many people have left the land, leading to urban unemployment and housing shortages, reduced agricultural production alongside increased population, a dangerous increase in dependence on foreign countries for food, and, finally, a check to industrialisation because of the shortage of foreign currency and inadequate outlets in agriculture for industrial products. This underlines the lack of popular participation in the working out of development policy. The same analysis can be extended to the traders, who have sabotaged domestic trade in agricultural products by insisting on making as much profit as they can from the surplus which is due to the farmer. It is widely recognised that, in the absence of any radically new structures, it is very difficult to organise the supplying of the towns efficiently by means of public trading.

None of this was inevitable. The political set-up, the removal of the Congress of fellahs in 1963, the lack of any really revolutionary party, and probably many other factors, make up the explanation. However, this gives us the key to future possibilities: will they involve a more radical agrarian revolution and the imposition of real workers' power in the socialist management of businesses, or will they involve the establishment of a leading class of technicians (who exercise effective economic power at the moment by means of the state production apparatus) and lead towards ill-defined or dangerous alliances between classes? There are many indications of the importance today of these internal struggles.

But it would be quite wrong to minimise the barriers erected in the way of the process of industrialisation by the advanced capitalist countries, particularly the ex-colonial power. This is not just a matter of high cost materials bought abroad and delivery delays. It is more important to concentrate on the contradiction between trying to go quickly (through the turnkey contracts and 'products in hand' contracts where the seller provides factory and workers and sets it up before receiving his money) and keeping control of industrialisation in a situation where developed countries contrive to maintain the monopoly of engineering knowledge and their firms act for profit quite independently of any specific attention to the needs of development.

We must, however, also acknowledge that Algeria is definitely an exception amongst the ex-French colonies. (Clearly Vietnam is on a quite different level, with industrialisation taking place in the context of a hard-fought war, demonstrating the potential power of a people's political will.) It may be said that other French ex-colonies do not have Algeria's oil resources, and that this is why they can establish neither industry nor independence. But this will not do. For one thing, Algeria began its development in 1972, when oil was still fetching a low price, when none of the other oil-producing countries, far richer than Algeria, had made any efforts in this field; the importance of political will cannot be denied. What is more, many French ex-colonies – not Gabon alone – have abundant raw materials. The problem is not the possession of such resources; it is wanting to use them for industrialisation and independence. This is not an economic problem, but a political one. This explains why Gabon allows itself to be robbed and why Mauritania and Togo decided to recover control of their natural resources. But even nationalisation of mineral deposits, however important, does not guarantee independence.

However, it would be mistaken to put all the blame on the ex-colonial power. Naturally, we cannot study the policies of all France's ex-colonies. However, it is worth looking at Ivory Coast, for this is always taken to show that independence can be established in the framework of capitalist policy in close co-operation with the ex-colonial power. No one can deny that countries such as Brazil, Iran and Hong Kong have reached a certain level of industrial development. The question remains whether they have laid the basis for real industrialisation, that is, a process of building an autonomous base of 'home-made' accumulation and a process of distributing income so that the majority of the people benefit from the productive results of their own labour. Here again, politics and economics cannot be considered separately.

The list of the industries set up in Ivory Coast since independence excludes practically all branches which could constitute a material basis for growth. The main ones are in food (34.5 per cent of the industrial turnover in 1974) and textiles (12.6 per cent). The wood industry concentrates on exports (9 per cent). The chemical industry (plastics, rubber, etc.) only involves goods for domestic use or exports (21.2 per cent). The mechanical and electrical industry includes the assembly of vehicles and bicycles (9.8 per cent). Mining is currently limited to diamonds (0.6 per cent). The best examples of growth are in the construction industry (2.6 per cent); a small rolling mill (0.7 per cent), a 40,000 tonnes fertiliser factory, a ship-repairing scheme, and the setting up of a small electric cable plant. Agricultural diversification mainly takes the form of the development of plantations and products for export (coffee, cocoa, bananas, etc.) and an increase in rice-growing and market gardening. None of these industries are controlled by the government of Ivory Coast, nor even by its own capitalists. Although most of the limited companies belong to Ivory Coast formally, this means very little in fact. Even in the food or textile industries we can find the same international companies mentioned earlier in connection with Cameroun. Construction materials are under the control of French cement companies. When Ivory Coast offered the exploitation of iron deposits it was to the United States within the framework of a syndicate of metallurgy companies including Japanese, United States, and European interests.

Banking is mainly French- or European-controlled. Since the reform of the statutes of the West African Monetary Union and the Central Bank of the States of West Africa in 1973, the Ivory Coast has managed, through its National Monetary Committee, to play an active part in issue policy. The liberalisation of exchanges world-wide has reduced the importance of the currency pool. The Malagasy experience shows that the rules of accounting practice can be far more flexible than might have been thought. However, all these countries are affected by fluctuations in the franc, which are decided exclusively by Paris. On the other hand, Franco-European (and American) involvement is considerable in banking, even though the share of the Ivory Coast is increasing.

With regard to commercial banks, there are three local banks which are 40 per cent Ivory Coast owned,[4] a branch of the Paris BIAO (International Bank of West Africa) which alone handles 25 to 27 per cent of the trade in coffee and cocoa, and five branches of other foreign banks. Ivory Coast is a majority shareholder in two development banks and the National Savings and Credit Bank (housing and plant) is a State-owned company. But Ivory Coast holds a small minority of shares in the main development bank and owns only 49 per cent of the capital of the Financial Company of Ivory Coast, the main business bank in French-speaking Africa. Ivory Coast possesses its own financial establishment, SONAFI (the National Finance Company of Ivory Coast). Only one quarter of the capital of SAFCA, a French group including Renault, the French West African Company and the West African Trading Company, is held by Ivory Coast: this group also operates in other African countries.

There does not appear to be any way in which the government of Ivory Coast or Ivory Coast capitalists acting in concert could organise financial channels and use them to bring about growth in Ivory Coast of a national policy of integration. Indeed, it is obvious that nearly all the surplus production from the Ivory Coast economy goes abroad. To get a clearer picture, we should examine the tax system, the distribution of private and public investment between profitable and non-profitable areas, the links between the Ivory Coast middle-class and international capital, the fixing of prices for agricultural products, and so on.[5] This is the framework in which the concern about the Africanisation and training of management staff should be judged. A committee on localisation was set up in 1973 by the PDCI-RDA (Ivory Coast Democratic Party and African Democratic Rally) as was an official committee in 1975, but 35 per cent of the wages earned still goes to expatriates. International capital can only support those attempts (financed by public administration) which will allow it to decrease its payment of salaries and will remove the employment bottleneck.[6]

Finally, it must be noted that even if we assume that in general this model might be effective in gaining independence, it could scarcely hold for Ivory Coast and neighbouring countries, because it assumes that the domestic market of the industries brought into Ivory Coast is the market of this region. The trading surplus of Ivory Coast over its neighbours has gone from 2.4 to 18.5 thousand million c.f.a. (African Financial Community) francs. What is more, we can see how French capitalism (and European and international capital) can, through Ivory Coast, strike a blow at the neighbouring countries' desires for independence. We can also appreciate how it was able to profit from the change of regime in Mali: during that period, Ivory Coast exports to Mali went from 802 to 7,710 millions c.f.a. francs.

We may now turn to analyse the development of the *foreign trade* of France's ex-colonies. Some general statements are possible concerning the geographical elements of this trade. First, all the ex-French colonies have, without exception, reduced France's share in their foreign trade. This was, with the exception of exports from the Congo and Upper Volta, in excess of 50 per cent at the time of independence, and subsequently dropped to about 40 per cent: less than 30 per cent for exports from Tunisia, Ivory Coast, Upper Volta, Togo, the Congo, Chad, Cameroun, Mali and Mauritania, and only more than 50 per cent in Algeria (oil), the Central African Republic and Senegal; it is never less than 30 per cent for imports, and is still over 50 per cent for imports into the Central African Republic, the Congo and Gabon. As a general rule, France's ex-colonies have increased their trade with EEC countries. The exceptions are Chad, and exports from Congo and Gabon.

But this increase, except in the case of imports into Togo and Gabon, has not made up for France's reduced share. No general tendency can be discerned in trade with the United States (increased in 18 cases, reduced in 9) whose share exceeds 10 per cent rarely (exports from Tunisia, the Ivory Coast and Madagascar, imports to Mauritania and Gabon); nor for any of the other OECD countries (a reduction in 18 cases, an increase in 10), this share often being less than 10 per cent in any case. With perhaps only one exception (exports from Benin) the share of other countries in trade is still growing, sometimes most spectacularly. The share of socialist countries is usually less than 5 per cent (exceptions are Morocco, Algeria, Togo, Madagascar and Mali). The share of Asian underdeveloped countries is, with the exceptions of Madagascar and Senegal, less than 3 per cent (an overall average of 3.7 per cent). Except in Gabon and Morocco, the share of Latin American countries never exceeds 3 per cent. On the other hand, the amount of trade with other African countries – though not South Africa – varies very much according to country (from less than 5 per cent in Algeria and the Central African Republic to a much greater share in Mali and Upper Volta, where the role of Ivory Coast is very important).

However, to judge the significance of these figures we have to ask further questions. For example, what local control, public or private, exists over international trade? Algeria has nationalised it completely. However, one of the accusations made against A. Ben Salah was that he wanted to control it. Senegal had to give up its

Groundnuts Trading Office in 1961. Togo has nationalised its phosphates, and Mauritania its iron and copper, but do they really control the trade in them? Again, what is the role of transnational companies in this international trade? Their simultaneous intervention in several countries within the same area is a form of permanent blackmail. What is more, diversification can just be a means of extending the markets of these firms and increasing their influence on countries, which only appear to be diversifying 'their' own foreign trade. Further, how and how soon does the repatriation of funds from exports take place and what government control is exerted over such transactions? Who fixes the prices of exports for the producer?

It is not possible to give realistic answers to these factual questions, which just goes to show the lack of information available on the operation of present-day capitalism. These questions show that the problem of dependence on metropolitan France cannot be separated from that of dependence on foreign capital. This rather takes us back to the first questions we asked. Can we, in the framework of international capital, distinguish capital by its nationality (always presuming that capital can have a nationality), and must we speak of dependence on France just because more capital comes from the French bourgeoisie than from any other bourgeoisie?

There is another aspect of international trade which relates to the type of product imported and exported. This aspect of foreign trade is not independent of industrialisation, nor is it entirely dependent on it. The most striking point is that for the majority of France's ex-colonies in Africa south of the Sahara, the main group of imports has scarcely changed. If we look at the share of various groups of products in total imports in 1959–60 and in 1971–72, we find that food products have dropped slightly (except in Cameroun where they have gone down by 50 per cent) or remained the same (Ivory Coast) or have increased, mostly very slightly (except in Togo where they have increased by one third). The same applies to consumption goods, whose share was more than 50 per cent, except in Togo (20 per cent), and the Congo (43 per cent) in 1959–60, and whose share was never less than 40 per cent in 1971–72, and was often more than 50 per cent (70 per cent in Benin). Energy often went down to about 5 per cent or less, except in Ivory Coast (6.4 per cent) and in Mali (9.5

per cent). The share of raw materials and semi-finished goods rose (except in Benin and in Cameroun), sometimes dramatically (doubling in Gabon and tripling in the Central African Republic) to reach between 20 and 25 per cent (6 per cent in Benin). The share of finished goods for industry rose little in Ivory Coast, Benin and Gabon (where it reached the exceptional figure of 34 per cent), rising more in Cameroun and Madagascar, but it dropped in Togo, the Central African Republic and the Congo, where it was more than 30 per cent in 1959–60. Now it is usually about 25 to 30 per cent (20 per cent in Benin and Togo).

Calculations for exports are very similar. More than 90 per cent of these exports are products of agricultural origin or raw materials in an unprocessed state, except in Cameroun (82 per cent), Togo (82 per cent), Senegal (76 per cent), the Congo (66 per cent) and the Central African Republic (62 per cent). The case of the latter is, however, different, since diamonds, which make up 36 per cent of its exports, do not count as raw materials. In addition, the vast majority of exports depends on a very small number of products, mostly the same now as in 1959–60, with the exception of the development of raw cotton (Benin, Upper Volta, Mali and Niger to some extent) the discovery of uranium (Niger and Gabon), of oil (Gabon), of phosphates (Togo) and an increase in the exploitation of the forests (Ivory Coast, Central African Republic and Cameroun), which can take the form of destructive over-use (Congo).

There are two exceptions to the general pattern. Cameroun is beginning to transform its wood and aluminium industries to make parts for the aeronautical industry, but this is a completely export-based industrial process. Senegal, on the other hand, is a country with a slightly diversified economy, exporting manufactured fertilisers, semi-finished textile products, cement, various minor engineering products, basic materials for transport and some finished products (clothing). There remain the potassium fertilisers from the Congo (13 per cent), timber or plywood (Congo, Gabon), diamonds (the Central African Republic and the Congo) and various textile products.

Thus we have the typical picture of countries completely dependent on foreign countries, and as we have seen, still mainly dependent on their former colonial power. Because of their climate, position, and natural resources, and the kind of colonisation they underwent, the former colonies in North Africa have always had a more diversified economy. But their structural development too has been much more marked than that of Black Africa. Whilst the three countries of the Maghreb at independence devoted more than half their imports to consumption goods, of which food made up two-fifths or a half, these figures were practically halved by 1972–73. During the same period, the share of raw materials, semi-finished products and plant had increased by 50 per cent. With regard to exports, particularly from Algeria, sales of crude oil were the means of financing imports of equipment, and the desire to carry out industrialisation at home did not allow any dramatic development in exports. Nevertheless, significant exports of manufactured products did take place, which guaranteed the quality and relative competitiveness of domestically manufactured products.

Thus, we can see how trading relations between France's ex-colonies and the industrialised world (especially France) can be viewed as an organised system for transferring surpluses; from this point of view, we emphasise that trading companies of French origin operating between these countries and the industrialised world constitute an essential element of this system.[7] We will just make two comments on this. Firstly, the importance placed by Algeria both on the nationalisation of its foreign trade and on the need for changes in the rules governing the world market is quite understandable. This constitutes an essential element of independence. Secondly, we must mention the interesting possibility of a detailed and quantitative study of this transfer of surplus. However, this would be difficult since the price on the world market does not necessarily represent the value of these goods (just as the price of French agricultural products is less than their value), but allows wages to stay at a level where the rate of profit can remain stable, or even increase, in industrial economies. Moreover, the market price must be differentiated from that paid to the producer, and account must be taken of all the intermediaries involved.[8]

It is understandable that *emigration* may seem inevitable in the majority of over-populated Third World countries, where the traditional economy decays – dramatically as in the Sahel drought – without a modern economy really being developed (in spite of economic domination by transnational companies). At the time of independence, Algeria was the main provider of an immigrant work force for France. Tunisian and Moroccan contingents have grown from small beginnings at that time to become considerable (150,000 and 270,000 respectively). And the number of emigrants from Black Africa (more than 60,000 from Mali or Senegal) has increased to a point where the government of Senegal itself was forced to take notice of it.

Initially Algeria was quite unable, in the dilapidated conditions which she inherited from the colonial period and war of independence, to do anything to halt the flow of migrants. Indeed, at the time of the crisis, brought about by France during 1969–71 and leading to the nationalisation of oil resources, emigration became the only way of carrying on at all with the development programme. However, after much internal discussion, and because of the racialist attacks on immigrant labour in France, the Algerian government felt able to suspend emigration in October 1973. At present, employment prospects for the next ten years are such that the Algerians are thinking of going back to emigration, although this would have to be done with great care.

III

If it is relatively easy to see that situations of dependence still exist, or that a process is just beginning which may lead to economic independence, it is much more difficult to discover the respective responsibilities of the political and economic powers in the ex-metropolitan country and the dominant social classes in the ex-colonies. In reality, they are closely linked. The example of Algeria proves that the metropolitan power resorts to hostile delaying tactics when it is faced with a popular demand for independence. But, on the other hand, the dominant social classes in most of the ex-colonies could not have stayed in power if they had not had political, economic, financial, and sometimes even military support from leaders in the ex-metropolitan power. Here, too, however, it is no good trying to separate the attitude of the ex-colonial power from the process of the internationalisation of capital, in which this power is trying to maintain its own independence.

The history of Franco-Algerian relations since 1962 has many aspects. It is in part the history of all France's attempts to stop

Algeria from launching and then developing its industrialisation programme by its series of refusals:[9] to build the third pipeline (1963); to build the steelworks, although this was part of the Constantine Plan (1964–65); to develop a real industrial co-operation policy (part of the 1965 oil agreements); to carry out the Arzew petrochemical project (1967); to raise the price of Algerian natural gas; to raise the price of Algerian oil (1969–71).

It could be shown that in each case France's refusal gave Algeria the opportunity to take yet another step towards political and economic independence. It is therefore surprising that France should have persisted in its attitude, as if to show the world that Algeria's industrialisation was being carried out from beginning to end in the face of France's opposition. This is particularly striking since these obstinate refusals have at times been contrary to France's immediate interests. For France had a great advantage in Algeria over its competitors in that Franco-Algerian commercial links were of very long standing. However much an ex-colony wants to diversify its customers and suppliers, it takes time, due to the importance of language, commercial habits, and so on. France could have kept its edge over other countries, but this would have required that it come to terms with the needs of the Third World and be prepared to buy products from its ex-colony – though this would admittedly have aided the ex-colony's industrialisation. During 1975 the Algerian government drew the French government's attention to the risks involved for relations between the two countries if this state of affairs continued: the French government's reply – which it transmitted indirectly in December 1975 – was to stop oil extraction in Algeria.[10]

This French attitude is not limited just to Algeria. We obviously cannot go into the complete history of France's relentless struggle against nations trying to implement an independent policy, such as Guinea since the 1958 referendum, Mali from the break-up of the Federation of Mali up to the coup d'état in 1968, and Tunisia from 1956 because of its support for Algeria's fight for independence from 1956 until the coup d'état of 1969 against A. Ben Salah, when it gave up support for any kind of socialism. This has been the policy of all French governments since Mendès-France, in both the Fourth and Fifth Republics. We are led to ask how it is that the French public take so little interest in these questions, and why movements which

support the Third World have not revolted against this flagrantly
neo-colonialist behaviour by the French governing class?

Of course, at the same time, France gives aid to those countries
which are submissive. This is the point where links between
internal political structures and the policy of the metropolitan
power are strongest. It cannot be said that France imposes 'co-
operation' by force: it made no attempt, for example, to
reconquer Guinea, even if some of its agents would have been
satisfied, to say the least, by the success of a certain coup d'état. If
the groups in power are not able to keep themselves there, they
need the 'aid' of a foreign power. France's interests, too, lie in
keeping in power those groups whose domestic policy is in line
with the interests of the local capitalists. France's help has not
been forthcoming for any other policy. Nor would any group
with a different policy have asked for such aid.

This explains, in my view, the institutions and working of the
franc zone. It also explains the apparent contradiction between
discussion and reality as regards 'aid' policy in France.

France has in fact had a fairly explicit discussion on aid in
comparison with other powers. General de Gaulle elaborated on
the virtues of decolonisation. France should have an 'Arab policy'
and keep its distance from Israel. Apartheid was condemned. The
concept of 'aid' was regarded as old-fashioned and was replaced
by the idea of equal co-operation. France was to lead a 'new
world economic order'. He even stated, in a country which was a
copper producer, that France was not opposed to an increase in
some raw material prices. Complaints against France were
described as mere misunderstandings – the proof of this was
France's readiness to sell arms to practically any country!

However, actions speak louder than words; during this period
France was using the consensus procedure at the United Nations
to avoid being in a minority and expressed 'reservations' (similar
to those of the United States) to the Final Declaration of the
Special Session in the spring of 1974. It abstained in the vote on
the Charter on the Economic Rights and Duties of States. For as
long as it could do so decently, or undetected, it sold arms to the
white governments of Southern Africa. It supported, though less
openly, the representatives of these governments in Angola, after
voting on the side of fascist Portugal within the UN. France
remains, in addition, one of the last actual colonialist powers,

even if it uses referendums or *départements* as strategems. It takes no part in the International Energy Agency, but continually protests against rises in petrol prices and refuses to pay more for other raw materials.

From this point of view, the latest government report entitled 'French co-operation policy' deserves a detailed analysis, since it is the ultimate example of this contradiction. We will, however, only deal with it briefly here.[11] This report – the Abelin report – takes as its starting point the magic words, 'New International Economic Order'. Strangely enough, however, it neither defines this term nor refers to any of the criteria by which the Third World usually defines it since President Boumedienne's speech at the UN Special Session in 1974, nor does it even refer to the Resolution passed then. Indeed, it maintains practically total silence on all the main points.

Thus it makes no reference to the principle of the nationalisation of the exploitation of natural resources nor to the control of price-fixing mechanisms. It shows no sign of being ready to see an increase in the price of raw materials. How in 1976 can a co-operation programme be credible if it is based on stable prices which allow a large surplus to be transferred to the power which is supposed to be a source of aid?[12] There is indeed some reference to industrialisation in new states but it is conceived only in the vague context of 'raising Gross National Product and making social improvements'. At the same time the report is all too clear that industrialisation is not to upset present structures: it will entail 'calling on the experience gained over 150 years by the industrialised countries, France in particular, whose private sector is widely represented in Africa. This industrial experience can only be passed on by those who have actually known it – that is, the industrialists themselves'. When it moves on to 'industrial co-operation', frankly described as 'the intervention of private partners from France' it talks of course of 'reciprocal interests resulting in equal profit for both sides' but the main feature seems to be that French industrialists should be associated with and in control of all that goes on. Nor is this surprising; it merely reflects the policy of the co-operation Conference organised in the spring of 1975 by the Ministry of Industry on the subject of industrial redeployment. Ministerial solidarity is complete. Who is giving aid to whom?

The report recognises that French aid in 1973 only amounted to 0.58 per cent of French G.N.P., only just half the target of 1 per cent and still below the 'pseudo target' of 0.7 per cent, but nowhere suggests that either target would be reached. Nor is any reply given to reasonable Third World claims about conditions of aid. It is not so much a question of 'untying' aid nor of 'globalising' it. Rather, the more important problems are how to plan aid over a number of years so as to fit in with African development plans and how to reduce the burden of debt but neither is seriously discussed.

Finally there are two further matters of importance. First, Abelin is completely silent on the subject of immigration. Yet immigration certainly on the one hand benefits French capital directly and indirectly through markets subsequently opened up in the countries of origin, and on the other hand underlines the lack of development in those countries without being of the slightest benefit to them, except in so far as their workers use their time in France to obtain professional qualifications. But on the whole the workers who come to France illiterate, unskilled and healthy leave it illiterate, unskilled and sometimes sick or injured. Who, then, is giving aid to whom? Second, there is a serious ambiguity as to what lies behind the often stated desire for co-operation with other industrial powers to give aid to ex-colonies. It is, of course, an acknowledgement that France is no longer the only power in French-speaking Africa. But it also means giving up any notion of policy other than that of imperialism in general – no doubt recognising that if France by itself can no longer hope to have a really powerful grip on its ex-colonies this is at least a way of retaining a shared grip!

But this last point has a much wider bearing. The position of new states in the world has changed greatly in recent years. This is to be seen not merely in the fact that developed countries no longer lay down the law in the UN, but in other more important ways. 'The Group of 77' has overcome its preliminary problems – caused by the presence of countries with privileged relationships with an imperialist metropole – and has developed the unifying concept of the 'least advantaged'. This unity has become stronger and more radical at various summit meetings, in the Secretariat of Non-Aligned Countries, at UN Special Sessions, at Conferences on the Law of the Sea and on Food, in the UNCIO

Council, the Council on Population, and so on. Here, Algeria has played a dynamic role, avoiding very radical positions in order to gain an increasingly solid base for unity and strength. It is now recognised that the leaders in France's ex-colonies cannot cut themselves off from the Third World; they can keep up their links with France only if French policy permits them to believe (or to appear to do so) that such links do not contradict their belonging to the united Third World movement. France, too, knows that it can only safeguard its domination by taking account of this – which no doubt explains the new co-operation agreements signed with all the countries concerned. While it may be too soon to judge these, it is certain that a force has arisen which can only be favourable to the independence of these countries in the long run, unless capitalism finds some unforeseeable way of protecting itself.

We have already referred to the internationalisation of capital which affects both France and its ex-colonies. French multi-nationals rely on the French state to help them in their hard-fought struggle against international competition; for them this is definitely not the time for additional costs such as would result from accepting the need for increases in raw material prices or from increased aid (unless it involved cornering markets!). Of course, there is a small sector of public opinion which campaigns for a more generous policy towards the Third World, although very often it is just a case of campaigning for more aid rather than for a quite different sort of aid. This sector of the public tends, however, to be moved by sentiment without trying to analyse basic political and economic reasons and current situations, and without understanding that it is the logic of capitalism which is basic to the problem.

The reaction of the French authorities, and sometimes of private groups, expresses this contradiction in its own way. If France does not maintain its position, other powers such as the United States or Japan will take over. And, of course, France's failure in recent years to gain large industrial contracts with the oil producing countries (in advance technology industries, the mechanical and electrical industries) hardly encourages it to allow its ex-colonies in Africa to follow an independent path. French policy in Africa is determined by its need to maintain its relative position within the international capitalist economy. It has had to concede de-colonisation; it now tries to keep a privileged position for itself within the general context of domination of the Third World by the industrialised powers, always in the hope that this position will improve that of its own industry with regard to its rivals.

I have two final comments to make. First, it would appear that, with the exception of Franco-Algerian relations, the relations between France and its ex-colonies are at once altered and yet strangely familiar. It is no doubt a mistake to over-estimate the change involved in formal independence; but equally we must not under-estimate this change, for it has released new forces both within the ex-colonies in the form of various social conflicts and within the Third World as a whole as it seeks a unified stance in a genuinely new international economic order. But although these forces are real, and are an important cause of capitalism's present crisis, it is sobering to recall that capitalism has always shown considerable adaptive power. Nevertheless it is also possible that we are nearer than ever before to an alternative to capitalism. In any event the future of relations between the metropolitan power and its ex-colonies must be sought elsewhere than in an analysis of those relations alone.

Secondly, the tendency to under-estimate the new forces has been encouraged by the slow pace of development. Moreover, if independence from the metropolitan power in the end only leads to another kind of dependence on all industrialised countries, or rather on the multi-nationals, we have to ask if this is a phase in the development of metropolitan-colony relations or, rather, a stage in the development of capitalism itself. Here, too, there are two possible attitudes. I take the position, for example, that despite internal and external problems and contradictions, Algeria is moving towards economic independence, although it has not yet reached its objective. The alternative attitude would be to say that at a given moment in history no social force or class can break free from the historical conditions in which it finds itself. Since all social systems seek to ensure their continued existence, it follows that dominant countries will try to retain the bases of their dominance over others and thus see to it that dependent countries do not follow their 'dream' of independence.

We are therefore forced back towards an analysis of the historical conditions which can create favourable conditions for those social forces which seek independence and which carry out the struggles necessary to this end against dominant capitalism attempting to ensure its continued existence and expansion. This conflict evolves both within industrial economies (the role of the workers' movement) and in the relations between these economies and those of non-industrialised countries. This, in any case, is the context in which the subjects we have been discussing have to be viewed.

NOTES

1. For obvious reasons we cannot go into a detailed analysis country by country. The general nature of the analysis may therefore give rise to some doubts. We must note in particular that lack of sufficient statistical information on Guinea means that we cannot refer to this exceptionally interesting case. Also revolution in Madagascar is too recent to permit serious analysis of that case. These are both countries where politics has been strongly influenced by forces which felt that their independence could not be guaranteed within the framework of the links proposed by the ex-colonial power.

2. France itself could be in this position in Zaire. She has the same language but enjoys two advantages over Belgium – no taint of colonialism there and greater industrial power.

3. I am not speaking lightly. Amongst the 'thirty largest industrial companies' in the Cameroun, according to the classification in *Afrique Industrie* of 15 July 1975, there are three companies in which the Cameroun state has a majority holding (electric power, water, state plantations) and six private undertakings in which the majority or the whole of the holding is held by the National Investment Company or by private Camerounians who may be indirectly linked with French companies, in food or timber industries. The remainder, the vast majority particularly if we take account of sales figures, is owned by the Bank of Indochina, the Rivaud group, the PUK, the Barry group, de Bastos, de Finsider, de Lafarge, the Grands Moulins de Paris, Unilever, Cellulose du Pin. Very often the same companies also have interests in the Central African Republic, Gabon, Congo Brazzaville, Chad, Ivory Coast and Liberia. Almost all Cameroun business activity is therefore organised in a framework of 'plunder' – with no Cameroun strategy in sight.

4. Shares in these are held by the Crédit Industriel et Commercial, the Société Générale, the Banque Nationale de Paris, Crédit Lyonnais, the SFOM, Banque Lazard, Banque de Paris et des Pays-Bas and by a dozen European and American banks.

5. An excellent study of this question dealing with Senegal is Monique Anson-Meyer's *Mécanismes de l'exploitation en Afrique: l'exemple du Sénégal*, Cujas, Paris, 1974.

6. The policy of educating management varies in significance and effect according to the framework within which it is implemented.

7. Whilst relying on internal trading networks which keep a share of the surplus gained from the primary producer for themselves.

8. The BCEAO index is very interesting but it arbitrarily takes 1966 as a basis and it is not clear which of these prices it is using.

9. We are summarising the list given by P. Judet in his article in *Le Monde Diplomatique*, February 1976, p. 9.

10. P. Judet, *loc. cit.* shows that by doing this France lost the chance of industrial sectors gaining contracts in Algeria. What could have caused such a decision? Inefficiency, lack of contact with reality, or was it a political decision? It must be admitted that industrialists wanted France to buy oil elsewhere, where they could get special advantages. This brings us back again to the role of the state and monopolies in present day capitalism.

11. However, see also the contribution to this volume from Jean Poirier and Jean Touscoz.

12. The Lomé Agreement only deals with stabilising resources, which is not sufficient here.

I. The share of various countries in the total imports and exports of France's ex-colonies.

	Togo				Ivory Coast				Upper Volta				Niger			
	Imp. 1960	Imp. 1972	Exp. 1960	Exp. 1972	Imp. 1960	Imp. 1972	Exp. 1960	Exp. 1972	Imp. 1960	Imp. 1972	Exp. 1960	Exp. 1972	Imp. 1959	Imp. 1972	Exp. 1959	Exp. 1972
France	51.3	35.6	62.3	26.9	70.5	47.1	52.4	29.1	71.2	46.8	1.9	19.2	63.7	46.6	85.3	38.4
Other E.E.C. countries (the Six)	13.4	22.8	16.5	56.9	9.1	19.4	15.3	31.3	3.5	9.9	3.6	9.9	8.4	15.7	0.1	n.d.
of which: Germany		10.7		11.3		6.9		10.9		4.7		2.3		8.0		n.d.
Italy		2.7		2.5		5.4		10.7		2.0		7.1		2.4		5.2
Benelux		9.4		43.1		7.1		9.7		3.2		0.5		5.3		1.2
United States	1.5	5.5	7.1	2.0	3.6	6.1	15.1	13.9	0.4	2.5			1.1	4.9	2.8	2.0
Other O.E.C.D. countries	25.1	16.6	9.6	3.5	5.1	8.9	2.2	5.2	18.6	2.8	91.2	6.9	18.3	5.3	9.8	2.3
of which: United Kingdom		9.0		0.9		2.0		2.7		0.1		2.3		2.6		1.1
Japan		4.3		1.8		2.8		1.6		1.8		1.5		0.9		1.1
Other countries:	8.7	19.5	4.5	12.7	11.7	18.5	15.0	20.5	6.3	38.0	3.3	64.0	8.5	27.5	1.9	51.9
Developing African Countries		6.3		3.9		7.7		8.4		23.1		58.4(2)		18.0		34.4(2)
Developing South American Countries		2.8				0.1		0.2		1.2		—		2.8		1.8
Developing Asian Countries		4.3		0.5		2.1		0.5		1.2		—		2.5		—
Socialist Countries		5.3		8.1		0.4		1.3		2.5		—		2.4		6.7

(1) of which 48.5% is for the Ivory Coast; (2) of which 27.5% goes to Nigeria.

II. The structure of imports (as % of total imports)

	Togo (1959)	Togo (1971)	Ivory Coast 1960	Ivory Coast 1972	Upper Volta	Niger
Energy	19.7	5.5	5.9	6.4	7.4	4.9
Raw Materials	9.2	20.1	17.5	21.0	14.5	8.9
Finished Products - (Plant, Equipment)	32.9	21.1	23.3	25.7	18.9	15.5
Consumption of goods	20.3	53.3	53.3	46.9	59.2	70.7
of which food	14.5	19.1	17.0	17.0	11.7	32.1

I. The share of various countries in the total imports and exports of France's ex-colonies

	Algeria Imports 1960	Algeria Imports 1970	Algeria Exports 1960	Algeria Exports 1970	Tunisia Imports 1956	Tunisia Imports 1973	Tunisia Exports 1956	Tunisia Exports 1973	Morocco Imports 1956	Morocco Imports 1973	Morocco Exports 1956	Morocco Exports 1973	Benin Imports 1960	Benin Imports 1971	Benin Exports 1960	Benin Exports 1971
France	83.9	42.4	80.8	53.6	66.1	36.7	55.1	27.7	49.6	31.8	52.7	33.7	58.2	38.3	67.0	41.5
Other E.E.C. countries (the Six)	3.4	23.0	5.1	20.0	6.9	22.5	13.5	25.1	13.4	18.8	18.1	25.1	6.2	16.2	9.8	24.7
of which: Germany		10.0		12.9		8.9		6.9		8.2		9.8		6.3		13.2
Italy		7.3		4.2		8.1		15.8		4.6		6.9		2.5		3.8
Benelux		5.7		2.9		5.6		2.4		6.0		8.4		7.4		7.7
United States	1.4	8.0	1.1	0.8	4.6	9.3	0.7	14.8	8.5	10.6	3.7	1.4	2.1	5.9	-	3.2
Other O.E.C.D. countries:	2.8	9.5	7.0	6.5	4.3	16.0	15.24	4.2	9.9	11.0	11.0	9.3	10.1	12.5	2.8	14.1
of which: United Kingdom		3.3		4.1		8.9		2.3		3.4		4.7		5.0		5.1
Japan		1.1		0.3		1.0				2.2		1.3		5.1		8.9
Other countries:	8.4	17.1	6.0	19.1	15.1	15.5	15.39	28.2	18.6	27.8	15.6	30.5	23.4	27.1	20.4	16.5
Developing African countries		3.0		3.8		1.6		8.8		4.7		5.8		2.5		10.9
Developing South American countries		3.0		3.0		2.7		1.7		6.5		1.8		2.9		-
Developing Asian countries		1.0		0.4		6.6		2.6		2.5		2.6		4.3		0.5
Socialist countries		6.4		8.6		4.5		1.0		7.6		10.8		5.0		3.6
II. The structure of imports (as % of total imports)																
Energy													9.7	3.6		
Raw materials													15.6	6.0		
Finished products (plant, equipment)													18.2	20.3		
Consumption of goods													55.5	70.1		
of which food													17.0	15.7		

I. The share of various countries in the total imports and exports of France's ex-colonies.

	Chad				Cameroon				Congo				Central African Repub.			
	Imports		Exports		Imports		Exports		Imports		Exports		Imports		Exports	
	1960	1971	1960	1971(3)	1960	1973	1960	1973	1960	1972	1960	1972	1960	1971	1960	1971
France	52.4	44.4	69.2	16.1	58.4	47.4	57.0	28.5	66.0	53.8	28.0	15.3	60.5	61.7	65.6	56.1
Other E.E.C. Countries (the Six)	16.1	9.6	4.4	0.3	8.6	18.0	27.3	40.1	9.1	14.6	54.8	38.9	14.5	16.7	12.2	18.0
of which: Germany		3.2		0.2		9.5		9.9		1.4		14.6		6.1		4.3
Italy		2.2				4.2		3.9		3.0		4.1		4.8		1.2
Benelux		4.2				4.3		26.3		10.2		20.2		5.8		12.5
United States	2.4	3.2		0.01	4.0	9.0	6.3	7.5	6.0	8.5	1.5	1.2	6.0	5.6		0.6
Other O.E.C.D. Countries	19.4	4.6	18.6	0.5	11.6	6.8	3.6	7.2	9.6	6.6	5.9	7.3	12.2	6.1		3.2
of which: United Kingdom		2.3		0.4		2.9		1.1		1.9		2.0		3.0		2.6
Japan		1.3				2.0		4.6		1.9		2.9		1.8		0.3
Other Countries:	9.7	38.2	7.8	32.6	17.4	18.8	5.8	16.7	9.3	17.0	9.8	37.3	6.8	9.9	22.1	3.6
Developing African Countries		26.8		32.1		9.0		10.8		4.1		6.3		4.5		
Developing South American Countries		3.8				0.8				1.1		0.4				
Developing Asian Countries		3.0				3.9				0.7		1.0				
Socialist Countries		2.5				3.3		1.2		2.9		12.8	1.5	0.7	0.6	0.2

(3) The destination of 50.8% of the exports in 1971 is not known.

II. The structure of imports (as % of total imports)

	Chad	Cameroon (1960)	Cameroon (1971)	Congo (1960)	Congo (1970)	C.A.R. (1960)	C.A.R. (1970)
Energy	12.0	6.6	5.2	6.5	2.0	8.7	1.6
Raw Materials	15.2	20.1	17.0	10.8	17.4	6.5	19.3
Finished Products, (Plant, Equipment)	16.8	17.0	27.2	39.7	27.2	31.8	27.2
Consumption of goods	56	56.3	50.6	43.0	53.4	53	51.9
of which food	20.9	19.4	10.5	17.2	19.5	16	17

1. The share of various countries in the total imports and exports of France's ex-colonials.

	Gabon Import 1960	Gabon Import 1972	Gabon Export 1960	Gabon Export 1972	Madagascar Import 1960	Madagascar Import 1973	Madagascar Export 1960	Madagascar Export 1973	Mali Mauritania Senegal(5) Import 1959	Mali Mauritania Senegal(5) Export 1959	Mali Import 1971	Mali Export 1971	Mauritania Import 1971	Mauritania Export 1971	Senegal Import 1972	Senegal Export 1972
France	59.0	58.3	51.2	36.7	55.7	49.0	55.9	37.3	65.7	81.6	44.4	20.1	36.5	20.6	49.2	58.2
Other E.E.C. Countries (the Six)	10.2	18.3	25.7	17.0	6.9	14.6	5.9	9.1	9.3	2.0	8.3	4.4	11.9	39.0	14.7	10.0
of which: Germany		10.4		5.9		7.7		4.0			3.6	1.0	4.8	11.0	6.1	1.2
Italy		3.3		2.1		3.1		1.9			1.8	1.1	1.0	11.3	3.9	3.7
Benelux		4.6		10.0		3.8		3.2			2.9	2.3	6.1	16.7	4.7	5.1
United States:	12.6	11.2	2.5	8.4	2.9	7.5	12.8	17.5	3.9	0.1	5.5		15.5		6.0	0.5
Other O.E.C.D. Countries	8.6	5.5	7.8	5.8	2.4	3.6	5.1	9.2	5.3	6.0	4.9	4.7	8.3	23.8	3.8	5.3
of which: United Kingdom		3.0		2.0		1.6		2.0			2.4	1.6	6.7	15.8	1.4	1.9
Japan		1.3		1.6		0.2		6.4			1.6	2.7	0.1	7.5	0.4	0.9
Other Countries:	9.6	6.7	12.8	32.1	17.7	25.3	20.3	26.9	15.8	10.3	36.9	70.8(6)	27.8	16.6	26.3	26.0
Developing African Countries		1.9		10.1		3.5		13.7			19.5	51.2(7)	15.0	3.7	11.9	20.4
Developing South American Countries				14.7		0.2		0.3			2.9	-	0.3	1.4	1.4	0.6
Developing Asian Countries		0.2		0.6		9.5		7.1			1.1	1.8	3.0	-	7.5	
Socialist Countries				0.7		5.5		0.8			13.1	1.7	1.7	1.0	3.6	0.5

(4) 45.8 if we include Reunion; (5) These three countries were covered by the revised reports of the franc zone in 1960
(6) of which 14.5% is not allocated; (7) of which 27.2% is for the Ivory Coast.

II. The structure of imports (as % of total imports)

	Gabon (1970)	Madagascar (1971)	Mali Mauritania Senegal 1959	Mali 1971	Senegal (1971)
Energy	7.6	4.6	5	9.5	6.2
Raw Materials	12.9	19.6	12.1	21.4	18.5
Finished Products (Plant, Equipment)	30.0	17.5	15.1	19.3	21.5
Consumption of goods	49.5	58.3	67.8	49.8	53.8
of which food	20.0	16.7	33.9	27.5	31.1

III. Main exports (as % of total exports)

Algeria 1960		Algeria 1970		Tunisia 1960		Tunisia 1973		Morocco 1958		Morocco 1973		People's Republic of Benin 1960		People's Republic of Benin 1971	
wine	53.6	oil	67.3	wine	20.3	oil	30.9	phos-phates	21.1	tinned foods	40.8	palm cabbages	48.2	cocoa	24.1
iron	7.3	wine	14.6	phos-phates	12.9	olive oil	15.5	citrus fruits	10	phosphates	22.8	palm oil	17.9	cotton	19.0
citrus fruits	6.2	pig iron	2.5	olive oil	14.5	manufac'd. fertilisers	7.4			non-ferrous metals	5.6	ground-nuts	15.1	palm oil	26.9
		citrus fruits	2.3			phosphates	6.7								
		iron ore	1.8			wine	5.5								
	67.1		88.5		47.7		66.0		31.1		69.2		81.2		70.0

Togo 1960		Togo 1971		Ivory Coast 1960		Ivory Coast 1971		Upper Volta 1960		Upper Volta 1971		Niger 1960		Niger 1971	
cocoa	38.5	cocoa	27	un-roasted coffee	50	coffee	34.7	cattle	70.7	cattle	36.4	ground-nuts	58.1	ground-nuts	32
un-roasted coffee	17.7	un-roasted coffee	15.6	cocoa	23.4	cocoa	20.9	fish	11	vegetable oil	21.9	cattle	13.6	cattle	18.5
palms	13.5	phosphates	30.6	wood	17	wood	23.2	karite	8.8	cotton	18.9	ground-nut oil	11.7	uranium	18.6
cotton	10.1	palm cabbages	5.8											cotton	5.3
		cotton	1.7											ground-nut oil	9.1
	79.8		80.7		90.4		78.8		90.5		77.2		83.4		83.5

contd.

III. Main exports (as % of total exports) continued ....

Chad

	1960		1971
cotton	62.4	cotton	65.5
cattle	12	cattle	4.2
leather	6.5	leather	1.1
meat	6.1	meat	20.2
	87		91.0

Cameroon

1960		1971	
cocoa	33.9	cocoa	28.9
un-roasted coffee	19.2	un-roasted coffee	25.5
aluminium	18.4	wood	11.4
		cotton	3.9
		aluminium	9.1
	71.5		78.8

Central African Republic

1960		1971	
cotton	44.8	cotton	23.1
un-roasted coffee	24.9	un-roasted coffee	23.8
diamonds	12.1	wood	10.5
		diamonds	35.6
	81.8		93.0

Congo

1960		1971	
wood	63.6	wood	44.1
palm cabbages		plywood	11.4
palm oil	9.5	sucre	11
		potash fert.	13.6
		diamonds	6.6
	73.1		86.7

Gabon

1960		1971	
wood	72.7	wood	23.9
crude oil	20.9	plywood	6.4
		manganese	19
		uranium	3.1
		oil	45.2
	93.6		97.6

Madagascar

1960		1971	
un-roasted coffee	31.5	un-roasted coffee	26.5
vanilla	8.9	vanilla	8.7
rice	6.4	cloves	14.1
cloves	1.6	rice	5.0
		meat	4.6
	48.4		58.9

Mali/Mauritania Senegal

1959	
groundnuts	38.7
groundnut oil	38.0
cattle cake	7.6
	84.3

Mali

1971	
cattle	20.9
sheep	5.1
groundnuts	11.3
cotton	23.6
groundnut oil	5.9
	66.8

Mauritania

1971	
fish	6.5
iron	79.6
copper	4.0
ships	6.2
	96.3

Senegal

1971	
phosphates	10.9
groundnut oil	21.3
groundnuts	5.3
oil products	5.6
	43.1

Sources: Reports from the franc zone 1960– 1971 –1973.
International trade statistics (U.N. 1972-73).

IV. The structure of Exports from Nos. 5, 6, 7 and 8 of the Standard International Trade Classification in % of total exports

Countries	Year	5 Chemicals	6 Manufactured goods classified chiefly by material	7 Machinery and transport equipment	8 Miscellaneous manufactured articles
Algeria	1970	0.4	4.3	1.6	0.2
Tunisia	1973	11.1	10.5	0.4	1.4
Morocco	1973	3.2	7.0	1.01	3.3
People's Republic of Benin	1971	0.3	3.3	2.0	0.7
Togo	1972	1.5	10.6	5.0	0.9
Ivory Coast	1972	0.8	3.7	0.9	0.4
Upper Volta	1972	0	3.4	1.8	0.8
Niger	1972	0	1.5	1.8	0.4
Chad	1971	0	0.9	0.8	0
Cameroon (1)	1973	0.6	12.2	3.4	2.6
Congo	1972	13.6	19.2	1.2	0
Central African Republic (2)	1971	1.1	36.3	0.2	0.2
Gabon	1972	0	6.5	0.9	0
Madagascar	1973	2.5	2.2	3.2	0.8
Mali	1971	1.1	5.9	0.9	1.0
Mauritania	1971	0	0.7	7.3 (3)	0
Senegal	1972	4.2	9.4	5.1	4.5

(1) Products derived from wood and aluminium under (6),
Under (7) the aluminium industry, including aircraft parts,
Under (8) finished textiles

(2) Under (6) diamonds
(3) Ships

Source: U.N. statistics of International Trade 1972-73

V. Development of the Geographical Structure of Mali's imports and exports after the coup d'etat of 18.11.1968.

Countries of origin or destination	IMPORTS					EXPORTS				
	1967	1968	1969	1970	1971	1967	1968	1969	1970	1971
FRANCE	29.7	31.6	38.8	38.4	44.4	8.6	16.3	16.0	17.1	20.1
Other E.E.C. Countries (the Six)	4.3	5.3	8.4	10.7	8.3	2.8	11.5	0.9	4.6	4.4
United States	0.9	1.0	2.6	3.7	5.5	-	-	-	-	-
Other O.E.C.D. Countries	8.1	3.8	5.9	3.6	4.9	3.2	6.6	7.9	6.7	4.7
of which: Great Britain	6.2	1.6	1.2	1.7	2.4	0.5	-	1.1	2.6	1.6
Japan	1.7	1.9	0.7	1.4	1.6	1.9	6.2	4.6	3.9	2.7
Other Countries	57.0	58.3	44.3	43.6	36.9	85.4	65.6	75.2	71.6(1)	70.8(2)
Developing African Countries	16.6	21.1	21.4	20.4	19.5	85.3(3)	55.3	71.3(4)	62.2	51.2
Developing South American Countries	0.9	0.7	2.0	1.5	2.9	-	-	-	-	-
Developing Asian Countries	0.4	0.8	0.9	1.2	1.1	-	-	-	1.1	1.8
Socialist economies	38.6	34.7	19.4	20.0	13.1	-	7.3	2.7	1.8	1.7
TOTAL IMPORT & EXPORT in millions of dollars	34 190	34 298	38 912	44 799	59 265	11 055	10 733	17 310	35 456	36 012

(1) 5.9% not allocated
(2) 14.5% not allocated
(3) Ivory Coast 27.6, Senegal 32.0, Ghana 15.4
(4) Ivory Coast 39.2, Senegal 4.8, Ghana 21

6

Dependence, Independence and Interdependence in Economic Relations

Guy Caire

The new nations came into being in the unique historical context of decolonisation,[1] and the course of their historical development was shaped by this fact. The kind of national independence (or at least what we may provisionally label as such) that was achieved in each case depended on how each new nation made the break with its metropolitan country – i.e. whether by armed struggle as in the case of Algeria, or by more peaceful means as was the case for francophone black Africa.

Decolonisation also determined where frontier lines were drawn. Administrative boundaries inherited from colonial powers were often ethnically absurd and economically debatable; although they usually guaranteed a measure of short-term stability, they were sometimes a source of difficulties in the long run. Moreover, decolonisation determined the form that new nations' institutions were to take: administrative institutions in the political sector, professional bodies in the social sector and organisations for planning and management in the economic sector.

But leaving aside for the moment the subtle dialectics of dependence and independence which begin to come into view, it seems clear that political independence, even if it is achieved, merely puts on the agenda economic independence which is much more difficult to attain. Political independence, even if it is too often embodied only in a national anthem, a flag and an

136

airforce, is readily understood to involve ideologies, rituals which express a system of values, symbols of membership of the collectivity and norms – but what is really to be understood by economic independence?

Although we cannot provide an exact definition of economic independence, we are sure (hence the title of our paper) that the general understanding of economic independence is too often ideologically dependent on ideas developed for other, quite different, times and places. We feel that, unless full account is taken of the actual conditions in which economic independence is sought, anachronistic and misguided policies will be formulated and followed. Therefore our aim in this paper will be to investigate the relations between the ideological assumptions about independence which are unconsciously made at the level of economic planning, the actual dependencies that are revealed when one examines the constraints surrounding real action, and the very limited room for manoeuvre (in the formulation of strategies) if national autonomy is to be obtained.

The Ideology of Economic Independence

Economic independence may be considered in terms of doctrine, analysis and policy. Under these headings we shall be able to show the ideological dependence of which the under-developed countries are victims. 'Practical men, who believe themselves to be quite exempt from any intellectual influences, are usually the slaves of some defunct economist. Madmen in authority, who hear voices in the air, are distilling their frenzy from some academic scribbler of a few years back.' Despite reservations that one could have about the general validity of Keynes' well-known appraisal, there is certainly no denying that its truth should be acknowledged by the founders of new independent nations whenever they act as economists. In this context two doctrinal legacies deserve emphasis.

First, mercantilism. If one understands this simply as a doctrine directed towards the accumulation of wealth through international trade, this is certainly a misunderstanding of the doctrine's basic meaning. Keynes' rehabilitation of mercantilism in Chapter XXIII of the 'General Theory' enabled us to see in this doctrine an anticipation of the theory of effective demand. The emphasis henceforth placed on long-term growth rather than on short-term boosts to the economy produced in turn fresh views on the subject. 'The mercantilists' main objective in the theory of development', wrote Spengler,[2] 'was the acceleration of the rate of growth of the total product rather than the per capita product. This objective was to be realised directly by full employment and the productive and intelligent use of the available factors of production (in particular labour), and subsequently by increasing the stock of these factors and by technical and economic improvement in their use'. The ideology of independence comes in this way to be sustained by themes closely linked with industrialisation, with the essential role of the sovereign state, and with national solidarity, sometimes tinged with xenophobia; all this recreates the essential nature of mercantilism which, if we are to believe G. Schmoller, lies in the total transformation of society and the state, in the replacement of regional and local economic policies by nation-state policies.[3] But if mercantilism really does bring to the fore the role of the state and its instruments as central to economic life, we still need an account of the tasks to be accomplished.

Second, the historical school. When List formulated his nation-based system of political economy, he provided the ideological weapons that countries gaining independence and seeking development were to seize upon. The chosen framework was the nation, the mobilising plan was the agrarian-manufacturing-trading state, the mechanisms set in motion were the forces of production, and the determination of governments was expressed in constructive protectionism; here was the impetus to the national effort. In the service of the goal of national integration, this doctrine reintroduced considerations of economic structures focused on national interest as opposed to particular interest, and also emphasised the dimension of time. It was already List who, ahead of the main debate on the ideological leanings of classical theory, was making the point that they served excellently the dominant interests of the established industrialised countries but not at all those of new aspirants. 'The infant industry argument simply exploded liberal logic', François Perroux tells us, 'in fact a protest against the kind of dependence that is the outcome of uneven development'.[4]

It is true that national independence movements have seldom

been primarily conceived in economic terms.[5] Nevertheless, the ideological elevation of the state and the emphasis on industrialisation as a vehicle for national integration are inherent in the doctrines of mercantilism and the historical school, whose legacies are unconsciously assumed and accepted.

Turning from doctrine to analysis, clearly if there is to be independence then some economic content has to be given to the concept of the nation. On this point economic analysis wavers between two alternative sets of ideas.[6] According to one point of view, the nation is a system of prices in imperfect communication with the outside world; national space is thus just an administrative district bounded by customs barriers. Then the nation is a system of factor supply; capital and labour are mobile within the frontiers, but only products cross over the frontiers to the outside. The immobility of factors may be relative or absolute, but in an analysis of international economic relations, it is nonetheless tempting to view the nation as a firm.

Consequently, the variables to be taken into consideration (factors, prices and quantities) and the optimum goals set are all to be found within the framework of the nation. The nation-mass is called upon to face the outside world, and this fosters controversies of the kind that occur within international organisations, in particular UNCTAD, concerning the deterioration of exchange rates, fluctuations in commodity prices, etc.

Viewed from a different angle, the nation is a complex structure composed, on the one hand, of activities that are heterogeneous in nature and form and varying in sensitivity to fluctuations, susceptibility to technical progress, productivity, etc., and on the other, of agents (households, firms, professions, social groups, representatives of the state, etc.) with usually incompatible plans. The nation is thus, in the words of François Perroux, a group of groups. It is subject nevertheless to state authority which manifests itself in organised and legitimate public control. So it may be defined as an 'organised and structured complex of material and human resources, heterogeneous and independent activities subject to the combined action of normally incompatibly inclined micro- and macro-units, dominated by the politically sovereign state'.[7]

Viewed in this way, the nation becomes identified with the

development plan. With his usual perspicacity, Waterson pointed this out clearly when he stated that 'today the national plan is a symbol of sovereignty and modernity in the same way as the national anthem or flag'.[8] Of course it remains a question whether this structuring of behaviour and the emergence of a nation-group implied by planning are not matters of myth, as some writers have claimed.[9]

The two analytic interpretations of the nation which we have just sketched briefly and which have been inherited from Western tradition play a part in the formation of strategies by the new nations. Thus in Africa 'national independence very often seems to be synonymous with economic development. Sometimes, however, the formula is not spelt out very explicitly and one can see that it signals a double intent: equilibrium of the trade balance and Africanisation of trained personnel'.[10] The connection between economic analysis and policy, however, requires to be examined more closely.

Ideological dependence also exists at the level of the economic policies. We know that one of the first choices to be made in national accounting is between the territorial viewpoint (agents living in a particular area) and the national viewpoint (agents or factors at work overseas to be included); one calculates the latter from the former by adding to the domestic product the net foreign income from the rest of the world. In imitation of their respective colonial models, the Anglophone African countries chose the former type, and the Francophone countries chose the latter. But specialists have been quick to point out that both approaches are inappropriate to the national accounting needs of developing countries – hence the attempts to remedy the situation by Peter Ady and Michel Courciel, Henri Leroux and Jean-Pierre Allier.

But even if everything is done to sort out meaningful data – e.g., physical counts of products and stocks that bring out significant relationships (co efficients of capital and labour) for programming purposes; production tables that distinguish between production for own account and production for sale, modern production and traditional production, private production and public production; calculation of the co-efficient of dependence by branch and product, import and export trends to account for dependence on foreign countries in employment and resources accounts[11] – one can hardly say that great progress has been made towards achieving clear separate national accounts, even allowing for all the statistical difficulties that are involved.

The links are well-known between Keynes' ideas and their expression in accounting terms which have been applied to consumption, investment, production and national trade. We also know that Keynes intended to replace the cosmopolitanism of the classical economists with a focus on the nation, by showing in particular how national policies (notably those of full employment which could entail exporting one's unemployment to preserve full activity at home) may sometimes be mutually incompatible. Finally, in his argument against the perfect harmony of equilibrium analysis, Keynes was able to show (to use Joan Robinson's rather extreme phraseology) how the 'invisible hand' could sometimes lead to strangulation. National accounting, a national frame of reference, and a national will – these concepts were enough to ensure that Keynesian analysis would be held in high regard even in those countries where, on account of their disjointed structures, it has little hope of corresponding to the underlying realities.

One ends up with the paradox that an instrument designed for analysing economic trends is transposed to a situation where the problems to be handled are essentially structural. This is perhaps in spite of and contrary to Keynes' own ideas. In fact, as E. A. Lisle has pointed out, 'the quasi-downgrading of the *Treatise* to the benefit of *Theory* has created the paradox that "Keynesian analysis", as understood and propagated with such success, has become an intellectual system where the only elements that enter are fluctuations in the well-known national accounts aggregates of product, income, consumption and savings. The effect on the economic behaviour of agents of changes in the amounts or forms of wealth is completely ignored, in defiance of explicit statements by Keynes himself'.[12]

When legacies of doctrine and political analysis and recollections of policies are made to serve the aim of economic independence, this makes sense only on the ideological level. The consequence is that in the case of Africa for instance 'one cannot think seriously about national independence without also giving some thought to the content of such independence in terms of state- and nation-building, the basic directions of economic reconstruction, the development of a new culture and also relations with the rest of Africa'.[13] If a plan is to succeed, then, it must first take account of the constraints acting against it.

Constraints and Economic Dependence

'Do not all nations aspire to that contemporary form of freedom, national independence? But do not they all also seem to be subject to the absolute law of dependence?'[14] Before we can attempt to answer these questions, however, we will have to examine the forms and mechanisms of dependence and the contemporary framework in which it is manifested.

Economic dependence can be measured statistically. Thus we have M. Michaely's proposal for calculating the ratio of imports and exports of goods and services to the gross national product[15] which, as Kuznets pointed out, is a function of the size of the nation and increases in proportion to the decrease in size of the economy. However, in the case of poor countries the relation is more irregular because of the greater difficulties that poor countries have in obtaining world resources.[16]

Economic dependence manifests itself in many different ways which may be conveniently, if roughly, classified as occurring in 'upstream' and 'downstream' situations.

'Upstream' situations for new nations are characterised by dependence on the inflow of goods and services, especially manufactured goods but sometimes also foodstuffs, which they can only obtain from the dominant nations. Their patterns of consumption are determined by these imports. Examples of this (ranging from whisky to cars) are so well-known as not to require elaboration. Dependence on external sources of financing can cause greater damage since the very fate of the nation may be compromised by investment. A caricature-like illustration of this danger is provided by Allende's Chile, where loans from international institutions (World Bank), foreign national institutions (American AID) and private banks (Eximbank) were suspended from one day to the next. More difficult to define but equally constricting is technological dependence, which, as C. Vaitsos demonstrated for the Andean Pact countries, has wide-ranging economic consequences, the transfer of technology (which he prefers to call technology commercialisation) being accompanied by tied imports of intermediate products, machinery and equipment, technical skills and know-how, systems of production (turn key plants) or even market or distribution systems, whilst the transfer negotiations often entail restrictive clauses for the export of products manufactured locally with the help of foreign techniques.[17]

The second kind of dependence, in 'downstream' situations, manifests itself in exports which are usually limited to just a few products that are subject to major currency fluctuations caused by changes in the economic situations of purchasing countries and also by monopsonistic or oligopsonistic conditions in which the purchase is made. Dependence may also be expressed in overseas indebtedness. Lately this has been explained away as a reflection of the particular stage of development reached, but in his speech to the UN on 10 December 1972 Allende pointed out that the annual servicing of the Chilean foreign debt (of 4,000 million dollars) represented more than 30 per cent of the value of the country's exports.

. A study of consequences of dependence for a country's development opportunities reveals the difference between Marxist or radical theorists on the one hand, who stress the dramatic consequences of dependence for developing countries, and the neo-classical theorists on the other, who emphasise its positive effects. The former theorists predict that economic dependence will have a negative effect on economic growth, while the latter come to quite the opposite conclusion. The only way, then, to decide which view is correct is to conduct a statistical test, and this is what Christopher Chasedun did recently.[18] Two kinds of international economic dependence are studied: investment dependence measured by the penetration of a country by foreign capital, and debt dependence, which is the dependence of a government on foreign credit. The technique employed is sample regression analysis, a flexible statistical method of testing causal relations which allows the introduction of multiple independent variables and which, because it employs data at different points in time, reduces the likelihood of false inferences due to reciprocal causality. The dependent variables studied are gross national product per capita, kilowatt hours of electricity consumed and the percentage of the male labour force not employed in agriculture. The statistical data refer to the years 1950 and 1970. The conclusions of the analysis are relatively unequivocal: the hypothesis that dependence by lowering incomes and raising profits causes the unequal distribution of income is verified. It now remains to see whether we can uncover the mechanisms at work.

Traditional analysis depends on the category of the nation-state, seen as the basic 'atom' unit of the international economic system, a rational, self-conscious unit that continually seeks to maximise its advantage under internal and external constraints. More recently, the growth of the multinational corporations has brought about a shift of emphasis to the problems of the non-coincidence of territorial collectivities and of the centres of decision-making that determine their future. Thus it is necessary to examine the operation of these two categories of agents, taking account of the state of economic dependence of the new nations.

As regards first the relations between nation-states, the forms and degrees of dependence can vary enormously, ranging from total domination that amounts to colonisation to leadership that results from voluntary imitation, with intermediate positions of unilateral influence operating in a specific area and partial domination expressing a more permanent and complex state of affairs. Apart from a typology of the combinations of asymmetrical effects that one could draw up, various attempts have been made to offer fundamental explanations by introducing such concepts as domination or structural take-over (François Perroux) or 'the development of under-development' (G. Frank) – although of course these two sets were designed to fit into quite different general bodies of thought. In order to elucidate them, we need some preliminary investigation of these powerful forces that Myrdal's 'backwash' effects were attempting to account for. A recent and quite original analysis has taken a step in this direction. Using estimates of the income per capita for 45 countries surveyed by Kuznets, Woytinsky, the UN or various other writers, J. R. Lassuen and F. Wasservogel showed[19] that differences in classification between nations (analysed with the aid of the Spearman and Kendall co-efficients) are ephemeral and very relative. By adjusting the domestic product growth curves, they show that the overall level of growth of the domestic product increases more rapidly in rich countries than in poorer ones; they also show that the relative distance between the two groups of countries moves cyclically around a trend value, thus leading to the hypothesis that the development of a country is determined essentially by the developmental characteristics of the whole system of nations.

These structural distortions, from which the peripheral nations suffer (Amin, Don Santos, Frank), manifest themselves in specialisation in raw materials, which inevitably leads to weaker growth than would be achieved in a more differentiated economy (Galtung), by means of outward oriented infrastructures which effect integration towards the centre (Ehrensaft), to whose benefit the foreign trade multiplier operates (Singer). In traditional economic terms, one would say that the weak differentiation of economic activities and the weak integration of the national economy lead to a system of exploitation of resources that retards economic development. In the more usual language of systems theory, mastery over energy and information works to the advantage of the dominant nations and to the disadvantage of the dominated ones.

In less esoteric terms, the dependent nation, having only a few industries but no real industrial machinery or financial market for foreign exchange dealings, suffers the disappearance of its capital; having no modern universities or research centres, it is a victim of the brain drain; being unable to provide work for all its nationals, it has to condone their migration; having no market of its own, its products are subject to trade restrictions, monetary manipulation, fluctuations in the exchange rate, and so on. If we can go back now to the analysis of François Perroux who states that foreign trade is conducted between strong and weak structures,[20] we are now in a position to set out the asymmetrical effects which manifest themselves:

—in classical exports (caused by price differences) or non-classical exports (influenced by the State, e.g. the sale of nuclear arms or even agricultural surpluses), which may be direct or derived (e.g. after-sales service);

—in direct investment, which attracts tied loans;

—in monetary fluctuations, which are a manifestation of the phenomenon of power, for when a country has exhausted its credit reserves and facilities, the limits of aid granted by the IMF vary according to the country's size and the IMF keeps the national policies of underdeveloped countries under far

closer surveillance than those of the USA or Britain – and
are at the same time an instrument of power (via reserve
currency).

We may now turn from nation-states to the multi-nationals. In
taking the world market as their objective, in tending to organise
production, distribution and selling activities with as little regard
to national frontiers as possible, by manipulating transfer costs
and shifting the production of components or finished products
from one country to another, the multinational corporations are
employing a strategy that is full of consequences both for the
location of branches in host countries and for the types of activity
carried on there.

In his study of the problems of 'localisation' (in terms of
personnel and geographical location) S. Hymer used Chandler
and Redlich's typology of the forms of organisation of large
corporate structures to show that the strategies of multinational
corporations were organised on a three-tier system.[21] At the
lowest level of day-to-day operations, location depends basically
on the availability of manpower, markets, and raw materials; the
management of enterprises can easily be left in the hands of the
nationals of the host country. At the intermediate level, at which
tactics are planned, activities tend to concentrate in large cities
(which may still be in underdeveloped countries), because of the
need for white-collar workers, communications systems and
information. At the highest level where strategy is planned,
activities tend to be even more concentrated, for they must be
located close to the capital market, the media, and the
government; the possible places are limited in number (New
York, London, Paris, Bonn, Tokyo), and the senior men must be
nationals of the home country. The patterns of income and
consumption will tend to parallel those of status and authority.

As regards choice of the type of activities, the strategy of the
multinational corporations is motivated by wage costs. The
transfer of activities, at least in countries where sophisticated
technology may be combined with unskilled labour, has the
advantage of low wage costs in these countries, and this more
than compensates for the lag in labour productivity in relation to
the home country. Thus we find the migration of declining labour
intensive industries (textiles), industries with longer product-life
cycles, the labour intensive portions of technology-based

industries (electronics), mass consumption industries with labour intensive operations (automobile industry), industries which are subject to environmental controls in the home-country even if they are capital intensive (chemical and paper industries), and the transfer of industries to a low-wage area in order to offset customs tariffs, etc.[22] An increasing number of countries are involved in these types of activity – originally it was Taiwan, Hong Kong and North Korea, more recently Singapore and Malaysia, and now Indonesia, India, Brazil and Mexico. The result of these developments is the creation of real enclave industries, economic and structural dependence on developed countries for which the products are often manufactured, and dependence on the sub-contracting firm, leaving the host-country with little room for negotiation.

We will now take a look at economic independence in its present setting, with a word first on the internationalisation of capital. Dependence theory, the 'development of underdevelopment' theory, theories of the core/periphery opposition and of world-wide pauperisation, all place great emphasis on the world system as the unit of analysis. Consequently, whether with reference to Baran, Franck, Amin or Emmanuel, Boukharine's concept of the world economy crops up time and time again. For him, imperialism combines on the one hand internationalisation (of which international trade is the most primitive form and the trust, with interpenetration of industrial and banking capital, is the most sophisticated) which entails intensive and extensive growth of capital on a global scale, and on the other hand, nationalisation which at once entails centralisation of capital, emergence of finance capital and amalgamation of capital and the state.[23] One must, therefore, examine the circulation of social capital and its different component parts, as C. Palloix does using Marx's analysis of cycles of reproduction of capital. Even though merchant capital has always operated internationally, it was only recently recognised that not only merchant capital (through international investment) but also production capital (through internationalisation of manufacturing industries) can have an international dimension.[24]

The consequences of this type of analysis have been elucidated very clearly by H. Radice:

on the one hand, this means that the appropriation and redistribution of surplus value cannot be understood solely in terms of the circulation of commodities (trade), nor of the circulation of money (financial flows), nor of the production process (international division of labour); the accumulation of capital involves all these. On the other hand, the 'function' of imperialist relations for capital in an advanced capitalist country has to be seen in terms of the relevance of the national economy as a basis for continued accumulation and the reproduction of capitalist social relations, within the world economy. There is a 'surplus of capital' or a 'surplus value which cannot be realised', in relation to the accumulation of capital on a national basis, and hence capital must reconstitute itself at a world level, incorporating the resources, labour and commodities produced in other areas of the world under its sway, pushing the internationalisation process further.[25]

If the law of value can only be fully comprehended at the world level because of the growing internationalisation of capital, does it follow that nation-states are no longer the primary structures of the international economic system, or must we postulate a *de facto* annexation of weak nations by strong ones, or indeed imagine the law of value to be controlled by some supranational entity? This brings us in fact to Kautsky's ultra-imperialism thesis to which Lenin gave his well-known reply. However, the controversy has recently been reawakened. R. Murray, who considers that 'nation states are becoming entities without substance' believes that 'in spite of the underlining of the trends of accumulation and centralisation of capital, and in spite of the political role of the state, Marxist theory has not brought these two aspects of analysis together to clarify the problem of the nature and significance of nation states in a period of international centralisation and concentration';[26] he is of the opinion that the growing divergence between the activities of nation-states and multinational firms, which are the economically dominant institutions of the capitalist world, has tended greatly to weaken states and their ability to control firms. B. Warren, on the other hand, believes that the power of the nation state vis-à-vis the large firms is greater now than ever before and that there are always links between capital abroad and its home government, though this is not to say that there are no contradictions between states and firms or that such contradictions are always resolved in favour of nation states.[27]

In this controversy, Magdoff, Nicolaus, Jalee, and up till 1971 Sweezy, support the super-imperialism thesis of the increasing power of the US and American firms, while Kidron, Mandel, Rowthorne and, since 1971, also Sweezy, stand on the other side, taking the opposite view that American hegemony is being challenged by European and Japanese capitalism supported by their nation-states. The differences of view depend primarily on two things: on the one hand, the importance attributed to American capitalism based on the size, rate of accumulation, and research and development activities of the country's firms, and on the other hand, the prominence given to rivalries between national capitalisms in the struggle for markets through the export of products or capital, while recognising that, as the case of Britain shows, the power of a nation's capital and the autonomy of its home state may not coincide.[28]

If one believes, as Palloix does, that the implementation of the law of value is simultaneously in the hands of the various nation-states which are the product of the internationalisation process, then one can already begin to discern the degree of freedom permitted to independent states in their formulation of strategy.

Strategies for National Autonomy

It is appropriate to begin the third part of our essay by quoting Vigny's statement: 'independence has always been my goal and dependence my destination'. This seems to be quite an accurate characterisation of the dialectics of the national behaviour of states in which what is at stake is national sovereignty. Somewhere between autarchy, which is not realisable for the majority of states, and dependence, which is morally unacceptable, lies sovereignty, a strong form of interdependence combining the preservation of a more acceptable structure with a certain degree of autonomy. In other words, what we call national independence entails thinking of the nation as an economic concept and of sovereignty as economic practice.

The nation, as distinct from the people and the state, has been defined in many different ways, all of which, however, seem to oscillate between two extreme poles. On the one hand, we have 'objective' definitions, for example the one given by Stalin: 'the nation is a stable and historically constituted community of people, created on the basis of a community of language, territory, economic life and psychic identity which is expressed in a community of culture'.[29] The absence of one of these elements means that the nation ceases to exist. However, in addition to this listing of elements, Stalin's analysis stresses the historical nature of the nation: embryonic in the pre-capitalist period, it does not become a reality until the era of capitalism, it increases in importance with the appearance of the national market and the resulting economic community, giving rise to the oppression of minorities within and expansionist attempts without, and will cease to exist when socialism has been victorious on a world-wide scale and the conditions are ripe for the fusion of nations in a global socialist economic system. We have, on the other hand, 'subjective' definitions of the nation, of which G. Burdeau's is a fair example: 'Since the nation is not a directly observable phenomenon, finding expression only in the feelings and attitudes that it arouses in people, we are forced to regard it as an idea, a representation made by individuals of the collective being which they themselves constitute, in other words a myth'.[30]

The first definition paves the way for the structural interdependences of the (non-Marxist) concept of integration. The second leads straight into the dynamics of the task to be accomplished, already suggested in 1882 by Renan[31] and again in 1926 by Malraux when he referred to the nation as 'a dream community'.[32] In this way the nation becomes a fundamental idea that among other things involves on the economic level a 'capacity for sacrifices'.[33] This may take the form of transfers (public services) and postponement of consumption (investment). It is also a frame within which are contained and encouraged certain dynamic objectives such as development (or progressive transformation of structures), integration (defined by the intersecting elasticities of a relevant market), and the goal of a desired future society.

It is possible to theorise about national sovereignty in political terms. E. Sicard for example describes a ten-stage process: 1) on the basis of the dissolution of empires, one may 2) reject the coloniser's ethnic privilege, whereby 3) the intelligentsia, shaped by the dominant power and now discovering its own special character, plays an essential role, but must, however, 4) gain the support of the masses in a charismatic and militant act of fusion, out of which the nation is truly born; then 5) the nation recaptures a past that has been idealised by the collective memory, and this constitutes a solid foundation for nation-building; 6) the recovery of national territory is more difficult in so far as the territory called for by the economy is incompatible with the frontiers fixed by politics; 7) recognition from outside is claimed by those groups who have invested themselves with political power; 8) there is the emergence of a constructive group with mystique and a programme; 9) the State can then institutionalise the nation; and 10) individuals become conscious of their personal identity and the national identity of the collectivity.[34]

But is it also possible to theorise about national sovereignty from the point of view of economic practice? First of all, one can put forward the idea that in principle 'national sovereignty implies independence and dies away if the authorities cannot choose an economic objective and, to implement it, arrange for suitable means to be placed at the disposal of the citizens and the State'.[35] Any listing of means, however long, will always be necessarily incomplete: this is the case, for example, with Murray's six primary functions of the capitalist state (guaranteeing of property rights, economic liberalisation, economic organisation by controls and economic planning, provision of inputs, intervention for social consensus through legislation or ideology and management of external relations) and the five subsidiary functions (maintenance of effective demand, taxation, aid to particular monopolies, 'first aid' to key sectors, absorption of surplus).[36] On the other hand, one can easily foresee what the objective to be pursued might be: 'Economic autonomy of an area is only possible if, on the one hand, one or several enterprises in operation in the territory fulfil functions or provide services which are technologically (or financially) necessary for several countries and if, on the other hand, the area itself is not dependent on too limited a number of enterprises and on foreign research centres, which perform functions that are irreplaceable in prevailing market conditions by the rest of world production'.[37]

In short, then, independence is a powerful means towards an interdependent system in which the search for a better equilibrium of powers puts a check on the satellisation of weak structures by strong ones. It may be attained in two complementary ways. The first may be called negotiated independence or managing the rules of the game. 'The industrialisation of new-born nations can and must be effected by a methodical co-ordination of multinational industrial centres and territorial economies.'[38] This was written by François Perroux at a time when states had recently attained political independence. He went on to draw up a programme of the tasks that lay ahead of these states. In his view, their activities should proceed in three principal directions. First, basic commodities should be stabilised, instability in its various forms being one of the mechanisms through which domination is perpetuated and which the quasi-colonial type of stabilisation policies are not capable of overcoming. Second, foreign investment should be organised in accordance with a collective formula within the framework of a development programme. Finally, there should be a renewal of technical co-operation which, in its bilateral and multilateral forms, is an aspect of inter-system competition. Thus we can perceive the full significance of negotiation as a means of managing the rules: 'Since each individual actually lives through his relations with the rest of society or the world, independence is most certainly not an absolute and illusory absence of dependence; independence is the concrete result of accepting a multiplicity of dependences, the conscious choice of alliances and subordinations. Independence is a calculated interdependence'.[39]

There is no lack of examples clearly illustrating this kind of negotiated co-operation, the characteristics of which the dominant powers are attempting to define at present.[40] One solution to the problem of dependence lies in the attempts made by the periphery to control inputs from the core and make them consistent with balanced development:[41] thus Mexico, India and Yugoslavia have produced legislation on investment with the aim of maximising advantage while minimising costs, but the scale of the multinationals' operations is so vast as to guarantee them undeniable superiority over the little peripheral nations.[42] The transfer of technology may also give rise to a negotiations strategy, but the limits of the maximum or minimum advantages that may be expected are determined by the amount of information available.[43] Migration of manpower is also the subject of concerted efforts, whose favourable outcome for the home countries depends on how co-ordinated their policies are, as illustrated by the very different cases of Turkey and Algeria.[44]

There is often keen competition among underdeveloped countries for the transfer of activities from industrial countries; for example, Indonesia, India, Brazil and South Korea have entered the race, probably following the example of Hong Kong and Singapore who are now diversifying their production towards high-productivity capital intensive goods.[45]

An alternative strategy for new states can be that of changing the rules of the game. It is very often the underlying assumptions of the rules that are the cause of dependence. As Myrdal pointed out, much of the economic theory on which the implicit codes of the international institutions regulating the world economic order are based 'is a rationalisation of the dominant interests in the industrial countries where it was first put forward and later developed'.[46] Therefore 'underdeveloped countries utilising their newly won independent status can by deliberate policies manage to alter considerably the direction of the market processes under the impact of which they have hitherto remained backward'.[47] Now we find ourselves in a world where the traditional tools of the economist no longer seem to apply. At the very most, the economist may find a few useful concepts in game theory, oligopoly theory or the theory of collective negotiation; then he is forced to introduce into his analysis 'the use of force, threats, promises and other mean tricks'.[48]

Thus we can see the gradual emergence of a new international division of labour which, contrary to the old one, rejects the most favoured nation clause, cancels the convention of reciprocal concessions, sanctions recourse to protectionist measures, and adopts the watchword of 'double morality'.[49] Examples of the new behaviour of independent nations trying to assert themselves are the diversification and the break-up of alliances instigated by Egypt when it wanted to build the Aswan dam, the fusion of the interests of the block of '77' initiated at the first UNCTAD conference, now extended to other international organisations, and the co-ordinated management of the prices and quantities of key products pioneered by OPEC. Since they are aware that the distribution of resources has always been effected under strong and sometimes violent pressure on the part of those destined to reap benefit from it, and that it is therefore difficult to accept serenely the idea that the desired distribution of wealth might now be effected on the basis of the solidarity of mankind, the underdeveloped countries may conduct themselves 'well' (i.e., in accordance with established rules) in their relations with industrialised countries or multinational firms. They are, however, just as likely to have an interest in 'indulging in bad behaviour in order to make their presence felt, and this policy line may be followed individually, and, better still, collectively. The co-ordination of underdeveloped countries' policies considerably increases the extent to which they are able to make a nuisance of themselves, should they choose to do so, and it also strengthens their bargaining power. To exercise their bargaining power, they make use of a whole gamut of means ranging from the simple union of sellers to political incitements involving their considerable powers of blackmail by means of which they play off rival industrial powers against each other'.[50]

*   *   *   *   *

We may conclude by making two remarks. The first concerns the definition of economic independence. Economic independence cannot be described as a *fait accompli*: it is at most a victory that could be shaken and perhaps toppled at any time, but which must nevertheless be defined: 'Although it is true that interdependence is the rule, this interdependence can lead to independence on one condition only – and this condition is that the interdependence must be multiple and diversified. The most realistic definition of independence is the diversification of interdependences'.[51] The second remark concerns method. If our analysis appeared to be over-cynical that is simply because it could not have been otherwise in a world where relations between nations are far from perfect. For too long a prisoner of Walras and Bastiat, economic thinking must now be converted to Clausewitz. But does realism necessarily entail the abandonment of all ideology? Certainly not, for rejection of ideology would be tantamount to misunderstanding its real meaning: whether treated as a system of representations or misconceived consciousness, ideology always has 'an existence and a historical role in any given society'.[52] This also holds for the ideology of national independence.

NOTES

1. Though it could be argued that this birth of nations out of the dissolution of colonial empires is just a repetition of a process that occurred twice in the past: once at the end of the eighteenth and the beginning of the nineteenth centuries when the Spanish and Portuguese empires were crumbling apart, and again in the mid-nineteenth century and at the beginning of the twentieth century during the break-up of the Russian, Austro-Hungarian and Ottoman empires. Cf. E. Sicard, 'La construction nationale' in *Encyclopedia Universalis*, Vol. II, pp. 568–569.
2. 'Mercantilists, physiocrats and growth theory' in B. F. Hoselitz, *Théories de la croissance économique*, Dunod, 1970, p. 69.
3. G. Schmoller, *The mercantile system and its historical signification*, New York, 1931, pp. 50–51.
4. G. Perroux, *Indépendance de la nation*, U.G.E., 1975, p. 15.
5. See for example: Y. Benot, *Les idéologies des indépendances africaines*, Paris, Maspero, 1972.
6. J. G. Merigot, 'La nation dans la pensée économique', *Economie contemporaine*, June 1950, pp. 7–14, September 1950, pp. 7–14.
7. *Economie contemporaine*, September 1974, pp. 8–9.
8. Waterson, *Development planning, lessons of experience*, Johns Hopkins Press, 1965, p. 28.
9. 'A plan must be at once a strategy of options, a coherent basis for decisions and a brake on the economy to ensure control over operations and their effects. In Africa, however, these three factors are absent. As regards a strategy of options, the centres of decision-making are external to the State. A plan must be a concerted programme between foreign private investment, the foreign countries providing aid, and the State. As regards the coherence of decisions, present models are inappropriate, for a plan would necessitate sectoral and regional accounts that are at present inadequate. As far as the question of control is concerned, African countries do not have control over the strategic variables that make regulation of the system possible.' Ph. Hugon, *Analyse du sous-développement en Afrique: l'example de l'économie du Cameroun*, Paris, P.U.F., 1968, p. 265.
10 M. Gaud, *Les premières expériences de planification en Afrique noire*, Cujas, 1967, pp. 143–144.
11. Idem, pp. 108–133. A. Pichot, *Comptabilité nationale et planification*, Paris, Cujas, 1968, pp. 185–199. O. Arkhipoff, *La comptabilité nationale et ses applications au Tiers-Monde*, Paris, Cujas, 1969.
12. E. A. Lisle, *L'épargne et l'épargnant*, Paris, Dunod, 1967, p. 68.
13. Y. Benot, *op. cit.*, p. 123.
14. P. Clair, *L'indépendance petrolière de la France*, Paris, Cujas, 1968, p. 9.
15. M. Michaely, *Concentration in international trade*, Amsterdam, North Holland Publishing Co., 1962.
16. 'Economic growth of small nations', in E. A. G. Robinson Ed., *Economic consequences of the size of nations*, Macmillan, 1963, pp. 14–32.
17. C. Vaitsos, *Intercountry income distribution and transactional enterprises*, OUP, 1974.

18. 'The effects of international economic dependence on development and inequality: a cross-national study', in *American Sociological Review*, December 1975, pp. 720–738.
19. 'Quelques aspects du processus de développement du système des nations: stabilité, polarisation, diffusion' in *Revue d'économie politique*, March–April 1970, pp. 330–439.
20. F. Perroux, *Indépendance de la nation, op. cit.*
21. S. Hymer, 'The multinational corporations and the law of uneven development' in J. Bagwati Ed. *Economics and World Order from the 1970s to the 1990s*, Macmillan, 1972, pp. 113–140.
22. G. Adam, 'Multinational corporations and worldwide sourcing', in H. Radice, *International firms and modern imperialism*, Penguin Books, 1975, p. 89.
23. Boukharine, *L'économie mondiale et l'impérialisme, esquisse économique*, Paris, Anthropos, 1967.
24. C. Palloix, *Les firmes multinationales et le procès d'internationalisation*, Paris, Maspero, 1973.
25. *Op. cit.*, p. 17.
26. R. Murray, 'The internationalization of capital and the nation state', *New Left Review*, May–June 1971, pp. 84–109.
27. B. Warren, 'How International is Capital?', *New Left Review*, July–August 1971, pp. 83–88.
28. B. Rowthorne, 'Imperialism in the 1970s – Unity or Rivalry', *New Left Review*, September–October 1971, pp. 31–51.
29. Stalin, *Le marxisme et la question nationale*, Paris, Ed. Sociales, 1948.
30. 'Nation', *Encyclopedia Universalis*, Vol. II, p. 565. According to the author, this myth would fulfil two functions: 'an integrative function bringing about a spiritual cohesion overcoming all conflict of interests, and a disciplinary function which makes power sacred and thus bestows authority on force'.
31. Renan also listed the elements constituting the nation, adding: 'To have common glories in the past, to have a common will in the present, to have done great things together, to wish to do so again; these are the conditions that are necessary for being a nation'.
32. A. Malraux, *Tentation de l'Occident*, Paris, Gallimard.
33. *Relations économiques internationales*, Paris, Dalloz, 1971, p. 5.
34. *Loc. cit.*
35. F. Perroux, *op. cit.*, p. 7.
36. *Loc. cit.*
37. J. Attali, *La parole et l'outil*, Paris, P U F, 1975, p. 207.
38. F. Perroux, *L'économie de jeunes nations: industrialisation et groupements de nations*, Paris, P U F, 1953, p. 15.
39. P. Clair, *op. cit.*, p. 15.
40. 'Rapport sur la politique française de coopération', *La Documentation Française*, 1975.
41. S. A. Morley, 'What to do about foreign direct investment: a host country perspective', in *Studies in Comparative International Development*, 1975, 10, pp. 45–66.

42. T. H. Moran, 'Transnational strategies of protection and defence by multinational corporations' in *International Organisation*, 1973, 10, pp. 273–301.
43. C. Vaitsos, *loc. cit.*
44. A. Benhadji, 'Retour et réinsertion des travailleurs migrants dans leur pays d'origine', *Bulletin international d'études sociales*, 1974, No. 12.
45. G. Adam, *loc. cit.*
46. Myrdal, 'Théorie économique et pays sous-developpés', *Présence Africaine*, 1959, p. 118.
47. *Idem.*, p. 83.
48. J. G. Cross, *The Economics of Bargaining*, Basic Books, 1959, p. 120.
49. G. de Lacharrière, *La nouvelle division internationale du travail*, Paris, Droz, 1969.
50. G. de Lacharrière, *Commerce extérieur et sous-développement*, Paris, P U F, 1964, p. 266.
51. P. Clair, *op. cit.*, p. 71.
52. L. Althusser, *Pour Marx*, Paris, Maspero, 1966, p.238.

7

Neither Partnership Nor Dependence: Pre-Decolonisation, Inertia, Diversification and Para-Protectionism in Indo-British Relations since 1947*

Michael Lipton

I

Since Independence in 1947, many Indo-British relationships continued along paths of disengagement commenced long before. In 1947–57, India and Britain became slightly less important to each other in trade, finance, education and defence: but not much faster than in 1880–1947. After 1957, the process accelerated sharply as post-colonial inertia broke down; the breakdown acquired its own momentum (i.e. powerful interests were vested in continued breakdown); and, by 1970–75, Britain and India had weaker links than made sense given the interests of elites or masses[1] in either country. Section II summarises the process.[2]

It is a process that the two standard international theories (of 'decolonisation followed by partnership in development', and of 'neo-colonialism, dependence and the development of underdevelopment'[3]) fail to explain. Yet the process underlies the post-Independence history of the most important colonial relationship in modern history – perhaps in all history. Hence the failure to explain the delayed, but sharp, Indo-British disengagement represents a challenge both to liberal-Fabian and

* I am grateful to Prof. G. Fischer, Dr. R. Luckham, Prof. W. Morris-Jones, Dr. R. O'Brien, and Prof. B. Schaffer for valuable comments on an earlier draft. My debt to John Firn's co-operative effort on our joint book is large and self-evident. In all cases, the usual disclaimer applies with regard to this paper.

158

to structuralist-Marxist analysts of the international system. To this challenge there are three possible responses.

First, it could be argued that features *special* to India (Section III) or to Britain (Section IV) accounted for the scale, timing and pattern of their post-colonial disengagement. If so, standard international theories might remain relevant to other links between ex-metropole and ex-colony.

Second, India (Section V) or Britain (Section VI) might have disengaged as they did because they exhibited features *general* to ex-colonies and ex-colonisers respectively. If so, rejection, or at least drastic revision, of standard theories is required.

Third, factors *external* to Indian and British experience, such as the position of the superpowers, might explain the post-colonial history of the Indo-British link (Section VII). This might or might not require drastic modification, or rejection, of the two standard theories. It would depend on the permanence of such factors; on their importance in affecting other bilateral ex-colonial links; and on the scope for modifying standard theories to account for them.

*   *   *   *   *

That summarises the structure of this paper (the conclusions are presented in Section VIII). The cumbersome title, however, indicates an argument which I could not fit neatly into this formal structure. Since this argument bobs up rather disconcertingly in several parts of the paper, it may be useful to state it here, and to consider some of the problems that it raises.

In India, as elsewhere, the colonising elite − chiefly British bureaucrats, businessmen, and army officers, who gained cash or status or power from colonisation − had in 1857−1939 to defend its position on several fronts. In the metropolitan country, the colonising elite was threatened by businessmen (and sometimes bureaucrats) who opposed taxes to support the diversion of investment and infrastructure to the colony, especially where such diversion might assist competitive (even if metropolitan-owned) business there. Also at home, there was an increasingly articulate popular opposition to the cost and personal danger, and (rarely) to the illiberalism or brutality, of colonial ventures. Sometimes, there was popular protest in the colony. But much the most important attacks on colonising elites were − and are − from two rival elites, both damaged by the legally sanctioned self-protection of elite colonists' rights that is the essence of colonialism. The indigenous elite sought more access to government, trade, professions, and ownership. Third-country elites sought to end the colonising country's privileged access to its colony for exports and sources of raw materials, and sometimes also sought to rival that country in political, military or cultural influence on its colony.

The usual method of the colonial power, in resisting these threats, was to buy off part of the indigenous elite – the assimilados, the beni-oui-ouis, the Indian knights. Whatever the aims of this buying-off, it leads to a process, here entitled *pre-decolonisation*, in which the colonists' power in the colony is diluted. This happens partly because the bought-off sections of the indigenous elite develop a taste for power; partly because their success proves the permeability of the colonial structure, and hence encourages more radically nationalist groups; and partly because the increasing costs of buying-off weaken the 'will to colonise' of the metropolitan paymasters. The process of pre-decolonisation is of varying length and intensity (in India too long, in the Congo disastrously short). After political independence, the bought-off groups loom large in the successor elite. They find it in their interests to preserve many of the laws and institutions, previously created by the colonists to defend their own interests.[4] Yet such laws and institutions are the soft underbelly of the post-colonial body politic. They are slimmed away by two processes, reflecting the two elites – indigenous and third-country – whose interests are rivals to those of the old colonial elite and its inheritors.

The unassimilated part of the indigenous elite – dissident nationalists, small and medium businessmen, local 'big men' outside the national and provincial capitals, in short the men of power who before independence did *not* help run the government, big or metropole-based business, parliament, courts, or trade – not merely seeks at first to run them and later to remould them to suit its own interests. More basically, it seeks to establish that whatever the indigenous elite can, or might in principle, produce, or teach, or invest in, shall not be provided by foreigners. This 'in principle' principle, analysed elsewhere (LF, pp. 221–2), is a form of protectionism extending far beyond trade, and here termed *paraprotectionism*. This is everywhere attractive to the part of the successor elite which, during the late colonial period, remained relatively unassimilated; but it is likely to prove practicable in ex-colonies in approximate proportion to their economic size.

Third-country elites, especially those without major colonies or ex-colonies, seek to penetrate the markets, supplies, investment prospects, and political options opened by the colonists' withdrawal. To these pressures correspond some general interests, and many special interests, in the ex-colony. This leads to *diversification* of its trade, military contacts, educational and cultural influences, and political goals and alliances.

Normally, as will be argued on p. 190, diversification and paraprotectionism are alternatives, sought by (and tending to benefit) distinct groups in the ex-colony. However, the attainment of either alternative damages the former colonial power, whose interests in the ex-colony – having been to some extent protected artificially, and even promoted violently, through colonial presence – are especially vulnerable once that presence is withdrawn. The past artifice, the past violence, render some measure of paraprotectionism and of diversification desirable for mass welfare in the ex-colony. However, the processes acquire their own ideological momentum, corresponding to new interests vested in them, and therefore tend to be pushed well beyond the point where mass welfare begins to suffer.

More surprisingly, perhaps, analogous processes are at work in the ex-metropole. Usually it has stayed in its colonies long after the costs of so doing, for the metropole as a whole, came to exceed such benefits of its relationship to the colony as could not have been achieved without direct colonisation. This lag suggests that the metropolitan interests vested in continued colonisation – its beneficiaries in the bureaucracy, the army, the professions, and to some extent in trade and investment – must have been stronger, better-organised, or more aware of their advantage than were the more diffuse taxpaying, consuming, and business interests that paid the increasing bills. As in the colony, so in the metropole: well-organised beneficiaries of traditional links maintain them for a decade or so; then counter-pressures burst the wall of inertia. Not merely do persons, administrations, skills and capital redirect themselves away from the former colonial market once their old special, artificial advantage there has gone. Diversification away from, and paraprotection against, the ex-colony are carried much further than the general interest in the metropolitan country – as crudely indicated by, say, the inter-country allocation of a given volume of trade that would maximise GNP in the metropole – would warrant.

These processes, symmetrical in ex-colony and ex-metropole, may well be common to all ex-colonial links. They are rooted in patterns of interest, inertia and organisation: patterns that are more pervasive than particular class-relations. However, there were important factors in the British-Indian case making the post-inertial disengagement especially rapid and excessive. Both countries suffered slow growth and poor balances of payments. Both faced changes that required regional realignment: Britain, the growth first of NATO, then of EFTA and EEC; India, the increasing need for close links with one or other of the regional nuclear superpowers, China and the USSR. However, these factors could well have induced India and Britain to concentrate their scarce extra-regional energies and resources on each other. That both instead diffused them – in Britain's case, toward such extremely unlikely mini-clients as Malta and Mauritius! – must be traced to two sources. The first is the deeper, and more generalisable, process of realignment and diversification outlined above. The second is the failure of policymakers, in business as well as government, to review strategically and take systematically the selective decisions required to adapt to, or if desired against, this process.

*   *   *   *   *

The above account is presented as an explanation of the course of relations between India and Britain after Independence in 1947. I shall argue that, despite special features of those relations, the account also provides a *general* model for the likely sequence of post-colonial events. In either case – as special explanation or as general model – the account is open to three criticisms. These must be raised here, though they cannot be treated at all fully.

First, how can one explain the growth of paraprotection: of walls to defend domestic activities, often inefficient and sometimes purely hypothetical, against trade, migration, capital movements, even ideas, between ex-colonist and ex-colony? India and Britain have been neither so small as to render this process impracticable, nor – usually – so neurotic as to push it to extremes. Yet, given its probably harmful impact on output and welfare, it is odd. The power, at Independence, of persons and classes and organisations that had worked with the colonial 'partner' makes it odder still. So does the growing strength of transnational organisations: in business (especially international trade), in management of concessional capital flows, in the bureaucracy, in education and culture, and to some extent in labour movements.

Second, I argue that the diversification of overseas links by ex-colony and ex-metropolis away from each other takes several years after independence, and then – having gone too slowly for the welfare of either people – goes too fast and too far. Both the inertia and the momentum need explanation. What determines the length of the delay, and the strength and speed of the diversifying reaction from it?

Third, how do these processes of pre-decolonisation, diversification and paraprotection relate to interests, conflicts or compromises, and decisions? I speak of an 'elite', in (ex-) colony and (ex-) metropole, in each case with emerging awareness of an overall 'interest' that reflects its changing structure, and of the scope and limits of its power to implement that interest. However, this sounds bloodless, and its relationship to political or economic accounts of conflict or interpenetration – among classes or institutions – is not clear.

These three theoretical issues will be discussed briefly in the Appendix. First, however, the specific Indo-British processes of disengagement, and their typicality or otherwise of ex-colonial events, must be explained.

II

Figs. 1–4 (reproducing LF, pp. 406–7) indicate the trends in Indo-British trade. There was a slow decline in India's and Britain's role in each other's trade, from peaks reached around the turn of the century. Between Independence and 1957–58 or so, the downtrend did not accelerate – on some indicators it slowed down. From 1958 to the early 1970s, the downtrend accelerated

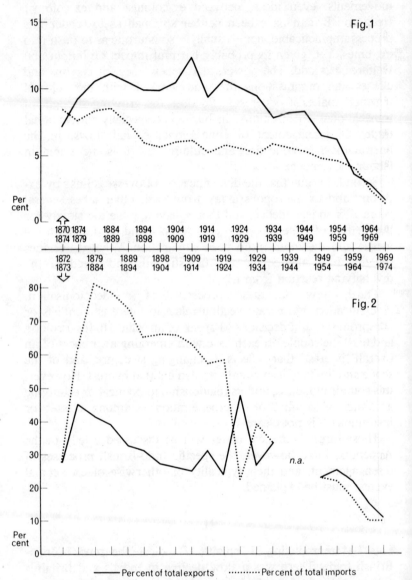

FIG 1: British Trade with British India, 1870–4 to 1964–9, 6-year averages
FIG 2: British Indian Trade with Britain, 1872–3 to 1964–9, 6-year averages

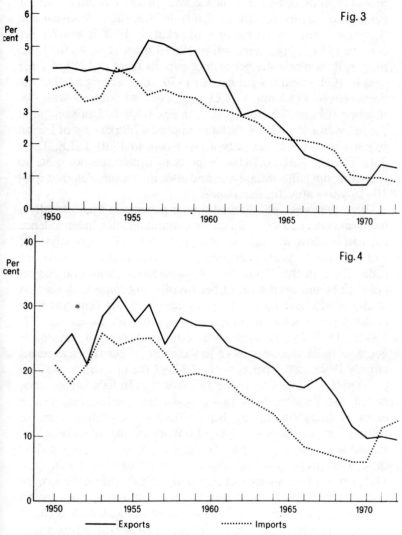

FIG 3: Share of Total British Trade held by India, 1950–70
FIG 4: Share of Total Indian Trade held by Britain, 1950–70

at a rate which, for overtly friendly major trading partners, is probably unprecedented in peacetime. In 1879 Britain sold 9.1 per cent of her exports to 'British India' (including Pakistan and Bangladesh but not Burma or Sri Lanka); in 1938 it was 7.1 per cent, in 1956 5.1 per cent, and in 1969 1.6 per cent. As for India proper, Britain sold 4.4 per cent of exports there in 1950, 4.1 per cent in 1960 – and 0.9 per cent in 1970, representing a fall in the decade from £152 mn. to £73 mn., even without allowing for inflation (LF, p. 209 and Table 3.1). From the Indian standpoint the fall was also massive: Britain supplied 17.9 per cent of Indian imports in 1960–1, but only 8.1 per cent in 1970–1 (LF, Table 3.4). The declines for Indian exports to Britain are not quite so dramatic, but still substantial – and also, in essence, deferred until 10–15 years after Independence.

Other relationships followed similar patterns to trade, usually a few years later: patterns, that is, of continuing after Independence the earlier slow attenuation that went with pre-decolonisation, and only 10–15 years later embarking on a dramatic downward slide. Thus, in the 1960s, British transactions about doubled on both credit and debit sides of her invisibles account with the rest of the world, and India's grew by about 40 per cent, yet their dealings with each other remained stagnant (LF, Tables 5.2, 5.7, 5.8). In 1959–61, the share of British private foreign investment going to India was very close to the share of her overseas assets already there, at 6.1 per cent; by 1970–1 the proportion was 1.6 per cent (LF, Table 6.6). In the 1950s, half of India's foreign trade deficit was financed by running down the 'sterling balances' – debts to India run up by Britain during the closing years of colonialism, in the Second World War; by the late 1960s, net British aid covered less than 10 per cent of India's trade deficit, though the proportion later increased somewhat (LF, Table 7.15). 11.7 per cent of foreign students at British universities were Indian in 1947 8; 12.2 per cent in 1960; but only 4.7 per cent in 1970–1 (LF, Table 9.3). In other statistically measurable areas of mutual involvement – defence, journalism, diplomatic representation, population movements – the same pattern of delayed, then avalanche-like, acceleration of disengagement can be traced also.

The great political adaptations behind the statistics are familiar. From 1958, Britain's long *rapprochement* with continental

Western Europe, first through EFTA and then through successive approaches to EEC, was so conducted as to erode not just Commonwealth preferences but also the Commonwealth itself. This was less a sensible realignment than an attempt to attract new partners by showing disloyalty to, and losing goodwill from, old ones. Meanwhile, India expanded first its aid and trade link with the USA (from 1956 to the mid-1960s), and then, massively, its barter dealings with the USSR and Comecon; bunkering facilities, friendship treaties, and political realignments (stopping far short of subservience) followed as naturally as the flag usually follows trade. However, India's failure to develop a major EEC-UK option, alongside her new Soviet semi-alignment and in the wake of her worsened relations with the USA, is as puzzling as Britain's failure to develop Asian alliances as options to, and strengtheners of, her new European connections.

It is impracticable, in a brief paper, even to summarise the process by which the Indian and British interests vested in continuing the old special (protected, privileged) relationships (a) maintained these relationships from 1947 to the late 1950s, but (b) crumbled thereafter. It is, however, important to stress three points.

First, the apparent political turning-points − Suez; US involvement in the finance of Indian planning after the exhaustion in 1956–8 of India's sterling balances; the Indo-Soviet treaty of 1971; British accession to EEC in 1974 − are *ex post* records of achieved political and economic processes, much more than causes in themselves of Indo-British disengagement. That is true both in the narrower, statistical sense that the graphs of Indo-British trade, aid, educational movements, etc., show no sharp 'blips', and in the wider sense.

Second, it is relatively easy − but can be misleading − to identify the process of sharply accelerated disengagement (and the strengthening of interests benefiting from it) most clearly in one or two concrete economic relationships. For example, the severe erosion of India's free access to the British market for her textile exports after 1957 plainly helped powerful and inefficient textile producers in Britain; conversely, the sharp parallel fall in British defence sales to India helped analogous Indian manufacturers, mostly in the public sector. But an economist should beware of overstressing the concrete. It is probable that more importance attached to the inertia, and delayed decline, of *institutional* influences (such as that of the old Indian Civil Service, and in Britain of the 'old India hands'); and to the growth of powerful ideologies of disengagement, whether in the form of Indian advocacy of not letting others do what might 'in principle' (and at almost any cost in time and money) be done in India, or in the form of the British elite's sometimes barely sane desire to treat its historic links and advantages as lumber to be discarded, rather than as dowries to be offered, to its new European partners. Such ideologies, however bizarre, have served some interests admirably, and have recruited in their support some sincere intellectuals who might have known better.[5]

Third, even in a world of perfect competition (or one that behaved like such a world[6]) in the economic sphere, there is no process by which the political clash of interests accompanying a national realignment – whether a *renversement des alliances* or an adjustment by ex-colony and metropole to decolonisation – need produce an outcome consistent with the welfare of the people of the country as a whole. India's realignment towards the USA in the 1950s was primarily a response to an acute need for cash (and food) to fuel the Second and Third Plans after the sterling balances had been exhausted; her later tilt towards the USSR was largely a response to the strategic need for very close links with at least one of the two nearby nuclear powers; her persistent paraprotectionism was a response to internal pressures, mainly from large industrial houses but also from State suppliers, academics, and senior officers, all seeking to enlarge their roles. Each set of policies was accompanied – in some cases preceded – by adjustments in laws affecting trade patterns (or affecting their analogues in such fields as capital movements, industrial licensing, or regulations about who could get foreign exchange to study what where). The conditions and signals surrounding individual responses were thus affected by the shifting political balance (itself due substantially to past economic power). Even if those responses were always rational, and even if they took place in a quasi-competitive framework enabling them to be therefore socially optimal given the conditions and signals, there is no process for 'optimising' the outcome – for, say, a tariff structure – of the power struggle deciding the conditions and signals themselves. Exactly analogous remarks could be made about

Britain's adaptation – and over-reaction – in 1960–70 to the weakening position of interests that had traditionally defended the Indian connection.

It is in practice surely clear that by 1976 Britain and India had pulled further apart, at least economically, than the interests of elites or masses of either country can justify. India has interests in an EEC option that could enable her to bargain more strongly with the USSR, currently a very large presence in trade, diplomacy, and perhaps defence. Britain has interests in efficient trading options, and in an EEC expanding its trade emphases in the 'Third World' beyond the range of traditional French concerns.[7]

III

In both India and Britain, diversifying and disengaging changes in the pattern of trade generally preceded changes in other relevant variables – capital flows, 'defence' relationships, diplomatic representation, etc. In asking whether features special to Britain and India, rather than features general to ex-metropolis and ex-colony, explained the delayed but astonishingly rapid pulling apart after the late 1950s, it is to factors affecting trade that one naturally turns first. The reader can easily amend the following discussion to apply to other variables of the relationship.

A country's capacity to move away from traditional overseas suppliers and markets – assuming the shift in interests described in the last section, and hence the will to make such a move – depends on several factors, considered below. These include (a) its economic size; (b) its internal economic diversity; (c) the availability of alternative overseas partners; (d) the nature of finance for trade with different partners; and (e) the extent to which growth and structural change alter the pattern of goods traded, and hence possibly of trading partners. Given any particular level of will and capacity to disengage from Indo-British trade, the amount of disengagement that happens will depend on its costs and benefits to, and the relative freedom of choice (and power) of, rival groups *within* the trading nations. These considerations can largely be decomposed into (i) the extent to which late-colonial trade owed its size to artificial stimulation and protection, and (ii) after independence, the conventional economic categories of change, in the trading partners' incomes, prices, tastes and technology. On balance, the strength in India and Britain of such factors affecting the capacity to disengage, and size in India and Britain of benefits (relative to the costs) of disengagement, probably go some way to explain why the role of Indo-British trade shrank after 1960 so much more rapidly than that of Britain's trade with countries that became independent later than India, or of India's trade with developed countries other than Britain (LF, Tables 3.1, 3.6, 4.1).

However, most of the explanation must be shifted onto time-factors. India was decolonised long before Africa, so that the interests in the old Indo-British link by the mid-1960s had had twenty years to decline or realign, while the new interests in (say) Indo-Soviet or British-EEC connections had had a similarly long period to organise their case for replacing the old links. This suggests that metropole-excolony trade from Africa will in the early 1980s feel much, though because of special Indo-British factors not all, of the chill blast that hit Indo-British trade in the 1960s.

*   *   *   *   *

(a) India's *economic size* certainly helped her to move away from the British relationship without incurring new binding dependencies. However, the contribution may well have been small. It achieved little before the late 1950s. Moreover Brazil, an economically larger country than India (i.e. with a higher total GNP) despite its smaller population, in the very period (1960–75) when the Indo-British link eroded so much, became *more* dependent on her main, traditional overseas metropole, the USA. Nor should India's large area and population lead us to overstate her economic size (her GNP is less than Belgium's). Finally, the contribution of economic size to the capacity to alter trade patterns depends partly on the mobility (in response to either incentives or physical controls) of factors of production among uses, and especially into and out of exporting and import-substituting sectors of the economy; but India has been perceptively described as a 'stagnant economy in progress', with about 70 per cent of workforce in agriculture at every census from 1921 to 1971, very slow rates of net rural-urban migration,[8] and major barriers (ranging from linguistic diversity through rural bond-slavery to skill shortages) to quick adjustment. (All this suggests that an ex-colony, if seeking rapid post-colonial realignments, should stress measures that ease internal factor mobility, to exploit its economic size – and, if it is small, regional cooperation to simulate a larger economic size.)

(b) These last barriers to adaptation also restrict the power of India's great *economic diversity* to account for India's approach, neither partnership nor dependence, after 1960, both to Britain and to her successive partial replacements on the trade front, the USA and the USSR. We shall see that the changing structure of trade as a whole has little power to explain the decline of Indo-British trade in particular. Smaller still, *a fortiori*, is the explanatory power of the fact that India's economic size or diversity may have facilitated changes in that structure.

(c) As for *alternative partners*, India's problems were plainly in the field not of general trade, but of defence imports, food imports, and exports competitive with products of developed countries. The problem with defence imports was the reluctance of Britain, in common with other Western suppliers, to provide spares or replacements in 1965 for India and Pakistan to use against each other; but this accelerated rather than caused the attenuation of Indo-British links, for it *followed* a diversification towards US and domestic defence supplies, and, indeed, the beginning of growth in Soviet supplies. As for food imports, India is not special but typical of many ex-colonies (and other poor countries) in that (i) net food exports were long turned into growing net food imports by rapid population growth, some growth in income-per-person, and inadequate attention to small-scale farming – as regards investment, incentives and institutions alike; and (ii) the growth of net grain imports then shifted import structures away from Europe towards the USA. India has shared with a few other countries, notably Pakistan, Bangladesh and Egypt, the acute foreign-exchange shortages, the obvious needs, and the political skill to get US and other food imports largely on concessional terms. The widely-shared wish that such food aid, which has serious drawbacks, should be temporary, however, probably rules it out as a major source, special to this group of countries, of post-colonial diversification and realignment.

(d) *Export access* is another matter. The special advantages accorded in British markets to EFTA after 1957, and to EEC and its associates after 1973; the conclusion of successive rounds of trade-freeing negotiations under the GATT, largely confined in impact to trade among rich countries; periodic, but in their impact on India ratchet-like, bouts of specifically British protectionism, especially in cotton and jute textiles: all eroded the value to India of Commonwealth preferences, and in particular of the British markets, from the late 1950s on. To ascribe Indo-British disengagement to such trends (and their obvious analogy in capital movements, migration, defensive alliances, etc), is, however, to reverse cause and effect. The issue is: why should India's export access – rather than Malta's or Nigeria's, let alone Ireland's or Denmark's – to the UK market have so sharply deteriorated?[9]

(e) Britain's effective provision to India of *import finance* fell drastically with the near-exhaustion in 1956–8 of India's sterling balances. As tied US aid came to replace these, a push was given to India's import structure (though not nearly enough to explain the huge fall in British exports to India in the 1960s). But again one has to ask what was cause, what effect. The question is given focus by the events after 1967, as it became clear that US food and defence aid were not to be replaced by similar amounts of other US aid; despite Britain's devaluation relative to India's other possible suppliers, it was not to Britain, either in its own capacity or as a key to EFTA or EEC, that India turned for import finance. Instead a series of very large barter deals with the USSR and other Comecon countries was entered into. Moreover, the terms of British aid rendered it a more important source of import finance, relative to others, after 1967 than the crude flow data suggest (LF, pp. 108–12); yet other donors attained much higher trade/aid ratios in India than did Britain.

(f) Was the type of *structural change* a factor, special to India, attenuating its links with Britain? If Britain had supplied India with the same share of Indian imports in each of the nine major commodity groups in 1970–1 as in 1960, Britain's share of *total* Indian imports would have fallen hardly at all – by at most 8 per cent of its actual proportionate decline (LF, p. 33). Conversely, if India had retained its share in British imports of each major commodity group from 1960–1 to 1969–70, India's share of *total* British imports would have fallen by at most 6.6 per cent of its actual proportionate decline (LF, p. 45). More detailed analysis might show different results, but it does not look as if India's changing trade structure can be a major factor affecting the British connection.

*   *   *   *   *

Apart from these special features of the Indian scene, were there specially high benefits, or low costs, to powerful groups in India, likely not to apply to ex-colonies considering rapid disengagement from the metropole? To the 'soft underbelly' issue we return in Section V. Suffice it at this point to note that India's extensive pre-decolonisation, and (by 1947) large national bourgeoisie, render it *prima facie* unlikely that Britain can by 1947 have been getting away with as much, in terms of trading or other practices aimed at her advantage to the colony's cost, in India as in most of the more recently independent colonies.

More significant is the fact that India's total growth rate, and – a linked consideration – the growth of her exports and imports, was in the 1960s slow, both in volume and in value terms, by the standards of less developed countries. On its own this need not have reduced Britain's role, but the point is that Britain was doing similarly badly by the standards of developed countries. 'The various countries, including Britain, dealing with India [expanded their transactions with India] at rates retarded by India's slow growth ... [E]xactly similar tendencies also depress[ed] Britain's share in India's various transactions, to the benefit of other nations growing more rapidly than Britain' (LF, p. 225). Two slow growers, two nations raising their export prices relative to their competitors, as were India and Britain (LF, pp. 25–7); two countries, consequently, with poor foreign-exchange positions – such entities face a double handicap in their transactions with each other. Faster-growing, slower-inflating, and more healthily endowed with foreign exchange, 'third countries' – mainly the USSR in India's case, mainly EEC in Britain's – face only a single handicap, the poor performance of *either* India *or* Britain. Hence they tend to replace each in the other.

This gravity-flow model, in which the fate of international links depends on the changing economic 'mass' of the partners and hence on their capacities to attract each other, has real attractions, transcending pseudo-physics. However, like most of the arguments that India or Britain is special, the model begs the questions of causation. How far does Britain's relatively poor economic performance since 1950 stem from reactions – first of delay and later of panicky, unselective little-Europeanism – to loss of empire? How far does India's stem from analogous failures, first to attenuate the British links in 1947–57, then in 1957–75 to decide how best to use what remained to develop new options?[10]

IV

Possible special explanations of delayed disengagement by reference to the peculiarities of Britain's position can be dismissed much more briefly than those referring to the Indian situation, for the following reason. India is one of seventy-odd ex-colonies to become independent since 1947, and in several ways apparently distinct – size, earliness and 'preparedness' of decolonisation, etc. Britain is one of a small number of significant ex-colonial metropoles, and was much the most significant colonist by any measure. Thus, although general social laws applying to 'ex-colonies except India' could perhaps make sense, such laws for 'ex-metropoles except Britain' could not.

The fact remains that the considerations underlying the gravity-flow model, discussed in the last section, suggest that Britain, with its relatively poor post-war growth and balance-of-payments performances, was especially likely to lose ground to third countries, in India as elsewhere. Moreover, the factors underlying Britain's slow, random and undirected responses to loss of empire – factors connected with early 'maturity', in particular with a share of workforce in agriculture that fell fast and soon and did not leave a 'pool' of rural-urban migrants responsive to incentives; and with levels of welfare and public outlay, highly desirable in themselves, but able temporarily to rest on an insufficient tax base only because traditionally supported from imperial tribute – induced, in particular, inertia with regard to the use of resources formerly involved in the Indian connection.

Before 1914, one-tenth of Britain's national product comprised 'net factor incomes received from abroad' – crudely, net colonial tribute. By 1960 the share was one-hundredth. Yet clearly the interest-groups, created and nourished by that one-tenth, long possessed the political influence to defend themselves. The surprise, then, is less that inertia affected Britain's relations with India, but rather that the acute balance-of-payments pressures on British diplomacy, military policy, and marketing compelled readjustment as soon as they did. Britain's experience vis-à-vis India after independence — first 10–15 years in which most of the statistical series show little change; then a decade of almost panic disengagement — is an extreme case all right. But subsequent decolonisers such as France and Belgium, having experienced more recent industrial revolutions, are likely to feel in due course the 'maturity' (i.e. exhaustion of the rural labour pool), and the impact of lost special advantages in ex-colonies, that for Britain have together made adjustment difficult and inertia significant.

V

Four features of India's post-colonial situation, which arose in a particular time-sequence, are generalisable to most subsequently independent ex-colonies. First came the 'soft underbelly', created before decolonisation (and supported by colonial institutions), of residual factors serving principally the ex-colonists' interest; in result though at least initially not in intention, pre-decolonisation created, well before independence, powerful (if ultimately vulnerable) groups willing to act after independence as supporting corsets for that 'soft underbelly' of British-orientated practices and organisations. Second came the delayed reaction of the indigenously orientated part of India's elite[11] into para-protectionism; this is extensible to fewer sorts of activity (but still likely to be tried) within smaller and less diverse ex-colonies. Third, partly competing and partly supporting, was the incursion of third countries into formerly colonial preserves in India. Fourth is the management of these twin transitions by an elite of changing, cross-pressured bureaucrats and politicians: half-tied to the Indian rich, but increasingly with interests and power of their own; half-tied to the British education, culture and style that once helped them to advance, but increasingly realigning themselves towards the newly-popular (though mutually inconsistent) alternatives of indigenism and cosmopolitanism. During these changes, the political system was driven, both when maintaining the 'soft underbelly' and when undermining it, by elite-group interests; mass pressures to 'deliver the goods' (subsidised food imports, protected jobs in making fertilisers or ball-bearings to replace imports) acted as constraints or goads, rather than as primary motivations, in determining both the rate of movement away from Britain, and its direction as between paraprotection and diversification.

The persistence in India after 1947 of a 'soft underbelly' of institutions, practices and traditions, initially set up mainly to satisfy the interests or styles of the British, could be demonstrated in many fields: from the Managing Agencies, through Chambers of Commerce and the British role in such product areas as chemicals and motor vehicle assembly, to the choice of overseas locations for higher training in medicine or engineering or the methods of war. The problem created by such a 'soft underbelly' – supported by institutions (such as those of the law, the English-language press, and the Indian Administrative Service) decolonised well before independence in personnel, not long afterwards in interests, but much later, if at all, in attitudes and procedures – is the subtle one, documented briefly in Section II above (and at length in LF), of delayed response followed by overreaction. For example, those in India who buy wool-tops, or license their import, continued for many years to 'buy British'; partly out of habit, partly because of intra-firm and inter-firm connections, but partly because particular key personnel, and attitudes, stayed the same after independence. One day, one link in the chain of the decision snaps: a civil servant or a businessman thinks again, or is replaced, or pressured, or does a new set of sums; and there is a new view, India-wide, of the costs and benefits of alternative sources of supply. Instead of a smooth adjustment we see a sudden, delayed, and total switch of orders to a new supplier, in this case Australia

The risk to the ex-colony is that delayed reactions are often over-reactions. Many of the 'British-style' IAS procedures, for instance, have been of developmental value: in recruiting a large cadre of people, selected for their ability and not their region or caste or relatives; people in themselves strictly executive and apolitical, and thus flexible, loyal and responsive in face of policy changes (such as those around the areas of public ownership and 'panchayati raj'), and largely honest and uncorrupt. Probably the British often fostered these values selfishly, in order to serve the interests, or at best imitate the ideals (rather than the practices) of the metropolitan bourgeoisie of the nineteenth century; but so what? Such values would remain valid in an independent, democratic and socialist India, and challenges to them are likely to come from rather different sorts of ideological stable. Until the late 1960s, criticism was rightly directed at the need to make the IAS's values subserve not merely 'administration' but development. Since then, however, the idea of a truly Indian IAS has in some quarters been abused, regrettably, to argue for an increasing erosion of the values themselves. Elsewhere also — in domestic matters such as law and dealings with the press, as well as in international links affecting trade or capital flows or education — *some* aspects of a colonial connection can, with careful selection, help the ex-colony after independence: help not merely its elites but its people as a whole.

*   *   *   *   *

Thus, even apart from India's need for an overseas option — Britain to offer alternatives to the USA's influence in the 1960s, EEC to balance the USSR's today — it is hard to see that India's paraprotection was or is of general benefit. Paraprotection covers measures going beyond simple tariff and quota rules, in two senses: that of preventing, not just deterring, international dealings in several areas; and that of extending protection from trade to such areas as technical assistance, education, and overseas investment finance (whether private or through inter-governmental aid). In all these areas, one can document an Indian policy of 'not "let us do what we are good at", but rather "leave to us all we are in principle able to do" — the "in principle" principle' (LF, pp. 219–20). In imports, this meant, for example, refusing to license engineering imports, above a very small sum, unless there was *no* Indian response, however uncompetitive to advertisement (LF, p. 31). In education, it meant that undergraduates were not trained abroad unless no courses of comparable quality — in the opinion, inevitably and rightly, of Indian administrators advised by Indian educators — were available at home. And so on. It was because the British underbelly in India was soft that Britain was most affected by such policies.

However, five objections to them must be made from a strictly Indian standpoint. First, some such policies must for many years be high-cost. Second, while the adoption of such policies in a few areas can be defended on infant-industry, economies-of-scale or learning-by-doing grounds, in all areas at once it cannot; it is a fallacy of composition to argue that, because the principle of doing things for myself can be practised in a few areas, I can practise it in all, let alone that I can make an 'in principle' principle out of so doing. Third, the glow of vicarious pride that an administrator feels in indigenism, in any activity, provides a misdirected (albeit genuine and honourable) motive if the costs of error or inefficiency are borne by others, especially the poor. Fourth, a generalised quest for self-sufficiency − if it implies increases in the requirements for (but not in the incentives to the efficient use of) scarce forms of capital and of skills − is likely to waste foreign exchange, not to save it, and to reduce employment in the process (especially as the foregone exports, implicit in a programme of general encouragement to import substitution, are usually more labour-intensive than the activities that replace them).

Fifth, in an international context, India has the power and diversity to render autarkic policies, if not low-cost, at least (misleadingly) credible to other, smaller poor countries in which the costs of greatly extending such policies have, notably in Latin America, proved very high. However, that very power and diversity also permit India to set an example of open, option-preserving international relations with little or no risk of neo-colonial outcomes. The latter path would surely increase India's overseas options as well as her domestic welfare, income and employment.

If the part of the elite that benefits from paraprotection has been able in India to ensure that it *eventually* prevailed in the post-colonial period, there are likely to be similar results elsewhere. The comparative lack of open, 'liberal' frameworks for democratically-organised counter-pressures or exposés will in most of Africa make it easier for such elites to disguise their self-interest in paraprotection as 'socialism' or 'nationalism' than was possible in Nehru's India. The comparative lack of economic size and diversity, on the other hand, will make it more difficult.

*   *   *   *   *

If an elite is confident, in a newly-independent country, of satisfactory growth and external economic relations – and such confidence depends *inter alia* on non-protectionist and non-neocolonial conduct by developed countries – it will react to the ex-colonist's 'soft underbelly' less by paraprotection, with regard to imports or capital supply or foreign education and treaties, than by diversification of overseas links, perhaps accompanied by outwardly-directed policies. Diversification towards the surrounding region – as typified by, say, the Central American Common Market and the Andean Pact as attempts to escape the trade and investment dominance, respectively, of the USA – was made difficult for India: by political conflict with Pakistan, which reduced their inter-trade after 1950 to a trickle and after 1965 to even less; after 1962, by similar conflict with China; but, more fundamentally, by the fact that the South and East Asian countries had similar exports, imports, projected output structures, labour surpluses and capital deficits, and hence relatively little prospect of integration, whether through liberalising trade or through harmonising investment plans.

India thus diversified first towards the USA in 1957–65, in the shadow of the exhaustion of the sterling balances and the growing need for concessional food imports; and, after 1965, towards the USSR. It is popular to see this latter realignment as (a) political in spirit, being encapsulated in the Indo-Soviet Friendship Treaty of 1971, and (b) not involving dangers to India because of her size and power – Soviet troops in Delhi (with snow on their boots) are a rightly-derided scenario. However, in reality, (a) Soviet involvement – like British colonisation and disengagement, and US involvement and withdrawal, before it – was trade-led, well before political relations followed the lead; and (b) the political analysis of international relations is, here as elsewhere, befuddled by the 'fallacy of misplaced concreteness' that underlies scenario-building and scenario-exploding alike. India's growing reliance on the USSR for trade, military supplies, and diplomatic support must find expression in Soviet demands for a *quid pro quo*, as in any bilateral relationship, with unbalanced advantages, that prevails for long between powers whose elites are neither angelic nor grossly incompetent. What 'scenarios' could have predicted the Soviet instruction to India in March 1976 forbidding the promised and agreed delivery to Egypt of MIG-21 engines – constructed for (and hence legally, if not legitimately, controllable by) the USSR, under licence – because the Egyptian government had offended the USSR?[12] If the future were precisely predictable by social science, it would not be the uncertain outcome of probabilistic behaviour in risky situations. Because it is, the destruction of options by a delayed, then exaggerated, retreat from metropolitan links is a route to new risks of dependence, on new 'partners', in new and unknown situations not usefully describable *ex ante* in 'scenarios'.

That is especially the case in a post-colonial world dominated by superpowers who are not the old colonists. The old metropoles are London, Paris, and to some extent other European capitals. Excessive diversification from those capitals (in both senses of the word) means risks of excessive reliance on the new power centres: Moscow, Peking, Washington (or New York?). Nobody, except an ideologue, would be unhappy that India should have good relations with the USSR, or Indonesia with the USA, or Cambodia with China. But anybody, concerned that people (or even, let's face it, national elites) should be able to decide their own nation's fate, should be unhappy if any very poor country develops close relations *uniquely* with one superpower. The EEC, now an 'alcoholics anonymous' of ex-colonialists, could well help: if it moderates its stress, historically accidental and not in its own or even its business elites' interest, on Africa; if it accelerates the decline of neo-colonial features within the ACP relationship, a decline assisted by part (not all) of the Lomé accord; above all, if it sees links with poor countries, especially in trade liberalisation, as a question of mutual advantage and not of reluctant concession. Failing EEC action along such lines, much of the Third World will follow India's path after decolonisation: through inertia, via exaggerated diversification, to unwilling and half-planned impalement upon one of the three poles of superpower political and economic struggle.

VI

Because Britain, unlike India, represents a majority of the world's ex-colonial links, analysis of facts about Britain, generalisable to other ex-colonial relationships, becomes in part analysis of 'the British problem'. Such analyses are usually obtuse, boring and silly, and I wish to avoid them (save only to point out that growth and redistribution – admittedly supplemented by foreign borrowing – have raised Britain's mass welfare, in the three decades of post-war decolonisation, at a rate never approached, for any period of comparable length, during the preceding three centuries of colonial tribute). Questions analogous to those asked about India, however, can be constructively asked about Britain too. Was there an India-orientated 'soft underbelly' that delayed, and hence eventually exaggerated, necessary realignment? Was there a para-protectionist reaction? Did diversification, Euro-regionalist or other, go too far? And – an important question not discussed here – do changes in Britain's elite structure help account for the delayed collapse of Indo-British links?

*   *   *   *   *

Investment by British firms in India was concentrated after 1947 on 'defensive' ventures by big firms – Unilever, ICI, British Leyland – yet seems to have shown post-war rates of return fairly average by world standards (LF, pp. 93–4), suggesting little inertia or emotionalism about placements. Trade was a different matter; the maintenance of India's 'colonial' share in British trade during the 1950s does suggest a 'soft underbelly' in Britain (as in India).

Political perceptions as usual lagged behind economic changes. By 1964, when Harold Wilson claimed that Britain's 'frontiers were on the Himalayas', the collapse of Indo-British economic links (and indeed of Britain's economic capacity to afford world-wide military presences) had been under way for at least five years. Often the very same British politicians and senior civil servants, who relied too long on Commonwealth connections that they did little to render beneficial to affected parties, suddenly overcorrected – when they realised the gap between reality and illusion – into a 'Europeanism' as undiscriminatingly anti-Commonwealth (especially non-white Asian Commonwealth) as their earlier complacency had been passively and uselessly pro-Commonwealth. To this political folly, unfortunately, fate was kind. While France was forced by crises to prepare a post-colonial presence in Africa and to diversify into Europe through one and the same series of events (the 1956–7 negotiations leading to her signature of the Treaty of Rome), Britain, partly through EFTA and partly through the improving terms of trade and the consumption booms of 1952–60, was encouraged to retain the illusion that she need choose neither Europe nor the open sea. The 1950s were Britain's dog-years; colonial nostalgia is not her only 'soft underbelly' then nourished and later uncomfortably shrunk.

*   *   *   *   *

It might seem odd to seek paraprotection in the delayed British reaction against the Indian connection. Britain, in EFTA and EEC, adhered to two trade-liberalising bodies whose trade creation effect demonstrably exceeded their trade diversion effect. She participated in the successive liberalising GATT 'rounds'. When she entered EEC, about 4 per cent of British GNP was spent on Third World imports, as against 3 per cent in EEC and 1 per cent in the USA and USSR-Comecon.[13] And British education, military relations (including arms deals), media, and policy on factor movements all appear to be still outward-looking. Yet these appearances are deceptive. When she entered EEC and still today, Britain should be classified as a country with a legacy of fairly 'liberal' (albeit in origin colonialist) overseas economic relations, but of relations that began to turn sour and gradually paraprotectionist after about 1957. Conversely, the EEC 'Six', by long tradition paraprotectionist, have gradually (as the 1957-Yaoundé I-Yaoundé II-Lomé sequence shows) become less so.

Britain, in joining EFTA, created more trade than she diverted; but EFTA included some countries, such as Portugal and Austria, producing goods directly competitive with (and gradually given advantages in the British market over) Indian and other Third World exports, expecially cotton textiles. The GATT rounds did little to free access, to Britain or other rich nations, for such exports, concentrating instead on trade among industrialised nations. Membership of EEC meant phasing out of Britain's

Commonwealth preferences, in return for vague promises of goodwill, and an Indo-EEC framework treaty that still has little real content. (That Britain's unfavourable treatment of India is no 'special case' is shown by the fact that other Asian Commonwealth countries did not even get a framework treaty.) Meanwhile increasingly restrictionist, albeit nominally agreed, restrictions on cotton textile exports bore harshly on India after 1957.

A case that all this was part of a move towards *para*protection vis-à-vis the less developed world can be made. Outside the trade field, the British tax laws were made increasingly unfavourable to British overseas investment (a situation eased for Europe, first by the Eurodollar market, and later by the impact of Britain's accession to EEC). Fees in British higher education were gradually raised to overseas students, in a way likely to deter only the poor. Above all, immigration laws were made steadily more restrictive, especially – in effect and presumably in intention – towards non-white immigrants.

*   *   *   *   *

Thus Britain's involvement in close alliances, going far beyond military matters, first with the USA and then European countries, can be seen in part as diversification away from links with poor countries, in part as paraprotection against them. Is this a precedent for other ex-colonial links? In my judgment it is. The neo-colonialist 'French' Africa of M. Foccart is retreating into history. Neither France nor Britain can long buy security for its capital in Africa by 'budgetary support' that, in the guise of aid (normally technical assistance), means overseas paymasters for the civil servants and teachers of the recipient countries. A tough and fairly united ACP stance on Lomé, led by a large country that was an important oil exporter (Nigeria), produced an outcome that is many removes from the 1960s, with their reverse preferences, EEC barriers to processed African products, and applications for aid by Gabon that had to be rejected by IBRD on the grounds that the main beneficiaries were not poor Gabonais but wealthy Frenchmen. An OAU concerned to maintain unity, even at the 'cost' of accommodating radical states and attitudes, reinforces these trends.

Yet, desirable as such trends are in many ways, they also mean that the gains to EEC from the old games – concessions-language combined with the practice of surplus extraction through investment, and excessively[14] unequal exchange of labour-power through cartel-manipulated trade – are becoming as sparse in ACP states as they have long been in South Asia. Hence EEC, the ex-colonialists' club, can choose: either gradually to attenuate, almost to do without, major economic links with poor countries (and the weakness of some neo-Marxist analyses is their failure to see how easy that option is – how small is the proportion of EEC's GNP needed to compensate the losers from, and replace the gains yielded by, the old imperial connections); or to move from concessions-language and disguised exploitation to mutual bargains about joint, shared advantages from expansions of trade, capital and labour movements, education and travel, political and defensive arrangements. The British precedent, of delayed then headlong diversification away from India towards regional huddles in Europe, shows the first, wrong route. The 'Foccart path' is untenable. Can EEC produce a post-colonial policy based on the bargaining option – a whole better than the sum of the pasts?

VIII

This question implies my main conclusion: that the factors underlying the delay, and the subsequent exaggeration, of the erosion of post-colonial Indo-British links – although sharpened by special features such as Britain's 'maturity-induced' balance-of-payments problems, and India's size and diversity – are general to most links between Britain (or France or Belgium) and her ex-colonies. There remain to be considered, however, external factors, possibly more specific to Britain and India than the fact that the new superpowers are not the old colonists (a fact conditioning all excolony-metropole relations).

India is within striking distance of two nuclear superpowers with sophisticated delivery systems. India's leaders, whoever they are or represent, must conduct foreign policy, in large part, with a view to neutralising the threat *potentials* created by that fact; for no Indian government could responsibly assume that yesterday's leaders and intentions in China or the USSR could be extrapolated to infer these countries' non-violence towards India, especially an India without deterrent power, tomorrow. The only practicable policy for India, especially after US withdrawal from the Asian arena, is one of extremely close links with one of the nearby superpowers (whose mutual hostility, given their long Siberian border, constitutes a major Indian interest). Moreover, India's accelerated disengagement from Britain, and her growing closeness first to the USA and then (as the USA sided with Pakistan and later withdrew from South-east Asia) to the USSR, coincided closely with China's nuclear development. Can the Indo-British disengagement therefore be treated, after all, as a special case, because of a regionally special consequence of geopolitics?

For two reasons, I believe that such a treatment would invoke the external factor incorrectly. First, it fails to explain why, given the great and historically obvious risks of military reliance on one power, India did not seek to strengthen the British and EEC alliance into a major political option, but instead rendered the (inevitably one-sided) Soviet relationship even more 'special' by giving it major trading, diplomatic, educational and cultural components. Second, too much can be made of accidents of geography in the Polaris-Minuteman-MIRV era of long-distance, rapidly-mobile and realignable nuclear weaponry; if by 1960 it was clear that India's geography implied close links with China or the USSR, by 1976 it seems likely that many African ex-colonies face similar compulsions. The wish of such countries' elites (unless 'comprador' to a degree quite implausible outside the world of rhetoric) to preserve freedom of action does not depend on their class base; the mystery of the surrender of 'European' options, which increase the scope of free action, does not vanish when one mutters the spell, 'threat potential'; and, if my earlier analysis is right, the pressures that led India to abandon those options had little to do with her geographic closeness to China and the USSR and will sooner or later be replicated in the ACP and elsewhere in Asia.

Analogous arguments refute attributions to external pressures on *Britain* of the disengagement from India. The view that the USSR's threat potential – as expressed in action in Poland in 1946, Czechoslovakia in 1947 and 1968, Hungary in 1956, etc. – required some deterrent force in Western Europe is one which any Western country's governing elite, including a partly Communist elite (as in Iceland) or even a wholly Communist one, would have had to take in the 1950s and 1960s, and in my judgment still has to take. Britain's major role in SEATO and CENTO, however, in the 1950s involved a particular, globalist interpretation of the USSR's threat potential that had no obvious justification, in historical precedent or in Soviet action or motivation, save blurred memories of the 'Great Game'. It isn't, I think, the wisdom of hindsight to say that the revolts against Western strategy by Iraq, Pakistan, and to some extent Turkey, and the alienation of India, were implicit in the SEATO-CENTO approach; plenty of people (including at times Sir Anthony Eden) were saying this in the 1950s. The illusion of negative anti-communism, supported by a global, conventional military system, had much to do with post-colonial nostalgia. To explain the pulling apart of Britain and India in the 1960s, it will not do to invoke a particular, wrong response (to the USSR's very real threat potential) that was the offspring of Dulles and Blimp; why was such an offspring conceived, in disregard of the world's biggest democracy, its only major experiment in liberal-democratic development? Are not similar unwise conceptions much more likely in future, in Africa or elsewhere, because (as compared with Asia in the 1950s) EEC economic interests are engaged more directly, liberal-democratic indigenous alternatives less credible, and Soviet (or Cuban or Chinese) involvements outside the 'Atlantic theatre' much more direct and visible?

Perhaps it is not 'political science' to ask such questions. Shouldn't it be?

VIII

This paper is already too long and too speculative. Its central conclusion is, however, clear. Until 1947, India and Britain were locked into the most important relationship in modern, perhaps in all, colonial history. Until about 1956, the quantitative indicators of that relationship declined little, if at all, more quickly than in the long period of pre-decolonisation from the 1870s to 1947. After 1960 the interests supporting inertia realigned themselves or weakened to such an extent that the whole relationship collapsed, trade-led, into an exaggerated depression, from which in the

1970s there have been some slight stirrings of recovery.

Neither the inertia nor the subsequent exaggerated decline can be attributed mainly to features special to India or Britain, though both were helped along by such features. The factors in the decline that were due to external forces, too, are likely to be replicated in other post-colonial situations. Revulsion against the colonial legacy is in many ex-colonies likely to be more deeply and widely felt than it was in ex-British India; as for the metropole, the argument for disengagement, that both late colonialism and post-colonial inertia involve the metropole in net losses in GNP, and in major transfers to particular favoured investors and traders from the rest of the bourgeoisie and from taxpayers as a whole, carries much greater conviction in (say) Franco-Senegalese relations than in British-Indian relations.

The pattern of EEC-ACP disengagement and ACP-superpower, unipolar, option-reducing alliances – following the Indo-British, then Indo-US, and later Indo-Soviet pattern – is therefore at least plausible. To prevent it and to recreate mutually advantageous links with South Asia are, at least in the attitudes and policies required, complementary goals for EEC and not, as the Lomé Convention (with its exclusion of 'non-associables') implies, competitive ones. Whether EEC, or some of its member states, can or will develop relevant overseas policies – aimed neither at UNCTALK nor at exploitation – remains an open question.

Appendix: Some Theoretical Issues

On pp. 160–2, I raised for explanation certain parallel trends in ex-metropole and ex-colony. In each, paraprotection has grown to an extent, and in activities, where it reduces both general and elite welfare. In each, the drive to diversify away from the former colonial 'partner' was first delayed, later exaggerated. In each, the relations among classes, elites and masses require classification with regard to the impact on them of decolonisation, especially as it has affected the groups that were privileged on account of the late colonial nexus – and the rivals of such groups. I hope that both this paper and the book (LF) on which it is based may help to show that the Indo-British 'case' is not so special as to prevent it from providing a large part of the answers to these three

questions. In this brief Appendix, they can be tackled through a few
hints, though I hope systematic ones.

*   *   *   *   *

There are two approaches to the first puzzle, that of exaggerated
paraprotection. Excessive, generally welfare-reducing paraprotection
may be attributed to incorrect perception (by classes, elites, other groups,
or individuals) of their own interests – so-called 'false consciousness'; or
to correct perception, by a particular group of the powerful, that
paraprotection advances its interest even though retarding general
welfare. As usual, the former explanation, while satisfying to the social
scientist's self-esteem (how much better he is, he tells himself, at
recognising other peoples' self-interest than they are themselves!), is
unconvincing. Admittedly elites, especially urban elites seeking peasant
support (in the colony)[15] and liberal sub-elites seeking working-class
backing (in the metropole), try to enlist mass pressures on behalf of anti-
colonialism through appeals to self-sufficient indigenism; this, whether
tribalist or little-England, does involve 'false consciousness' and contains
the seeds of later support for paraprotection. However, there are
sufficient, increasingly powerful, forces that gain from paraprotection to
render unnecessary attempts to attribute it to persistent error.

First, big domestic capital – able to obtain import licences even if they
become scarcer, interested in displacing foreign rivals – gains from
simple protection, while small domestic firms lose correspondingly;
analogies for other components of paraprotection are obvious. Second,
to exploit the gains from paraprotection and to avoid (or impose on
rivals) the losses, access to the licence-allocating, exception-making
bureaucracy is crucial; those who have such access, and the powerful
bureaucrats who gain more power (or money) from manipulating
paraprotective controls, will favour paraprotection. Third, international
contacts, notably trade, would increase the demand for – and hence the
power of – those who provide a country's abundant resource, labour in
a poor country and capital in a rich one; hence the initially powerful,
whose power depends on controlling *scarce* resources, may well oppose
such contacts.

Fourth, specific and powerful interests within an economy are
damaged by open relations with very *different* economies. The free
inflow of products and knowledge, both chiefly industrial, from the ex-
metropole threatens the ex-colony's powerful urban elite, and improves
the terms of trade for its less articulate rural masses. Thus the condition
of urban bias, which characterises most poor countries, sustains and is
sustained by paraprotection (a linkage discussed in detail elsewhere).[16]

Conversely, decolonisation promises welcome relief to disproportionately powerful producers of labour-intensive products in the ex-metropole.

Fifth, professional groups, especially those (like lawyers and academics) where standards of entry and performance are often hard to establish, are assisted by paraprotection to claim, without tears, supposedly 'international' standards with minimal foreign overview or competition.

* * * * *

If paraprotection has too many competing explanations, the trouble with our second puzzle – the initial inertia, and later exaggerated momentum, of diversification – is how to explain it at all. Delays in changing an 'ex-colonial' pattern of external economic links which is unfavourable to general, or elite, welfare in a country are made likelier, and longer, if the interests damaged are weak or dispersed, and the types of damage concealed are small, relative to the interests and damage involved in maintaining the pattern after independence. But two main difficulties impede us in getting an explanatory theory out of this near-tautology. First, what can be said if the ex-colony and the ex-metropole differ widely in these respects, as do India and Britain? (India, though internally bigger and more diverse than Britain, was far more concentrated upon the 'partner' than Britain; Britain, being relatively smaller and more specialised, has featured far higher ratios of external trade, capital flows, etc. to income than has India). Second, how can our near-tautology help to explain the great variety among historical experiences? There are clearly 'conjunctures': Australia as well as India discovered the possibilities of diversification away from Britain around 1957–63. And there are clearly no *simple* laws relating the size of the 'partners' to their delay in post-colonial diversification: the USA (to which foreign economic relations mattered much more after 1783 than to India after 1786) took 70–80 years after Independence to diversify the links with Britain to the extent achieved by India in 15–20 years, although the USA enjoyed much greater affluence and strength relative to the world 'then' than does India 'now'.*

Some generalisations, however, seem possible. Normally a country's capacity to reduce its risks of 'dependence' by diversifying – and hence disarming (or turning against one another) – strong partners in trade, investment, culture or politics, increases with four sets of variables. The first set indicates the country's economic size and diversity. The second relevant set indicates the initial weakness or conflict within the

* I am grateful to Dr Fieldhouse for drawing this point to my attention.

transnational nexus affecting the flows of goods, factors, or ideas that most concern the country. Third, the speed and scale of diversification increase with the extent to which it can be used as a transitional stage towards building up indigenous capacity, without unacceptably costly (para)protection. Hence, fourth, diversification will proceed fastest in activities relatively immune from economies of scale, and hence from inbuilt tendencies to favour monopoly and penalise diversity.

Whether, and over what time-span, 'diversification' prevails over 'paraprotection' within both ex-colony and ex-metropole (as the influence of the forces strengthened during the colonial period dwindles) depends above all on the relative strength of different sorts of business and labour interests. Those in firms that are major *users* of producer-goods prefer diversification of their sources. Those in firms that, actually or potentially, *make* producer-goods seek protection, against the ex-colonial 'partner' and third countries alike – indeed, they probably fight the latter harder than the former, since the colonial partner is often less of a competitive threat to them than new entrants (competitors from Taiwan, Korea and Hong Kong worry British firms making textiles, a producer good for the clothing industry, much more than competitors from India and Pakistan do).

*   *   *   *   *

The third puzzle, and the deepest and least tractable, concerns the relationship between delayed Indo-British diversification – surely no more an autonomous process than, Carlyle notwithstanding, was the French Revolution – and the changing structure of power among classes and sub-elites within Britain and within India. What, institutionally, decides whether, or when, a power-group with interests in 'interdependence' (or 'exploitation') *loses* to a rising power-group with opposed interests in paraprotection, or in diversification towards a geographically contiguous region – EEC for Britain, the USSR for India? Do not the same firms, the same civil services, the same people, often have one foot in each camp?

These difficult questions might be evaded by accusing those who ask them of a form of category-mistake: a confusion between analyses designed to show what happened, when and with what results, on the one hand, and analyses of the interests and power of gainers and losers, on the other. Certainly the former analyses do not logically necessitate the latter; but they are rather dull without them. Indeed, I suggest outline 'who whom' analyses at several points in this paper.

In general, I would stress the role of the *training* of an elite. The skills and attitudes, required to do well as a member of a colonising (or in part pre-decolonised) elite, are likely to become counter-productive after Independence. Those trained in such skills and attitudes grow older, reach the top of the firms or bureaucracies in ex-colony or ex-metropole, and are replaced by younger *rivals*, suspicious of their predecessors' geographical prejudices and of the value of the associated special knowledge. It is in such ways that conflict, not of classes or even of capital, but within an institution, may most significantly swing both ex-colony and ex-metropole away from their old links, once the people who sustained such links have gone.

NOTES

1. These terms are not used in the specific context of Weberian, Marxist or other class theory. Elites are merely interlocking, not necessarily conspiring, top decision-takers in government, business and possibly labour movements, together with their main influences from universities, journalism, and the learned professions: see C. Wright Mills, *The Power Elite*, Oxford, 1956.

2. Section II in particular, and the paper as a whole, rests heavily on M. Lipton and J. Firn, *The Erosion of a Relationship: India and Britain Since 1960*, Oxford RIIA, 1976 (incorrectly dated 1975 in the book). References in the text to 'LF', followed by a page number, are to this book.

3. The *locus classicus* for the former is probably L. Pearson et al., *Partners in Development*, Pall Mall, for IBRD, 1968; and for the latter A. Gunder Frank, *Capitalism and Underdevelopment in Latin America*, Monthly Review Press, 1969. More profound and self-critical expositions can be found, however; of the former, in the reports (entitled *Development Co-operation*) of the OECDs Development Assistance Committee (Paris, annual); of the latter, in C. T. Leys, *Underdevelopment in Kenya: the Political Economy of Neo-colonialism, 1964–71*, Heinemann, 1975.

4. This is not to say that such laws and institutions are necessarily against the mass interest. In India, some were (e.g. Princes' privy purses) and some were not (e.g. the beginnings of multi-party parliamentary democracy).

5. Where most Marxist accounts of ideology seem to me misleading is in their identification of it with the self-justification of a single, coherent *class*. Both colonialism and these subsequent disengagements featured ideologies claiming to justify what were, above all, transfers of income within the British, and within the Indian, 'national bourgeoisie' – between sections of each that gained from a close (and specially favoured) international link, and sections of each that lost from it.

6. M. Friedman, 'The methodology of positive economics', in his *Essays in Positive Economics*, University of Chicago Press, 1953.

7. M. Lipton and P. Tulloch, 'India and the enlarged EEC', *International Affairs*, January 1974.

8. A. Bose, 'Migration streams in modern India', in International Union for the Scientific Study of Populations, *Papers and Proceedings of the 1967 Sydney Conference*, 1971.

9. If one answers in terms of the greater strength, in Britain as elsewhere, of producer than of consumer lobbies – together with the fact that India's exports, unlike those of most poor countries, posed a threat to those producer lobbies – one implies that Britain was in 1957–75 most restrictive to those nations with most to offer by way of competitive imports: in general, plainly false.

10. The *costs* to India of attenuating British links never exceeded the direct costs, plus those of possible (but unlikely) *economic* retaliation. France was able to increase the analogous costs to some of her former African colonies for several years after decolonisation by retaining a military presence. However, any 'Dulles-Arbenz' (or indeed Brezhnev-Dubcek) tactics in non-colonies, including ex-colonies, have become, in several ways, increasingly costly to the metropole engaging in them. Hence the 'direct cost only' situation, that characterised Indian action against (say) British tea plantations in Kerala, is likely to prevail generally in ex-colonies, at least of non-superpowers.

11. The firms (and administrators) who gain more from encouraging production for the home market by restricting – or licensing – imports than from promoting exports; the politicians more at home with their 'mass support', and its languages, than with Westernised English-speaking intellectuals; the part of the 'clerisy' that advocates protection for old, or new, Hindu or Moslem or Indian institutions or ideas.

12. *Financial Times*, 26th March 1976, p. 5.

13. M. Lipton, 'Europe and the Third World', in *Europe Today and Tomorrow*, ed. by Peggotty Freeman, Longmans, 1977.

14. A. Emmanuel, *Unequal Exchange*, New Left Books, London, 1972. His argument is that (in a world of mobile capital but immobile labour, where profit rates but not wage-rates in different countries tend towards equality) poor nations, by trading freely, commit themselves to exchanging unequally rewarded labour-power (because their relatively weak labour organisation leaves rich nations to determine, through their trade unions, the wage-rates that export revenues from trading partners must cover). It can reasonably be objected that (a) trade increases employment, even if not wage-rates, in poor countries, and (b) *some* inequality in wage/profit ratios among nations is the major cause of trade, which *does* benefit the trading partners. The strength of Emmanuel's case, however, lies in the probability that much international trade, due to trade-union (and other cartel) power within the richer nations, is at price-ratios that are very close to those of the poor country. Trade at such price-ratios concentrates most of the gains from trade in the rich country, and reduces the rewards of the poorer nation's labourers, *relative to the richer nation's*, much more than is needed to induce the trade in the first place.

15. F. Fanon, *The Wretched of the Earth*, Penguin, 1957, esp. p. 125.

16. M. Lipton, *Why Poor People Stay Poor: Urban Bias in World Development*, Temple Smith, 1977, pp. 321–4.

8

The Military Relations between Great Britain and Commonwealth Countries, with particular reference to the African Commonwealth Nations

Anthony Clayton

The British Empire was generally accepted at the turn of the century to be an entity in which a major attack on one part would be construed as an attack on all, with an obligation for all to defend. With the emergence of self-governing dominions the theory evolved that a major war involved the participation of all, but the degree of participation was a matter for self-governing dominions to determine. In 1939 South Africa's government was divided on the issue of whether it was bound to participate at all in a war in which the rest of the Commonwealth and Empire was involved; indeed if Britain had gone to war with Germany over the 1938 Sudeten issue South Africa, and very probably also Canada, would have remained neutral. Germany's 1939 attack on Poland provided the Old Commonwealth and Empire with a last flicker of unity. By 1945 the trend towards national individual foreign and defence policies which had emerged in the 1920s had reached a point at which it was clear that neither Britain nor any other self-governing Commonwealth member saw itself necessarily committed to mutual defence. The attainment of independence by the Asian nations, India, Pakistan, Burma and Ceylon (Sri Lanka), with their very different defence perspectives marked the finish of any total imperial defence unity. The British government made it clear it would assist neither side in the India–Pakistan conflicts, nor did it feel the need to offer more than weapons and diplomatic support (India's specific requests) when

193

China attacked India in 1962. Britain did assist Malaysia with troops (a force of division size) in the Indonesian 'confrontation' operations[1] but was not prepared to join Australia and New Zealand in their provision of units to fight in South Vietnam. Equally Britain found herself without any Commonwealth military support, and very largely without even political support, at the time of the Suez intervention in 1956. It is then the existence of self-governing dominions, to use the pre-1945 term, or fully independent Commonwealth members, therefore, that makes the pattern of British military relations with her former imperial possessions so very different from those of France. In matters military, these nations formed initially a pattern, later sometimes as an English-speaking assistant or surrogate, and sometimes a rival in the process of Asian and African decolonisation. And it was only by the free determination of several Commonwealth governments (but not all, as Pakistan and Ceylon did not participate) that the Commonwealth contribution to the U.N. Force in the Korean War came into being.[2]

Service in action together – in two World Wars and Korea – provided a major historic reason to reinforce links of the imperial era. Military and naval men in the original Commonwealth wished war-time associations and camaraderie to be maintained, officers and political leaders in countries advancing to independence were impressed by the success of British systems and saw – at first only in some cases – no need to consider alternative models. All were agreed on the British concept of a 'non-political' army. Most too agreed on the desirability of a volunteer force rather than obligatory national service, and the recruiting and morale value of many of the exchanges and liaisons remains a major reason for the continuance of many links. From the British point of view other reasons for the maintenance of traditional links were a paternal concern, seen as being in the interests of both Britain and the territory concerned, a strategic interest in good relations with friendly governments together with the use of facilities and the support of economic investments overseas – this strategic interest was of course heightened by the Cold War – and also an interest in future sales of defence equipment.

The links have taken and take varied forms: a very few specific Commonwealth military arrangements, participation of some members in various regional defence pacts, a few specific bilateral treaties and formal agreements between Britain and a particular Commonwealth country, a very much larger number of much less formal arrangements, the retention by many successor nations of the essentials of British military organisation, and lastly a small number of sentimental links conveniently summarised as *mystique* or *esprit de corps*. It is also possible to discern a general evolution of these links in three stages – an initial pre-independence foundation-laying stage; a transition stage in which Britain supplied arms and sometimes unit commanders, squadron and ship commanders, commandants of schools and other specialist staff and training missions; and a developed stage. These stages occurred at various times – in the cases of Australia, Canada and New Zealand 19th century to 1914, 1918–1939 and post-1945 respectively; with the Asian Commonwealth members and the Sudan pre-1939, 1945–54, and post-1954 (with Malaysia a few years later); and in the cases of the African Commonwealth countries pre-1952, 1952–64–5 and post-1965.[3]

The few purely Commonwealth links fall into two groups, the first being British metropolitan military involvement in various forms arising from the imperial past – the defence of Malaysia already referred to is the major example, but the British defence of Belize (formerly British Honduras) against Guatemalan claims, involving a battalion or so of troops, is a second. The present position of Gibraltar and the Falkland Islands is one entirely dependent on British military support, and a garrison is an important element in Hong Kong's status. A very small force of British troops was sent into Anguilla in 1967 to restore order after the breakdown of Anguilla's relationship with St Kitts. In theory Britain remains responsible for the defence of a few remaining colonies and other polities named 'associated states'.[4] Some of these maintain very small forces of their own, in all cases British-trained and equipped. The other purely Commonwealth military associations have been the increasingly vague inclusion of defence matters in various Commonwealth Prime Ministers Conferences in the 1940s and early 1950s, and a series of Commonwealth Chiefs of Staff Studies held in Britain at two yearly intervals from 1959 to 1967.[5]

Britain has a number of links with Canada arising from joint membership of NATO; co-operation with Pakistan under

CENTO (earlier Baghdad Pact) arrangements was very close in the 1950s but declined somewhat in the 1960s; while SEATO has provided an opportunity for the continuance of British links, mainly naval, with Australia and New Zealand.

No British parallels exist to the complex co-operation, monetary and defence treaty arrangements entered into by France with some of her territories at independence.[6] The most noteworthy[7] was the Treaty of Defence and Mutual Assistance between Britain and Malaysia in 1957; this provided for Britain to maintain naval, land and air forces, and for a Commonwealth strategic reserve in Malaysia and for British assistance to Malaysia in the event of attack.[8] An agreement (not a treaty) with Kenya in March 1964 provided for the use of remote areas of Kenya territory for British Army training and naval facilities at Mombasa.[9] The only other agreement providing for a British garrison was that with Malta in 1964, though the 1968 agreement with Mauritius also granted Britain certain naval facilities in the southern Indian Ocean.[10] Apart from these there are no permanent British bases in independent Asian Commonwealth countries, and neither bases nor garrisons in African states.

The less formal arrangements have included the provision of British Army − and other services' − training teams and missions and single instructors for special subjects, and the large-scale provision of places in a very wide variety of British Armed Forces training schools and establishments.[11] In the cases of the original Commonwealth countries similar arrangements also provide for a number of officer and a small number of warrant officer exchange appointments.[12] The training so provided does, of course, tend to reinforce the organisational legacy. Only a few Commonwealth countries have attempted totally to recast the British organisational mould of military units[13] − their approximate size, regimental organisation and the different responsibilities of officers and non-commissioned officers, Regulations and disciplinary procedures, training methods, roles of the various arms of a service (i.e. the difference between army engineers, electrical and mechanical engineers, signals and pioneers − all of which are separate corps in the British Army and have generally been reproduced as small separate corps in new nations), and perhaps most important of all, command and staff procedures. A number of countries have found that officers trained outside the

British system have found it difficult to adjust on their return; this difficulty led several African countries to seek Canadian, Indian or Pakistani help since these nations followed the overall British pattern.

The links of *mystique* and *esprit de corps* are very difficult to pin-point but are nevertheless real. Corps and regimental badges, belts and uniforms may be adaptations based upon British origin; service and mess customs, the significance of regimental Colours, the special raising of flags at particular occasions, parade ritual and music, even service humour all may contain some element of British inspiration; the names of barracks and camps may commemorate World War victories in which local troops and British troops fought side by side.[14] Personal friendships formed with British officers during cadet training, maintained perhaps by staff training together, all have significance. Although, obviously, officers of those states which have become republics no longer owe allegiance to the British Crown, the British Monarch is still held by many soldiers in a very special regard.[15] For nations who remain part of the Sovereign's realms some British military decorations may still be awarded – Australians were awarded the Victoria Cross for bravery in Vietnam. Finally many British regiments have regimental affiliations with Commonwealth regiments, though these in practice amount to little.[16]

It should however be noted that the pattern of these arrangements is not exclusive to the Commonwealth – armies such as that of Jordan follow many British organisational patterns, training missions have served in a variety of different countries, a very large number of countries send personnel to Britain for training, British officers are sent on exchange to a number of West European armies and to the U.S.A., and British regiments have also had European affiliations.

Despite the trauma of partition India was fairly well-prepared for an independent military existence in 1947, and Pakistan not far behind; the bloodshed, recriminations and hostilities of the period have tended to overshadow the reality of the preparations. The British imperial Indian Army had been designed to be a separate and distinct field army with its own complete range of logistic support services, depots, training establishments, ordnance installations and staff training.[17] The British officers were on an Indian Army establishment making their careers in

India, entirely separate from the British Army. Indian cadets had begun to train at Sandhurst shortly after World War I, an Indian Military Academy had opened in 1933.[18] The expansion of the Indian Army in World War II had accelerated the move both to self-sufficiency and Indianisation; by the end of the war there were a number of brigadiers and colonels, well-trained and with very recent combat experience. Partition gave Pakistan a number of very capable officers, but left India with many of the major installations (except the Quetta Staff College) and all the arms factories. The quantities of military equipment in the sub-continent, a legacy of the war, ensured an initial adequacy for both nations.

The actual partition of assets was undertaken – among the military – with surprising ease bearing in mind that regiments had to be broken up as they had been structured, since the Indian Mutiny, on the basis of companies organised by race, caste and creed, though with officers of any origin. In the circumstances of shared war experience and trust this proved a strengthening factor. In addition the British were popular on account of their willingness to depart, their impartiality was accepted, and the Kashmir question had not then become acute. India retained some 300 British officers initially, the number falling to some 65 for the period 1949–1952. These officers were seen as being on contract terms; a few held major appointments such as Commander-in-Chief, Commandant of the Staff College and arms directors, others were technical specialists. In Pakistan a few unit commanders were British at the outset, and rather more officers were retained in the same type of duty as in India. But both armies had dispensed with British officers by 1953, and the last metropolitan British troops had left the sub-continent in 1948. No formal military treaties were signed by either country with Britain, and both immediately began to pursue their own foreign policies. The only British military constraint was a directive that no British officers were to participate directly in the Kashmir fighting. Since their independence, India has purchased British, Czech and Russian equipment (and some French aircraft), while Pakistan has acquired British, American, French, West German and Chinese material.

Neither Ceylon nor Burma had maintained any sizeable military establishment prior to 1939; Ceylon's wartime expansion provided foundations for her post-independence army for which British and Soviet equipment has been purchased at various times. Burma experienced particular difficulties on account of the Japanese occupation. Burma, Ceylon and Pakistan used training facilities in Britain, the first two nations extensively, in the early post-independence years; though Burma ceased to do so in the mid-1950s. Its large army is poorly trained with obsolete World War II equipment. Pakistan sent selected cadets to Sandhurst until 1970[19] and still continues to use Staff College and Royal College of Defence Studies facilities. Ceylon resumed sending cadets to Sandhurst in the Senanayake government period but ceased to do so on the return to power of Mrs Bandaranaike. Bangladesh has sent a very small number of personnel to Britain following her secession from Pakistan. Malaya also had only very small pre-war forces[20] and the Japanese occupation prevented any development of them; Malaya's military progress was therefore delayed but the exigencies of the insurgency movement in the late 1940s then led to a very rapid expansion; from 1948 to 1957, the year of independence, eight new battalions were raised. There had been Malay officers before the war; in the late 1940s and 1950s sizeable numbers were sent to Britain and Australia, and with British assistance a military cadet academy opened. New Zealand assisted in certain fields, notably survey. The Malay government saw no urgency in Malayanisation, a British general was still Army Commander in 1962, and British officers retained in key appointments for two years beyond that date. The expansion continues – the Malaysian Army now has 29 battalions, and British armoured cars, artillery and anti-tank weapons. Of all Commonwealth countries, Malaya was the most heavily dependent on British military help and support on its emergence as a nation; without this support a very different type of nation would have appeared.

Malaya became Malaysia in 1963, Singapore seceded as a separate state in 1965. Singapore has pursued a more varied defence assistance policy. Israeli help and advice, and the Israeli pattern of a largely part-time force, trained in a period of national service but which can be quickly called out, have been the basis of Singapore's defences, though the Israelis themselves have now returned home. British assistance was and still is also used for cadet, staff officer and radar installation training, Australian help is also used, and light tanks have been purchased from France. British military forces, steadily diminishing in size to one battalion in a combined Australian, British and New Zealand brigade only from 1968 onwards, were finally withdrawn from the Malay peninsula in 1974, although a British Gurkha battalion remains in Brunei at Brunei's wish and expense.

The major military difference between British Asia and British Africa (and between British Africa and French Africa) is that of scale.[21] Britain never saw her African possessions as an important source of military manpower,[22] nor was there a large established institutionalised Army as in imperial India; even after Indian independence when an expansion in Africa was for a time considered such a scheme was rejected. A very small number of British officers served on two or three year secondments, there was no British African officer corps. Certain other general conditions also made for very different transition arrangements. Except for Mau Mau in Kenya[23] the political transition, while exciting, was free from any large-scale violence – either anti-colonial or communal. As in India and Pakistan, but not as in Malaysia, there were not seen to be any vital strategic facilities which Britain must retain;[24] Britain vaguely hoped she might maintain a peace-keeping role in the Indian Ocean, but the political unacceptability of this policy (particularly after Rhodesia's declaration of independence) and the cost led to its abandonment. Lastly, although British African units had been loosely grouped together – the Royal West African Frontier Force in the West and the King's African Rifles in the East – the battalion units were in fact organised and recruited by territory,[25] each colony having one or two battalions. Further, although within these battalions certain ethnic groups thought to be 'martial' might be preponderant, the battalions were not affiliates of any traditional religious or political structure: they were therefore quite well placed to be seen as agents in the building of a new nation. The transition period in Africa then essentially saw three devolutionary processes – an africanization of the officer corps, the start of the conversion of local battalions equipped and trained for an internal security-gendarmerie role into a combat army, and the provision of light artillery (usually mortars), engineers, and support units.

At first the British Command Generals in Africa were cautious towards change.[26] There were political difficulties, particularly in East Africa, and also legal problems in each territory, but transition began in West Africa in 1951. A few general if unrelated features of the transition merit mention at this point. It is possible to note three types of officer – the very few (Gold Coast only) commissioned in World War II, promoted warrant officers and sergeants, and young school leavers trained (usually) at Sandhurst. Sandhurst's courses have never been very testing academically and the colonial school systems were, after a slow start, able to produce men well able to deal with them. Particular problems arose with technical and administrative units which had sometimes been centralised by region – i.e. East Africa – so that each service had to be split and then rebuilt; on the other hand regional groupings enabled certain services, e.g. initial officer training and some technical training, to be undertaken regionally. In these difficult and complex situations many political and military leaders inevitably turned to the British, who at least knew the background and had some realistic idea of what was possible; after independence it was normally only Britain who posted a Defence Adviser (Attaché) to its mission in the newly independent capital. These officers were often very influential in the early years.

West Africa was particularly fortunate in the foresight of the British West Africa Command General, Sir L. Whistler, appointed in 1951. He urged an immediate increase in African N.C.Os and a programme of africanization of officers to produce captains in five to ten years, and majors in ten to fifteen years.[27] Places were reserved at Sandhurst – which at first could not all be filled – and preliminary training courses for potential officers begun at Teshie, near Accra, for both Nigeria (to 1960) and the Gold Coast. The first Nigerians arrived at Sandhurst and at other British officer cadet schools in 1952, the first Gold Coast cadets a few months later. Because of settler prejudices in Kenya and the Mau Mau campaign, East Africa was much slower, the first warrant officers[28] being given commissioned status under the title of *effendi* in 1957 after a course run for all three territories in Kenya. Northern Rhodesia and Nyasaland were even more delayed by their inclusion in the Federation of Rhodesia and Nyasaland, dominated by Southern Rhodesian prejudices, their first officers not being commissioned until 1964.

The Gold Coast achieved independence, as Ghana, in 1957, but its army was still commanded by a British general, a number of important staff posts and all battalion commanders were British.[29] President Nkrumah found himself on the one hand irritated by the presence of British officers, notably during the period of the presence of Ghana units in the UN Force in the Congo where these officers (and also their Ghanaian colleagues) worked to UN directives in preference to his own, and on the other hand anxious to double the size of his army from one brigade to two. The foundations had, however, been well-prepared and Ghana's army was able to survive the dismissal of its British commander and the return to Britain of almost all the British officers in 1961.[30] Even before the return of the British officers Ghana had begun to diversify; some cadets were sent to India, and British assistance was replaced, on a much reduced scale, by Canadian officers in the case of the army and Indians in the case of the Navy. Ghana continued to send a few cadets to Britain, however, together with officers for training at the Staff College. One or two cadets were sent to Pakistan and India. Israel and the Soviet Union both promised military help but apart from the provision of some very out-of-date Soviet equipment this assistance appears to have been negligible. On the other hand Nkrumah drew substantially on East German and later Chinese help in his intelligence organisations. After the fall of Nkrumah there was an increased use of British facilities, particularly with a small parachute unit (later disbanded by the Busia government). British arms, including armoured cars, were also purchased, though Israeli mortars were preferred.

Nigeria's case was more complex due to its internal political condition. The post-independence Nigerian government felt the need for a more specific arrangement with Britain, and a formal defence agreement was signed, setting out British military assistance in return for the use by Britain of certain air staging facilities (but no garrison). This agreement led to large popular street demonstrations and had to be abrogated in 1962.[31] However the retention of a British Army general (on contract, in this case) was seen as necessary, again largely for internal reasons.[32] At independence Nigeria had some fifty local officers; after independence officers were sent for training to Britain, Pakistan, Canada, the USA and Ethiopia (whose military academy had been established and organised with a considerable

amount of help from India). With the collapse of the civilian
government and the commencement of the 1967–70 civil war,
the Federal government drew heavily on British help in the
supply of ammunition, other military stores and medical
equipment and, later, *Saladin* armoured cars for the greatly
expanded army. Britain, however, refused to supply additional
artillery (Nigeria had already some British 25-pounder pieces) or
any bomber aircraft. The British formula for the aid was
'traditional in kind' (i.e. the type of material supplied previously),
but no limit was placed on the quantity. Nor would Britain supply
bomber aircraft. Bombers and field artillery were then obtained
by Nigeria from the USSR. Britain supplied no British army
personnel.[33] Since the end of the civil war the Nigerian Army has
returned to Britain as its source for the purchase of light tanks and
armoured cars, but the air force has continued to purchase strike
aircraft from the USSR.

Sierra Leone was similarly dependent on Britain in its early
years of independence. In 1961 only eight out of the thirty-seven
officers of its army were local,[34] and the first Sierra Leone officer
was sent to the Staff College as late as 1962. Sir Milton Margai
saw no urgency in africanisation and appeared to prefer a British
army commander. Personnel, in very small numbers, were sent
to Britain and to Ghana for training; Israeli facilities were also
used. The Sierra Leone army then became involved in the
nation's politics to its detriment, and after the return to civilian
rule the Siaka Stevens government found it necessary to request
the help of Guinean troops in 1971. These have now returned
home, and Sierra Leone's chastened army has resumed sending
individuals to Britain for training – probably the most cost-
effective option open. Weapon purchases, however, have been
made from several countries, perhaps the most noteworthy being
Switzerland.

The stages of Sudan's military progress equate more to those of
West Africa than those of her southern neighbours. At
independence, the replacement of British officers by Sudanese
was complete – in part a reflection of Foreign Office anxiety to
forestall Egyptian ambitions. In its first decade of independence
Sudan purchased equipment simultaneously from Britain, the
USSR and Yugoslavia, sending personnel to a variety of countries
of which Britain was one for training.

Tanganyika was the first of the three East African territories to gain independence in 1961, and in consequence the least well prepared – her first Sandhurst products having only just returned and with British officers commanding units and in staff appointments. British officers had prepared plans to complete africanization by the end of 1964 but were overtaken by the mutiny of January 1964.[35] The mutiny coincided with President Nyerere's reappraisal of his nation's development strategy, and after brief usage of Canadian, Ethiopian, Nigerian and Israeli assistance,[36] Nyerere came increasingly to view the military as being involved with the nation's overall development. The Tanzania Peoples Defence Force's officers are expected to be party members, their duties may include civilian administration or political work tours, the country's national service provides for a military option by fit young men rather than a 'volunteer professional army' and a peoples' militia has been formed as both a general and a political reserve. British models came to be seen as irrelevant, or even elitist and harmful,[37] and only Chinese assistance and facilities are now used; the Chinese apparently demanded and obtained a monopoly position.

Kenya gained – in relative East African terms – from being the last of the three territories to become independent in 1963. Unlike its neighbours Kenya had a British garrison for reasons already noted; this garrison had served two additional purposes. It had served to reconcile Kenya's whites to majority African rule by a reassurance of help if it were needed; its presence had acted as a restraint on Somali ambitions in N.E. Kenya while the Kenya Army was being built up. Both President Kenyatta's overall policy of national unity and reconciliation and his immediate military needs led him into a more close military relationship with Britain than either of his neighbours. The defence agreement with Kenya has already been noted – after its signature the British garrison returned home. At independence the first Kenya officer to command a battalion was appointed,[38] but Kenyatta retained the services of a British army general (on secondment) either as Army Commander or Chief of the Defence Staff until 1969. A very large British Army Training Team operated in Kenya until 1970, though these personnel had been withdrawn from unit or sub-unit command appointments earlier. Some British born officers were also appointed on contract.[39] Although a few Kenya

Army personnel have been sent to countries (Israel being perhaps the most noteworthy) other than Britain for training, these have been a minority. In 1962–65 a very large number of Kenyans passed through Sandhurst and Mons Officer Cadet School;[40] smaller numbers continue to do so, and also attend the Royal Military College of Science, Staff College and Royal College of Defence Studies courses. The *Shifta* operations – against Somali insurgents – of the early post-independence years required some expansion of the army and also greatly improved its morale and efficiency. Kenyatta has seen benefits without constraints upon his military and foreign policy as a result of the British alliance – he was the first of the East African leaders to seek British help in suppressing a January 1964 army mutiny, he firmly rejected the Soviet Union's offer of some elderly *T34* tanks as a gift and refused to accept into the Kenya Army a number of cadets trained – under private arrangements – in Bulgaria.[41] Almost all Kenya's military equipment has been purchased from Britain, but Kenya's Air Force is now ordering American strike aircraft – probably because the USA offered easier credit terms.

Kenya, and since 1965–66 Tanzania, have followed a consistent path in their military policies. Uganda's policies have veered from one direction to another. At independence in 1962 Uganda's first cadets had returned from their training in Britain, it also had some promoted *effendis*. The Army commander and the battalion commander of Uganda's one battalion were, however, British, as were its Regimental Sergeant Major, its Paymaster and some other officers. In 1963 a second battalion was created, again with British help and key personnel. The mutinies of January 1964, again after unheeded warnings by a British commanding officer and put down by British troops flown in from Kenya, led to the removal of most British personnel from the battalions, and then, by late 1964, the final departure of British personnel from Army Headquarters as well. Uganda then found herself in the same situation as Ghana, very anxious to expand her army to six battalions (two brigades) as a result of both external and internal problems,[42] and accepting assistance from a variety of sources. Cadets and staff officers continued to go to Britain for training, Israeli training staff arrived, some use was made of occasional Russian and Chinese help, and when the decision to mechanise the infantry was made in 1967 Uganda army officers and warrant officers were sent to Brno to learn how to operate the large, costly (and totally unsuitable) *OT64* Czechoslovak armoured personnel carriers. After the military coup, Amin expelled the Israelis and then sought British help. Finding that realistic payment arrangements were required for this, and immersed in his quarrel with Britain over the Uganda Asians, he turned first to Libya, who sent troops for the defence of Uganda,[43] and thereafter, after a brief and apparently inconclusive flirtation with France, to the USSR.

Somalia's military problems were those of the fusion of two different colonial legacies – a new force had to be created from an Italian-style gendarmerie, and the British police and a small military unit. At first Somalis were sent to Britain for training but this was discontinued in 1963 after the break in diplomatic relations; since then Soviet and recently Cuban assistance has steadily increased.

Zambia found itself very poorly prepared for an independent military existence, largely as a result of the Federation government's blocking of the training of African officers and also the return to Southern Rhodesia of most military equipment of value at the dissolution of the Central African Forces of the Federation; the situation was worsened by the necessity to use military forces to cope with the Lumpa religious sect. Guns to fire the independence salutes had to be imported in great haste. Zambia sent cadets for training to Britain from 1964 onwards, drew on the advice of a British Army Training Team until 1968, and employed on contract a number of white officers – many born in Central Africa – who had been officers in the Federation's forces.[44] President Kaunda had at first no quarrel with the British system, his son and nephew were both sent to Sandhurst; as the difficulties created by the Rhodesian situation worsened, however, pressures for a rapid africanisation built up, and at the end of December 1970 the Army Commander (an ex-Federation Army officer on contract) and almost all the remaining seventeen contract officers were dismissed. The white officers, both contract and British, posed particular problems. The contract officers were found to be disloyal, some supplying intelligence to Salisbury. The British government limited the use of British officers to training. Zambia's needs were for good battalion officers who could contain border incursions by Portuguese forces. A new local Army Commander, an African officer who had only left Sandhurst some five years previously, was accordingly appointed. Thereafter, apart from some technical assistance in connection with the purchase of British *Rapier* guided missiles, Zambia began to seek training assistance and facilities elsewhere, in particular Ireland and in Canada and also Tanzania, with Italians assisting the Air Force. The Zambian Army was planned to expand to thirteen battalions, but only four have so far been established. Malawi, too, was handicapped by the Federation arrangements at independence, but like Kenyatta, President Banda opted for an almost exclusively British assistance and training pattern. British officers on secondment assisted at first, later replaced by British and other white ex-officers of British origin but in some cases central African birth, residence or military service, employed on contract. Cadets were sent to Mons, occasionally to Sandhurst, and officers were sent to Britain for staff training, but Dr Banda saw no need to hasten specific africanisation; an African battalion commander only appeared in 1970 and an African Army Commander in 1972.[45]

These specific transition arrangements constitute dependence and independence at one level. It is perhaps worth mentioning a few general and disparate matters arising from this period which may have some bearing on the overall relationships. Britain, of course, retained no troops in Africa other than those from Kenya briefly engaged in internal security work in Swaziland in the mid-1960s, and a battalion operating under UN authority supervising the referendum in the former British (Southern) Cameroons, in 1960–61. Only in Kenya did the British legacy, carefully realigned but maintained by Kenyatta, provide for another military force of any size – the Police General Service Unit. The colonial units had always had a small role as a vehicle of modernisation;[46] this tradition and the exhortations of new political leaders to soldiers to see themselves as agents of nation-building reinforced a British-transmitted attitude of armies being custodians of true patriotism at a soldier's level. The British vocational view of an officer's calling has led some commentators to observe that military officers formed a very important part of a post-colonial élitist structure in Africa – a section of the élite with guns.[47] Certainly the first and generally very conservative generation of African officers were often less nationalist (when

nationalism was meant to equate with radicalism) than their
political leaders; many saw their professional links with Britain as
strengthening their own position *vis à vis* political leaders who
had hoped their armies would turn into armed political support
groups. These political leaders then began to pressure their armies
either by starvation of funds, the creation of rival units or a total
theoretical reappraisal of the role of the army, all policies which
led to tension.

Sometimes difficulties would be created by unauthorised
actions of individual ministers – notably in Kenya, and in Uganda
where bribery played an unattractive role in the arrangement of
military assistance to replace the departing British. One or two
minor oddities in the British system, inconsequential in Britain,
occasionally became serious on transplantation to African
countries – excesses of regimental loyalty, suspicions of officers
trained under short-service arrangements towards the long-
service Sandhurst regular, the friction between the youthful
inexperienced Sandhurst subaltern and the experienced sergeant
or sergeant-major,[48] some suspicion among military officers of
their police opposite numbers, some anti-academic attitudes and
the traditional slowness of military men to adjust to changing
political situations, worsened perhaps by their continuing need to
work with expatriates. On the other hand the innate overall
British respect for military men and military rank seems also to
have been transmitted in some measure. One final paradox, again
African rather than Asian: military strength seems to play very
little part in African international political leadership rivalries or
in OAU prestige ratings.

Following the end of the transition arrangements, British
official military (as opposed to private commercial assistance
occasioned by weapon sales) assistance to overseas countries has
been on a very limited scale, a limitation reflecting the United
Kingdom's own economic difficulties and in some cases doubts
on the stability or ability to pay of countries requesting help. It is
in general pragmatic – it is not governed by any all-embracing
statement of government policy; it makes little difference between
Commonwealth and non-Commonwealth states in theory,
though in practice a Commonwealth country may have a slight
advantage in any competition for a particular facility by virtue of
longer or some previous usage of that facility. Assistance is given

after a request for it has been received. The assistance falls under four general headings, the first being after-sales support for defence sales where advisers and training staff may be sent for the introduction of new equipment. In this context new equipment refers to material manufactured in the Royal Ordnance Factories (or built or refitted in the Royal Dockyards in the case of ships) and is therefore a government to government deal; the two largest of these commitments in 1975–76 were the sale of *Chieftain* tanks to Iran and Kuwait (neither of whom are Commonwealth members).[49] The second pattern of assistance meets the need of a very large number of countries for staff training and certain other specialist military advice or training.[50] At present Britain is supplying instructional help at the Sudan Staff College, and a number of officers have been sent to Nigeria and Ghana for the establishment of Staff Colleges. These two spheres of activity in respect of army matters are administered by the Director of Military Assistance Overseas, a Major-General whose office is situated in the Ministry of Defence; this appointment was created in 1968–69. He has a very small staff, nothing in any way comparable to the complex arrangements and special training courses for officers to serve overseas operated by the US Military Assistance Institute.[51] British military personnel sent overseas on either of these two spheres of activity are known as Loan Service Personnel; the cost is borne by the receiving country.[52] The officers or non-commissioned officers concerned serve for a tour of duty and may then be replaced by others on British LSP terms or sometimes by retiring or retired British officers on contract.[53] The arrangement is almost always ended by the receiving country when the need for it has been filled.

The third sphere of activity is the continuing provision of training facilities in Britain. The vast majority of these arrangements provide for the attendance of overseas military personnel at courses primarily designed for the British Army – senior officer courses at the Royal College of Defence Studies, the Staff College,[54] Royal Military College of Science degree courses, Royal Military Academy officer training courses, specialist infantry, engineer, ordinance, signals, military police, bandsmen and musicians, Women's services, military medical, and parachute courses, etc.[55] The courses cover almost every aspect of military life except recruit training; for almost all courses many more bids are received than can be accepted. A few separate courses exist, usually for one country's personnel in suport of a particular weapon sale such as that of *Chieftain* or *Scorpion* tanks,[56] or in a particularly sensitive subject such as intelligence.[57] The agreements that arrange these facilities are concluded at a relatively low level – British Defence Adviser or Attaché to an Army Chief of Staff for example; they may be simply memoranda or an exchange of letters. It is perhaps worth noting here that New Zealand provides comparable facilities for Fiji, though Fiji also send cadets to Britain for training.

A final and very small sphere of activity is one whose principal purpose is to provide a volunteer army with an outlet for energy and travel, but with goodwill and the maintenance of tropical expertise also included – minor development work. Small teams of Royal Engineers have recently been at work building bridges in Zaire,[58] at road and bridge-building in Kenya, Malawi, Sudan and Ethiopia and at drilling boreholes in Botswana. These very minor schemes are British-paid and equipped.

With the older established Commonwealth countries the wheel has turned full circle. The Jungle Warfare School in Malaysia, established by the British Army, is now entirely in Malaysian hands with one British exchange instructor; a small quota of British students is accepted. On account of the heavy strains of the Ulster situation on the British Royal Military Police, small detachments of the Royal Australian Military Police assist in the patrolling of the British home garrison centres of Aldershot, Catterick and Tidworth. Australian, New Zealand and Canadian officers are exchanged as training school instructors and sub-unit (i.e. company or squadron) commanders.[59] British units train regularly in Canada. The newer Commonwealth countries find foreign exchange shortages preclude this, but two exchanges of battalion-size units were arranged at Ghana's request in 1968 and 1969; British units have training rights in Jamaica and, as already noted, in Kenya; units are also to train in Gambia.

Britain has also assisted a number of Commonwealth countries with naval training. In the cases of Canada, Australia and New Zealand naval training arrangements have existed since the last decades of the nineteenth century, Australia and New Zealand sending their cadets to the Royal Naval College, Dartmouth for training, and officers of all three countries attending a whole variety of courses in British naval establishments and ships. These arrangements were maintained for the first years after the end of World War II; their nature then began to change. On the one hand some facilities came to be considered more in the context of regional defence treaties than Commonwealth, and with the reduction of British sea-power both Canada and Australia began to use United States Navy facilities in addition to those of Britain. In the case of Australia this extended to the purchase of American-built ships and missiles. On the other hand Australia and Canada both also developed their own training and construction facilities, culminating in Australia's ceasing to send cadets to Dartmouth for their initial training.[60]

After independence India and Pakistan also ceased to use British help in general terms, but frequently did so and continue to do so at present with the introduction of specific equipment, most notably with India's aircraft carrier which was British-built and the *Sea-King* helicopter, and for higher grade technical and staff training. As with military links, in the case of Australia these are now becoming more those between equal partners, Australia having developed the *Ikara* missile system, which has been purchased by Britain.

Immediately after independence British naval missions assisted in the training of the Kenyan, Nigerian and Ghanaian Navies; in the latter case as already noted Indian Navy instructors were also present. Malaysia, Thailand, Singapore, Jamaica and Trinidad regularly send officers to Britain for training, and Algeria, Kuwait and Egypt do so at irregular intervals; Ethiopia and Libya also did so prior to their respective revolutions.[61] In the late 1960s and 1970s Iran has been the recipient of the largest amount of British naval assistance, a number of officers being trained in RN ships and establishments. Australian, Canadian and New Zealand officers continue to serve on exchange loans with the RN and specialist officers such as constructors, aviators and technical staff are sent for training.

Naval assistance has sometimes posed particular personal relationship problems – the British Army could draw on colonial experience in respecting local susceptibilities, an experience the RN generally lacked; naval discipline is more formal and superficially less friendly (in Britain Army officers address each other by Christian names, naval officers by appointment). Crises, when they occur at sea, can arise very suddenly in conditions which may be tense; there is no room for more than one person in command. RN officers have in consequence been regarded in some countries rather more as efficient commanders, and later instructors, than as fellow members of a club.

The RAF has supplied assistance and training facilities to Ghana, Kenya, Nigeria, Zambia, Malaysia and Singapore, but the assistance offered by this service has been less than those of the Army and the RN as much British equipment has proved too sophisticated, complex and costly for former colonial territories. Zambia, for example, while using RAF training and British aircraft help initially, opted for Italian aid, and Yugoslav, Italian and Canadian aircraft. Kenya used Israeli facilities. Nigeria has a number of Soviet aircraft, a link established in the civil war; prior to 1966 they had used West German training aircraft and aid and also Italian aircraft, with British helicopters. Kenya and Ghana have some Canadian transport machines, and Ghana some Italian light jet strike aircraft. An RAF squadron was sent to Zambia for a brief period after Rhodesia's declaration of independence as a defensive measure.

Lee notes the continuance of British patterned intelligence structures in independent African states immediately after independence;[62] these had taken the form of a Central Intelligence Committee composed of representatives of the administration, police Special Branch, Labour Ministry and other relevant ministries. Here the Head of Government or other Minister simply replaced an outgoing colonial Governor;[63] Lee also notes that the British Security Service and Police Special Branch began to offer courses for colonial officers in 1950.[64] In some cases British officials remained a member of or were associated with this committee for a brief period.[65] Most states however appear to have recast their intelligence structures to conform with their new domestic political alignments within a few years of independence; President Nkrumah sought Indian and East German assistance, but his disparate organisations were dismantled after the 1966 coup. Several countries retained a number of British police officers for varying periods of time, in some cases in very senior posts, notably in Lesotho and in Kenya, where Sir Richard Catling remained Kenya's Inspector General of Police after independence. For the most part, however, officers retained for the early post-independence years were specialists such as finger-print or ballistic experts.

British administrations had expanded police training facilities in the 1950s including local courses in both West and East Africa for ordinary police officers and some specialists such as CID and Special Branch.[66] No need to send all or any junior police officers on first appointment to Britain was therefore perceived and training in Britain was reserved for meritorious officers with a number of years' experience to their credit. These came to be sent to the British Police College, first at Ryton and Dishforth and then in its new location at Bramshill, Berkshire. In response to requests from many countries, Commonwealth and non-Commonwealth, an 'Overseas Command Course' was instituted in 1970 and it is perhaps the most noteworthy of the present-day British police training facilities. The course is of three months' duration and has been attended by some 252 officers from 52 countries, a number of whom had already attended some earlier police training in Britain.[67] The Course syllabus includes Police Management, Crime, Traffic, and Internal Security and Public Order. Many graduates of this course have been appointed to very senior posts on their return home. Other police training provided by Britain includes lower level instruction on CID and traffic duties.

In conclusion it must be emphasised that military independence is a very remote prospect for almost all nations. Only the USA and the USSR can make any real claim to the full status. Even when a nation has equipped and trained its armed forces it may find severe constraints upon its policies imposed by mundane matters such as spare parts, fuel supplies and ammunition – Egypt and Ethiopia afford two very clear recent examples of this.[68] The repair of aircraft and the dry-docking of warships can pose even worse problems (Ethiopia, for example, finds it necessary to use Malagasy dock facilities). One or two anglophone African states, in particular Uganda, have the capacity to launch an attack on a neighbour (providing that attack produces the desired results very quickly); most have forces of defensive value only.[69] In the process of decolonisation and the establishment of independent states from former colonies Britain provided newly independent states with the right to choose their military links. In the early years of independence governments or parliaments in a number of countries felt the need to assert this right as a sign of independence, or in response to specific domestic criticism of continuing military relationships with Britain. In the 1970s many countries have passed this early post-independence stage, some have had discouraging experiences with military assistance from elsewhere. The very informality and straightforward nature[70] of the assistance now offered has led many countries, Commonwealth or non-Commonwealth, to maintain, return to or establish military links with Britain.

NOTES

1. It is perhaps appropriate to note here, in the context of territories not self-governing at the time, that troops from Northern Rhodesia (Zambia), Southern Rhodesia, Kenya and Fiji were used alongside British and Malayan units in Malaya in the 1948–55 campaign. This however represents the only use of non-metropolitan troops on British imperial commitments since 1945 (with the exception of Gurkha battalions, a very different relationship and one outside the scope of this paper.)

2. This force, of division size, included British, Canadian and Australian infantry, New Zealand artillery and an Indian medical unit, with a South African Air Force squadron and British, Canadian and Australian naval support.

3. It is perhaps relevant to note here that a few small but wholly independent Commonwealth countries deliberately opted for no armed forces at all, or at most a very small barrack police gendarmerie. Gambia, Botswana, Lesotho and Swaziland have followed this course in Africa, leaving them in defence matters dominated by Senegal in the case of Gambia and South Africa in the case of the other three.

4. These include Ascension and St Helena, Belize, Bermuda, British Virgin Islands, Brunei, Falkland Islands, Gibraltar, Gilbert and Ellice Islands, Hong Kong, New Hebrides, Pitcairn Islands, Seychelles (to be independent in 1976), Solomon Islands and certain small West Indian Islands. Rhodesia remains legally in this category, but lies outside the scope of this paper, nor does the paper examine in any detail the considerable British military involvement with and assistance to the Persian Gulf states which had been linked to Britain by treaty relationships in the imperial era. These treaties had given Britain control of defence and foreign relations, but they had not been annexed to the British Crown.

5. These were known at first as *Uniflex* and later as *Unison*. At first all Commonwealth countries sent their Chiefs of Staffs or senior representatives. These studies discussed technological advance and staff procedures at a very philosophical level. At the last, in 1967, Tanzania and Uganda were not represented at the British government's request, the subject of the study being counter-insurgency.

6. In considering a theme of dependence and independence it is perhaps

relevant to note that it was British diplomacy, backed up by a military presence in British Guiana, that secured the treaty in 1966 with Venezuela by which the latter abandoned certain territorial claims. Independent Guyana has maintained military links with Britain since independence, although purchasing some small arms from West Germany.

7. Others included agreements with Australia covering nuclear weapon testing in the 1950s and an agreement with the Maldive Islands providing for the use of Gan.

8. It is perhaps noteworthy that when 'confrontation' actually occurred Australia remained neutral despite Britain's involvement.

9. The agreement also covered military assistance for the training of Kenya's forces, these are examined later.

10. Britain has also had a number of agreements with South Africa over the ownership and use of the Simonstown naval base. This was leased from South Africa, and transferred to South African control in 1955, Britain continuing to use its facilities whenever required. This arrangement, modified in some respects in 1967, was finally terminated in 1975. British military relations with South Africa are outside the scope of this paper.

11. Perhaps the most formative of these was the R. M. A. Sandhurst. For a description of the effect of Sandhurst on a young Ghanaian see Colonel A. A. Afrifa, *The Ghana Coup*, London, Frank Cass, 1966, 49–52.

12. There are also very few Indian exchange appointments; an officer is, for example, posted to the British School of Infantry.

13. President Nkrumah attempted to break the British mould with his creation of the 1st President's Own Guards Regiment, a Russian-equipped political unit bitterly resented by the Ghana Army. Tanzania has attempted to align the Tanzania Peoples Defence Force much more closely with the nation's overall development policy; Singapore has an entirely different defence structure, both of these are noted later. Guyana is also developing a politically oriented army.

14. There is not universal acceptance of the British tradition. An important element in Canada's decision to unify her armed forces and provide a common – and entirely different – uniform was a need, particularly among French Canadians, to create a Canadian tradition. Occasional criticism of British tradition appears in Indian and Pakistan military journals. At a more personal level and particularly in African armies officers who have not benefited – by travel or education – from such links may well be jealous of those who have.

15. General Gowon of Nigeria is a notable example, but the regard is not confined to African officers (nor, of course, to soldiers – President Nkrumah may also be seen in this light). A francophone equivalent would appear to be the charisma of General de Gaulle.

16. These links extend to Australian, New Zealand, Malaysian, Canadian, some West Indian and some African units, but very few are with India, Pakistan or Bangladesh, a curious survival of the old jealousy between the British and Indian Military establishments in imperial days. They really only assume any practical form when personnel of a regiment are serving anywhere near their affiliated unit.

17. There had been one or two omissions, notably artillery (except mountain artillery) until the mid-1930s, a legacy of distrust dating from the Indian Mutiny.

18. There were two curious brakes on the process of indianisation – the Indian non-commissioned officers, particularly those elevated from the ranks to 'Viceroy's Commission' status, were not always receptive to the young Indian school-leaver subaltern, and the British War Office retained the right to fill half the staff appointments in India with British Army officers for reasons of experience and career structures. These brakes had in fact put the Army behind the police and the Civil Service where indianisation was complete at almost all levels. But already by 1939 the Indian Army had some 450 Indian officers out of 3,000. I am grateful for the opportunity given to me by Lt Col A. A. Mains, late Indian Army, to read his unpublished manuscript which contains much useful information both first-hand and following research in the former India Office archives.

19. Only a small number of cadets were sent each year, the bulk being trained at home. This pattern of sending two or three cadets designed to provide a cross-fertilisation of ideas, is one adopted by many countries. It has considerable military value to the sending army but should not be taken as any measure of dependence after the transition stage. Countries with policies sharply critical of Britain, for example Iraq, continue to send one or two cadets per year to this day.

20. These, further, had been Malay only, and at the outset from certain states only. In the 1930s recruitment was extended to all states, but Malay Chinese and Indians only became eligible to serve in 1953, subject to a rule that Malays must hold 80 per cent of the officer appointments.

21. In the inter-war period France maintained some 40 African battalions, Britain fewer than 10. Britain maintained no peacetime metropolitan troops south of Khartoum from 1914 to 1952.

22. The structure of the system, although complex, illustrated the policy. The British War Office paid some contribution to forces which might prove useful as a nucleus for expansion in war, but colonial governors were overall responsible for their own territorial units. The Command generals in West and East Africa were responsible only for training, military supplies and military administration.

23. And of course the turbulence and revolution in Zanzibar; Zanzibar however had no military forces at independence in 1963.

24. For a while the British Ministry of Defence planned for permanent military and air bases in Kenya (a large barracks was built for this in the late 1950s), but the retention of this was not seen as indispensable in the face of the growth of nationalism.

25. It should be noted that in practice recruits did sometimes come from other territories; the Gold Coast Regiment (of the RWAFF) attracted a number of its soldiers from Niger and Volta. The African battalions did not follow the Indian pattern of racial/ religious companies.

26. J. M. Lee, *African Armies and Civil Order*, 1969, 38–9, notes that in 1947 the British Cabinet said there could be no objection in principle to African officers. But their powers over white NCOs remained a problem.

27. Sir J. Smyth, *Bolo Whistler*, 1967, 199.
28. Among this course was Idi Amin, and products of other early courses included the two first Kenyan generals, Ndolo and Mulinge. The status was seen as equivalent to the Indian Viceroy's commission. It should perhaps be noted that platoon commanders in the KAR units were often warrant officers.
29. By the end of 1960 Ghana had two brigadiers, and three out of the four battalion commanders were Ghanaian.
30. In addition British training assistance was present in a number of activities – for example the creation of the Ghana Military Academy and junior staff courses. A very few British regular officers remained in appointments such as brigade administration for a further year or so; one made an accidental discovery of one of Nkrumah's freedom fighter training camps during a morning ride and reported it to his brigade commander (the later General Ankrah), to whom its existence was a surprise. (The late Major R. Alers-Hankey to the author, January 1972.) A few other officers remained on contract terms.
31. Political opposition was heightened by the fact that it was one of very few matters on which Nigerian politicians could parade a show of unity.
32. The senior Nigerian officer was an Ibo and distrusted by the Northern-dominated government; the presence of a British general was seen by many politicians as a safeguard against a coup.
33. The issues here were very complex. Britain had a considerable political and economic stake in Nigeria which the British government perceived best preserved by the continued existence of the Federation. The supply of arms was, however, politically unpopular in some quarters in Britain. Nigeria could almost certainly, at some inconvenience, have purchased these 'traditional' supplies elsewhere but wanted the diplomatic boost that British supply afforded. British public criticism was offered the formula of British aid not being more than fifteen per cent of Nigeria's total weaponry purchases. This formula has been alleged to have served to conceal the quantities involved, as the cost of Nigeria's purchases of guns and aircraft from the USSR was so much greater. For an examination of this subject see J. St J. Jorre, *The Nigerian Civil War*, 1972, 296–305. The point in sum is that Nigeria needed British weaponry for political rather than military reasons, and Britain wanted to see Nigeria survive as a nation; the dependence was mutual. Some former British servicemen, in particular pilots and airfield staff, were recruited by the Federal government on contract, they also recruited Egyptians.
34. 'Sierra Leone and her Army', W. Gutteridge, *British Army Review*, October 1961.
35. The British battalion commander of the first unit to mutiny had warned Tanganyika's Minister of Defence, Kambona, of trouble impending but no action had followed; the reasons for this inactivity were those of internal Tanganyikan politics; Kambona believed that he might profit from a breakdown. Ostensibly the difference of opinion between Kambona and his British officers had been over the use of army units for developmental work; the real reasons were more personal.

36. A battalion of Nigerian troops was sent to maintain order in Dar es Salaam; the British Royal Marines from an aircraft-carrier who had in fact restored order after the period of anarchy sparked off by the mutiny were not acceptable on political grounds. A photograph of President Nyerere inspecting the Marines does, however, exist, and at that point in time his dependence was almost total. Russian, East German and later Chinese assistance was provided to assist the small gendarmerie of post-revolution Zanzibar. West German assistance was made available to the Tanzanian Air Force, this and Canadian facilities also lasted only briefly.

37. Tanzanian cadets were sent to Britain as late as 1967, however – despite the break in diplomatic relations.

38. Kenya also had over 35 officers who had been commissioned under the *effendi* arrangements together with its first British products.

39. Contract officers or NCOs are usually former British Army personnel; their advantage to a government is that they are usually cheaper than British regular officers supplied on secondment (for which the receiving government usually pays). Their disadvantage is that their knowledge may be out of date. In some subjects such as pay, quartermastering, etc. this does not matter, but with a subject such as anti-tank missiles modern expertise may be very important.

40. This school, designed to produce short-service officers for the British Army, has been much used by foreign countries anxious for officers quickly – in the 1960s the Mons course was under six months while Sandhurst took two years – or by the poorest countries such as Malawi. It has now been amalgamated with Sandhurst.

41. Both these matters were related to Kenya's internal politics at the time. The USSR had been supporting Kenyatta's former Vice-President, Oginga Odinga, a Luo by ethnic group; the cadets trained in Bulgaria were apparently nearly all Luo sent there by Odinga. The story is a complex one and can only be briefly summarised here. The Israeli training arrangements appear also to have been kept secret and may well have been known only to the President and a limited circle of ministers.

42. The external problems were those of the Simba rising in the Congo (Zaire), the difficulties of Rwanda, Burundi and the Sudan – refugees from all spilled over into Uganda; the internal problem was, of course, the Buganda Kingdom.

43. The threat, as perceived by Amin, appears to have been a British military intervention to extricate the Asians.

44. Zambia was not able to appoint a Zambian as a battalion commander until 1970.

45. The reader may need to be reminded of the original army sizes at this point. Zambia's army was one battalion size at independence in 1964, at which time Malawi also had one battalion; this has now been expanded to two.

46. Many battalions ran schools and dispensaries, the wives of senior NCOs would as 'lines managers' induct the wives of recruit soldiers into Western methods of housekeeping and child care.

47. For an extensive development of this theme from a Marxist standpoint, see R. First, *The Barrel of a Gun*, 1970, *passim*. Another variant of this pattern

of thinking argues that colonial forces supported the efforts of colonial governments to govern by ethnic balances, rather than by revolutionary doctrines. This cautious approach was, it is argued, inherited by successive military leaders leading them to look askance at innovations such as youth services, national services corps, Workers Brigades and attempts to align military leadership with political guidance.

48. In colonial units officers commanded by orders, often brief, while NCOs might engage in a lengthy palaver if circumstances permitted. Difficulties arose where young and inexperienced African officers adopted their predecessors' methods. NCO frustration was a major internal cause of the East African mutinies of 1964, and a contributory cause to the breakdown of discipline in Nigeria's army in 1966.

49. Sales of equipment, both by government factories and private commercial companies, can be seen at one level to be profit-making, and are designed to be so. At another level, however, the profit represents some contribution towards the equipment's research and development expenses, resulting in lower unit costs for all concerned. British commercial firms design and produce military and naval equipment specifically for Third World countries (i.e. equipment not suitable for Britain's own forces, e.g. the Vickers *Vijayanta* tank purchased in large numbers by India, the Short and Harland armoured personnel carrier, the BAC *Strikemaster* aircraft in use in Kenya, Singapore and New Zealand, the Folland *Gnat* aircraft used by India and various corvette designs purchased by African and Asian navies); but the British Ministry of Defence does not produce such equipment – in contrast to France where sometimes the French Armed forces are later constrained to purchase and use such equipment even though it may not meet their own particular preference.

50. For example Sudan receives some assistance from specialist tank officers, other countries are assisted in a variety of 'middle-management' technical fields.

51. An Appendix to this paper shows the total number of British Army, RN and RAF personnel serving abroad on loan, exchange or in training and advisory duties.

52. In a very few cases some Foreign and Commonwealth Office funds may be made available to assist.

53. The British government may assist in the recruitment of officers on contract but does not always do so. These are contracts between the individual and the government concerned and are not underwritten by Britain, though arrangements for their implementation may be made by the Crown Agents.

54. The British Army's Staff College at Camberley, for example, has taken in two recent years officers from USA, Canada, Australia, New Zealand, S. Africa (discontinued), Greece, France, Netherlands, Belgium, Denmark, Italy, Yugoslavia, Norway, Philippines, Pakistan, Malaysia, Brunei, India, Nepal, Jordan, Thailand, Brunei, Japan, Indonesia, Israel, Sri Lanka, Singapore, Egypt, Zaire, Kenya, Nigeria, Ghana, Ethiopia, Sudan, Sierra Leone, Zambia, Malawi, and Peru. Naturally some of these need to be seen as exchanges but the majority reflect difficulties that many countries experience in staff work.

55. The Appendix to this paper lists countries with personnel training in Britain.
56. These courses tend to be at technical non-commissioned officer level where language weakness may be an additional reason for a special course.
57. By this is meant military intelligence only, covering such subjects as air photograph interpretation, operational intelligence and security of military personnel against espionage, sabotage and subversion.
58. 'Bridging in the Congo', Majors P. E. Morrison and S. L. Rooth, *British Army Review*, August 1969 describes one such operation.
59. A visitor to British Army of the Rhine is quite likely to find, to his surprise, that a tank squadron or artillery battery of a British regiment may be commanded by an Australian major on a two-year exchange.
60. Australia and New Zealand, although ceasing to send their school-leaver entry for primary training, continue to send somewhat older sailors selected for commissioning to Dartmouth and most young officers on certain specialist courses, for example anti-submarine warfare. Missile specialists, on the other hand, go to the US Navy.
61. It should also be noted that a number of Latin American countries receive British Naval training assistance.
62. This practice, too, followed the Indian example. The (imperial) Indian Joint Intelligence Bureau was taken over by the Nehru government; the Bureau's Karachi branch formed the nucleus of the Pakistan intelligence structure. Both have of course now been totally re-shaped.
63. Lee, 63–4.
64. *Ibid*, 31.
65. *Ibid*, 63–4.
66. *Ibid*, 43.
67. These include all the present Commonwealth African countries with, in addition, Sudan, Egypt, Ethiopia and Tunisia, and all Commonwealth Asian and Caribbean territories with in addition Burma, Thailand, The Philippines and Dominica. I am grateful to the Police College, Bramshill, for supplying me with this information.
68. This is a very complex topic. In sum it can be said that India assembles *Vijayanta* tanks and some aircraft (but not her main interceptor force of Soviet fighters) under licence, and can manufacture light artillery, small arms and vehicles. Neither Pakistan nor Malaysia has any manufacturing capacity though they can assemble and repair smaller weapons. No anglophone African state (except South Africa) has any weapon or ammunition manufacturing or repair capacity at all. On the other hand, as a result of arms sales to the Middle East, and NATO standardisation in the case of rifles and ammunition, spare parts and ammunition for British equipment is often available from a very wide variety of sources, some of dubious repute.
69. Uganda's forces have recently been re-equipped with Czech and Soviet equipment, which includes modern armoured personnel carriers and assault river-crossing equipment; *The Times* 27 June 1975 carried photographs of Soviet *GSP* tracked pontoon ferries on their way to Uganda, wrongly noting them as missiles. Uganda has a border dispute with

Tanzania, the Kagera river would be a natural Tanzanian defence line.

70. A staff officer of a large Asian army recently remarked that he hoped his country would continue to draw on British facilities as, unlike other foreign advisers, his country's experience had been that if British experts felt that British-made equipment was not the most suitable for his country, they would then actually propose foreign alternatives.

Appendix

I *British Armed Services Personnel serving on loan, on exchange or in training and advisory duties overseas*

Personnel totals: Numbers at year ended 31st December

	1971	1972	1973	1974	1975	Currently Serving
Australia*	159	120	136	107	89	86
Bermuda*	4	4	4	4	4	4
Brunei*	52	49	58	64	90	90
Canada*	96	88	90	87	81	76
Fiji*	—	—	1	—	—	—
France	7	7	7	7	8	8
Germany (FR)	4	4	6	11	14	14
Ghana*	1	—	—	—	—	—
India*	1	—	—	—	—	—
Italy	—	1	1	3	1	1
Iran	21	48	36	62	71	74
Jamaica*	1	—	—	—	—	—
Kenya*	104	28	14	31	18	18
Kuwait	106	112	112	118	118	118
Libya	71	14	—	—	—	—
Malawi*	29	22	19	4	—	—
Malaysia*	209	165	87	51	19	16
Nepal	1	1	1	1	1	1
Netherlands	7	9	9	10	10	10
New Zealand*	4	5	7	9	7	7
Nigeria*	12	9	7	3	—	7
Norway	2	2	2	2	2	2
Oman	92	121	154	170	235	216
Pakistan	1	1	1	1	1	1
Peru	—	8	—	—	2	2
Qatar	—	—	—	1	8	8
Saudi Arabia	6	5	6	6	6	6
Singapore*	79	91	89	42	13	13
South Africa	1	1	1	1	1	1
Sudan	—	5	6	9	8	8
Union of Arab Emirates	121	105	77	53	43	44
United States of America	137	154	186	191	191	195
Zaire	—	9	9	—	—	—

*Commonwealth Member

Source: *Parliamentary Debates, Commons,* 23 February 1976

Notes

1. These figures show personnel from all three Services, separate Service figures are not available. The Army would, of course, form the large majority of the totals.

2. The figures include neither NATO nor other regional pact garrisons or headquarters staff, nor do they include military, naval or air attachés, nor the small Royal Engineers development project teams.

II *Foreign Armed Services Personnel Training in Britain at the end of January 1976*

Countries of Origin

Algeria	Lebanon	
Argentine	Libya	
Australia*	Malawi*	
Bangladesh*	Malaysia*	
Barbados*	Mauritius	
Belgium	Nepal	
Brazil	Netherlands	
Brunei*	New Zealand*	
Burma	Nigeria*	
Canada*	Norway	
Chile	Oman	
Denmark	Pakistan	
Ecuador	Peru	
Eire	Philippines	
Egypt	Portugal	
France	Qatar	Total number involved
Gambia*	Saudi Arabia	approximately 2,250
West Germany	Sierra Leone*	
Ghana*	Singapore*	
Greece	Sri Lanka*	
Guyana*	Sudan	
Hong Kong*	Sweden	
India*	Switzerland	
Indonesia	Thailand	
Iran	Tonga*	
Iraq	Trinidad and Tobago*	
Israel	Turkey	
Italy	United Arab Emirates	
Jamaica*	United States of America	
Japan	Venezuela	
Jordan	Yemen	
Kenya*	Zaire	
Kuwait	Zambia*	

*Commonwealth Member   Source: *Parliamentary Debates, Commons*, 23 February 1976

Notes

1. As in Table 1 these figures include soldiers, sailors and airmen, the largest number again being soldiers.
2. National totals are not available.

9

Aid and Cooperation: French Official Attitudes as seen in the Jeanneney, Gorse and Abelin Reports

Jean Poirier and Jean Touscoz

Since a collective work reflects the views of its authors, we may begin by seeing who was entrusted with the delicate task of evaluating and making recommendations on cooperation policy, which of course entails making assessments of development problems. The first striking feature – see Table I – is that members of all three Committees were mainly leading figures of the French establishment. One might have thought that a major qualification for these 'wise men' – as they were often called – would have been some actual overseas experience; instead it can be seen that only a minority of members had any overseas experience.[1] This is astonishing, for it must be acknowledged that the nature of the problems in developing countries can scarcely be grasped by those without first-hand experience on the spot. It was also disappointing that there was so little representation of the social sciences, especially of anthropologists who could have provided an understanding of the social context of development and the social implications of policies of aid.[2]

Since the Committees were fairly similar in composition,[3] it is not surprising that all three reports are on similar lines, a certain difference of terminology reflecting mainly the different timing as we move from the relatively traditional Jeanneney (1963) through Gorse (unpublished, but 1971) to Abelin (1975). All three documents proceed in the same orderly fashion from general principles, through appraisals of projects completed and in progress, to

TABLE I

COMPOSITION OF THE COMMITTEES

Members	Jeanneney	Gorse	Abelin
Politicians	J. M. Jeanneney J. Bertaud M. Lemaire		R. Monory R. Schmitt A. Voisin
Administrators (metropolitan power)	J. Baillou J. Sadrin	P. Dehaye Marjolin Y. Roland-Billecart	J. P. Benoit J. de Chalendar P. Dehaye J. Doublet J. Ripert Y. Roland-Billecart P. Toulemon M. Viaud
Administrators (overseas)	G. Buis J. Chauvel L. Pignon P. Rondot	Gal B. Cazelles M. Gorse	B. Clergerie S. Hessel
Social scientists	G. Balandier		G. Balandier G. Blardone
Historians			J. Devisse
Lawyers	J. Donnedieu de Vabres R. Gregoire		M. Flory M. Niveau P. Sabourin
Economists	F. Bloch-Laine Cl. Gruson L. Malassis S. Nora F. Perroux	J. Ripert	Y. Berthelot G. Caire
Health			
Scientific research	P. Auger		D. Dollfus
Private or semi-public sector	R. Charadame J. de Precigout		J. Audibert R. Colin J. P. Gardinier P. Galoni Y. le Gall J. Sagne

TABLE II
ATTENTION GIVEN TO VARIOUS TOPICS IN THE THREE REPORTS

	Jeanneney	Gorse	Abelin
1 General trends	XXXX	X	XX
2 Agriculture	X	XX	X*
3 Industry	XX	XX	X
4 Health, Demography	X	X (demography)	–
5 General education	X	X	X*
6 Technical education	X	–	X
7 Literacy programme	–	–	–
8 Rural training	–	–	–
9 Research	XX	X	XXX
10 Financial situation	XXX	XX	X
11 Legal framework	XX	X	XXX
12 Status of cooperators	XX	X	XXX

– indicates that the report did not deal with this problem
* indicates that these problems were the subject of a 'mission of dialogue' sent overseas.

recommendations for the future. The Jeanneney report approaches the problem from the historical angle and discusses the significance of colonial rule and decolonisation. The Gorse report is more pragmatic and, wrongly perhaps, pays less attention to the major policy choices – e.g., should aid be tied or free, concentrated or diversified – and more to detailed diagnoses and specific recommendations. The Abelin report bravely raises the important problems but seems to hesitate over solutions, while providing a number of practical suggestions for changes in ways and means.

On the fundamental question there is complete agreement in the three reports as to both the legitimacy and the necessity of aid and cooperation on grounds of international solidarity as well as the interests of developed countries who can in this way increase their influence and prevent confrontation between rich and poor countries. Accusations of neo-colonialism made immediately after decolonisation are discussed in the Jeanneney and Abelin reports and rejected. The former is particularly emphatic in justifying the action of the developed countries; it argues that aid should be a process of material development founded on the interests of receivers and donors alike. The Gorse report takes a similar line, arguing that the Third World has become of marginal importance to the industrialised world whose economy in fact does not require its cooperation. While the meaning of cooperation – this term is generally preferred to 'aid' – is not analysed by the two first reports, the Abelin Committee explicitly states that 'the world in 1975 no longer accepts the classic ideas of aid and assistance and this fact gives the idea of cooperation a new dimension' (p. 13); it also mentions accusations of 'cultural imperialism' made increasingly by the Third World. However, it makes little constructive use of these signs of awareness.

New factors arising from political and economic changes are recognised in all three reports. Jeanneney analyses the decolonisation process, emphasising the end of any kind of imperial cohesion and solidarity and the need for this to be replaced by the development of new kinds of solidarity. Gorse deals more briefly with these problems, just mentioning the disappointing results of the first decade of effort and concluding that bilateral actions will not suffice. On the other hand, Abelin stresses the importance of recent economic changes – the new situation following the increase in oil prices and the emergence of the 'Fourth World'; political changes – the time has come for choices to be made since France cannot do everything, and donor countries have to respect the varying policies of the sovereign developing countries; and changes on the cultural front – giving recognition for the first time to the importance of a real cultural dialogue in view of the desire of certain countries to find their own cultural identity.

The main policy choices are set out in all three reports though in quite contrasted terms. Thus, should aid be bilateral or multilateral? Jeanneney hardly discusses the matter, so firm is its unquestioning commitment to bilateral cooperation. Gorse supports France's participation in 'international cooperation', and recommends increasing the French contribution to the UN Development Programme from 2 per cent to 5 per cent, along with more support for the International Association for Development, the Asian Development Bank and the Interamerican Bank. Even so, the report is still almost completely dedicated to dealing with bilateral cooperation. On the other hand, Abelin emphasises the importance of international cooperation (the UN Development Programme to which France in 1975 contributed 3 per cent of the budget, the World Food Programme, the European Development Fund, the World Bank, the UN Food and Agriculture Organisation, etc.) and points out that the new states 'even if they state their preference for bilateral aid, still keep a watchful eye on the positions taken by us in international organisations dealing with population, environment, industrialisation, food, agriculture, health, education, the law of the sea, raw materials and trade and development. Even if France's friendly position on these subjects appeals to them, they still watch very closely the amount of our contributions to the particular funds and programmes' (p. 44). However in the end Abelin pleads for a regionalisation of the French effort, in effect seeking at once a concentration of bilateral aid and an increase in multilateral aid.

Should aid be concentrated or dispersed more widely? This problem was posed in 1963, with Jeanneney giving a list of arguments for and against, and concluding that there was much to be said for both and that 'cooperation with Africa must remain a major but no longer exclusive priority' (p. 76).[4] Gorse, noting that aid to African countries has decreased proportionately, advised that this tendency should not go any further and recommended a one-third increase in the percentage of aid given to the African states and Madagascar. It stated, though not quite in so many words, that attempts to help non-French-speaking countries were of less importance. The Abelin report considers that cooperation with African countries should still get relatively high priority but that, due to the new economic situation, France should, from now on, 'recognise its limits ... approached by people from all over the world, it must make choices' (p. 16); at the same time the report hopes that French efforts will be united with those of other developed countries to add to multilateral aid. On the whole then it seems that whatever the general public may have thought, and in spite of attempts to disperse aid more widely, a considerable consensus still exists in favour of a cooperation policy which is more concentrated than dispersed.

Should aid be tied? The reply to this question depends on whether cooperation is seen as disinterested, with the beneficiary regarded as an equal partner able to make its own choices, in which case aid should be given without imposed conditions. It is to be noted that the 'untying' of aid may happen when the donor country either does not require precise advantages in return for its money or when it does not wish to be tied to a given aid flow for a particular project. Current ideas and developments are constantly bringing us closer to the complete 'untying' of aid.[5] Jeanneney comes out frankly in favour of tied aid (pp. 111–12), commenting that in the last analysis tied aid is simply aid in kind; nothing is said about the reactions and views of the assisted country. Gorse does not deal with this question directly anywhere – a strange oversight – but from its general trend it would seem to be in favour of a progressive 'untying'. This is true of Abelin too, which says more on this subject in its general philosophy than in precise terms; it does not believe it necessary for assisted countries to keep among their demands that for untied aid,[6] and merely remarks that 'the leaders of cooperating countries are ready to discuss the allocation of funds to the projects they consider most important' (cf. p. 67). On the whole, therefore, the Committees gave this problem little attention, in our view a grave error of judgement since this is, rightly or wrongly, one of the basic issues in the eyes of developing countries.

Should aid be in the form of grants or loans? To some extent money given without any return is a problem from several points of view; although the recipients prefer it, they also see it as being more prejudicial to their national dignity; on the other hand, loans with a very low rate of interest are practically grants anyway due to the depreciation of money, while in some cases moratoria have been called or debts have been totally cancelled (as by President Pompidou for African countries). If in addition one adds that these facilities will have to be renegotiated because the burden of debt on the Third World is already considerable, the difference between the two types of aid can be seen to be less than might have been thought. Jeanneney alone analyses this problem in any depth, concluding that aid when given as an outright grant can be a danger to the donor and lead to complications. Gorse is silent on the matter while Abelin merely remarks that events have destroyed the traditional concept of 'aid'. In fact, no real attempt is made to debate the actual differences between the various concepts of aid, assistance, loans and cooperation. Here again a knowledge of traditional cultural values is essential to understand the attitudes of the recipients. For these people it is an insult to their dignity to receive without giving for their social life is made up of a rhythm of gifts and counter-gifts. Thus non-reciprocal aid is a non-starter. It is humiliating to be merely 'assisted'. Different countries react variously but usually on one or more of three lines of defence: they may deny the reality of the gift, calling it a reparation for the sufferings under colonialism; or they may denounce the false generosity, saying that technical assistance is neo-colonialism which benefits the donor country far more than the recipient; or they may demand a revision of aid policy – with all too often the result that terminology changes from 'aid' to 'cooperation', but without any real change in relations. This problem has yet to be solved; as we will see below, opinion surveys and additional enquiries in assisted countries would give us some valuable information.

The function of cooperation is to help bring about change in various sectors of these non-industrial countries. Of these none can be more important than agriculture, and more generally, the rural economy including animal husbandry, fishing etc. which represents from 80 per cent to 90 per cent of the economy. However, this is not always the view held by the assisted countries who often want to promote industrialisation without admitting that rural 'modernisation' is an essential prerequisite for industrialisation. Nor do our three reports, which agree on the importance of this sector, seem fully to understand its indispensability for development. Jeanneney mentions agriculture among the five priorities which it lists (health, agriculture, industrialisation, training and the promotion of crafts) without placing any special emphasis on its importance. Nor is it emphasised in Gorse either, although its proposals for rural development are interesting, being realistic, intelligent and novel. Gorse regrets that aid in education (often inappropriate – see below) is three times that given to rural modernisation. It reminds us that intellectual training often cuts young people off from reality[7] and recommends that no action should be undertaken without consulting traditional leaders. It lists a number of measures, not excluding the need for property reform. However the gap between the Minister's office and the field of operation is very wide and these fine words have not yet been put into effect. The Abelin report, unlike the others, does not deal with the problems of rural development directly (except in a mere appendix[8]) but concentrates on the perspectives of the 'new cooperation' of industrial promotion.

Industrialisation is the source of many misunderstandings in Third World countries; it is both the driving force and the symbol of development and as such it is often included in plans to the prejudice of less spectacular rural efforts. It copies the Western model, in spite of declarations proclaiming the African or Zaïre models. None of the three Committees attempted a definition of overall industrialisation; they keep to criticism or suggestions which, whatever their importance, remain limited in scope. Jeanneney extols 'industrial regionalisation' (in the framework of agreements between countries with complementary economies) and the stabilisation of raw material prices, whilst hoping that customs laws might be modified to allow a more open market in developed countries for industrial products from developing countries (cf. p. 96 ff.). Gorse presents a different view, emphasising that attempts should be made to encourage industries producing substitutes for imported products, so as to improve the poor countries' balance of payments. It also recommends the forming of regional groupings, emphasises the lack of private investment and as a new departure recommends that more should be done to adapt technology to the needs of the recipient countries. The Abelin report deals with the 'industrial environment' and asks for the setting up of a Centre of Research and Innovation, but does not propose any actual strategy, limiting itself to a study of the legal and administrative aspects of industrial cooperation.

Hygiene and health are dealt with only briefly: this is an extraordinary gap particularly since this is the area where actual results have been forthcoming and where all the developing countries continue to request aid. The problems involved are also far from being solved (all health policy now needs to be reorientated towards prevention). Jeanneney alone shows some interest, but has just part of a page on the exemplary achievement of the colonial period (p. 15) and another on the fact that the problem still exists (p. 86 plus appendices 13 and 14[9]). Otherwise there is a brief mention in Gorse of demographic problems and a cautious recommendation in favour of reducing the growth rate and setting up a research organisation.

On the other hand, education is the subject of much discussion, but each of the reports is only interested in one of its aspects. This, as we have seen, is where much of the money goes and it merited a more detailed examination. Four very different areas are to be distinguished: general education (primary, secondary, higher[10]); the various sectors of technical education; teaching of literacy skills and basic education; rural instruction. There is nowhere any overall evaluation of these four areas, a real gap to be filled in future. Scientific research is touched on in Jeanneney but only in the context of the status of technical assistants. Abelin also shows little interest in education itself; in what it says on scientific research, it seems to have been overtaken by events and reveals no awareness of the serious problems in this area which have become evident since 1975. Gorse deals more seriously with education problems, emphasising in particular lack of adaptation and excessively theoretical content.

When, finally, we come to the administration of aid policies we find that all three Committees give substantial attention to this aspect. They underline the decreasing amount of aid and its progressive diversification and although they are not able to go far in the delicate direction of 'real' aid (which would entail looking at such matters as disguised aid in the form of military expenditure and the 'repatriation' of capital), they do however deal in some detail with organisational and personal problems involved in implementation.

Since cooperation followed on the heels of colonial rule, the tendency of French administrators has normally been to give the responsibility for aid administration to former colonial officers though with adjustments of service structures. This was logical since it made use of the previous experience of those whose careers had developed overseas. However, it was in fact opposed to the desire – expressed with varying degrees of force – of ex-colonial countries to rid themselves of the colonial relation. The relationships between ex-colonial power and former colonies have always been officially described as satisfactory but they have in fact developed in an ambiguous atmosphere full of uncertain understandings and contradictions. In fact we have still to understand the complete revision of policy which needed to be made from the early 1970s when the Third World already entered into the third phase of its post-colonial history. The first stage, that of political independence, came to an end around 1960; the second, that of economic independence, is still in progress. The Third World's dramatic problem has been to attain international status at a time when neither of these kinds of independence could be totally achieved. But the real problem arose during the third stage of decolonisation, when cultural independence made its appearance with such ideals as a return to one's roots, cultural integrity and 'authenticity'. It was completely impossible for these multi-cultural societies to repudiate Western values; it was not just their technology which depended on them but their languages, legal systems, ethics, ideologies and religions. It is this very problematical political context which has shaken the organisation of cooperation and indeed of 'development' to its foundations.

The reports pay little attention to these new factors. Jeanneney, whilst emphasising the drawing up of international conventions rather than bilateral assistance, does not question the administrative structure of the time (1963) which was made up of an unwieldy bilateral structure of a Ministry of Cooperation on the one side and a General Secretariat for the Community and African and Malagasy affairs. (There is also however a 'General Secretariat responsible for Algerian Affairs', and the specialised departments of the Ministry of Foreign Affairs also play a role, with competition from the Finance Ministry and other technical Ministries, with no real coordination between any of them.[11]) Gorse develops this by proposing the creation of a General Commissariat or a General Delegation attached to Foreign Affairs, suggesting the nomination of a Minister-Delegate for Aid and Development, who, with the Prime Minister, would control the workings of an Interministerial Committee coordinating the responsibilities of the various interested administrative bodies. Abelin does not suggest any changes to current organisation, but makes three important suggestions. First, coordinated activities should be provisionally planned for several years ahead (without affecting the principle of the budgetary year) and the FAC (Aid and Cooperation Fund) should be kept better informed of current projects and activities. To this end, an annual report covering French intervention in each country coming under the Ministry of Cooperation should be presented to the FAC whose Management Committee should be enlarged and assisted by a select committee which would examine particular cases in detail. Finally, a new organisation should be set up: the 'Centre for Development Research and Innovation' whose task it would be to promote and coordinate all research in this field.

It would seem therefore that the Committees felt that administrative restructuring was a problem, without being able to find a solution for it. It may well be unfair to criticise them unduly on this point for there are real uncertainties and difficulties. For example, while some Third World countries wish to have their privileged position in relation to the ex-colonial power recognised through a special administrative framework, others want to assert their sovereignty and tend to see any special relation as part of neo-colonialism. It is probably true that in any case institutions in this field matter less than people; cooperation will be whatever the cooperators do.

As regards the relevant 'actors' in the exercise, above all those on the spot, the three Committees attach different degrees of importance to the problems raised. Jeanneney suggests that personnel employed abroad as 'technical assistants' should be administered by a 'Management Agency'; they should form part of French administration in order that their rights and careers should be guaranteed. For this purpose there should be established a 'Cooperation Service' which would allow a certain number of young people called up for military service to be excused this obligation in return for working (after training) on cooperation projects abroad for a fixed period of from twenty to thirty months. This new scheme has been widely applied with varying results but unfortunately the organisation of the preparatory training has been deficient.

Gorse pursued this matter by emphasising the need for both relieving and renewing the personnel on the spot, the former involving the smooth replacement of European technicians by national technicians and the latter being aimed at preventing the cooperators from staying too long in the country and getting stale. Gorse also approximates the position of the cooperators to that of agents from the private sector and favours a university training for future cooperators with more careful selection at the outset. Abelin makes a detailed examination of the legal problems and position of VSN (National Service Volunteers) and expresses the wish that these should be better recruited, better trained and more carefully supervised. Their duties and rights should be laid down precisely in a 'charter' agreed with their country of destination. Abelin also repeats the emphasis on retraining. Abelin additionally examined the higher education and research fields with regard to personnel exchanges.[12]

In actual fact it would seem, strangely enough, that many of the Committees' recommendations have been followed. The serious deficiency is in the area of the training. A considerable number of organisations have been allowed to proliferate – centres, institutes, associations – with all the consequences of different standards and overlapping activity that one would expect. Even a minimum training is often not ensured. This gap explains the disillusionment of some cooperators and the failures or mistakes of others. There is an urgent need for reorganisation in this field. The various branches of the service need to be defined and their training put in the hands of training teams on site but with every branch given a general orientation course to help with acclimatisation in the recipient country. Young Europeans can easily have misconceptions about men and matters abroad. They need an in-depth introduction into the society where they will be spending several years; applied anthropology should play an important role in this education, since only a knowledge of the specific values of these very different societies can give the cooperators the basic understanding which is indispensable to the human contacts they have to make.

In spite of the importance of the work carried out by the three Committees, a number of problems have been left untouched, either due to lack of information or for political reasons. Without trying to fill these gaps, we would in conclusion just like to mention a few salient points.
1. The reports did not propose any general cooperation policy based on clear principles and worked out in detailed programmes. They were most probably not equipped to do so.
2. Indeed, these three analyses, often profound, are too concerned with legal matters and do not make enough effort to put the facts in a total social context. The Committees failed to make adequate use of the social sciences, in particular anthropology.
3. These methodological shortcomings can perhaps explain the fact that the Committees appear indifferent to one crucial kind of information – knowledge of opinion, or rather of opinions

in all their diversity and complexity, in the countries being assisted. True, the special 'dialogue missions' sent out by the Abelin Committee gave rise to interesting documents, but they do not replace proper local enquiries. Knowledge of people's reactions, of their desires and criticisms, would certainly have caused a few surprises.[13] For example, we note that a part of the intelligentsia is genuinely very hostile to French cooperation policy, being convinced that it is part of a Machiavellian plot by ex-colonialists; several years ago attention was drawn to the existence of a real 'myth of cooperation'.[14]

4. It is time to conduct our discussion with new states in a language shorn of euphemisms, to try to make an honest assessment of the advantages and difficulties which the various methods of cooperation may cause for both sides, above all to recognise the new forces which have recently come into play. It is necessary to acknowledge, for example, that the claims of cultural independence and authenticity have often degenerated into xenophobia; plain speaking is necessary for an effective exchange of views.

5. From this point of view there should be in-depth discussions of two important problems. First, the size of the return on capital. This is seen as resulting either through tied aid or otherwise in a constant flow from Third World countries to European countries. But in any proper overall accounting of this process, the multiplier effect of investments has to be taken into account; this means that even if invested capital is returned intact to the investing country, it can still have fulfilled its function of creating economic progress. Second, the protection of investments. Reports of bankruptcies come in from all sides. Obviously it is within the responsibility of sovereign countries to decide to nationalise companies set up in their countries, but it is then no good failing to give investors real guarantees and at the same time complaining that foreign investors do not come forward. It would appear that only action can find a solution.

6. Honest discussion of the results of cooperation should lead to a more balanced judgement. Mistaken methods explain most of the failures to date of development. The first priority must be that of rural development, which determines all other

development, since industrialisation requires, by definition, a market which can only be provided if a surplus is available (and this too cannot be divorced from the primary sector of the economy).[15] In the field of education profound structural changes are called for in the organisation of teaching; it is not enough to condemn present structures as inappropriate. It must also be acknowledged that current teaching, which is too remote from the real rural world of the majority, simply speeds up the rural exodus; more emphasis should be placed on the technical branches of education. Finally, health programmes need to be completely rethought; it is ridiculous to spend money on building a modern hospital (to save at best hundreds of lives each year) which could be spent on sending out travelling health vans (to save several tens of thousands of lives); preventative medicine should have clear priority over curative medicine.

We therefore consider it necessary to make an attempt to rethink the basics of cooperation, its methods, problems, the choice of priorities and, more generally, its end effects. We cannot go on transferring non-transferable experience or techniques which are ill-suited to the actual situation. Of course political choices often affect decisions. But there is a very wide consensus that recognises – beyond all egoism – a profound solidarity uniting nations despite their ethnic and cultural differences. The three Committees agreed on the need for and the legitimacy of cooperation; it still remains to give cooperation its real basis; a truly international one which alone will allow cooperation to realise its full potential.

NOTES

1. These are only the actual signatories; they certainly received assistance through consultation and special cooption, but this does not affect our comments.
2. There were two anthropologists among the twenty members of the Jeanneney Committee, none on the Gorse Committee and one on the Abelin Committee.
3. These Committees were perhaps supposed to be 'think groups' but in fact they turned out to be bodies designed to tackle quite particular problems.
4. Arguments for concentration: the existence of privileged relationships, a common language, France's responsibilities towards its previous colonies,

the wishes of the people concerned who want special treatment, the presence of French-educated elites, relative geographical proximity, greater efficiency. Arguments for dispersal: risk of being accused of paternalism and neo-colonialism, the need to be present in areas of world importance, an end to 'zone of influence' policy.

5. Usually aid is described as 'tied' if it consists of money which requires a direct reciprocal supply of various products; 'specific aid' (as opposed to 'general aid') refers to money which is given for a particular project without the receiving country being able to transfer resources elsewhere. These are two different types of cooperation, but as far as the recipients of the aid are concerned, they both represent a restriction of their freedom.

6. The priorities of the Abelin report are: the diversification of trade; the end of the monopoly of commercial and intellectual influence; the in-depth study of traditional culture (back to the grass roots); the speeding up of Africanisation in every area.

7. 'The primary school pupil is definitely lost to traditional society ... The process of education seems to make pupils less able to do productive work than the illiterate ... so school, which should help to lift traditional society out of underdevelopment, paradoxically acts as a brake on growth.'

8. Where, in a rather contradictory way, they are listed as of prime importance (p. 71). Matters of importance are not usually dealt with in appendices and the report as a whole puts the emphasis on industry not agriculture.

9. Annex 13: 'Some principles of technical assistance in public health matters'.
   Annex 14: 'Multilateral technical assistance by the WHO and cooperation on health in Africa and Madagascar'.

10. Obviously each level has its own problems: the extent of cooperation varies very much according to level.

11. The report does however welcome, in an Appendix, the attaching of Cooperation (in the shape of a Commissariat) to the Ministry of Foreign Affairs and the creation of a Cooperation Council which would lay down basic policy guidelines.

12. It notes that up to now the most frequent visitors to the Third World universities have been young people at the beginning of their careers; experienced lecturers should be encouraged to go out, with a guarantee of return to their university after their contracts have expired.

13. Research should for that matter also have been carried out in France where polls on the subject of aid are rarely taken. Various strands of African opinion could have been examined systematically by content analysis of daily papers and periodicals.

14. Cf. J. Poirier in L'homme devant l'échec, ed. Jean Lacroix, Paris, PUF, 1970.

15. If the following two conditions are met there should be no problems in financing development: the stabilisation of prices of raw materials exported by the Third World, guarantees for private investment.

III

INSTITUTIONS
AND
CULTURES

10

Private Law in the New Francophone States

Eugène Schaeffer

The subject raises at least two problems of definition: the meanings to be given to the concepts of 'private law' and 'dependence'. In the case of 'private law' the difficulty is not in determining which branches of law are to be covered but in deciding whether to consider law as the body of formal or codified enactments or to expand the definition to cover law as the people of these states experience it, that is, to include traditional or customary law. This choice depends on one's philosophy of law; for this will determine whether the law of a state is seen as consisting solely of what issues from the duly constituted law-making authority or is regarded as including all those rules which govern behaviour and are accepted as constraints by the members of the society. Legal realism requires that we adopt this second definition; for it is customary law which shapes the lives of virtually all the citizens of these countries and which also influences most of the processes of law in these societies. This more general approach has the advantage – as well as the complication – of going beyond a static analysis and, by adding another dimension, takes us into the sociology of law.

This wider concept has the further merit of fitting in better with a concept such as dependence which at once obliges the lawyer to adopt a broad and flexible approach. Of course it is true that the legalistically-minded can find precise criteria laid down in international law for the 'independence' of a state. Moreover, it cannot be denied that the new African states satisfy these criteria; they are sovereign states, legislating independently in the domestic sphere with which we are dealing, and their laws are not subject to foreign control. From that point of view, the independence of these states as regards private law is complete and the supposed puzzle would simply not arise. But by now we are well aware that law and fact must not be confused; equality in law need not mean equality in fact — and the same applies to independence. The formal features of economic independence may disguise actual economic dependence. The appearance of cultural independence — an attribute seen as appropriate to every sovereign state — may hide an actual cultural dependence.

We may at this point raise the question whether economic and cultural dependence are of the same kind. (This question must not be regarded as alien to a lawyer; law is a social phenomenon and as such no stranger to either economics or culture.) It seems to us that economic dependence — perhaps because it is concrete and its effects are obvious and inevitable — differs from cultural dependence. Capital, technology, management — these cannot be borrowed without incurring reciprocal obligations. This does not apply to cultural dependence, where the borrowing takes place quite without payment; it appears as voluntary, chosen for its usefulness or convenience, or simply imposed by events and subsequently not rejected. More than that: through cultural contact over a period a foreign culture may become second nature and then neither desire nor ability exists any longer to shake it off. Only one more step is required to reach the furthest point of dependence, where the foreign culture becomes completely absorbed into the domestic one.

From this view point the problem of independence and dependence in private law seems to resemble much more the same issues as they arise in terms of culture than in terms of economics. To the extent that law is concerned with ethics, it forms part of the area of cultural dependence and appears as a secondary effect of culture on society. To the extent to which law regulates the economy and depends upon it, it is under almost the same constraints, either directly or through the medium of the social sphere which is partly controlled by the economy and must be organised by the law. Under such complex conditions, the degree of dependence or independence of the law in relation to a foreign legal system is difficult to assess, especially if one also considers the number of institutions and the variety of countries to be covered (from the Islamic Republic of Mauritania to Cameroun, and from the Ivory Coast to the Congo). Moreover, we have to bear in mind the continual development of the law and its content, and the fact too that its implementation and impact varies over time and from place to place – in ways which are all too little known. It follows that our aim must therefore be to attempt a definition of a trend.

Indeed all forms of dependence or independence must be analysed in the context of time, in movement and in development. A static analysis would be not merely limited but even misleading, for example presenting one variable as dependent on another which if seen over time would disclose elements of independence. In economic relations, for instance, the technological dependence of the Japanese or the financial dependence of the Germans on the USA in one phase of the post-war period was no more than a temporary means towards their eventual greater independence. Or, again, in cultural relations the colonisation of North America by Great Britain does not seem to have created in the USA any permanent dependence on the English.

This overall, dynamic approach to the question lacks, it is true, any revolutionary qualities. Those interested in influencing action and making direct political impact tend to ignore the subtle effects of time – of yesterday and tomorrow – on men and on institutions. This was surely the case with ideologues of decolonisation before independence. Independence constituted an end in itself for them – decolonisation had to be complete. Any borrowings from the colonial power would be a sign of hateful or suspicious dependence. Liberation was to be freedom from all external influences in all areas; cultural, social and therefore and above all, in terms of the legal superstructure.

Opinions differed however when it came to a decision on the resources to be used in constructing the new state. According to Franz Fanon it was necessary to destroy the legacies of both colonisation and the pre-colonial past: 'Fighting colonialism, fighting sterile traditions ... the newly independent nation evolves during its early years in the atmosphere of a battlefield'. This is the cultural revolution to perfection: the new man brought to life by revolution. On the other hand, the African independence fighters, as supporters of black culture, wanted to return to the sources of Africanism, admittedly not simply in order to return to their traditions but to derive therefrom a creative impetus. Camara Laye, Sheikh Anta Diop, Sheikh Amidou Kane, Albert Tevoedjere all wanted an Africa free from cultural alienation and put their trust in the power and conviction of black culture. Leopold Sedar Senghor, at once poet and politician, was for that reason divided 'between the call of my ancestors and the call of Europe, between the demands of Negro-African culture and the demands of modern life'.[1]

In fact the quest for revolutionary effect in the discussion ignored most of the political reality. Once independence had been obtained the new leaders were soon forced to take account of this reality. They saw immediately that the independence proclaimed in the new states needed at least two conditions to be effective: economic development and national political unity. In addition both these conditions required, in their view, a modern, unified law; this entailed the elimination of the diversity of traditional laws and customs which were not adapted to the technological society which was to be developed. Such a modern law was readily available: it was, for numerous reasons which are worth examining, the law of the old colonial power. So the setting up of an African State which was to be modern in economic and political terms seemed as though it would have to take place through the extensive use of French law and the dismantling of customs. The battle for independence was going to have to be fought all over again.

In these new states, already shaken by the revolution which was independence, the struggle over law is not over. After the pendulum had swung from a pre-independence stress on African tradition to an immediate post-independence leaning towards modern law, it is now returning to the authenticity of tradition. Its movements, however, seem to become less extreme, as if law is trying to find that position of equilibrium where the people understand their law because the law understands the people (to paraphrase Ihering). African private law today reflects the contradictory trends and opposing needs of modernity and Africanism. These are expressed with varying intensity according to the area of law under consideration. It will therefore be useful to review these areas before looking for an explanation of their degree of dependence or independence.

Development

In political, administrative and legal terms the new states which had achieved independence without violent struggle were forced initially to set up house with the old furniture inherited from the colonial power, even though they did not want to accept this inheritance except for its balance of benefits and had planned the outlines of a new legal structure. It is a separate task to analyse the basic rules governing relations between individuals in their daily life. These are dealt with later but only in sketchy form.

The French administration which, at the very beginning of the process of colonisation, had intended to introduce French private law into Africa, soon gave up the idea of applying it generally. It realised the impossibility of imposing French law on people whose lives were governed by their own habits and customs and rooted in a totally different economic, social and cultural context. The administration therefore found itself creating a dual system of law. The 'French law' sector applied to Europeans, to 'privileged' natives or to those who opted for 'modern law' for a particular legal case. The sector of traditional law – 'local law' – covered the other Africans. In this way in matters of private law custom continued to control the legal affairs of the bulk of the colonial population. These two sectors of law had two more or less corresponding structures of courts: one of the French type for 'French law' which was subject to the control of the French Cour de Cassation; the other one which was indigenous, for 'local law', was usually presided over by a colonial official assisted by indigenous advisers who knew the customs.[2] It is true that the French colonial power, moved by the crusading spirit of Christianity, humanitarianism, Rousseauism and egalitarianism and by belief in the superiority of their own law, still retained as its ultimate aim general application of French law. But this had to wait until education and exposure to French culture had made their impact. In the meantime, French private law hardly impinged on the customs which continued to rule everywhere outside the elitest circles of *evolués*. Its role was confined to filling the gaps left by custom, to removing anything regarded as contrary to public order, by making use of adaptations of French law; only in certain areas (e.g., criminal law) was custom replaced. On occasion provisions were even made to protect custom from the impact of colonisation (as in decrees relating to dowry).

It can be argued that, as a result of this careful policy and the very slow progress of legal assimilation, the new states in effect had complete freedom of manoeuvre when they attained sovereignty. Traditional law survived French colonisation intact, despite the fact that, on account of colonialist long-term aims, little or nothing had been done to establish or perpetuate it.[3] It would thus have been possible to mark independence and celebrate Africanism by encouraging this traditional sector, with a view to developing it subsequently, and introducing modern laws only where they were essential for economic development. However, it was the opposite choice which was made in practically all the new states, though it is true that there were certain variations. The urgent need for economic and political development secured priority over respect for traditional values; it seemed too difficult to reconcile the two.[4] The beginnings of some freedom of manoeuvre came in the French constitution of 4 October 1958 which in article 78 gave the Community control over justice and made each state responsible for the organisation and administration of its courts.[5] Immediately each state proceeded to set up its own system of courts – on the French model but still retaining the dualism of the colonial system.

Independence and the establishment of new sovereign powers marked a period of change but, since independence had not been won on a battlefield, change took place with continuity, in a peaceful takeover of the state. In order to prevent a legal void, the new states laid down, often in their constitutions, that the legal provisions or regulations existing at the time of independence would remain in force unless repealed. As a result they began, during this transition, to bring up to date the wording of the texts taken over and to codify them, though for practical reasons without making any real changes.[6] This was all no doubt necessary, but (for that reason!) not necessarily of any great significance.

Much more important as an indication of the influence of French models was the reform of legal institutions and the role which was to be given to traditional law. Almost all the new states rapidly began to modernise the organisation of justice. They removed local law courts fairly systematically and integrated them into the modern law courts, which thus became courts of common law, to which all the people were subject from that time onwards. The dual system of the colonial era was regarded as a sign of segregation, which had to be done away with.[7] Where local courts could not be absorbed at once, for practical reasons such as personnel problems, they were nevertheless integrated into the unitary system by being submitted to the control of the Supreme Court of each new republic.

It is true that the unification of the courts, even on the French model, does not in itself predetermine the law which these courts will apply: modern, traditional, or one which mixes local traditions with French legal techniques.[8] It must however be pointed out that the belief of African leaders in the need for a united, hierarchical system of administering justice, and in its universality, is not rooted in African tradition, but belongs to modern French ideas on the organisation of justice and the state.

More revealing is the choice made by the new leaders with regard to the role of custom, discernible particularly in texts relating to the organisation of the judiciary or the setting up of Supreme Courts. Custom is never praised, but neither is it reduced to a mere fact of life; instead it constitutes an element of the legal system, it is a kind of law. Thus the Supreme Courts have to recognise the violation of law *and* of custom.[9] However the application of customary law is only a secondary function for the modern law judge. Customary law is only applicable in personal matters and covers a limited field. It is gradually being cut back by new laws which M. Lampué calls 'laws of general application'. Thus in most of the states the realm of custom is limited in terms of both *ratione personae* and *ratione materiae*;[10] in addition, the idea that certain customary rules work against public order has been retained and included in various laws.

Briefly then, modern law must spread, by virtue of the increase in laws of general application, the requirements of public order which are invoked when necessary, the gaps in custom, the choice of the litigant and, finally, the priority which modern law is sometimes given in cases of conflict of laws. Traditional law on the other hand seems destined to disappear, its area of application contracting at the same time as that law itself becomes blurred with the passing of time. The hope of the leaders is to speed up the introduction of modern law, regardless of its French origin.

There are two comments which might be made on the positions taken here. It has been repeatedly stated that a unified system of courts and a unification of laws are necessary for the economic and political development of the new states. This could be disputed. The fact remains that the African leaders have not done so, nor do they question the need for development or the very concept of development. This shows that the idea and the model — both of which are Western, and the latter French, in origin — were unhesitatingly taken over on independence; this applies even to the political framework of justice which in France was the outcome of development (but not its cause!).

The second comment concerns laws of general application and their relation to custom. Law of general application is often described as modern but this does not mean that it must necessarily involve a complete break with the traditional past. It is modern because it has its source in legislation and because it is general, but it could very well incorporate custom. (It is true that national unification of customary rules would in itself constitute a considerable reversal of tradition.) Indeed, that is what has been done by those states which have affirmed their faithfulness to Africanism most strongly and have at the same time opted for law of general application.[11]

Despite this, customary law still remains in existence. M. Keba M'baye speaks of a 'base of traditional law' on which modern law rests. This base is large and strong. The majority of legal cases are still decided by traditional law, either because the people concerned have not yet fully accepted the state courts[12] or because the law to be applied is special to given groups, or because of a gap in the laws of general application.

If, for a moment, one disregards this hidden role of customary law, the degree of dependence and independence in the private law of the new African French-speaking states with regard to the law of the ex-colonial power may be judged by the influence of custom, on the one hand, and on the other by that of French law, on the actual provisions of these generally applied laws. This seems to be the real crux of the matter. On this point, M. Miyoulou[13] believed that 'the marriage of Congolese customs and

French legal techniques can only be considered valid to the extent to which the traditional principles of the Congo are respected ... Only on this condition will justice be brought within the reach of the Congolese people, who are mostly illiterate, and for whom custom is an integral part of life'. But G. A. Kouassigan[14] notes that 'In every case, the new African laws, which have been deliberately drawn up as instruments for development, demonstrate − in their direction, their techniques and their formal expression − the desire to substitute European legal standards for the provisions of traditional law ...'

What is actually happening?

Present situation

One of the first tasks of all new states was to legislate on *nationality*. Naturally they used French law as a basis. They borrowed terminology, general layout and techniques. All the same, there is considerable variety in the criteria used for determining nationality, each state making its own distinctive selection of criteria in such a way as to fit in with their own general policy towards citizenship. Could they have gone further in their legislation in this area? On this subject a non-African author writes: 'Written law should have been adapted to African realities ... There was nothing to prevent the problems of nationality, which were new to Africa and Madagascar, being viewed differently from in France or Belgium, in the interests of these new states themselves'.[15]

International private law (of which, according to the African concept inherited from France, nationality law is only one branch) has remained essentially a matter of case law in these countries, as it has in France.[16] The opportunity was thus available for development to take place quite independently of the French model. But as a French author writes with regret: 'Although French jurisprudence and doctrine should have been used only as a guide, they were too often regarded as the sources of positive law ...'[17] This is certainly an area where African sources are rare or even non-existent (the old rules of interstatute conflict have scarcely been studied). In addition, the technicalities of this field and the possibility of awkward come-backs discourage hasty new departures, even in France.

Another branch of the law which cannot depend on African tradition is the *law of contract*. Certainly rules of custom exist which regulate some types of contract and so-called non-contractual responsibility. Such legal relations, if they arise in a traditional context, are always ruled by custom. (Occasionally a general law may have taken over the content of the traditional one.) However, as regards the law in the area of contractual obligations, most of the French-speaking states are still governed by the provisions of the French Civil Code; those who have published new laws in the area are the exceptions.[18] This law of contract is closely linked to the imported economic model whose complicated legal nature and whose legal philosophy is radically different from that of traditional African law. It is usually added to, rather than substituted for, customary rules. With its Roman origins it spread throughout the West and was subsequently exported by the West all over the world; as such it was taken over by the African leaders not as specifically French law, but as law of universal legal validity.

Similarly, little new law has been developed in the area of *commercial and company law*. Traditional law is more or less silent here. Moreover, the rules involved in this field arise – except in the case of small traditional businesses – from links between the economy of these countries and the industrialised Western world. It is therefore an area where the safety of tried and tested laws is preferable to improvisation, and an area where inter-African harmonisation seems more desirable than individual national expression. Retaining the provisions laid down by the old colonial power is not regarded as a sign of dependence, but as the adoption of useful legal techniques. However, in this branch of law, as in that of law of contract, a clear divide has opened up between African laws and French law. The new French laws (legislation on companies in 1966; legislation on the disposal and liquidation of assets) and recent French jurisprudence, have had practically no effect in Africa. The systems are beginning to develop along separate lines.

In *labour law* dualism continues to exist in spite of the law. Traditional law has survived intact in the labour relations of the peasant and rural world and even in domestic services in the urban areas between natives. It survives in the shadow of the law.[19] The legislation itself was modern and uniform in all the

French territories at the time of independence (e.g., law of 15 December 1952 on the labour code of Overseas Territories and Decree of 24 February 1957 on compensation for industrial injuries).[20] This code, drawn up by the French but in advance of French law on the subject, had been adopted at the request of the representatives of the Overseas Territories and therefore looked like modern law adapted to African needs. In actual fact its aim was to regulate labour relations in industrial undertakings which were, at that time, seldom managed by Africans. This foreign import intended to govern labour relations with foreigners has been taken over as such by the new states. They have done nothing more than improve one or two of its provisions. The dualism which exists today in labour law is simply a reflection of the two types of economy (the industrial economy and the traditional economy) which still run parallel, rather than being merged, in Africa today.

Land law is a branch of law which clearly demonstrates the opposition of the needs of development and traditional rules. African legislators, almost without exception (Upper Volta, Benin, Congo), have for this very reason imposed laws of general application.[21] They have opted for law which is composite in the sense that it respects the application of custom whilst altering it, but at the same time it confirms the priority of new rules to encourage development; these rules have themselves been inspired by the African tradition of not owning land privately. Three points are particularly relevant. Firstly, the declaration of the community's right to the land negates the quiritarian ownership of land laid down in the French Civil Code. But the collective ownership principle is not inspired so much by African tradition as by the desire of the states to secure control of the land, so that they can get possession quickly of land necessary for development without coming up against objections from individuals or land speculators.[22] Secondly, on the other hand, the system of registration has been borrowed from colonial legislation; this permits the French type of ownership, one of its advantages being to provide security for credit which is badly needed to aid development. Thirdly, they recognise the existence of areas of lineage holdings where traditional rules continue to play a role, in the absence of new organisations either envisaged or still to be activated.[23]

If we look at the form, the terminology and a number of techniques used in these laws, they would seem to take their inspiration from French law. However they cannot be considered as imports, or as being culturally dependent on the French model. Although they have admittedly taken registration over from colonial legislation, this was already a special area of legislation, inspired by models other than the French one. This technique moreover now operates within a context which is mostly original in its working principles and philosophy. Land law in the new African states is therefore more an example of original, modern African law, which permits the coexistence of both 'tolerated' customary laws (of an African archetype but shorn of ancient purpose) as well as selected and adapted modern institutions. This law, to the extent to which attempts are made to improve it (these have been tentative up to now), is not well received by rural people, still living in close harmony with the land, whose customs have more to do with religious beliefs than with economic or legal reasoning.

We turn finally to *family law*. In view of the variety of customs in force at independence governing marriage and the family (the French colonial power had legislated only on the minimum age for marriage and the dowry and the French Civil Code applied only to those people subject to the French personal law), the new states were tempted to seek uniformity through new laws despite the sensitive nature of the subject. Would the new law be based on the development of a Western-type family, centred on monogamous marriage, and often considered an essential part of industrial society? Or would it, in the name of Africanism, limit itself to looking for a compromise between the various traditional laws in force in the territory, adopting in particular polygamous marriage and perhaps the matrilinear system? This problem gave some cause for thought.

In Mali, the Law of 3 February 1962 repealing local customs and statutes which had governed the various ethnic groups in Mali only altered these customs to a limited extent by Western standards (keeping the dowry and allowing the choice of monogamy though with the provision of being able to change one's mind) and drew much of its inspiration from Islamic law. In Madagascar the law took considerable account of traditional ideas (Order of 1 October 1962 on marriage, and of 20 November 1963 on filiation, adoption and rejection) and referred directly to custom on several points, in particular on marriage. The laws in Guinea (14 April 1962) also contained very few innovations. On the other hand, the legislators in the Ivory Coast chose legislation which was very close to the French model, suppressing polygamy and copying laws on divorce, separation, paternity, filiation and adoption (Laws of 7 October 1962). The Gabonese Law of 29 July 1972 was also modern, in its own way; it even regulated and gave a legal status to cohabitation! M. Lampué commented: 'This regulation seems avant-garde to us, but one can ask whether it will not finally ratify the customary rules which seemed to have disappeared'. At about the same time the Senegalese legislation appeared. This attempted a difficult compromise between Negro-Islamic tradition and the modernity of the West. 'An "à la carte" legislation, in which the citizen can apply the provisions of his choice' – this was the judgment of M. Backé[24] who added: 'These legal provisions really have the appearance of a futurist law for those familiar with our societies ... However the African is often called upon to act as a Messiah ... Legislation based in the community is not the prerogative of our laws ...'[25]

It is difficult in such a brief sketch – incomplete and full of generalisations – to establish the exact degree of dependence or independence of the law applied in these countries. It is obvious however that both exist, just as it is certain that customary laws and those of general application continue to exist parallel to each other. In other words, one could say that at present the influence of French law is very largely predominant in all laws of general application, but that, on the other hand, this influence and these laws are hardly to be seen in the daily legal relations of the great majority of the population.

But which factors have contributed and which will contribute towards dependence or independence? For it is the interplay of these factors which will determine the future of private law in these countries.

Dependence

The situation is complex and difficult to analyse. On the one hand there is African culture and the traditions and customs of a subsistence economy; on the other there is the influence of the modern economy – industrial and consumer-orientated – and the influence of French culture. Obviously each culture has links with its particular type of economy and vice versa. If it is difficult to separate one type of culture from its own type of economy, how much more difficult it must be to graft one type of economy, the industrial, on to a different, African, type of culture. Since it is generally agreed – though some controversy is now to be heard – that the decolonised countries need an economy of the industrial type, it is therefore this type of economy which is increasingly serving as a basis for introducing the corresponding culture – just as in the past and again today, modern culture has been a means of setting up an industrial economic model.

As already stated, law is rooted both in the economy and in culture. Since it is inconceivable that a type of economy could be introduced without its supporting cultural context and vice versa, it is even less imaginable that – in view of the time it takes for the economy to change its nature and the even longer time necessary for man to change in line with the economy – it would be possible to devise simultaneously, out of thin air and without lengthy planning, two new models, one economic, the other cultural. It can therefore be ruled out that, in the very short time between the birth of the new decolonised states and the present day, their governments following their acceptance of the need for development, could have worked out a system which was legally, economically and culturally quite independent. On the whole, they were bound to import law to fit both the economy and the culture they inherited.

Yet in the final analysis it is the people who make the law – the real law, which is lived – and they find it difficult to change – though more easily in their economic than their social behaviour. Also it is the people who unleash the forces of reaction against new economic and cultural models. Certain aspects are accepted, others rejected, and others still are integrated into the traditional system. Moreover, cultural and economic development brought about by external influence is accompanied by a genuine indigenous cultural and economic development. This releases forces which are biased towards continuity, towards a development which is 'authentic' and (let us use the word, though not without reservations) independent. These forces are combined with those whose impetus is towards an alien or 'dependent' economic and cultural development. A graph of these forces would show that over time the alien effect lessens more quickly as one moves away from the zero point of decolonisation whilst the forces of 'authenticity' only decrease a little. Experience will produce a meeting point. Thus we need to analyse the constituents of these two forces, beginning with the factors which make for dependence. Distinguishing them in a fairly arbitrary fashion, these are economic and cultural factors. But economic factors influencing the legal system seldom have any direct impact. That is to say, it is not actual, quantitive dependence which usually influences; rather, influence on law comes above all from the dependence on the economic model which has been reproduced; and therefore it comes from the cultural influence which has brought about the adoption of the model. Accordingly we have to begin with a description, unfortunately not all-inclusive, of the cultural factors causing dependence.

First of all there is the influence exerted by French culture on African elites: on their language, philosophy and religion. Education is obviously the chief purveyor; French education, in the case of the first generation of independence, went right from primary school to university, and even to a seat in the National Assembly. French legal concepts are part of the cultural message; even non-formal education serves as their carrier. So actual legal training falls on receptive ears. The message is received even more willingly since law in French teaching is usually presented as an instrument of social engineering available to all. Furthermore, the teaching is addressed to students who are ready to believe that it is French law which shapes French society and organises its ordered growth. French law comes to be regarded as a modern organisational technique of society virtually on a par with company law which organises industrial undertakings. Any suggestion that the courses should be changed to adapt them to conditions in the developing countries has long been regarded by Africans as a form of discrimination, and as training for an intermediate rather than an advanced technology. Also the recipients of this training, who have been culturally uprooted at an early age, have seldom got the African social background which would enable them to know about or be able to preserve an authentic African attitude to the customs and traditions of their country. They cannot therefore study French law from the comparative angle.

From their learning of the law, as subsequently from their experience of legal practice, the first generation of African magistrates, lawyers and administrators were very much assimilated into French law. When independence allowed them to legislate, they naturally thought and acted within the framework and according to the reasoning of the French legal tradition. They required considerable independence of mind to adapt certain institutions to the varying real needs of their countries. In the initial period, substantial French technical aid further contributed to dependence on French law: magistrates, officials, assistants, even trade unionists who went out to these countries either had no knowledge of Africa or else knowledge based only on experience of the colonial period.

Now, by the second decade of independence, the situation has already begun to change. There is far less cultural uprooting, since all education now takes place in Africa, with African teachers, even though French legal training is still the norm in African universities. But though the African student is still learning French law in African universities, he now learns it as the law of another country, useful certainly and still a kind of model. But he is not living in the society which is governed by this law, and as time passes, he knows less and less about that society. So he comes to be able to see the irrelevance of this law to the society in which he lives. It is true however that he still knows very little of local customary law or even national law. But his attitude to the training he receives has changed: he is becoming more critical of all legal institutions, since in a condition of cultural disequilibrium nothing appears as satisfactory.

The decline of legal dependence is also encouraged by the replacement of politicians – the products of French university law and humanities departments – by military men. Soldiers in all countries have a distinct dislike for 'legalism', and their training keeps them close to their origins. (The result in Africa has been a definite slowing down in the amount of legislation.) Finally, technical aid in the legal sector is decreasing rapidly.

Nevertheless, certain cultural factors will continue to contribute, for an indefinite period, to keeping these countries within the French zone of influence. One of these is the defence

by African legal experts of their modern knowledge against
traditional law, which they consider retrograde (compare the
opposition of the German Romanists to the German 'jus
asinum').[26] In addition there is the fact that African teachers and
researchers know French law whereas they know little of much
of traditional law. They therefore have a favourable attitude to
French law, or at least to modern law.[27] They prefer to think that
the opposition in traditional circles was directed against colonialism rather than against the modernity of the law.[28]

Finally, legal information and the opportunity to get to know
the law still favour dependence, and will continue to do so for
some time. One disadvantage of customary law is its diversity and
the fact that it is not written down. It is difficult to get to know it,
whereas it is easy to get access to French doctrine and precedents.

The science of law consists, for lawyers, judges and draftsmen,
in the accumulation of precedents. As long as French legal
records and collections of decrees are available and have no rivals
of equivalent scope and technical sophistication, dependence will
continue. But it will decrease in importance if and when the
French legal records are no longer renewed, or when the current
literature is no longer relevant. In fact, the development of
legislation in these countries scarcely follows that of France at all,
due to lack of information, lack of training, lack of interest in
French reforms, or because of the affirming of independence of
the French model. For these reasons we are getting close to a
situation where knowledge of French law and French legal
documents will be out-of-date in Africa.

The westernisation of the elites of these new states has been so
complete that no African has even questioned the advisability of
economic development on the model of the industrialised
countries. Although this model is not well known to the majority
of the population, who have only glimpsed its most tempting
aspects, nevertheless it has not been rejected by them. Neither the
supporters of Africanism or those of revolutionary independence
have questioned this model either, although they have chosen
different ways of putting it into practice, some preferring
socialism, others liberalism, and others again seeking an authentic
African socialism, the ideal of which is still an industrialised
society leading to a consumer society. Thus it is above all through
the attraction of the model of industrial development that the

cultural attraction of French law is reinforced; French laws appear to be needed to service the new economic system.

At the same time there are some influences in support of Western-type law which result from direct economic dependence. The need for foreign capital, business and technology requires the publication of investment codes and the existence of commercial and company law, labour law, even land law, directly based on modern law familiar to the West; only such a legal framework gives firms from capitalist countries a sense of confidence and allows credit transactions to take place normally. The French model is therefore naturally used, particularly since this is a field where the co-operation is with French industry. The requirements of international trade also make it necessary to make laws on transport, insurance, contracts and responsibility, among other things, which are as close as possible to a 'jus gentium'. Thus Western law is necessary in these areas too. The desire to attract foreign nationals, tourists as well as technicians, also encourages the adoption of law which is familiar and acceptable — as traditional law is not. As there is no question of reviving the system of 'Capitulations', preference has been given to legislation with general application which seems acceptable to foreigners (cf. the Egyptian experience), even if this legislation proves unacceptable to the native people.

In addition to all these cultural and economic factors making for dependence, there is also a political consideration. On achieving independence new states found it necessary to prove to the large international organisations that the new state was fit for modern international society — and this meant having modern law. For those educated in French universities, this meant a unified private law and a single pyramid-shaped judicial system to administer it. Since time was short and appearance was what mattered, they used 'demonstration' laws, which were only meant to be provisional, but which for various reasons have persisted.

It must be admitted that all these pressures nevertheless did not necessarily call for laws of specifically French origin. Naturally here it was the training of African jurists which played a decisive role; for them to draw on any other sources would have been enormously difficult. But in addition it can perhaps be allowed that French law was favoured on account of its world-wide

renown over the last century and a half. It has indeed its own
merits (well-tried codification, well-developed logical system of
doctrine and jurisprudence) which, since Napoleon, have given it
its considerable reputation in Europe and Latin America and even
a certain influence in the Near East and Asia. Thus, if French law
continues to be very influential in Africa, this is not due entirely
to the colonial prerogative, but also to its intrinsic value, its
Roman origin and its widespread distribution.

Independence

When we turn to the factors making for independence we find of
course – for such is the nature of law – that we look again at
economy and culture, but now discerning influences which
contrast and conflict with those which favour dependence. If we
list these independence factors, they emerge as fewer in number –
but of much greater weight. The desire of a people to continue to
exist and do things in their own way does not need to be
explained here; it is a fact of life and of history. The problem of a
Western-style development is precisely that of encouraging a
desire for change alongside this basic desire for continuity. The
main independence factor is rejection of any change which does
not respect the identity of the society in question.[29]

It would seem that decolonisation and independence have
almost imperceptibly caused a revival of traditional cultural
values. The true spirit of a people is expressed in its legal
institutions, which enshrine its real values. After these values had
been put in doubt by colonisation, the fact of being their own
masters again, of having only themselves to rely on – this feeling
being prompted by slow economic progress, major natural
disasters and the rhetoric for 'self-reliance' – all caused the revival
of these values. The African leaders have realised this and some of
them are beginning to act on it; they are those who talk about
'authenticity'. 'It cannot be denied that we have seen the birth of a
desire in Africa for an identity based on the norms and values of
authentic culture', said M. Van Rouveroy Nieuwaal.[30]

For this reason popular attitudes to modern law are different
from those found during the colonial era. Colonial law, like
colonial religion and power, did at least inspire respect, if not
obedience. The new courts and law inspire neither fear nor the

same respect as previously. The colonial's ignorance or criticism of African traditions was tolerated; but people do not recognise the right of their own children – now the judges and legislators – to disregard or do away with these traditions. The new law neither has the advantage of coming from a dominant culture nor does it correspond to people's own ideas. Moreover, behind the law there is mere power, rather than authority. The power is not deeply rooted, since the concept of the state is not widely grasped. The new social hierarchy is accepted, but the new values are mostly rejected. It is proving in some ways more difficult for a native elite to carry out the cultural re-education of a people than for the colonial power to do so directly. Both the elite and the power it represents run the risk of getting cut off from the people.

Resistance to 'dependent' law is increasing all the time. Modern law, which is supposed to regulate situations which used to come under traditional law, is either not known or disregarded or sometimes opposed (as with the regulations on land) – according to whatever people find convenient. Sometimes new institutions are in practice quite deformed as they are penetrated by men who adhere to traditional social patterns and are determined to domesticate the intruder institution (as has happened, for example, with the cooperatives). On other occasions, opposition by traditional authorities prevents people from being brought under the jurisdiction of the state, with the justice of the chiefs and traditional authorities taking first place over official justice.[31]

Legislators, judges and administrators in particular must take these factors into account. As a result of them, modern laws are not applied, or fall into disuse. Other laws become changed when applied, and others still are amended to make them more suitable. The framework, the terminology and the form of the law put up the best resistance. But increasingly the actual contents of the seemingly French legal 'cupboards' consist of locally woven materials. In 1968 M. J. Hilaire concluded that 'The idea of promulgating "shock legislation" has hardly any supporters any more: it will not be revived ... Codification remains more an outcome of the past than a creation of the legislator'.

It must also be said that as those who control legal matters have less and less intimate knowledge of the metropolitan culture, so the imported law is bound to become corrupted. Heresies are supposed to occur in the third generation of disciples. In legal matters this means that the law is increasingly altered to fit its new socio-economic context. Thus it gains in independence what it loses in conformity with the original model. Decreasing availability of French legal documentation and information has the same effect. Subscriptions to French specialist reviews are on the decline and indeed the French legal inheritance in Africa will become impoverished if France does not increase its aid in this area. However, our own authorities seem uninterested in maintaining the wide distribution of our law; they take no account of the prestige to be gained, and are not prepared to pay the necessary price for it. The Institut de Droit d'Expression française (IDEF), by setting up links between lawyers in all the Francophone states and regions of the world from Pondichery to Louisiana, from the Congo to Canada, has made a considerable contribution to providing a world role for French law, and laws inspired by it. France itself cannot be relied on to undertake this type of action.

Finally we have to note some economic factors which militate against modern, dependent law. In the first place, there is the permanence of the traditional, subsistence economy. Modern law simply lacks sufficient institutional support in some fields such as credit, owing to the lack of opportunity for mortgages on inherited agricultural land. Personal credit with modern institutions such as banks fails to work properly unless it is channelled along traditional routes employing collective social pressure. In other words, rural development is the decisive factor for all other development, and it cannot take place without institutions which are more biased towards a traditional economy than towards the economy of industrialised countries. It is therefore vital that these countries create their own independent procedures and institutions.[32] This seems to apply to all the basically indigenous sectors of development such as harvesting and sale of agricultural produce, crafts and small and medium-sized business. Similar considerations apply to all social and health legislation. Even family law cannot escape the economic constraints of a subsistence society, even if one was to ignore the negro-African cultural tradition. Polygamy in rural areas has economic as well as traditional support.

Last of all there is the questioning, only very recently begun, of the concept of economic development on the Western model. It is now being asked: is this a model whose long-term success is guaranteed, is it worth adopting, with all the sacrifices it requires from African individuals and society? The West too (in the Club of Rome) is asking this question. Africa is losing its faith in this model. It believes, in accordance with its tradition of economic subsistence, that social elements should take priority over economic ones; thus equality in a situation of improved subsistence is more important than fundamentally unequal competition between individuals.[33] These are the advance warning signs of an intuitive search for a different kind of society from that of the West today. This search is taking place in those societies which have tried to reject the absolute primacy of the state; it indicates perhaps that African socialism has every chance of becoming an original authentic socialism with its own ideals and its own law.

At the end of this description of the factors of dependence and independence affecting the content of private law in the French speaking countries of Africa, one may ask whether we are really drawing nearer to a 'harmonious synthesis' of tradition and Western law, as is the wish of so many African and French lawyers.[34] In the area of written law, dependence is predominant; in law as it is lived, independence is the rule. In the struggle for the law, the people always have the last word. The real question for the future is which model of society these nations will choose. After two decades of independence they are showing their wish to create a new society of their own, as independent as is possible in our interdependent, finite world. The degree of independence or dependence of their private law with regard to Western and French law will depend on how original their negro-African society – which seems to be at the beginning rather than the end of its development – can be, and how far it is integrated into the world community.

NOTES

1. See *A l'appel de la race de Saba.*
2. For additional details see P. Lampue, *Droit d'outre-mer et de la coopération* (Dalloz), also F. Luchaire, *Droit d'outre-mer et de la coopération* (Themis).

3. An example of an exception is the publication of *Coutumiers juridiques de l'Afrique occidentale*, 3 volumes, Dakar, 1939.
4. Cf. P. F. Gonidec, *Les droits africains – évolution et sources*.
5. Presidential Decision of 12 June 1959. See Hilaire, *Ann. Africaines*, 1964.
6. Cf. Keba-M'baye, 'Droit et développement en Afrique francophone de l'Ouest', *Aspects juridiques du développement économique*, p. 136.
7. Cf. Hilaire *op. cit.*, Keba-M'baye *op. cit.*
8. Cf. R. Miyoulon, 'Le congolais face aux techniques juridiques occidentales', *Revue juridique et politique*, 1966, p. 72.
9. Cf. Lampue, 'Les sources du droit de la famille', *Revue juridique et politique*, 1967, p. 20.
10. Cf. Hilaire, *op. cit.*, P. Lampue, 'La diversité des statuts de droit privé dans les états africains', *Penant*, 1961, pp. 8 ff.
11. Cf. Republic of Guinea, Ord. no. 47, PRG 29.12.1960, art. 5.
12. Yet there were 2,000 legal decisions in Senegal in two years arising out of the marriage law which came into force in 1973.
13. *Op. cit.*
14. *Quelle est ma loi*, Pedone, 1974.
15. A. Zatzepine, 'L'évolution du droit de la nationalité des Républiques francophones d'Afrique et de Madagascar', *Penant*, 1975, p. 147 ff.
16. See some unusual provisions in *Revue critique du droit international privé*, 1973, p. 392 ff.
17. P. Bourel, *Réalités et perspectives du Droit International Privé de l'Afrique Noire francophone dans le domaine des conflits de lois*, Clunet, 1975 p. 17 ff; cf. Francescakis, *Problèmes de Droit International Privé de l'Afrique Noire indépendante*, Cours La Haye, 1964, p. 275 ff.
18. Madagascar, Law of 2 July 1966; Senegal, Law of 10 July 1963 and 13 July 1966, including a Code of civil and commercial obligations largely inspired by French law. Cf. P. Bourel, 'Droit de la responsabilité civile extra-contractuelle en Afrique Noire francophone', *Journal of African Law*, 1973, p. 1–27.
19. Cf. E. Schaeffer, *Annales africaines*, 1962.
20. Gonidec, Cours, 1966; M. Kirsch, *Droit du travail africain*, 1975.
21. Cf. Conference of the IDEF, 1970: 'Le régime du sol', *Revue juridique et politique*, 1970, pp. 567–1335.
22. As in A. Ley, *op. cit.* p. 713; and *Penant*, 1975, p. 202.
23. Cf. P. Blanc, 'Nouvelles tendances du droit foncier africain et malgache', *Penant*, 1970, p. 97–127; M. Ducat, 'La réforme foncière togolaise', *Penant*, 1975, p. 291.
24. *Revue juridique et politique*, 1974, p. 777.
25. Cf. for family and inheritance law: Conference of the IDEF in *Revue juridique et politique*, 1967, pp. 3–208, 'La famille'; 1972, pp. 481–1411, 'Les successions'; 1974, pp. 541–863, 'Condition juridique, politique et sociale de la femme'.
26. Bodies of established legal knowledge are always thus defensive. Cf. Ribert, *Les forces créatrices du droit*; Hilaire, *Variations sur le mariage*, *Penant*, 1968, p. 147–193: 'Magistrates, by virtue of their office, are naturally led to advance the cause of "their law" '

27. Cf. M. Y. Nkouendé, 'Role de la jurisprudence dans les nouveaux états d'Afrique francophone', *Penant*, 1973, p. 22: 'Everything causes us therefore to retain law of a purely Western type. Thus we do not understand when those who are called upon to judge our decisions (in decrees) or our research (in our theses) reproach us for having listened to them, for having believed their teaching, when they advise us to keep our traditions etc …'
28. Cf. S. Melone, 'Le poids de la tradition dans le droit africain contemporain', *Penant*, 1971, p. 421 and *La parenté et la terre dans la stratégie du développement*, Paris, 1972, 220p.
29. Cf. E. Schaeffer, 'Aliénation, réception, authenticité − Réflexions sur le Droit du Développement', *Penant*, 1974, p. 311.
30. 'Droit moderne et droit coutumier au Togo', *Penant*, 1975, p. 1.
31. Cf. Congress of Francophone Lawyers in Dakar, 1967, p. 9.
32. Cf. Badouin, *L'agriculture de transition*, Pedone, 1975.
33. Cf. A. Teroedjere, paper published in Dossiers de L'ISJD.
34. Cf. L. K. Améga, 'Prière pour un Code civil togolais', *Penant*, 1966, p. 275.

11

The Maghreb Response to French Institutional 'Transfers': problems of analysis

J.-C. Vatin

The main aim of this paper is not so much to provide answers to questions about the nature and extent of dependence or independence to be found in the institutions of the Maghreb today – rather, we are concerned to explore the prior problem of ensuring that the questions themselves are suitably formulated. In particular we have to ask what is entailed in trying to assess institutional dependence by measuring 'distance' from a metro-politan 'model'.

'Institution' will be used here not in its wider sense of a set of social patterns of behaviour but in its more limited sense of political structures which serve at once to express governmental powers and to relate ruler and ruled. 'Dependence' is taken to mean relations of such inequality between the units concerned as to imply the virtual subjection of one to the other by direct or indirect means; 'independence', formal or real, accordingly entails the breaking of such relations in principle or in practice respectively. 'Model' is an ambiguous term in that while ordinary language suggests merely an example to be imitated or repro-duced, scientific usage refers to a simplified picture constructed of categories and variables and designed to focus attention on signifi-cant elements with a view to explaining the working of the whole. Both senses will be employed here, the second as a means of assessing the first. 'Institutional dependence', it goes without saying, cannot be approached as a discrete, isolated feature; we need to be aware of interactions with cultural, social, scientific and above all economic forms of dependence; equally we have to remember that relations between one former imperial power and its ex-colonies are set in a global context of several such relations which in turn form a part of present-day world politics. 'Maghreb' refers here to Tunisia, Algeria and Morocco (not Libya), the three countries of Arab-Islamic culture which experienced French rule in different degrees over periods from 50 to 130 years.

The plan of the essay is to confront a basic duality – and indeed inequality – in the subject matter. On the one hand there is the situation as seen from outside the area, notably from France itself; on the other there is the view from inside. The difficulty is that the eurocentric external pictures are so numerous and so well exhibited that it is hard to reach through to any genuinely inside view. In other words we can first present a more or less familiar version of the relations and this will be in terms of political necessities and copied models which will nevertheless have the appearance of experienced reality. But when, secondly, we try, as we surely must, to penetrate beyond to the insiders' own view of themselves and their institutions, we shall encounter relatively unexplored ground which poses theoretical difficulties and perhaps calls for new methods.

A. The View from the Metropole

The French understanding is that the Maghreb countries have generally passed through three broad stages as institutional models were first imposed, then transposed and finally differentiated. These categories take for granted that Maghreb institutions have been shaped solely by reference to French values and forms.

In the first phase, colonial rule successfully imposes itself. Thus, in Algeria, the French, once established, sought between 1830 and 1850 to make legitimate through law the victory they had won by arms. The colonial government presented itself as a continuation of the 'Turkish' state, taking over its heritage, exercising its prerogatives and enjoying its wealth. In Tunisia the protectorate moved in to replace the regime of the Bey. In Morocco in 1912 local hierarchies were treated more gently but on essentially similar lines. In all three territories the colonial power tended to drive a wedge into the local regimes, to penetrate bit by bit, to overcome them. Especially striking is the Algerian case where penal laws were purely French from the start and land law increasingly so and where a codification of rights only meant the imposition of restrictions on local customs and on the political liberties of local people. Moreover, with the extension of French law came also its gradual distortion culminating in the formulation and application of 'special' legislation for use in colonial territories. Similarly the export in general of the institutions of the colonial power gave way little by little to the creation of specifically colonial-type institutions. In Algeria a series of bodies quite peculiar to the territory – financial councils (1898–1945), financial assemblies (1945–1947), Algerian Assembly (1947–1954) – were simply instruments of colonial power. Municipalities entirely controlled by Europeans, municipalities with locally elected elements but run by French officials, whole areas in the South under direct French administration – all these devices adjusted local requirements to those of the overall colonial regime. Yet, in spite of everything, some indigenous institutions managed to survive, almost unnoticed by the colonisers; these were expressions of traditional solidarities, means of regulating internal conflicts, ways also of avoiding the use of alien administrative channels. Sometimes, however, time-honoured institutions – such as village *djemaa*, Muslim charitable trusts and Islamic courts – were salvaged only to be placed in the service of colonial domination.

In general, as colonial rule developed and became rationalised and modernised, so special institutions, imported or created, tended to gain the monopoly of power, making obsolete those which were native to the soil. The reaction against this began in the 1930s when nationalist political movements developing in these three North African countries called for institutions in line with the declared policy of encouraging and assimilating native inhabitants. Subsequently, most of these movements, while supporting an Algerian parliament at the end of the second world war, demanded for the future that there should be truly Algerian institutions – and thus a break with French institutions. From 1954 onwards, the war led to a kind of competition between the increasing number of colonial institutions (12 départements –

more than 1,500 communes), and the Algerian counter-institutions. The latter were aimed at destroying the French institutions by recruiting the Algerian population at the local level (*dechra, douar, kasma, daira* and *wilaya*); by providing a state apparatus at the top in the GPRA (Popular Government of the Algerian Republic), the CCE (Co-ordination and Education Committee) and the CNRA (National Council of the Algerian Republic); by supplying a means of national mobilisation in the FLN (National Liberation Front) or in group organisations among workers, traders and students.

At the moment of independence (1956 for Morocco and Tunisia and 1962 for Algeria) the nationalist counter-institutions did not cause the colonial forces to vanish by magic. This was hardly surprising since, especially in Algeria, their main task had been the organisation of the military and diplomatic struggle rather than the rebuilding of society, the construction of an independent nation and preparation for economic transformation. Each state found itself with a given institutional 'stock' of various bits and pieces and from this they had to try to find a way to a system of their own – in effect they had to take over their legacy while at the same time challenging it.

The inheritance of the first governments was patchy, to say the least. Some colonial institutions disappeared along with the regime which had supported them. With the departure of the European administrators, repossession of property took place (brutally in Algeria, more gradually in its neighbours), as did the accession to sovereignty in general terms. Some of the institutions taken over – e.g., the franchise and various forms of social mobilisation – contained modernising features; again, the colonial state had, of necessity rather than choice, speeded up the general process of political socialisation which enhanced national consciousness; it had also helped to bring about a weakening of traditional local authorities and thus assisted a centralisation and concentration of power. From this latter in particular, the new leaders would be the first to benefit – and yet they were obliged to deny that colonial rule had left behind anything of positive value. There were other kinds of surviving institutions which could be safely praised; these were those which colonial rule in search of means for its continuance had revived, retraditionalised, dressed up in folksy costume. But such institutions needed more than praise; colonialism was only able to feel safe with the moribund and these were now mostly devoid of any real meaning or living spirit. Thus by going through the motions of strengthening the *makhzen*, by setting the Berbers of the rural areas against the Arabicised cities, the French had put into effect policies which contradicted their other efforts, weakening the central apparatus and assisting a return at the periphery to the traditional leadership of the Kaids which threatened the development of a united Moroccan State.

The new nations found themselves in a paradoxical, if not false, position; they were forced to attack what was part of their strength, the state bureaucracy and the imposition of a single authority, because these had their origins in colonialism, and they had to emphasise the value of what often only had value as myth, such as ancestral structures already destroyed or worn out, the *acabiya* of another age, authorities and practices no longer relevant, empty of content, with no role to play. The only clear fact was legitimisation of the main opposition; the 'imprisoned' had come to power.

In deposing and deporting Mohammed V, France gave to the Sultan, now become monarch, an enhanced status and prestige. In Tunisia on the other hand the Bey's association with the colonial power improved the position of the members of the neo-Destour, who were systematically excluded from the government, arrested or exiled, and provided the justification for the removal of the Bey in a counter-coup and the setting up of a presidential regime under the most famous neo-Destour member, Habib Bourguiba. In Algeria, a provisional Executive with a powerful but complicated administrative machine at its disposal, could not carry out the transfer of power to the GPRA, which was soon to be stripped of its prerogatives by a Political Bureau which depended more on the army than on the divided Liberation Front. The regime and its leader, Ben Bella, seemed to survive the confusion more by the luck of the draw and faction fighting than by an authentic process of legitimisation. So, does the nature of the party system – single or multi – after liberation depend on the role played by the nationalist forces during the preceding period?

In spite of their stated desire to make a break with the colonial past, the leaders found themselves compelled to accept their inheritance without reservation. Consciously or subconsciously, they were obliged to proceed in more devious fashion: they stated that they were freeing themselves from the colonial system of organisation, whilst at the same time declaring their readiness to take over certain aspects of a European-style, that is French, institutional model. It was convenient for them to keep the 'positive' aspects of revolutionary France, the major principles of Western democracy, including the rights of man and of the citizen, whilst rejecting the 'negative' side of France as an imperialist power, colonialist France which had betrayed its idealistic statements and promises in practice by enslaving nations. But matters were already becoming more complicated. Neither Morocco nor Tunisia tried to claim that the reconstructed state was a 'national product' of the same sort as in 19th century Europe, that development of the Maghreb nation states in some way followed the routes taken in England, France or Holland. Nor did they claim that the problems with which the new states were faced were comparable with those of other nations which had obtained their political independence under different cir-cumstances. At the risk of some distortion, it can be said that the Maghreb countries were indeed nations, but that they still needed to set up the apparatus of a modern State and strengthen their internal coherence. In this sense, the European example of nations reaching political maturity within a firmly established geographical framework could not serve them as a model.

As for the institutions themselves, references to their French counterparts were more or less taboo, but it was conceivable that they might be reproduced, both because it was possible to differentiate between the institutions of liberal democracy and those of the previous colonial state, and because of the lack of any other examples to follow.

Taking legislation, for example, how could that in force at the time of independence be repealed without causing general confusion? In Algeria, indeed, the main laws were kept in force and it was 5 July 1975 before the law, according to those who drafted it, was free from the influence of the previous 'occupiers'. The fate of governmental and even political institutions presented a more serious problem, since these were the actual institutions of colonisation, of the monopoly of control and of domination. For several reasons it proved impossible to reject them, so another approach had to be adopted. Some institutions, however little suited to the new tasks of internal economic development, reorganisation of production and trade, political mobilisation and cultural education, were nevertheless taken over and 're-employed'. In Algeria, neo-Marxism clashed with the inherited state apparatus and the Charter of 1964 clearly stated the terms of the relationship between the instrument of the state and the will of the party (Part 3, Chapter 2, No. 4): institutions harbouring those who had obtained their qualifications under colonial rule were liable to act as a brake or a counter-revolutionary weapon in the service of a bourgeois bureaucracy which was unwilling to ensure the transition to socialism under the inspiration and control of the party. This condemnation of the state, and the whole tone of the Charter, showed how far away they had moved from the European model. An increasing personalisation of power, constitutions (1959 in Tunisia, 1962 in Morocco, 1963 in Algeria) diverted from their initial aims, difficulties in the functioning of the party system (whether the Tunisian neo-Destour, later Destour Socialist Party, the Algerian FLN or Morocco's many parties), infrequent or limited elections, assemblies curbed drastically or not being used at all, an unequal representation of interests, unclear methods of regulating conflict, local structures tardily set up: all these seemed to combine to emphasise the gap between the model and the originals, marking an end to imitation and instead the establishment of 'distinctive' institutions.

Confronted with a crisis of adjustment, the ruling groups in each state worked out a series of responses which, analysed from outside, showed that they were progressively abandoning the structures of the colonial state. Whilst the infrastructure of dependence continued, their economies still remained in the grip of world capitalism, more so in Morocco than in Tunisia and in the latter more than in Algeria. And it is precisely this threat from the outside world which is held to justify the decline of the 'classic' institutions. The need to contain the pressures of international financial powers, to create a domestic market, to plan the economy and to ensure political development explain the resort to 'modern' institutions, which fit such needs better than those of liberal democracy. Institutions must be adapted to increased production and to social mobilisation. When the situation is a delicate one, ensuring one's independence of the world involves increasing domestic potential by forging the tools needed: those of a 'new democracy'. There was no lack of arguments to support the growing ascendancy of the state, the increase in state control over society. These arguments are not always understood by outside experts, who readily measure Moroccan political methods or Habib Bourguiba's life presidency or the lack of a constitution in Algeria by the supposedly universal standards of liberal democracy.

The first point of attack is the popular base of the regimes as judged by the normal measuring rod of representation through elections. Now the Maghreb states have no regular elections and no effective party systems. Moroccan pluralism, laid down first in the Constitution of 1962, then in those of 1970 and 1972, would be nothing but a façade behind which the sovereign governs in an increasingly autocratic way, the withdrawal of the opposition parties from the 1970 elections merely underlining the pointlessness of the system. In any case, no ballot-box majority is necessary for the continuation of the government. The heart of the system lies elsewhere, in a direct dialogue between the monarch and the nation. In Tunisia the Destour socialist party has monopolised representation, and its main aim seems to be to secure confirmation of the dominant position of the President at the time of each presidential and even legislative election. The Algerian FLN, which is more a symbol of national unity than a membership party, has been in constitutional limbo since 1965, waiting for the meeting of a Second Congress, announced but not yet held. Whilst waiting for the next national election, it passes the time by drawing up lists with twice as many candidates as posts available for the local elections (1967 Charter), and the regional ones (1969 Charter) which are now being held for the second time.

A second line of comment focuses on those institutions directly linked to the exercise of power. Most observers note a discrepancy here between texts and facts, and in particular between the position ascribed to parties and that which has actually come to the leaders. President Boumediène for example has been in power for more than ten years, whilst the FLN seems merely to be in a permanent state of reconstruction. It exists without direct popular support and with no other form of legitimisation than a delegate body of national sovereignty, the Council of the Revolution, more than half the members of which are dead or expelled and which, although it continues to meet, still has only a vaguely defined function, despite the ordinance of 10 July 1965. In a changing Algeria, power is concentrated at the top of the political, governmental and party hierarchy, in the hands of the one man who is President of the Council of the Revolution, President of the Council of Ministers, Minister of Defence and effective leader of the party. In Tunisia the combination of offices is fairly similar, to the advantage of the one who is President of both Republic and party; there is just this difference that the party apparatus and that of the state, though merged at the top, still retain their own structures and powers, from the government to the political Bureau and right down to the electors and party activists, especially after the Ben Salah affair and the Congress of Monastir in 1971. On the other hand, the case of Morocco throws some doubt on the value of judging monopolisation of power by looking at the party position. The recourse to a state of emergency in June 1965 reintroduced the monarch in the job of head of the government, a state of affairs scarcely modified by the existence of a Prime Minister in name, nor by the constitution of 1972, which was promulgated but not applied. But this other example of concentration is not at variance with the spirit of a regime in which political parties have never had the same sort of role or responsibility as the single parties in Tunisia and Algeria.

What has struck observers most in recent years is the way in which tensions and conflicts have been regulated not within the framework of the institutions but within a ruling class, sometimes no more than a caste, certain elements of which have resorted to assassination attempts to get rid of their leader (in Algeria and more recently Morocco), whilst others concentrate on getting themselves ready for the succession (Tunisia). During open conflicts (the Ben Salah affair in Tunisia, the Skirat coup in Morocco, the Zbiri affair in Algeria) and during the hidden ones, institutions played a minor role and this tended to rebound on them. In Algeria only the army faced up to the crisis; the FLN, which might have improved its image, simply kept out of the affair and therefore only lost face even more; the Presidency looked elsewhere for support, for example during the agricultural revolution to the students who were used again as intermediaries for political socialisation. In Morocco, the growth of the power of the Sultan owes as much to assassination attempts as to party dissension. It is based today on a return to tradition, reflected in reliance on local elites as opposed to urban institutions and elites such as political parties. In Tunisia the tensions within the Destour party have confirmed the apparently irreplaceable nature of the 'Supreme Commander' and have in fact shifted the centre of the crises to more hazy, less public circles such as social groups competing for power.

Constitutional instability, institutional weakness and authoritarian powers; these are the elements which can be pointed to as contrasted to the standards of orthodox democracy. Those standards emerged from very different kinds of historical experience, yet they have been made into myths, set up as absolutes and put forward as models. The Maghreb politicians themselves pay homage to these standards, as if to reconcile their power with humanist ideals. For in Algeria, Morocco and Tunisia a discussion on legitimising power is beginning to take place along the most 'worthy' and 'approved' lines. Reference is very often made to the ideology embodying these standards in order to demonstrate the supreme value of a group of values called sovereignty, separation of powers, representation, pluralism and liberty. But the discussion should be accepted for what it really is: a justification for external use amongst the community of nations: it is also, however, the ideological result of power relations, of the political situation and of the economic position at a given time. The leaders, in their desire to show that their power is based on a unanimously recognised right, present themselves as the product of the general will, stating that they are acting in the public interest. Their opponents use just the same terms in their condemnation of and opposition to the regime (Ferhat Abbas and Ben Khedda in Algeria, Ben Salah or Mestiri in Tunisia, the UNFP (National Union of Popular Forces), USFP (Socialist Union of Popular Forces) and Istiqlal in Morocco), referring to the denial of individual rights, the personalisation of power, the impotence of the parties, the need to restore popular sovereignty, to return to the constitution, to guarantee liberties and institutionalise the opposition. They all use a vocabulary with special meaning, but this meaning is different – one thing for its users in the Maghreb, another among European analysts and with additional variations according to the specific context of each country. So it now becomes necessary to try to understand the reasons behind the words and the situation which gives rise to them, and in this way to understand what the people of the Maghreb themselves say and feel. In ignoring the participants in the drama and their own conceptions of their institutions, the explanations given up to now have run the risk of not being entirely relevant.

B. The View from Inside the New States

We will deal with some aspects of an approach from the Maghreb point of view, not using an a priori approach but examining various facts leading to the same conclusions. Algeria, Morocco and Tunisia have certainly produced outline ideas about their political systems, drafts of national plans and models of systematic thinking about the state which derive from their independent knowledge and understanding of institutions. This doubtless owes a considerable debt to European knowledge, or more precisely to French law, but it has amended the latter to suit itself and has made its own contributions to it. With the knowledge and means at our disposal it does not seem too early to attempt to define a formal model of the institutions in each country, and even to construct a rough draft which would apply to all three (the work of M. Flory and R. Mantran on *The political systems of Arab countries* being the first venture into this area), but it would be too complex a task to be undertaken in a few pages. It would be tempting to carry out an analysis of the content of legal teaching on constitutional law, for example, in the Maghreb universities (this would only yield a series of very formal references) or to read the legislation actually produced with a critical eye, starting with the explanatory notes to the main texts published in the Official Journals. But although such methods are necessary, they would still fail to reveal how individuals there regard institutions, what they expect from them, the relations they have with them.

It should be possible by means of an indirect approach, an 'image' approach, to gain access to the means by which the collective unconscious is shaped and reshaped and thus to grasp the way in which a community actually views events, facts or probabilities. From a whole world of myths, beliefs and opinions we need to penetrate to the idea which the Tunisians, Algerians and Moroccans had and have now of institutions in general and of certain institutions in particular; for example, the way in which they viewed the colonial authorities before and after independence, or how they now envisage the ideal institutions of their respective states.

A national memory carries the images of a glorified past, which is moreover used and embellished by those in power in order to ensure their own stability. As regards the range of institutions, the starting point is the community of religious believers, originally thought of as one of equals. There are several authors, such as the previous member of the FLNA, Mr Kaid Ahmed, who contrast Muslim democracy with marxist democracy, managing to find more socialism in the former. If such ideas cause a smile, that is not to say that they do not correspond to the inner beliefs, or to the desire to believe, of a considerable number of people. Next we find an idealisation of pre-colonial authorities. Liberated Algeria sings the praises of the *djemaa* of its ancestors, of the *khalifalik* and *aghalik* of Abdel Kader, and in doing so it emphasises certain favourable aspects in a partial analysis which provides it with the fiction of a supposedly balanced and harmonious world. This bringing of the past into the present, the unknown towards the known, presents a society made out of virtually nothing as being the true source of the modern Algerian community. This is so much the case that the observer has some difficulty in recognising the real institutions of the old Algeria through the misty descriptions provided by enthusiasts for Francophone Africa, or by yesterday's colonial glorifiers of Berbers or by those now praising Arab Algeria. But the new interpretation, this reference back to the original institutions, still matters, for it shows the Algerians' wish to find a place of their own in history, to see the past in terms of black and white, to discover pointers for their own ideology and to revitalise their roots. The assemblies of notables, the tribal or *douar* councils, which the colonial ethnologists (military and academic) expounded at such length, are reappearing now in writings by commentators and even from the mouths of officials, and they are presented as institutions which, in spite of the depersonalising and destructive impact of colonisation, can be rediscovered today. (See the Algerian Charters of commune and *wilaya*.)

An observer might imagine that since the institutions of the Maghreb's pre-colonial past are praised, those of the colonial past would be condemned. But it is not as simple as that. The praise given to the old *djemaa* has not prevented Algeria from setting up bodies on the municipal level which are quite opposite in character. Again, the centralisation of the state does not allow the organs of popular control to enjoy the same liberties and prerogatives as the *douars* did in the past. These new bodies are essentially instruments merely of deconcentration, and they act as links for a power whose structure and methods are almost totally based on current state norms and where some clear signs of the French type of system may be discerned. In its desire to 'restore the value of its institutions' (Proclamation of 19 June) Algeria is attempting to create its own framework, to break with the rules inherited from the pre-independence system and with the capitalist norms of the old colonial state, and to prepare for the construction of a socialist society in accordance with the Commune Charter. All the institutions need to be recast — in the true sense of the word, melted down and then run into a new mould — in order to promote the rebuilding of the state according to new norms, naturally leading finally to a truly Algerian state. So the rejection of the forms imposed by the colonising power involves making old structures dynamic again and reinterpreting them in the light of national ideology.

It must be admitted that the task remains of deciphering the symbols and imaginary pictures which individuals of varying social classes have in their minds of past institutions — colonial institutions, institutions of modernisation in general and the institutions of their own country in particular. We can move closer to this by taking a look at the expectations which people have of the state. This inquiry should be complementary to the 'image' approach, for behind every expectation there is a wish corresponding to the image created in the mind. What type of institution do the people of the Maghreb really want, what type do they express a wish for, and what in fact are they ready to accept?

However, expectations of the state, and therefore of particular institutions, vary from person to person. There are different expectations, a variety of images, which cannot always be reduced to a composite picture. The vision of the state, the 'institutional concept', varies according to the origin, forms and degrees of socialisation, the class position and the situation in relation to the state apparatus of the particular citizen. It is not simply a question of differences between the official and the *fellah* (peasant), although it is tempting to put it in these terms. The former, for example, would have an authoritarian, even Jacobin, concept of the role of the state as a centralising, interventionist body; that is, a view from 'above' of institutions which he sees mainly as intermediaries between power and the individual. He would moreover take advantage of his position within the state apparatus to look after his friends, building up an unofficial following or passing on his own support to a more powerful patron; he would see institutions as relevant only in terms of personal prestige or of state control, both of which would be seen as worthy of respect and perfectly legitimate. He would expect institutions to provide him with information and feedback, to be obedient instruments. The *fellah's* view of the state is equally affected by his own position; he would only see it as a far-off place with unfathomable power where decisions are made which affect him directly but which he does not understand. Always he would see the good of the community being used to explain decisions taken to the detriment of the individual. This state would be too strong in what it prohibits, too weak in what it allows, too vigorous in control, too lax in protection. The institutions would be seen as the intermediaries of a state monopolised by the bourgeois and the educated, by politicians and con-men. It would be better not to expect anything positive from the local or regional popular assemblies (provinces in Morocco, governorates in Tunisia, *wilayas* in Algeria) so as not to be too disappointed. The hope for better municipal, departmental and national structures (Councils of the Revolution or of the Republic, governments, presidents or kings, any kinds of councils, even assemblies where they exist and are still in use) would be tempered by long experience of doubts born of deception; the *fellah* would have come to turn in on himself. This indeed explains the lack of politicisation (rather than depoliticisation) to be found in these countries.

The only trouble with these specimens is that they reduce

society to extremes and caricatures. Any attempt at an in-depth explanation should involve detailed samples covering a representative section of as much of the population as possible. The setting up of a scale of attitudes would allow these to be interpreted as expectations. We might then be able to discover what the institutions of the past and present and those promised for the future really mean to the people, as well as to find out what people know of institutions in general and what functions they wish to see carried out by those institutions of which they approve. In the end we would doubtless find some traces left behind by the colonial structures and the potential power of the French institutional models. With the data gathered in, one would then compare fictions, expectations and realities.

But are there contradictions between the models and the needs and activities of men? One particularly striking feature commands immediate attention: the acceptance of the predominance of central institutions. We must emphasise again that the break with French cultural models has not been accompanied by any comparable departure from the norms of the political system. Efficiency, production, profitability, order, unity, progress, development: these have remained terms as widely used as in France – as any study of Maghreb political vocabulary will reveal. It would be a mistake to focus solely on slogans, theories, words and national ideologies in praise of the past and thereby to reduce everything to a confrontation level of 'East equals tradition' versus 'West equals modernisation'. Let us instead recognise that (a) power joins together the over-rated distant past, the rejected recent past and the desired future, or yesterday's capitalism, the situation today, and tomorrow's socialism; (b) the final institutional criterion is efficiency, which apparently settles down quite well alongside the idealisation of ancient ways; and (c) this mixture of styles seems to be acceptable and is confirmed by practice. So when President Boumediène insists that the test of profitability has to be applied to all 'self-management' farms* just as it is to the industrial sector, or announces the rebuilding of a strong, efficient party, or promises a national assembly that will

* ['Autogestion' made its appearance following the departure of the French. Their properties, mainly lands, were taken over and presented to those, mainly the peasants, who had worked upon them. They were now to run the farms themselves (though in fact the government appointed managers). – Eds.]

mirror the nation, he uses standards which obviously bear a close resemblance to those used in industrial nations. Nevertheless, no one includes the Algerian system in either the capitalist or the marxist categories of regime.

It would be interesting to know how ideology manages to build a sort of 'institution-mixer'. No less interesting would it be to see how words of praise and blame come to be applied, so that some things are good if they permit change in the real world (of production, consumption, trade, institutions as a whole and the international situation), and other things bad because they are irrational or contrary to the spirit of society. Without this, how can we explain the Jacobinism, the feeling for the state, the technocratic spirit, the status and mystique of the top official, the respect mixed with fear for everything concerning the state? How can we understand that, on the whole, the state is never challenged and certain aspects of its excessive power are accepted without a protest? The growth of the state's power, the increase in its personnel, the deterioration in its methods are seen as natural, as economic, political and strategic necessities. Thus the failure or relative lack of success of the institutions of 'self-management' in Algeria and of those connected with Bensalah's economic changes in Tunisia are attributed merely to the hurried nature of the venture, the lack of adaptation of the venture, the lack of adaptation of the forms of production, or the people's state of mind. If there are any regrets, hardly ever are these to the effect that the 'self-management' sector in Algeria should not have been widened, or that the Tunisian co-operatives should not have been developed.

Furthermore, the people of the Maghreb in general have simply accepted the paradox that it is the top of the political hierarchy which emphasises the need for decentralisation and praises the merits of autonomy and of local initiative. Does this acceptance come from the fact that the political elite is seen as the only group that achieved escape from the darkness in which the colonial state kept all Algerians for so long? Or does it stem from such alienation under colonial rule that men can no longer distinguish between what is good for them and what is dangerous? In fact, this cult of the state can, in part, be explained by the stress on national unity, always presented as the culmination of all the liberation struggles, to be preserved (and strengthened) at any price – and by what means if not by the state? The integration of the nation went hand in hand with the unity of the state, powers being concentrated in a few hands, individual institutions being given little independent power. Perhaps at this point we should ask: if a certain idea of the state involves an ideology of state growth and leads to practical steps towards that end, does not the resulting reduction in popular power ('self-management', i.e. less real, poorer representation, loss of effective control) gradually alter the nature of power itself and thereby alter the structure and role of the institutions?

Summary

1. The classic analysis of the Maghreb institutions has usually been set in a framework of liberal democratic categories. On these lines the study of the development of these states reveals three separate stages in the movement away from the French model. The era of assemblies and imitation of standards from 1956 to 1963 was followed by that of political parties, attempts at political representation and the building of autonomous institutions. Then we come to the era of leaders; they are symbols of concentrated state power and a centralised state apparatus, but they are also indications of regimes whose fragility is due to over-emphasis on personalities. In any case, they mark, in the contemporary context, a complete break between the system of the new states and that of the old colonial power.

2. A new line of inquiry would try to discover more about the specific nature of the institutions set up in each of the Maghreb countries and perhaps to pursue comparisons not with Europe but with other non-European systems in unindustrialised countries. By approaching them from the inside, through the way in which individuals visualise them (sometimes even as myths) we would discern people's expectations – ranging from everything to nothing. Ideas and expectations do not always correspond to the official ideology, which insists on the efficiency of institutions needed to promote development and modernisation whilst maintaining national unity.

3. On this last question, and amongst the many problems posed by the development of an informed model of the Maghreb's

institutions, there are some key issues: Which institutions are adapted to social change and can organise it? Can the same recognised political institutions (army, monarchy, political parties, the executive and legislature) achieve both social and economic changes or do these require different institutions? Could different institutions be accommodated or would they conflict? How then would the conflict be resolved?

12

Factors of Dependence: Senegal and Kenya

Rita Cruise O'Brien

Introduction

Scholarship on the application of models of dependence to Latin American and more recently African countries has made a very useful contribution to the understanding of underdevelopment in the world context. Specialist articles based on micro-empirical research have illustrated the dynamics of dependence in specific contexts,[1] yet within these and more general contributions on theory it is the *terms* of analysis around which most discussion has centred. And the debate has been dominated by neo-Marxists and (Latin American) structuralists. I do not wish here to summarise the debate (which has been well done elsewhere[2]), but to introduce a different perspective − one of comparison of two states in Africa which, though they have strikingly different social and economic histories, show a remarkable similarity in current policies and attendant problems. I offer this with a conviction that examining the empirical situation in comparative terms will feed back into a refinement of terms and add perhaps more perspective to the specifically African content of the characteristics of dependence.

The identification of the internal structural characteristics of a peripheral socio-economic system provides a starting point for analysis. First, the state in particular is very important in Africa as a consumer of GDP, as an investor in the economy, as a source of employment and therefore as an arbiter of class formation, as I

283

shall indicate. Scholars working on dependence in Latin America have begun to consider the role of the State in the periphery. But its position in post-colonial Africa is altogether different and requires fundamental research on a comparative basis in order to determine its precise importance as an instrument of external influence and a broker of internal interests.[3] Second, more work is required on class formation, in particular analyses of the new bourgeoisie. The capacity for local accumulation is limited in countries like Senegal and Kenya by the predominance of private foreign capital in certain sectors. The politico-administrative bourgeoisie (ruling class) has a predominant position, and the emergence of a professional class is somewhat circumscribed by its dependence on foreign standards and qualifications. Each of these sectors of the bourgeoisie is variously influenced (or buttressed by) the former colonial metropole and for each a common life style is emerging based on taste transfer from metropolitan sources. The identification of a bourgeoisie in Africa has thus far been confined to the Fanonist formula or an adaptation of Marxism.[4] The role of the State and its relationship to the bourgeoisie as well as other emergent classes is central to an understanding of the internal effects of dependence on a peripheral socio-economic system. While in both Senegal and Kenya a major proportion of economic power remains in foreign hands, the State which not only serves but encourages those interests is not just a cipher, nor can it be simply described as a 'comprador bourgeoisie' of those interests.

Scholars using dependence as a framework of analysis have identified three characteristics in peripheral economies: immiseration, marginalised growth or stagnation. Rather than apply these conditions to the whole structure of the economy it is possible perhaps to identify *all* of them at different levels or in different sectors. One of the arguments of this paper will find features of immiseration in the rural and urban working class, marginalised growth among small farmers and petty producers and elements of stagnation in the monopolistic features of the economy. In a situation of limited indigenous capital in Kenya and Senegal, the state has intervened to protect existing monopolies (foreign enterprise) or create new ones (policies toward local private investment and state investment).

Planning and state intervention in the economy has produced

in neither country an effective marshalling of local and natural resources. Although there has been growth in real terms since independence, much more dramatic in Kenya than in Senegal, the lack of an effective planning process has not been able to give an impetus to potential human and capital resources. Development in the periphery remains constrained not only because of the effects of sizeable foreign capital investment, but also because of local political options. It is not only the structural short circuits in terms of poor links between economic sectors, but also the social and political characteristics of a neo-colonial economy which explain the stagnation implied by dependence.

It may be useful at this point to present a list of composite characteristics of dependence which are applicable to the African situation. These characteristics are intended to be merely suggestive of features of dependence, not a 'check-list' against which dependence/non-dependence can be measured:

1. heavy foreign penetration through private investment;
2. use of capital intensive technologies (in sectors where less complicated ones might promote employment);
3. primary commodity production with overseas markets;
4. marked inequalities in income distribution;
5. consumption patterns for certain groups derived from advanced capitalist countries;
6. incomplete proletarianisation or absorption of peasant producers into the economy leading to marginalisation or marginal participation in the central productive economy;
7. import substitution industrialisation;
8. reliance on foreign aid and loans to finance many development projects;
9. weak legal or tax policies on the control of foreign penetration;
10. use of foreign standards in educational and professional spheres and imported modes of organisation.[5]

In his recent book, *Underdevelopment in Kenya*,[6] Colin Leys has identified peripheralisation in terms of the following characteristics, which complement the others, and in his view illustrate the difference between complete stagnation and confined growth:

1. external orientation with weak links between domestic sectors;
2. strong links between primary producing sectors and overseas markets;
3. monopoly capitalism;
4. non-generation of domestic development from economic surplus.

For the preparation of a Senegal-Kenya comparison, I have been most favoured by the recent publication of this book on which evidence I shall rely heavily. Evidence for the Senegal case is drawn chiefly from work contained in a collection of essays which has been prepared in collaboration with a group of scholars who have done recent research in Senegal (R. Cruise O'Brien, ed., *The Political Economy of Underdevelopment: Dependence in Senegal*, London, Sage Publications, 1979).

The comparison between Senegal and Kenya with their differing patterns of colonial exploitation and subsequent metropolitan dependence begins necessarily with different historical legacies. They both served as regional colonial centres, from which Kenya to some extent benefited subsequently, while Senegal has found its function as administrative and economic capital of the French West African Federation a considerable burden since independence. The contrasting economic base explains this – as Kenya has always had a richer and more diversified agriculture. Agricultural landholding in Kenya was based on two principal patterns – white settlers on large estates in the most productive areas (the 'white highlands') and peasant small holdings on the remainder of the land. In Senegal, the monocrop of groundnuts was grown on peasant small holdings; the base of the rural economy. African incomes in rural Kenya could therefore be wage or smallholder shares. Kenya also has a much larger internal market than Senegal and recently its capacity to attract import substitution investment, from a diverse group of multinational firms, is based also on its role as what Leys calls a 'peripheral centre' in East Africa. A striking difference between the two countries are different rates of growth of GDP. In Kenya between 1964 and 1970, the rate was 7.6 per cent with a solid contribution from the agricultural sector, where from 1964–1972 in Senegal the rate was 2.9 per cent, almost all accounted for in the rise in world groundnut prices between 1968 and 1971.[7] In contrast with the wealth of the highlands of Kenya and its excellent climatic conditions, Senegal is on the Sahara fringe and has suffered with other Sahel countries in recent years a severe drought which affected productive output of its chief export commodity, groundnuts. Political and nationalist traditions differ as Kenya had an armed rebellion and retains a strong element of violence in its political tradition, while Senegal made a very 'smooth' shift from colonial to politically independent status within the French orbit. Both countries enjoyed until recently (Kenyatta's death) strong political leadership in one man since independence – worthy of note in Africa today.

Both Senegal and Kenya have had a substantial local European presence in addition to the colonial administrative apparatus. The chief difference was that these were rural settlers in Kenya, while in Senegal French residents (who remained for their working life only) were urban wage and salary earners, managers, professionals and shopkeepers. Major divisions between the rural landholding group and the managers of urban commerce and industry in Kenya were to be apparent in the years prior to independence in addition to the colonial administrative apparatus. The definitive importance of these two resident groups during or after colonial rule has differed. Both countries have favoured positions in the French and British aid and technical assistance programmes respectively as large recipients. Both countries have had a foreign minority in middle-level trade and industry – the Lebanese and Asians – whose role has however been somewhat different. Neither country had an indigenous large landowning class from which surplus could be generated and therefore little potential for investment locally. There has been rapid growth in smallholder cashcropping in Kenya since independence and the new African bourgeoisie has taken over land previously held by Europeans. In Senegal growers' cooperatives have been formed. Despite these changes, however, neither government has radically altered the structure of agricultural production. Industrialisation, which until recently has been either primary product processing or import substitution, remains largely in foreign hands, which has meant retaining overseas linkages rather than generating domestic ones. In Senegal most investment has come from within the highly protected franc zone, while Kenya has had more diversified sources of investment. Each country has recently attempted to move into the highly competitive field of manufactured exports, although there are few signs that this move has been designed to stimulate many local linkages and therefore generate capital internally. It may be argued therefore that industrialisation has led to a consolidation of underdevelopment by being externally oriented and generating only marginal benefits internally. It would seem apposite to apply a framework of dependence to these two systems in order to better understand the internal constraints which, while allowing for growth since independence, have not enlarged the sources of local investment and may indeed in the long run have created greater impoverishment in the poorest stratum of the population relative to affluent groups. As the roots of this situation lie in the colonial phase, this will be the starting point of the comparison.

Roots in the Colonial Economy

The building of the railway from Mombasa to Lake Victoria just after the turn of the century was, as for the case of the Dakar-groundnut region rail link, the confirmation of the establishment of a colonial cash crop economy based on the export of primary products. Land on the rich highlands of Kenya was expropriated for white settlement, while Europeans served as trading agents to peasant producers of groundnuts in Senegal. In contrast to 2,400 acre plots[8] offered at a minimal price in Kenya in 1932, plantation farming was never seriously considered in the arid regions of the Senegal central basin. Europeans in Kenya benefited from investment in rural infrastructure, while the African peasants were compelled to farm less rich lowlands in order to pay government taxes. Colonial taxation was an important implement in shifting peasants from the subsistence mode of production in both countries. In the period between the wars the purchase of manufactured goods first from Europe, and later produced by local industries, destroyed traditional crafts and altered the employment structure in the rural areas, thus completing the shift to a cash-based economy. In both Kenya and Senegal a process of internal peripheralisation took place as regions not central to export production were deliberately deprived of infrastructure. In the case of Senegal, this led to migratory movements of labour from outlying regions to the groundnut basin or to the growing coastal urban areas between the wars, or later to migration of unskilled labour to France itself. In Kenya, land hunger became an acute problem and an impetus to later nationalism.

In the interwar period light industry in both Dakar and Nairobi was based first on the processing of food and later other commodities, which were exported to other colonies in the French West African and East African Federation respectively. The posts of trading agents for the colonial companies were reserved first for the French and later for the Lebanese. The Asian minority in Kenya controlled trade and credit on the coast for two centuries and opened wholesale and retail trade in the interior prior to colonial rule. By 1948, there were nearly 98,000 Asians[9] in Kenya whereas there were only 6,000 Lebanese in the same period and never more than 18,000[10] in all in Senegal. The Lebanese only began to be active in Senegal in a client relationship to French trading companies after 1900[11] and their interests were never so independent nor so substantial, as was the case of the Asians in Kenya. Leys calls the latter group 'a prototype of a national industrial bourgeoisie' for, when investments in commerce were saturated, they extended their interests to light industry and real estate. Thus by 1961 Asians owned more than 67 per cent of locally-owned industries with more than fifty employees.[12] There is no comparison with the Senegal case where less than a dozen Lebanese family firms held comparable investment. Much longer established and much more numerous (in comparison to the African-European balance of the population) than was the case of Lebanese entrepreneurs in Senegal, the Kenyan Asian minority has also been more circumscribed since independence in its activities, and (as elsewhere in East Africa) much more threatened.

Open migration within the French Empire and the encouragement of Frenchmen to migrate to Senegal between the wars meant that most of the job creation in the private sector, apart from unskilled labourers and apprentices, was reserved for Europeans, with negative effects on training and localisation prior to independence. Industrial and commercial development in Dakar was particularly favoured by the policy of local purchase by the expanding administration of the Federation of French West Africa. Both Nairobi and Dakar rapidly became enclaves of metropolitan society, with a foreign bourgeoisie of shopkeepers and service personnel. These enclaves remained divorced from the rural structure in some measure, parallel to it and maintaining a high cost of living because of protected import policies and taxation.

In Kenya, Europeans had a monopoly of production of the most profitable crops especially coffee, and a system of monopolies for marketing internally. In Senegal, by contrast, European monopolies remained solely with the trading companies which bought from the peasant producers (a role usually reserved for Asians in Kenya) and sold manufactured goods in return. These metropolitan companies with the colonial government were the two supports of imperialism in the colony, while in Kenya the agricultural base of the economy was much more complex. The Kenyan rural economy was arguably 'protected' from market forces by monopolies created after independence. Kenyan politicians accepted the necessity of maintaining the large-scale mixed farms which had been the basis of European settlement, and used them as a basis from which they and senior civil servants 'levered their way into the economy'. Marketing monopolies were then maintained after independence in order to prevent Indians from entering this sector. A parallel occurrence in the Senegalese rural economy was the creation of a state marketing monopoly for groundnuts (OCA, ONCAD) just after independence, thus replacing both the French companies and Lebanese agents, while creating peasant dependence on the state through a system of obligatory rural co-operatives, which have hardly been successful. While in Kenya marketing boards subsidized the settler sector (and later the African bourgeois owners) and protected them by high prices, the same institutions in Senegal were used to tax peasant producers to earn revenue for the State (as in Nigeria and Ghana).

Post-war prosperity in both colonies brought a rise in local purchasing power, confined to urban enclaves in Senegal. Food self-sufficiency was achieved in Kenya, while food so basic to the daily diet as rice in Senegal was imported from French Indochina, although subsistence farming remained important. In Kenya the prosperity of the non-agricultural sector was dependent on agricultural exports and this was also true for Senegal, at a much more modest level of expansion or diversification. Import substitution firms increased in number in this period to serve each of the colonial regions of West and East Africa.

Leys argues that when the Mau Mau Emergency called into question the colonial economy, foreign investment and in particular new commercial and industrial interests abandoned the settlers. Rejecting the notion that agricultural settlement was the predominant form of capitalism in Kenya, he argues that it was the urban interests which pressed the government to accept African demands for land, in order not to jeopardize the entire economy. His argument could be given a parallel case in Senegal (though its origins are structurally different) in the marginality of the *petit blanc*. As political activity in Senegal had from the nineteenth century been confined to the four coastal communes (which were regarded as part of metropolitan France) politics until the decade prior to independence had been dominated by African client politicians of the important French trading companies. Frenchmen, encouraged to migrate from the situation of post-war job scarcity, came in great numbers to Dakar after 1945,[13] but soon realised that they had no leverage on the economic system as they were in direct competition with the Lebanese, and even less influence on the political system in the colony or in France. They rapidly became marginal to the system as the hopes of building an integrated French Empire waned.[14] As a result of the Emergency in Kenya, in addition to the transfer of previously restricted land there was an opening of banking and credit facilities to African traders in 1952 – something which was not done in Senegal until twenty years later and then only by a half-hearted government promotion effort (apart from the recruitment of African trading agents for a partly state-owned retail consortium in the 1960s). Measures such as credit easing, access to mixed farms and the reservation of certain sectors of trade for Kenyans, had no parallel in Senegal and therefore what Leys was able to identify as an 'auxiliary bourgeoisie' in Kenya is minute in Senegal. Prior to independence, therefore, a major contrast would underline the relatively more diversified structure of the Kenya economy. Kenya will be considered in a later phase to have developed a more complicated level of dependence, contrasted with what might be considered in Senegal as only the rudiments beyond a stage of colonialism.

Nationalism and Post Independence Politics

The New Kenyan Group which was founded in 1959 by liberal Europeans and Africans may be viewed as the culmination of a process of the failure of colonial rule (already made obvious in the Emergency in 1952). The Group proposed policies which were adopted to ease the transition to independence by giving Africans access both to land and trade without structurally altering the basis of the economy. African members of the group included the sons chiefly of families who had access to mission education, and its European members were investors in the urban economy. Government policy was not to frustrate this group. A parallel in Senegal in political terms in the early 1950s would be the local branch of the French Socialist Party (the SFIO). It represented, on the whole, the urban indigenous and European business and professional interests as was the case of the NKG. In Senegal, SFIO leaders were the African deputies in the French parliament together with local elected representatives and it was regarded as a 'safe' interest group by the colonial administration. As the Kenya Emergency gave rise to the mass party, Kenya Africa National Union with its leader Jomo Kenyatta, mass politics was introduced in the Election of 1952 in Senegal by Leopold Senghor, who made an approach to the rural population and took as his party platform a stand to represent rural against urban communal interests for the first time. Conflict in tribal terms, as between KANU representing Kikuyu interests against the Kenya African Democratic Union which represented the minority tribes, was never important in Senegal. The spread of the market economy had led to a spread of the Wolof language and culture or a process of Wolofisation of the peasantry, more precisely.

Apart from Southern Senegal (the Casamance region in particular) ethnic differences always remained a minor factor in Senegalese politics, partly because of the division of the groundnut-producing peasantry into powerful Muslim Brotherhoods, which themselves organised the mode of production in the groundnut-growing region and had a subsequent influence on the clientele structure of politics in the countryside. As the early KADU platform represented interests in regionalisation, so did the political representative from the Casamance in the PRA (*Parti de Regroupement Africain*) in Senegal, but in neither case did these minority influences ultimately win favour as the centralising power of the single party state gained force.

Leys identifies the role of KANU as an arbiter among foreign interests, the local 'auxiliary' bourgeoisie and petty bourgeois interests.[15] It is tempting to see the *Union Progressiste Sénégalaise* (UPS) in the same brokerage role. In the early days of independence, both parties had a radical rump. In Kenya the radical challenge led by Oginga Odinga with some collaboration from the unions campaigned for an equality of opportunity based on two principal elements – free education and land for the landless. In Senegal, the first Prime Minister, Mamadou Dia, and his followers built their appeal on a socialist development strategy involving, above all, a radical reorientation of the rural structure – making it the focus of economic interest with not only co-operatives but community development efforts. In Kenya, the conflict was fought in multi-party electoral terms whereas in Senegal it remained based on clan following within the single party and was eliminated after the threat of an attempted coup in 1962. Part of the style of Senghorist politics has been the co-optation of the leaders of potential opposition parties, thus adding vitality to the clan struggles within the party. During the 1960s KANU consolidated its power by crushing the radical opposition, represented by the Kenyan People's Union (KPU) and reorganised its platform by 1965 to one of close collaboration with private foreign enterprise with an emphasis on rapid growth, allowing where possible for the support of local capital interests.[16] The same was true of a shift in orientation of the Senegalese government which based its growth in the 1960s on French investment in import substitution, while production in the agricultural sector was lagging.[17]

The consolidation of power in Kenya was achieved with the help of the following factors:

(a) availability of land to distribute to some of the landless and to rich farmers, traders and civil servants;
(b) trade of Asians to distribute to the African petty bourgeoisie;
(c) high rates of foreign investment;
(d) high rate of output from farming;
(e) good external relations for trade and aid;
(f) tactical weakness of the opposition.[18]

The factors in Senegal differed, since there was no land to distribute as property. There was only access to thus far uncultivated land in outlying regions for some of the peasant growers or maraboutic (Muslim religious) leaders or the settlement of new territories under government programmes. No Lebanese interests were offered to African entrepreneurs, and the only effort to curb their presence in Senegal was a law in 1964 which halted further immigration, which had in any case fallen to a negligible proportion both because of the nationalisation of groundnut marketing in 1962 (and the removal of half the trading business in the rural area) and the general recession caused by the departure of many French residents. Despite the necessary reorientation from acting as the commercial and industrial capital of French West Africa, the industrial sector in Senegal in the 1960s showed remarkable growth in this period, while output in the agricultural sector, in contrast to Kenya, was stagnant.

France, for example continued to subsidize groundnut sales over the world market price until 1967, which assisted government finances and the political stability of a regime which protected French investment interests.[19] The tactical weakness of the opposition was similar in both countries, but perhaps most marked in Senegal, which was a system with few benefits to distribute to its voters.

The political structure in Senegal has therefore had to bear the brunt of keeping the system together, a goal achieved by an elaborate clan structure through which local notables assert their claims on the governing elite, and a skilful balancing act is maintained by the President and other party leaders. It is a system which has been an effective means of patronage redistribution involving costs in terms of economic development.[20] Political stability has been achieved at the cost of internal economic stagnation. Although the French or British have little direct influence in domestic politics in either country, an important factor of administrative stability in both has been the presence of technical assistants from the respective aid agencies. Since neither model of administration was much altered after independence both British and French expatriates who had been well accustomed to running the system were useful to the governing elite. Regardless of how quickly localisation was achieved, the experience and skill of these administrators easily provided a parallel administration,[21] in an expanding administration often ill-prepared for the task of confronting the problems of under-development. Britain provided 60 per cent of the total of technical assistance personnel − 3,600 in 1971[22] in Kenya − while the French have had much more exclusive monopoly on the provision of technical assistance in Senegal.[23] In both countries the political system required numbers of expatriates on whom the ruling class could depend or who could keep a basically unreformed educational structure in operation. Though perhaps the latter is more dramatic in Senegal, the diploma-conscious Kenyan achievement system has also required a considerable number of British technical assistants per annum. Above all, the expatriate factor added a dimension to the political power of each regime in a situation of structural dependence.

Agriculture

In this sector differences in land ownership and endowments of soil and climate between Kenya and Senegal make an interesting background to comparison of the strategies adopted to cover the transition from colonial agriculture. Access to land and in particular mixed farms in the 'white' highlands was a concession awarded to Africans prior to independence while ranch land and plantations of very high capital value remained in European hands until later. Leys argues that 'in no other sphere was the transition from colonial political control to one of pervasive metropolitan influences − based on advice, technical assistance and credit − so clearly visible.'[24] Two central aspects of policy were evident: individualisation of land tenure and differential access to credit, to the benefit of the more prosperous farmers. The land transfer programme was achieved on two main lines: peasant farmers moved on to land alongside a small group of the African bourgeoisie (civil servants, traders and politicians) who aspired to take over the larger expatriate owned farms. Thus a structure of agrarian interests based on private property was created: land hunger on the white highlands served as a sufficient pole of attraction beyond which a restructuring of this rich resource was not considered.

The process of shift to African land ownership in Kenya was set up in the early 1960s when the British government was willing to 'pay a price to extricate itself from Kenya'.[25] The price in this sector was aid for debt-financing (until 1966) as the land was purchased. For smaller farmers debt repayment became difficult as the plot size was not necessarily viable. From 1964 money was lent through this scheme directly to entrepreneurs buying the larger firms. Sixty per cent of the total land occupied through these schemes were large farms often purchased by property groups of 2 to 3 owners.[26] Cooperative ventures on the larger farms proved unsuccessful. In 1970 the British grant for land purchase was renewed, and schemes through a state finance corporation favoured large landowners in particular (who could also acquire grants and British interest-free loans). This was an interesting pattern of the creation of a landed bourgeoisie within a protected financial environment in which commercial surplus was invested, and where politically important personalities were able to acquire a stake in the rural economy. The overlap of large farm ownership and political influence was apparent, with the obvious benefits of using government policy to continue to keep this process healthy, as well as withdrawing access (by eviction) to those who fell out of political favour.

The remaining land acquired by Africans in Kenya consisted of much smaller units but the overwhelming majority of owners began to have certain problems. Very few of them had the capital, experience or skills to operate efficiently. Finance schemes favoured the larger owners and the problem of debt repayment became so acute for small farmers that they became tenants of larger ones.[27] The whole scheme for the settlement of smaller farmers was perhaps in question owing to the dubious viability of the plot size. Having just provided land there was little other official support, as even government marketing board policies favoured the larger farm sector through greater concessions.

Land access was not a conspicuous public issue in Senegal. There is a very small proportion of large growers of groundnuts – usually Muslim brotherhood notables or other leaders with traditional status. Unlike the rich and varied agricultural output in Kenya, however, Senegal had to make considerable and largely unsuccessful efforts to diversify from its monocrop economy. One of the first efforts at diversification was in rice which had become a staple food, where in a very heavily capital intensive scheme the price of locally grown rice remained higher than even that imported from the Far East. All Senegalese efforts to diversify have been large costly state-managed projects with only long-term benefits, financed mainly through foreign aid, none of which injected any life into the agricultural economy during the 1960s. Growth was to some extent hampered by low agricultural planning priority and investment. As in the case of Kenya a metropolitan subsidy was crucial in the period of transition. A French subsidy was provided to the price of groundnuts above the world market price. It was a subsidy which was not passed on to the peasants but absorbed into the state purse.[28] While the subsidy was being reduced from 1965 a massive programme of (primarily French) technical assistance was provided to try to raise production per acre. There was a number of complicated reasons why the scheme was not altogether successful, not least of which was the poor weather conditions. Despite the disappointment, the subsidy was removed entirely by 1967, while for 14 years producer prices remained stable leading to greater impoverishment in a situation of rising cost of living (kept high to some extent by inefficient French import substitution firms).

The Senegalese government relies on groundnuts as its principal earner of foreign exchange. During the 1960s a system of rural cooperatives was introduced to complement the state marketing mechanism and make more effective the effort to raise production. Conflict of interest between cash-cropping peasantry and the state was a legacy of colonial rule, now reinforced and made more efficient. Cooperatives, which all farmers had ultimately to join (by 1968) provided seed, credit, fertiliser and machinery and the outlet for marketing of produce. Proclaimed as an end to colonial inequalities it in the first instance reinforced rural economic inequalities as the local cooperative officials – many of whom enriched themselves in the process – were the effective subordinates of the governing alliance.[29] The demise of the Diaists or radicals in the UPS within a few years after independence meant that the programme for the radical reform, participation and improvement of the principal agricultural sector was largely ignored, and the state apparatus became one of direct exploitation of the peasantry. The cooperatives organised the rural world and the state appropriated the agricultural surplus. The peasants become indebted to the system of cooperative credit chits for machinery and fertiliser which, for example, may have been prescribed by the Plan for their region. And cash was provided by the usurious practices of local traders (mainly Lebanese). Government practices effectively made a rural working class of the peasantry with no apparent leverage on the government institutions which oppressed them. Towards the end of the first decades of independence, a peasant consciousness of their objective situation led to a refusal to plant further groundnuts and a return to subsistence crops. This was a radical and ultimately effective short-term act. The *malaise paysan*, as it became known, began to cost the government revenue in serious proportions. An appeal to the European Development Fund of the Common Market with the active support of France brought a grant to the Senegalese government which allowed that government to use this so-called 'emergency relief' for a cancellation of peasant debts to the cooperatives. This grant (two million pounds) enabled the government to survive, assisted as it was further by an unprecedented rise in the world price between 1968–1973, at best one-fifth of which was passed on to the peasant farmer in 1973.[30] It could be argued that the peasantry in Senegal has been sacrificed to political stability and state enrichment, assisted actively by the aid policies of France. In the latter part of the 1960s a more serious effort was made towards provision of rural infrastructure and planning, but the high cost of consumer goods from local industries or imports has kept the peasant very poor. The neglect of short-term support for diversification of food production or the provision of non-agricultural employment in rural Senegal has kept the peasants tied to a market system in which they can ill afford to participate.

In Kenya the preservation of private property and settlement programmes can be compared to the state intervention in Senegal as a means of ignoring a radical alternative for improving rural production. The debt burden of large farmers in Kenya has been shifted to domestic consumers of farm produce. The Kenya government favours large peasant producers, potential capitalist farmers, the satisfaction of whose interests provides few political risks.[31] Foreign aid schemes to assist small farmers have been fairly unsuccessful as the multiplicity of donors (British, Swedish, Dutch, American) have imposed preconceived projects ill-adapted to local conditions. Too much emphasis was given to cash crops rather than food crops and employment efforts as well as infrastructure were similarly weak.[32] Above all agricultural potential in both countries has been sacrificed to patterns of industrialisation and commercial development, with little attempt toward integrated development and the added burden of high costs to rural dwellers.

Foreign Investment

Metropolitan trading companies which had established themselves in both Senegal and Kenya during colonial rule were consolidated into metropolitan groups or gradually diversified their interests into manufacturing. Foreign investment, formerly in land in Kenya, was also directed to manufacturing, as were Asian assets which were in commerce. In the transition period before and after independence there was a significant shift of ownership in internal trade as a number of sectors operated by Asians were reserved for Africans. Like the Asians, the few Lebanese capitalists invested in real estate, and manufacturing. Service industries like insurance are both being localised with local bank or state contribution. While Kenya's prosperity since 1967 in particular brought a considerable expansion of diverse multinational investments (with an average rise of £10.3 million[33] per annum in foreign investment), French interests in Senegal remain in a modern sector which is 85 per cent foreign-owned. Both foreign sectors are to date largely based on import substitution.

Import substitution is a traditionally short-term solution to industrialisation, in order to curb foreign spending and provide employment. But an import-substituting economy may block further possibilities for developing manufactured exports or keep the cost of local commodities so high as to contribute to a worsening in income distribution and consumption. And inefficient import substitution, far from generating further industrialisation, may actually inhibit the development process by increasing the costs of inputs to potentially forward-linked industries. This case exists in Senegal, largely because of the franc zone protection of relatively inefficient French enterprise which has not faced any competition.

A case in point is the farm-implement manufacturing company in Senegal, which has kept the cost of necessary farm machinery

very high, or the can-producing factory which is a major
impediment to the competitive export strategy of the country's
processed fish industry, for example. In order to attract foreign
investment, the concessions made in terms of taxation and import
regulations for components and raw materials have further
ramifications, as the growth of import substitution has reduced
government revenues from imports without any local tax
framework to compensate for the loss.

Kenya is, on the whole, a much more prosperous economy
with greater local earning and purchasing power. Despite
constraints on the development of local capitalism, which will be
discussed in the next section, the size of the local market has
permitted some 'filtering down' of this prosperity to local African
entrepreneurs, for example, who have become clients of the
foreign firms by providing satellite companies for either supply or
marketing. The multinational sector in Kenya has a critical role in
shaping demand through 'taste transfer',[34] while standardisation
allows for only a certain number of linkages with local industry.
Sophisticated product choice and technology reduce the
possibility of creating further linkages, while consumption
patterns establish preferences which are difficult to meet in small
scale enterprise. The MNC sector effect on employment in Kenya
is to encourage the emergence of a small, relatively well-paid
work force, which is very differentiated in income from the rest
of the labour force.[35]

In Senegal, by contrast, the difficulties of readjusting the local
structure of industry from its federal market in French West
Africa led to a recession in construction and all service industries
in the 1960s, which might otherwise have provided an
opportunity for local investment. Though the import substitution
industries showed growth of 6 per cent in this period it was only
achieved under very elaborate protection and concession schemes
which did not provide any structural growth in subsidiary
sectors, but rather kept the cost of manufactured goods extremely
high at a time when wages and salaries were frozen. Having
weathered the recession caused by the 'balkanisation' of French
West Africa and hence its markets for Dakar-based industries, the
government has renewed hope of moving into manufactured
exports, both for the European Common Market and newly
established possibilities for West African cooperation (particularly

among francophone countries). Growth rates in manufacturing were about 4.7 per cent in the 1960s[36] (which was four times better than the rest of the economy), but their growth somewhat camouflaged the cost of concessions as well as the support of certain inefficient French-owned industries. The recent investment code still offers substantial concessions to large investors but raises the problem of cost to the government of these investments in fiscal and other terms. The period of adaptation from earlier problems having been largely surmounted, the question remains whether the government will harden its conditions or perhaps reduce the oligopolistic import situation by differentiating its imports from French sources. New projects like a customs free industrial zone in Dakar or a tanker repair station, while providing local employment possibilities, do not appear to be geared to generating any linkages with local capital investment.

Tourism has in both Kenya and Senegal received a lot of government support since independence. In Kenya, it has replaced coffee as a major foreign exchange earner and in Senegal, although the sector is much smaller, a number of concessions have been offered to foreign firms which will provide a dubious contribution to local employment or investment. The proportion of capital expenditure to job creation is extremely high compared with other sectors. And the only major stipulation on foreign investment in tourism in Senegal, for example, is a required 20 per cent reinvestment of profits. While arguing that the sector will provide much needed employment (in minimal terms), the cost to the public purse in expenditure on infrastructure to serve tourist complexes far outweighs the small benefits.

While maintaining very favourable policies toward foreign capital investment, both the Senegal and Kenya governments have found it possible to nationalise assets in certain sectors, therefore increasing the government's share in locally generated surplus. In Senegal, socialisation of profits in phosphate production and groundnut oil refining was achieved without nationalisation of plant or equipment and joint earning from assets is shared by the company and the government. It has been argued that participation was the means by which the government gained information on assets in this vital sector, without the problem of managing the firms in question. While they were entirely in foreign hands it was difficult to know, for example, if tax assessment was adequate. Leys has pointed out that control on foreign investment through taxation has usually been under-administered and therefore easily ignored.[37] The Kenya government localised a monopoly of shares in the packaging industries, which meant the company sold old shares and repatriated receipts without any control. And Asian investors filled at least some of the local vacuum. Shares in oil refining were purchased by the government in Kenya, but Leys argues that the cost in terms of foreign exchange was high as was the lost opportunity cost of investing in other sectors.[38] Measures to control foreign investment (localisation of employment and assets) have in both countries served to further identify government interests with foreign capital investment.

The rate of employment in the foreign owned sector has not made a substantial impact on the shape of employment as a whole: in Kenya employment improved by only 2 per cent from 1964–69 in the modern sector (which remained largely foreign owned).[39] A significant structural feature of this employment was the rapidly rising wages to a small labour force, expanding much more slowly than the population. And in Senegal a similar problem is made more dramatic by the overproduction of primary and secondary school graduates, about 30,000 of whom join the labour force each year. In both countries the dependence on external models in the educational system remains striking. The emphasis remains on diplomas and formal qualifications and the medium of instruction is English and French respectively. Little has been done in either country to make significant changes in the educational system which would permit a more rational manpower policy related to employment opportunities.

Both countries since the mid-1960s have begun to insist on progressive Africanisation in foreign firms. The receptivity to expanding African management and professional staff has differed from firm to firm, the older longer established companies remaining most resistant. It was found in Senegal, for example, that the local managers of French multi-national firms which were keen to Africanise for political as well as budgetary reasons (expatriate staff and their maintenance remaining a high local cost factor) found that such policies were effectively blocked by local

expatriate managers who had little authority except in the sphere
of employment on company policy. Principal management roles
in both countries remain European. Efforts to develop specialised
training institutes, as in the case of Senegal the *Institut
Universitaire de Technologie* (IUT) founded in 1968 to train
principally middle management and technical staff, have faced
problems of integration of graduates. There were many features
of rapid employment mobility for Frenchmen during the colonial
period which have resulted in attitudes toward Africans which
remain counter-productive to localisation. Unlike Kenya, it
would appear that the socialisation of Africans serving in large
foreign firms is less developed in Senegal. This may be explained
by the more aggressive international policies of certain American
or Japanese firms operating in Kenya, compared with the
'colonial manager syndrome' which persists in most sectors in
Senegal, and which has continued deliberately to exclude its own
local African management staff from major discussions. Leys
writes about localisation:

> When all is said and done, it is difficult to know just what can be
> expected from Africanisation of management in large companies
> anyway. There may be some tendency for wage settlements and
> fringe benefits to become more liberal, and for the style of
> management to change in some respects, but it can hardly lead to a
> disregard of profitability or of capital growth and it is not likely that
> the foreign owners will allow local management to determine the
> fundamental issue of the use of company profits in the long-term. In
> retrospect what strikes one as significant is that in the course of many
> discussions no senior African executives mentioned this issue and in
> general it was the identity of views of African and expatriate
> executives that was remarkable, not the differences.[40]

Socialisation of this type can be achieved not only through
work. The IUT in Dakar, for example, which is based entirely on
metropolitan teaching methods, and management techniques used
at a French institution of the same name, can itself foster 'an
enclave mentality' in which its graduates come to accept certain
methods of work and forms of behaviour which are based
entirely on metropolitan management and which place demands
on the system or even a locally based foreign firm to satisfy them.
The issue is not therefore that such cadres may have the same

views as their expatriate counterparts, but the effect this has on an economy in which income and therefore standards and styles of living are so unequal. The policies of both Kenya and Senegal towards private foreign investment appear to support growth in each country, but the gains are very unequally distributed – favouring in particular the bourgeoisie or stable high-paid worker at the cost of the majority of the population.

African Capitalism

There has been pressure on the government in both countries to support local capitalism. Some examples have already been raised but the process – more limited in Senegal than in Kenya – has had some structural features in common: government policies award concessions, particularly in middle-level investment, which has begun to create certain local monopolies. These serve to support and complement existing private investment rather than replace it. In this sphere the role of the government as an arbiter of class formation has been clear. The level at which they have chosen to offer their support created in Kenya an 'auxiliary bourgeoisie' – that is, limited to those spheres which make it dependent on the central orbit of foreign investment. Kenya has been able to be more 'progressive' in its support of this group, as the economy is richer and more diversified. African entrepreneurs in both cases remain naturally totally dependent on foreign imports or local foreign firms for supply – almost no support has been offered to local petty production, which for example, in Senegal is blocked entirely from expansion beyond a very low level of capital turnover.[41] Among the concessions sought by African entrepreneurs have been fixed shares in specific markets – thus far achieved only minimally in terms of some urban services in Senegal, while awarded to African retail traders in the rural areas in Kenya (which moved from assistance in terms of loans to protection in terms of licence withdrawal from Asians in 1967). Other concessions were public loan funds or guaranteed credit and fixed suppliers and prices. In Senegal, a partial concession on loans was achieved by two government agencies offering assistance to industry and commerce, but the guarantees demanded for credit and the amount of initial capital required were so high as to be unrealistic in terms of the capacity of local capitalists, thus not improving much on the problems presented by foreign banking conditions and the acquisition of credit from these sources. The effort to restrict the Asian minority has not been entirely successful as Africans have not acquired the training and experience necessary to take over, the principal justification which is used in Senegal in defence of the Lebanese.

Local manufacturing has thus far had few inroads from African capitalists in either country. In service industries like construction, which require little capital outlay initially, however, more African investment has been apparent. In Senegal investment is usually made in multiple small enterprises. A common problem is the difficulty for small enterprise to cross the barrier, essentially technical and organisational, from the occasional odd jobs to business status. In Kenya, at least contractors have been assisted by a state organisation giving aid and advice, which has encouraged local entrepreneurs to operate as clients of the government in a fully protected relationship. Transport is also a likely area for local investment. In Senegal road transport is dominated by large local firms, many of which are owned by Lebanese entrepreneurs who have sufficient vehicles to transport the groundnuts after harvest at one particular time of the year, (the railroad having become very inefficient for this necessary seasonal transport). Urban transport has considerable local investment and in this sphere at least the single vehicle owner has in the past been able to expand from this basis. More recently, however, private urban transport has been threatened by the promotion of a state-run bus monopoly which will be less efficient and more expensive for individual passengers. Road transport in Kenya is often covered by a large number of single vehicle owners, who face competition from foreign operators. In neither case do government policies indicate support of local investment or entrepreneurial potential in this important service sector.

The drive for protection and the creation of monopolies to support African capitalism is apparent in Kenya, and becomes explicit in the Investment Code of 1972 in Senegal. These concessions will permit development of African entrepreneurship only within certain major structural parameters which are provided by foreign ownership. Thus, as the state formulates policies for the support of local capitalism, it is a critical instrument in shaping economic opportunity. In Senegal, government policy seems to indicate that the power structure does not yet wish to offer full support, being able to operate better with favourable foreign investment terms and an always potentially threatened Lebanese minority. In Kenya, by contrast, the government has permitted − often for its own personal enrichment − the development of a class which depends on the government for its continued concessionary support while providing an auxiliary to foreign capital, and, above all, posing no challenge to the existing order.

Conclusion

The key to understanding the dynamics of dependence in Africa lies not only in examining external influences and the lack of linkages between sectors of the local economy, which denote the weakness of an externally oriented economy of the type found in Kenya and Senegal; it lies also in a careful analysis of the policies adopted by governments since independence which affect class formation by awarding differentially the limited gains of economic growth. Most of the countries in Africa to which one would apply this analysis have, in my view, regimes which have necessarily constructed an economy which would serve their own immediate interests and their stability in the transitional period following independence.

Political independence has in some ways made for more effective external penetration while altering some of the most obvious structural features internal to the colonial economy. The changes which have been wrought have continued to enrich one class only in absolute terms − the new bourgeoisie, and to some extent highly paid workers in foreign firms. The deterioration in the rural-urban terms of trade has led to relative immiseration among rural dwellers made worse by inflation. Changes in the rural economy have in Kenya created great difficulties for smallholders, while enriching a few, and in Senegal they have served to tax the peasantry to increase state revenue. *Marginalised growth* is apparent among the rural and urban petty bourgeoisie, whose capacity to accumulate capital and expand is circumscribed by foreign investment and state supported enterprise owned or managed by local entrepreneurs. The *monopolistic features of the economy* have been strengthened by state protection and concession. Import substitution of often inefficient enterprises keeps local prices unnecessarily high. The burden of all these changes falls most heavily on the poor, in particular the rural poor.

Although Colin Leys has tried to apply an analysis based on what he calls 'underdevelopment theory' or a refinement of Marxist categories to current African problems, my approach in this paper has been somewhat more eclectic. In conclusion, however, I do wish to agree with his assumption that the importance of seeking a new framework of analysis, and of comparing specific cases, is to recognise that 'dependent capitalist development' resembles the old colonial system less and less[42] and has taken on new forces which require careful scrutiny. An assessment of the future direction of African countries requires a careful documentation of the structures and forces beginning to be shaped in this period, as they will give some indication of the potential realignment of socio-political forces in the future.

NOTES

1. See articles for example in the *Review of African Political Economy*, London, or *Qui se Nourrient de la Famine en Afrique?* Paris, Maspero, 1974.
2. See A. Foster Carter, 'Neo-Marxist Approaches to Development and Underdevelopment' in E. de Kadt and G. Williams, eds, *Sociology of Development*, London, Tavistock Publications, 1974, P. O'Brien, 'A Critique of Latin American Theories of Dependency' in I. Oxall, ed, *Beyond The Sociology of Development*, London, 1975, and S. Lall, 'Is Dependence a Useful Concept in Analysing Underdevelopment?' *World Development*, 1975, Vol. 3, Nos. 11 and 12.
3 See a very interesting attempt to apply one variant of dependency analysis to Kenya in M. Godfrey and S. Langdon, 'Parties in Underdevelopment? The Transnationalisation Thesis in the Kenya Context', *Journal of Commonwealth Political Studies*, 1976.
4. See S. McClelland, 'Political Economy and Dependence in Africa: An Annotated Bibliography' in R. Cruise O'Brien, ed., *The Political Economy of Underdevelopment: Dependence in Senegal*, London, Sage Publications, 1979, pp. 241–252.
5. This list is drawn from characteristics cited in Lall, *op. cit.*, S. Amin, *Neo-Colonialism in West Africa*, London, Penguin Books, 1973 and 'Contemporary Peripheral Social Formation, Unequal Development and Problems of Transition', U.N. African Institute for Economic Development

308   DECOLONISATION AND AFTER

and Planning, Dakar, IDEP/ET/2453, Feb. 1973 and M. Ikonicoff, 'Sous-Développement du Tiers Monde ou Capitalisme Péripherique?' IDEP, Dakar, ET/CS-2497, February 1973.

6. London, Allen and Unwin, 1975, p. 10.
7. Leys, *ibid*, p. 277; International Bank for Reconstruction and Development, *Senegal: Tradition, Diversification and Economic Development*, Washington, D.C., 1974, p. 13. Since 1974 the substantial rise in the world price of phosphates has considerably improved Senegal's growth rate.
8. Leys, *op. cit.* p. 28.
9. Leys, p. 44.
10. R. Cruise O'Brien, *White Society in Black Africa*, London Faber and Faber, 1972, p. 275.
11. R. Cruise O'Brien, 'Lebanese Entrepreneurs in Senegal: Economic Integration and the Politics of Protection', *Cahiers d'Etudes Africaines*, 57, XV–I, 1975.
12. Leys, *op. cit.* p. 45.
13. 12,000 in 1945, their numbers more than doubled in the subsequent ten years. R. Cruise O'Brien (1972) p. 275.
14. *Ibid*, Chapter 3.
15. Leys, *op. cit.* p. 207.
16. See discussion in Sessional Paper No. 10 of 1965, Leys, p. 222.
17. IBRD, *op. cit.* pp. 7–22.
18. Leys, *op. cit.* p. 253.
19. The technical assistance effort to increase production per acre was in part to compensate for the progressive reduction of this French subsidy from 1965–1967.
20. See Donal Cruise O'Brien, *Saints and Politicians*, Essays in the Organisation of a Senegalese Peasant Society, Cambridge University Press, 1975 for an explanation of how this clan system operates, especially chapter 5.
21. For an explanation of the importance of this phenomenon in the Senegalese case, see R. Cruise O'Brien, 'From Colonialism to Cooperation?', in H. Bernstein ed. *Development and Underdevelopment*, London, Penguin Books, 1973.
22. Leys, *op. cit.* p. 251. Kenya's capital aid sources are also more diversified than those in Senegal, with the US, Germany, Sweden and Canada (in declining order) providing the balance of the major contribution by Britain.
23. In 1975 there was a total of 1,100 French technical assistants serving in Senegal of whom 75 per cent were in education. Figures from the French *Mission de la Coopération au Sénégal*, 1975. There are not more than a few hundred from other sources, mainly Canada, Belgium or United Nations agencies.
24. Leys, *op. cit.* p. 65.
25. *Ibid*, p. 85.
26. *Ibid*.
27. Tony Moody, 'Peasant Agriculture, Commercial Production and Employment in Kenya', *Africa Development* (CODERSRIA, Dakar, 1977),

analyses the difficulties of peasant access to land and support, and the
failures of the cash-crop smallholder schemes.

28. In 1954, groundnuts were cushioned at 67 per cent over world market
    prices, declining to 26 per cent in 1963 and 16 per cent in 1964. IBRD, *op.
    cit.* pp. 138–142.
29. For an account of rural cooperatives, see D. Cruise O'Brien, *op. cit.*
    pp. 116–135.
30. IBRD, *op. cit.*
31. Leys, *op. cit.* pp. 113.
32. Report of the Institute of Development Studies, Nairobi, to the Minister of
    Finance on 'decentralising farming' (1975). Summarised in *The Guardian*,
    25 February 1976, p. 2.
33. Leys, *op. cit.* p. 118.
34. See S. Langdon, 'Multinational Corporations and Taste Transfer to Kenya',
    Review of African Political Economy, 1975.
35. M. Godfrey and S. Langdon, *op. cit.*
36. IBRD *op. cit.* p. 79.
37. Leys, p. 124.
38. *Ibid*, p. 131.
39. *Ibid*, p. 139.
40. Leys, *op. cit.* p. 124.
41. Chris Gerry, 'The Crisis of the Self-Employed: Petty Production and
    Capitalist Production in Dakar' in R. Cruise O'Brien, ed. (1979), *op. cit.*
42. Leys, *op. cit.* p. 27.

13

Arabisation and French Culture in the Maghreb

Christine Souriau

The use of a language is a guide to social and political relationships within a community as also between different communities. It is part of the intrinsic dynamism of social forces and has been part of their progress since well before what we call the beginnings of civilised time.

Language policy is therefore an area of complicated problems with wide implications. It is also ambiguous, depending on the way it is viewed, psychologically and politically, in the context of the balance of forces and interests. Its analysis is made difficult by the degree of ignorance prevailing. In addition, most discussions on the choice of language are biased: facts are selected and interpretations made on the basis of ideological positions, sometimes with the pretence of objectivity. But perhaps it is unrealistic to seek objectivity in this area which touches directly on the problem of identity and its affirmation, and where the reality of differences between people means that even if these differences are presented as complementary, nevertheless competition and hierarchies will always exist.

The use of terms such as 'transmission' or 'transfer' when discussing movements from one culture to another does not convey the implication that any loss is involved for the first culture (in fact this culture grows as it spreads) whilst it does imply a gain for the receiving culture. Thus the political and social significance of this process is disguised by disregarding not only the relationship between the influence exerted by one side and the effects suffered by the other, but also by ignoring the inequality and lack of reciprocity involved. Quite often, in order to justify this foisting of one culture on to another, it is regarded as 'progressive'; it is assumed to have had positive results, whilst no account is taken of any destructive or impoverishing influence it might have had in the context of domination and economic and political dependence. Cultural influence is just seen as part of the ancient logic of domination by power, force and a sense of mission, carried on from generation to generation in struggles to capture land, goods, power and knowledge. But in spite of this, cultural domination has, in the face of existing local interests, always given rise to reactions of all sorts, both for and against it, as we will see.

Reactions to what, precisely? Rather than enter into detailed research here, current academic thinking requires us to reply in terms of 'models'. This poses the problem of the definition of 'model': is it a Weberian ideal, a prototype of the kind Cuisenier constructed, or a simplified version of a system or process, as conceived by the sociologists? Or does it involve the moral idea of the model which *should* be imitated? This is most obvious in the idea of a 'cultural model'. The desire to make a culture universal is caused by this belief, that whatever is standard is correct and that its export is therefore justified. However, since these many 'universalist' cultures co-exist and compete — as do Western and Islamic cultures — their claims to be autonomous, and their attempts at domination, result in conflict.

By way of illustration, let us recall some historical examples of the changes in culture linked to the use of language. We will find considerable differences in developments and results in the struggles between social groups: indeed, the analysis itself will vary according to our own political or ideological standpoint.

1. Romanisation, Islamisation and Sovietisation are three examples of imperialism which resulted in Latinisation, Arabisation and Russianisation.

2. If we consider the Ancient Roman colonisation of North Africa, which in fact left far less of a Latin mark on this subcontinent than the colonialist West would like to think, one

will find that the analysis of a Mussolini or a Louis Bertrand, who used it to justify their right to dominate the people of the Maghreb, is quite different from that of our Moroccan contemporary Abdallah Laroui, who sees this as a period of slavery and cultural death for the Berbers.

3. An interesting case is that of the Bulgarian Turks, who came to 'Bulgaria' in the seventh century (hence the name), for they lost, at the same time, it seems, both their language and their religion, being made Christian and Slav in the ninth century. However, Western historians call them 'proto-Bulgarians', thus showing that for them history begins with Christian domination.

4. In the same period, written Arabic culture, which had spread with Islam, inhibited the growth of a written Berber culture south of the Mediterranean. Persian written culture, on the other hand, had managed to free itself from Arabic from the eighth century onwards and had taken over from it. Certainly there are Maghreb intellectuals who would find the first of these facts positive and the second negative, because of their belief in the superiority of Arab–Islamic culture.

5. Between the eleventh century and fourteenth century a struggle took place in England between the political, social and linguistic forces of the Britons, Saxons and Normans. This was resolved in favour of the English language of the London area.

6. Throughout Europe the growth of Latin in the Middle Ages and that of French in the eighteenth century as languages of culture can be interpreted either as evidence of the idea of universality or as a demonstration of organised domination by elites; this does not affect the fact that the other corresponding side of the story was the long neglect and underdevelopment of popular or national languages.

7. Finally, coming up to date, the Flemish living in a Flanders gallicised by the bourgeoisie in the nineteenth century have in this century included a militant element in their cultural campaign and have succeeded in regaining the status of their language in politics, law, the universities and literature. Their active participation in the economic development of North

West Europe now adds validity to their linguistic claims; so strong is their position in a dominant area that the Walloons now feel themselves threatened by Flemish dominance.

8. But now both of them, along with the French, currently experience their languages being subject to encroachment by transnational English, whose technocratic role is based on organised and predatory economic interests.

In France itself it is everywhere obvious from the press and the graffiti, from demonstrations on the streets and in universities and cultural centres that the theme of linguistic dominance or dependence is the subject of a fierce debate. People have become aware of language differences − with notions of superiority or inferiority − variations in language use according to class, region and occupation and language competition. This increase in general consciousness probably owes something to factors of widespread influence such as decolonisation, the conflict between political and economic hegemonies, and the expansion of theoretical knowledge amongst young people and its encounter with reality. But there is little logic in attitudes to language; for example, some people will denounce the influence of English in France and recognise the domination of French in the ex-French colonies, but will not see the dominance of the language of Paris over the rest of France in the same terms, considering it as normal. The French continue to place value on the classical model of their language; that is, on its written, scholarly, administrative, literary, educational and commercial uses, and it is this which they promote as an exportable product. But for the foreign consumer it is a finished product, not a raw material or a semi-finished product which they can adapt or transform to suit their own requirements. The French, who have the advantages of a living language in a constantly changing society, still do all they can to remain the popes of the sacred treasure, that is, controlling its development and directing its future (and their own) in the world. Customers exist for the importing of the French language, whether it is offered as a second-hand article or as surplus stock. But this unequal trade is offering the present or past of one society to another as its future. The metaphor of 'opening a window on to the world' is so widely used, particularly to justify the use of a foreign language (always a Western one in the third world), that it cannot help but distract attention from the interests involved and it betrays lack of any regard for its impact on the original culture of the dependent society at the receiving end. Such impact does to some extent hamper the development of the society in question. The imbalance is aggravated by the refusal of the influencing society to allow an equal cultural exchange, a refusal which reflects a superiority complex about its own language, a disdain for the language of the other country, and a strong reluctance to learn the other's language properly. These attitudes are of course the necessary pre-conditions for the exercising of cultural domination. Their result is to force the dominated society to change its culture; so the dominated have to become bilingual. However, it is true that under colonialism and present-day colonisation, the 'acculturation' of dominated societies has only benefited certain receptive classes who form an intermediate social group of intermediaries. Thanks to them development in these countries is channelled along lines of Western modernisation and French influence is thus exerted long after the French themselves have left. Shared hopes and interests have outlived physical separation.

In bilingual ex-colonies such as the Maghreb, the most important element in the method of distributing cultural products is the language used. The destination and circulation of such products is influenced by official policy on culture; the circulation itself takes place through the press, books, films, theatre, television, courses, conferences, manuals and technology, channelled through either the public or private sector. These products are not harmlessly neutral but have their own character; they come imbued with cultural or political significance; they are presented as either 'classical' (that is, unchanging, fixed), or 'modern' (up to date or in fashion), or 'avant-garde' (ahead of their time, or fictitious). Contemporary ideas also include a considerable ideological element which sometimes proves too heavy a burden for the French 'model' to carry successfully – with the result that the limits of tolerance at the receiving end are quickly reached. Indeed, the image of France today is not merely conservative, Republican, liberal or colonialist; it is also Marxist, left-wing, anarchist, regionalist, feminist, full of conflict – basically, it is heterogenous, quite the opposite of the original

picture of coherent centralism. If these new aspects of cultural
influence do find takers abroad they also cause misgivings. One
example would be the Maghreb view of French education. There
is something of a contrast here between on the one hand the old
model based on order and discipline, which the Maghreb parents
know and want for their children who are sent to mission
schools, and the horror which they see in the 'disorganised mess'
that came into existence in May 1968 whose effects on education
they mistrust – on principle rather than from experience.

These remarks lead us to consider la Francophonie as a prelude
to looking at the Arabisation movement which may seem to some
like a reaction to it. In fact la Francophonie constitutes one of the
transnational organisations which the modern world produces
out of its dominating centres. Born of an agreement between
official policies, it serves to institutionalise supplier–customer
relationships on the culture front, with the 'choice' of French as
the language used. The following four views from France about
this kind of project show the underlying conflicts:

1. Auguste Viatte, in *La Francophonie*, upheld in 1969 the real
chances of setting up an international cultural community united
through the use of the French language. He assessed the position
of the language in the world historically and at the present time,
the extent to which it had managed to penetrate and spread, its
chances of survival or even of further progress. He was aware
that the valued international status of the French language was
threatened by the leading position of English and he was
determined to prevent its decline.

2. Hyacinthe de Montera, in *La Francophonie en Marche* already
in 1966 showed the aggressive potential in la Francophonie. He
considered the battle between cultures as one which left few
survivors, but thought France should organise in order to make
sure she was one of them. 'We Europeans', he wrote, 'have
started it all. We were drunk with action, power and progress;
constantly aggressive and imposing our ideas, we overcame the
world, then we converted it. The converted nations became mad
at our touch'. However, he has a special view of future battles. He
regards the advent of the consumer society as universal and
irresistible. People care increasingly about material goods, not

ideologies. Accordingly la Francophonie is to be presented primarily as a great economic venture designed to secure material benefits for its members. Only in this rather indirect way can the battle for French be won. Of course, in his neat avoidance of ideological issues, he nevertheless gives no thought to the possibility that those who are to be manipulated might want to make other choices. In fact the argument is a restatement of the old colonialist ideas of Western Europe already found lacking. The snag in this kind of prescription is always that the patients refuse to remain passive.

3. Robert Lafont is one who looks at the situation from the patient's viewpoint. In *Clefs pour l'Occitanie* which came out in 1971, he analysed the type of aggression directed at the cultural communities (including Languedoc) in the South of France by the French speaking North. He gives the other side of the story of unification and centralisation in France; the French from the North organised their campaign of political and religious imperialism towards the South by means of a religious crusade, military conquest, law, administration, and eventually by crushing any remaining popular revolts, by education and by economic monopoly. As a result, the Midi became a dependent colony of Paris. The process is still continuing; perhaps the 'worst destruction of all' will complete it – the creation of economic provinces in the new Europe.

4. Louis-Jean Calvet widens our view of these socio-political struggles which use linguistic weapons – la Francophonie being only one case among many – by making the connection between the analysis of colonial domination and that of class domination. In *Linguistique et colonialisme: petit traité de glottophagie* (1974) he attempts to show that these constant conflicts are due to the hegemony which one class in power exercises over the masses or over minorities, for whom cultural assimilation would be fatal. Today, bourgeois ideology tries to hide its cultural and historical character; however, organising the transfer of a language, using it to transmit ideas and technology, setting up links which are profitable, both to the metropole and to the collaborating emergent bourgeoisie of the new nation – all this is the art of neo-colonialism, 'to get what it wants – which previously had to be got by force'.

These varied approaches to la Francophonie help us to approach 'Arabophonie' and the Arabisation of the Maghreb within a wider context, although all we want to do here is to touch on a few points. First of all, let us clarify what we mean by 'Arabisation'. Linguistically, it can just mean the transfer of terminology from non-Arabic languages to the Arabic language. However, it must be seen within its social, political and economic context. The concept of Arabisation, seen in this way, can have many meanings. For example Arabisation in Tunisia has been a historical fact since the eleventh century; the Arabisation of education in Algeria is underway at the moment; the Arabisation of industrial vocabulary is a translation technique; Arabisation in the sense of a renewal of Arab-Islamic culture has both traditionalist and modernist interpretations; and so on. Let us also remember that the long process of introducing Arab-Islamic culture in the Maghreb has its origins in the past, that before the seventh century there were no Arabs or Muslims in the North of Africa, and that now 70 to 99 per cent of them, depending on the country, are Arabic speakers. Islam and the Arabic language have therefore gradually increased in influence, taking over totally from older religions, and preventing, in part, the development of the Berber linguistic substrata. However, a fusion of Arab and Berber ethnic groups has taken place, and there are considerable bilingual areas where both the Arabic and Berber languages are spoken between Arabic and Berber speaking regions, with the Arabic written culture having helped to make the overall socio-religious organisations more homogenous.

From the thirteenth and fourteenth centuries onwards, power relations between the West European and the Arab worlds in the Mediterranean area were reversed, in preparation for the Europeans' future expansion into the Maghreb. This is 'modernity' in the sense which Baudrillard gives to the word, as it was used to encourage and justify increasing Western intervention, commercial and military and then industrialist and capitalist, in the Maghreb. However, we must recognise that modernity did not wait for the colonial presence to reach the Maghreb. From the nineteenth century the Maghreb has received two modernising influences, one coming directly from Europe in European languages (Italian, French, Spanish, English) but rarely in Arabic, and the other coming by means of the Near-East

(Ottoman, Syrian, Palestinian, Egyptian influence) coming in
Arabic or sometimes Turkish. Thus there was a modernising
movement taking place in Arabic before French colonisation,
though it did not go very deep, particularly in Algeria, where the
violent conquest came too early (1830) for this movement to
become established.

Pre-colonial modernisation through Arabic gave the Maghreb
people a chance to see their cultural heritage more clearly, and
presented them with a different view of their development. In
Tunisia from 1840 Western-type courses were taught at the Bardo
Military Academy, first in Turkish and later in Italian or French,
but they were also translated into Arabic. Arab translations of
literary texts or popular scientific works began to be imported
from Egypt and Libya; in 1858–1860 an official Arabic
newspaper began to appear regularly, printed locally; political
and legal reforms, inspired by French law, were also introduced.
Certainly one could describe all this as the beginnings of
dependence on Europe, but who can say whether modernisation
in Tunisia would not have given the people there more control
over their destiny if it had not been used for the profit of the
colonialists? However, in 1875, that is six years after the military
conquest of Tunisia by France, a cultural event revealed the lack
of such control. In that year Sadiqi College, a modernised
Tunisian Secondary School, was set up in Tunis for boys from
good families. In this College subjects classed as 'scientific' were
taught in French by French teachers whilst Arab-Islamic learning
was reserved for Tunisian teachers who taught in Arabic. As a
result, Arabic became linked of necessity with the so-called
'traditional' sector, which was considered less important than the
'modern' area of knowledge which was taught in French. The bilingualism which arose amongst the elite segregated the social
classes and colonisation brought about the creation of a new
social class which was Tunisian but whose cultural values were
French. Since then it has no longer been a question of
encouraging modernity – as the promoters of the Arab Institute in
Khaldouniya tried to do in 1896 – but of making use of modern
French ideas. This difference is essential, since it explains the
opportunities given to the French in Tunisia.

Things happened differently in Morocco. There was no
modern Moroccan education system before colonisation, but we

can take the methods used in introducing the press as an example. From 1880 to 1910 Tangiers (an international port) was the centre of Western political influence in various languages. During the first stage of development, locally set-up European language newspapers in English, Spanish, French began to appear. These were written by Europeans for Europeans and more or less ignored the Moroccans. There were however various Arabic papers imported from Tunisia or the Middle East. The French distributed copies of *Al-Ahram* from Egypt and *El-Mobacher* from Algeria because they made a profit. In the second stage, after 1889, the European papers sometimes included an extra page in Arabic for the Moroccans. Finally, in the third stage (1905–1911), the Europeans put out whole newspapers in Arabic, whilst promoting their own papers as much as they could. The Sultan of Morocco refused for years to allow the setting up of an official Moroccan newspaper, finally allowing one in 1908. Not until 1907 was an Arabic newspaper printed locally by some Lebanese; it included the modern ideas of political reform to be found all over the Arab world at that time. Moroccan private enterprise was not successful because of resistance in official circles, so they were reduced to sending articles to foreign Arabic newspapers. Thus before the colonial takeover in 1912, the dynamic nature of the Western press, particularly in French and Spanish, allowed the Moroccan Arabic press only a minor role; in other words, it was condemned to under-development, a condition that was then confirmed by the colonial laws on the press in all three countries.

In Algeria, where the violent conquest took place fifty-one years earlier than in Tunisia, and eighty-two years earlier than in Morocco, modernisation was mixed up from the outset with colonisation and the imposition of the French language. There was no merging of the races in Algeria any more than in any other country of the Maghreb; there were no common children of conquerors and Muslims, and no point of contact for the two cultures; on the contrary they met head-on in a conflict which still continues today. Expressions which qualify language and 'levels' of language, such as written, spoken, dead, modern, common, literary, scientific, dialects, pidgin/sabir, can be used as an additional way of indicating ethnic differences or contrasts of social class; such use often has a definite political function. In

Algerian Arab-Islamic society a distinction was already made
between the *fuçha* (the cultivated language used by the *khâçça* or
elite) and the *âmmiya* (the everyday language of the *âmma* or
people). Apart from the spoken Berber languages, there was also a
special type of Arabic spoken by the Jews, and many local
variations amongst the Muslims. However, within the total
spread of Arab languages, all these variations were regarded as
rooted in a common and ancient base, which was also felt as
living and vital by virtue of drawing its strength from Islam. This
idea was one which some European students of languages tried to
refute and undermine during the colonial era.

This, then, was the relatively homogenous culture into which
the French conquest tried to introduce, and on which it wanted to
impose, a foreign, minority language. The only way in which this
could be done was by cultural dominance, and in fact the colonial
power set about organising the blocking of Arab culture by
putting an end to the financing of local education, by down-
grading Arabic institutions and devaluing Arab-Islamic culture,
by replacing their personnel by people who worked in the French
language and in French ways, by relegating to inferior status any
administrative or legal functions which had been carried out in
Arabic. Only those Frenchmen who were forced into daily
contact with the Algerian population learnt Arabic properly (that
is, settlers, those in local offices, certain administrators and
traders), and then only when they could not get by by using
interpreters. Others knew only a little Arabic, and never the
written language.

The two cultures found themselves in conflict because of the
opposition of people rather than of basic principles. Both sides
had a strong belief in the special destiny of their own languages,
based on the Arab side on the transcendent importance of the
Koran and on the French side on the belief in the power of
reason. Both traditions had been built up during the so-called
'classical' period, and were strong enough to inspire the wish that
they should continue to exist untouched, should even, if
necessary, be imposed or resisted by force. Finally, both sides had
a homogenous written language which served as a norm and a
support for a social elite.

What, then, did the future hold for Algerian society after
colonisation? Linguistic diversification and cultural disintegration

went together with social heterogeneity. French became the means of communication of the colonising society, working for its profit and as the instrument of its power in a variety of forms – in institutions, legislation, political debate, military routines, administration, courts, police and the press. French became, above all, the language of technology and modern economic management, without any attempt to translate into Arabic. Nor was there any such effort in French secular education introduced in 1882. French was the language of command, of management, and of theoretical knowledge, and it also relegated Arabic to the language of the dominated, of those at the bottom of the ladder. It made it 'traditional', that is, it forced it to be associated with the archaic, the out of date, the common, the useless. Even worse, the Orientalist, W. Marçais, hoped for its 'natural' death on the basis of political reasoning which he believed to be scientific. The law encouraged this domination, too, by declaring Arabic foreign to Algeria in 1923; educationalists also helped by claiming that the Latin alphabet was better suited to modern needs than the Arabic one. The fact was, however, that the Latin alphabet increased the dominance of the Europeans, who made no effort to try to learn about the complex written culture of those they dominated, whilst they called it 'rational' to impose on those learning French the subtleties and inconsistencies of its spelling which were mainly due to the Latin alphabet itself which was not even really suited to French.

Thus, transfers of culture in a colonial context necessarily take place unilaterally. The Muslim population could only avoid de-Arabisation to the extent that more under-privileged Arabs were born. The effects of the imposition of French culture, although only on a minority, have increased, particularly since the Second World War, and still more during the war of liberation. They showed themselves in various ways: the creation of bilingual intermediaries in response to the need to control Muslim society; enrolment in the army; work on the roads or in large colonial towns; emigration to France; schooling up to university level for some. The main motive was either to earn a living or to get a steady job or an education. This is demonstrated by the fact that few women in this strict patriarchal society learned French.

In this case we might ask if the problems of the divisions and mobility of colonial society can be explained by means of languages. The following plan may be considered as a guide to colonial Algeria, admitting that it represents a synchronic approach and one more valid in 1945 than in 1900. (See Plan A).

In Plan A upward mobility in that part of society which is in the process of development takes place solely on the basis of the modern, French-speaking sector. It is for this reason that the sons of monolingual Arabic and Berber speakers learn French and become bilingual. However, the Algerians' access to the top is prevented by the presence there of Europeans; beneath them, an intermediary class made up of Algerians is formed. Those Algerians who do not know French constitute a mass sunk in under-development and unoriginality, *àmma* and *khàçça* (the elite) alike. Even the French-speaking Algerian elite come up against the ethnic barrier.

It was the consciousness of these divisions which gave rise to the 'Arabisation' movement, which had its roots in nationalism. This Arabisation embodies two main aims: first, a desire to fight the death of original culture politically, and second, to participate in modernity, wholeheartedly, without destroying the past. Amongst the French-speaking elite this only amounts to formal protests, since this elite continues to support bilingualism. The movement is far more active amongst the traditional elite and in certain popular circles where ideological positions are being politicised and radicalised; in cultural associations, unofficial education, the press, youth groups, political debates, preparation for revolution − here the operative language is mainly Arabic. Since independence, the ideological value which has been placed on Arabic has led to its being officially recognised as the one and only national language. The problem here is to make this effective in practice, to 'Arabise' everything which has been 'Frenchified', whilst still encouraging development in Algeria. In other words, modernisation involves using teaching, management and industrial techniques which depend on the use of French, but attention has to be paid to the Algerians' reaction to, and distrust of, their colonial heritage. As a result 'Algerianisation' has so far been a mixture of French and Arab influences.

The linguistic factor, however, remains an interesting indicator of the new divisions of society which have developed during decolonisation. The following plan is for Algerian society in 1970. (See Plan B.)

PLAN A

SUMMIT	Monolingual French: a small minority of privileged status, the dominant elite: (i) French from France; on temporary stays; no Arabic; (ii) Local French; born and permanently in Algeria; no Arabic learnt (or learnt and forgotten) so unable to speak or understand Arabic.

INTERMEDIATE
 	
 Developing ↑
 	
 Under-developed ↓
	French-speaking bilinguals and multilinguals: includes Muslims, Jews and Europeans; of very varied legal and political status; their population growing absolutely and as a proportion of the whole.
	 (i) Europeans:
	       (a) French with written Arabic: orientalists, officers from localities, some administrators;
	       (b) French with spoken Arabic: engaged in functions of command and political control with need to relate to subordinates and to rural areas;
	       (c) Spanish Italian or Maltese with French: in management, overseeing, modern technology.
	 (ii) Non-European but with access to French written culture: French-educated or self-taught minor officials, some liberal professions, teachers, journalists, politicians:
	       (a) Berber with French;
	       (b) Jewish Arabic and Hebrew with French;
	       (c) Spoken and written Arabic with French.
	 (iii) With some knowledge of French:
	       (a) Spanish Italian or Maltese with Arabic: small employers and manual workers;
	       (b) Spoken and written Arabic with spoken French: workers, domestic servants, emigrants.
	 (iv) Little or no French:
	       Arabic with Spanish, Italian or Maltese: farmers, fishermen, mechanics, small businessmen.

BASE	Monolinguals and bilinguals without French: the vast mass of the population with bare subject status:
	 (i) Written and spoken Arabic: the traditional monolingual elite: 'Khacca', controlling Arab-Islamic written culture: body of ulama, qadi, imam, qa'id, ukil, muderris, talib …
	 (ii) Illiterate 'Amma'
	       (a) Arabic with Berber: transactional contacts;
	       (b) Arabic, Muslim and Jewish: trade, crafts, customary law, popular literature and songs;
	       (c) Arabic or Berber: women, shepherds, agricultural workers, peasants, nomads.

PLAN B

SUMMIT	Bilinguals with dual written culture to university level; increased in number since 1970; in politics and top management: (i) Arabic with French (ii) Arabic with English (rare) (iii) French Arabic and English (rare)	English and French speaking experts, assistants, temporary stay, no Arabic
INTERMEDIARY LEVEL — Upper	Monolinguals with university education; modern sector posts: (i) French-speaking and educated in French (ii) 'Arabised', educated in Middle East	Arab assistants, temporary stay, no French
INTERMEDIARY LEVEL — Middle	Monolinguals, bilinguals and multilinguals: growing proportion of population; educated, self-taught, taught at work or trained; having French written education, primary and secondary, plus written Arabic (increasing with Arabisation); minor officials, teachers, lower levels in army, business, trade, nationalised concerns, public authorities.	
INTERMEDIARY LEVEL — Lower	Monolinguals with some education: Arabic only, learnt by traditional methods in past or recently; performing religious functions, teachers in the msid, scribes, rural officials.	
BASE	Illiterates, monolinguals, bilinguals, multi-linguals: the majority of the adult population (above all, women) and a minority of the educable population (above all, girls): (i) Arabic with French) (ii) Berber with French) workers, small business, migrants (iii) Arabic with Berber or vice-versa — as mass media and economic, administrative, political and travel contacts increasingly Arabise Berber speakers. (iv) Arabic *or* Berber only: women, shepherds, peasants, nomads, proletariat.	

The first difference from the previous plan is the marginal role now played by Europeans. The second difference is the decreasing importance of monolingual French speakers. The third is the social rise of Arabic-speaking intellectuals and scholars. The fourth is the triumphant rise of bilinguals who have gone in for applied studies. The fifth is the increase in social mobility due to the democratisation of education – now carried on in both Arabic and French – which has led to a considerable generation gap, which is maintained by the lack of any literacy drive. There is strong competition among both mono- and bilinguals for jobs in management in the modern sector.

We must now turn to Tunisia and Morocco and try to judge the differences between these two plans and the position in these countries, although our research on this is far from complete. With regard to the colonial period, Tunisia and Morocco would both have a column all the way up the plan to include the *khâçça* and *âmma* – those whose education was purely in Arabic but who had nevertheless not lost all chance of access to every social level (because of the continued existence of the Arab-Islamic universities of Zeitouna in Tunisia and Qaraouiyine in Fes). We must also include the competition which existed between those monolinguals educated in their own country and those who were educated in a more modern fashion in the Middle East. The existence of bilinguals educated in Franco-Arab schools should also be included here, in a vertical column running parallel to that above (but only from the division marking access to written French culture to that of being a European). In Tunisia, the Sadiqui and the French-educated students competed fiercely both with each other and with monolinguals for social position.

After independence, the Algerian plan is valid for all three countries, still excepting the *khâçça-âmma* column. In Tunisia this column is considerably reduced, particularly at the top, in comparison with the colonial period, due to the closure of Zeitouna and the reduction of Arab-Islamic teaching to a Department of Theology and a few hours of civic and religious instruction in the educational syllabus. In Morocco, on the other hand, it should be made larger, at the top too, with so-called 'original' teaching being kept alongside modern bilingual education at all levels.

In any case – and this is of paramount importance – the

colonial Protectorates set up in Tunisia in 1883 and Morocco in 1912 did not impose the same 'dis-Arabisation' as took place in Algeria, which after all constituted 'an integral part of French territory'. However the divisible way in which languages were assigned to the two sectors – Arabic to the traditional, and French to the modern – did put Arabic at a considerable disadvantage in all three countries. The introduction of the study of Arabic into the official colonial educational system gave rise to arguments about time-tables instead of discussions on the basic problem of domination itself (on which subject all colonial administrators were agreed anyway).

When independence arrived, and in the context of decolonisation, Arabisation fulfilled a profound need and desire, both on the part of the majority of the population – who wanted a social progress which did not deny their identity – and also on the part of the governments, whose task was to construct national states with direct access to the people. However, since it was a question of reversing the historical trend from Arabic towards French, the means to achieve this were limited, since working in French was still more reliable and profitable during the economic transitional period, and those who knew French were better able to take over from Frenchmen and do their jobs. There was, therefore, no way of approaching this problem head-on; so a reformist solution was sought, without any clear definition of stages or target date.

The three Arabisation policies vary according to the kind of society chosen by each of the three Maghreb systems. Thus the Tunisian choice of a policy open to the West can be equated with the introduction of bilingualism in principle, while political mistrust has kept monolingual Arab-speakers in the background. On the other hand, Morocco's choice of a co-existence in which the traditional and modern society are in constant competition has led to swings backwards and forwards, according to events, towards Arabisation, then back to French, within the context of the necessity of bilingualism. In both countries, however, there is practically no teaching of science or technology in Arabic, even at the most basic level. Few government ministers work in Arabic. But, even so, the continued use of French, reinforced by the number and importance of French experts and assistants who do not know a word of Arabic, does not prevent the Arabisation of the masses. This is spreading through urbanisation, everyday contacts, cultural life (religious and national celebrations, songs, music, literature, both popular and written), the mass media (press, radio and television) and public political debate. It is of course through education that the impact is most thoroughly effected. However, the choice of the classic form of Arabic creates a gap within Arab-speaking society between those who can only express themselves orally and the privileged few, mainly the young, who have mastered the written word.

Even if, in the years since Tunisian and Moroccan independence, social and political claims relating to Arabisation have been made from time to time, there has been no basic change in the system since the French of yesterday were replaced by today's French-trained leaders.

The same cannot quite be said for Algeria, where, from a far worse position for Arabic, Arabisation became one of the four aims of the Socialist Revolution (together with the control of resources, industrialisation, and agricultural reform). It was invoked as a symbol in 1962, actually defined in 1966, and put into effect in 1968 in education, even scientific education, and in 1971 in administration. The first National Conference on Arabisation in 1975 widened its aims to cover working and public life. Arabic could only progress as far as means were available, but those means which existed have been found and used. The doctrine of necessary bilingualism is not permitted. The aim is to Arabise ways of thinking, of management, of working, whilst still using French, but also English, Spanish and Russian, for the purpose of contacts with sources of modernisation overseas. So successful Arabisation is part of the struggle for national modernity and consciousness. This development is criticised for being too slow or too rapid, and involves all sorts of difficulties. However, it is constructive because of the unifying influence it has on the people, so divided by colonisation.

Under such circumstances can Arabisation in the Maghreb be considered as opposed to the transfer of French cultural models? Certainly not, in so far as the programme works on the basis of translations. This covers a very wide area; all the educational sector, including terminology, techniques, methods of learning. The transfer also takes place through imitation or assimilation. The limits to such transfers are indeed mainly set by the choice of the type of society and all that implies – indeed, in the way of life of the people of the Maghreb, their customs, their values, and in the Arab-Islamic way of thinking, which cannot be completely identified with the different strands of contemporary Western life. However, the way of life of certain social classes in the Maghreb is comparable with the West and gives rise to a certain affinity which transcends the differences.

In the opinion of all those people from the Maghreb whom we consulted, Arabisation is an essential feature of the future. They are, however, not agreed on the time scale, with some saying one generation is necessary, and others five hundred years. Arabisation would seem to be necessary if more is wanted than the development of just a middle class, or an elite. Experience up to now shows that it is practicable in spite of the problems.

We have no proposals to put to the people of the Maghreb on this point, since we are not responsible for their affairs. However, we would advise that in France the efforts lately undertaken to increase information about the Arab-Islamic world and encourage the learning of Arabic should be intensified. For, in a world where education is becoming more widespread, it becomes increasingly unfair to refuse cultural reciprocity to other countries. Indeed, in economic terms, it is a mistake, since the other country, knowing our language and culture, has a considerable advantage in negotiations. The monolingual French are therefore on poor ground, for even if they use an interpreter, he will usually be a bilingual Arab. We might ask whether such dependence is really necessary. Must the French become accustomed to losing control of their destiny on every side? There is no need for such outdated hegemony to be preserved. What is needed is a better knowledge of their Southern neighbours from the Maghreb, which would allow the French to come to terms with the world as it is today.

WORKS TO WHICH REFERENCE IS MADE

Baudrillard, article 'Modernité', *Encyclopedia Universalis*.

L. J. Calvet, *Linguistique et colonialisme, Petit traité de glottophagie*, Paris, Payot, 1974.

J. Cuisenier, *Economie et parenté, Leurs affinités de structures dans le domaine turc et dans le domaine arabe*, Paris, La Haye, Mouton, 1975.

H. Djait, *L'idéologie et le devenir arabo-islamiques*, Paris, Seuil, 1974.

R. Lafont, *Clefs pour l'Occitanie*, Paris, Seghers, 1971.

A. Laroui, *Histoire du Maghreb*, Paris, Maspero, 1970.

A. Laroui, 'Cultural problems and social structures' in *Humaniera islamica*, Vol. 1, Paris, Mouton, 1973.

W. Marçais, 'Rapport d'inspection générale' in *Articles et Conférences. Faculté des Lettres d'Alger*, XXI, 1961, pp. 171–192.

H. De Montera, *La 'Francophonie' en marche, La guerre des cultures.* Preface by Michel Debré, Paris, Sedino, 1966.

Ch. Souriau, *La presse maghrébine, Lybie, Tunisie, Maroc, Algérie*, 2nd ed., Paris, CNRS, 1975.

Ch. Souriau, 'L'arabisation en Algérie' in *Introduction à l'Afrique du Nord contemporaine*, Paris, CNRS, 1975, pp. 375–397.

A. Taleb-Ibrahimi, *Discours du Ministre de l'Education Nationale.* 3 Vol. Alger, SNED, 1965–1970.

A Viatte, *La francophonie*, Paris, Larousse, 1969.

14

La Francophonie with special reference to educational links and language problems

S. K. Panter-Brick

Introduction

La Francophonie is a term coined in the early 1960s to express in
a collective fashion the 'French-speaking' parts of the world; that
is, the countries or peoples making use of French, not necessarily
as a mother tongue but at least as a working language for some
basic purposes. It implies that therein lies a certain affinity, even
identity, which in turn invites the supposition that some formally
organised activity is both possible and desirable. This chain of
supposition is accepted by some but contested by others, making
la Francophonie a subject of some controversy.

The list of countries or peoples whose use of French puts them,
at least potentially, into *la Francophonie*, is long and varied.
Besides France itself it includes Luxembourg, parts of Belgium,
Switzerland and Italy; likewise Quebec and other parts of
Canada; French speaking communities in America and India;
islands in the West Indies, Indian Ocean and the Pacific; former
French and Belgian colonies in Africa; some Arabic countries;
and Indochina.

The list is surprising in its scope, especially if *la Francophonie*
is to be understood as having achieved a degree of
institutionalisation on a multilateral basis. What kind of enterprise
is this, it might be asked, which aims apparently at bringing
together such a diverse set of countries and peoples, founded, it
would seem, on their use of the French language?

Historical Antecedents

Although it is misleading to think of *la Francophonie* as nothing but a renewed attempt to salvage something from the wrecks of former Empires, there are elements of continuity, sufficient to evoke old dreams and inspire renewed hope. From the time of the French Revolution, it has been customary to make explicit, both in doctrinal and institutional terms, the nature of the relationship which links, or should link, France and its overseas possessions. A new constitution in France itself was usually the occasion for a reformulation of that relationship. It has been repeatedly re-examined and restated in a long series of such debates, notably in 1795, 1848, 1944–46, and 1956–58. The general corpus of principles enunciated on each occasion were not always followed in practice and the principles themselves were not entirely free from ambiguity and self-contradiction. Indeed, the only general consensus was perhaps in the order of preference for the two or three alternatives. These were, first, the integration of France and 'France overseas' under virtually the same set of institutions and laws; secondly, a union of autonomous states joined in some sort of federation; and, thirdly, separation. The first was very much the ideal, the second a possible necessity, and the last considered by many a confession of failure.

Unfortunately, from this point of view, history has been unkind. The colonies of greatest affinity to France, by race, language and culture – the colonies of settlement – those which might have provided the foundation for a close link between France and overseas, were largely lost in the wars of the 18th and early 19th centuries, also somewhat alienated by the Revolution, and in any case incorporated into other structures. Later, in the second world war, effective control was lost of important parts of the Empire: Syria and Lebanon became independent and associated themselves with the Arab League rather than any future French Union; French authority was never fully restored in Indochina; and the scattered possessions on the Indian sub-continent were unable to resist the attraction of Indian independence and the pressures of the Indian Government.

Neither the Fourth nor the Fifth Republic was able to stem the desire for independence on the part of the remaining Protectorates, Mandated Territories and Colonies. The attempt was made, in 1946, to create a Union of *Etats Associés* (enjoying a measure of autonomy), *Départments d'Outre-Mer* (declared integral parts of the French Republic), *Territoires Associés* and *Territoires d'Outre-Mer* (both categories a sort of half-way house between autonomy and integration, from which one could face either way in theory, both ways in practice). Neither Tunisia nor Morocco showed any interest in being Associated States, and achieved their independence in 1956. For a short period Laos, Cambodia and Vietnam consented to become Associated States, but the High Council of the French Union, in which these governments were associated with that of France, served no purpose, and the Assembly of the French Union, dominated in any case by representatives from France, was merely an advisory body. After the Geneva Conference of 1954, independence was achieved by all these countries.

The Fifth Republic, under de Gaulle's leadership, was in the end scarcely more successful. The Constitution of 1958 was a gamble with independence, for it offered the *Territoires d'Outre-Mer* their independence on particularly Draconian terms. Only those opting for autonomy within the *Communauté* could expect to retain close links with France and continue to receive its aid. Guinea alone took the risk and found that it had to pay the price. The gamble appeared to have succeeded, but it could not be repeated in the face of pressure for independence from Togo, Cameroun, Senegal, and the Soudan (the last two joined in the short-lived Mali Federation). Completely reversing previous logic and disregarding established constitutional law, de Gaulle decided to offer the Mali Federation independence without prejudice to membership of the Community; whereupon, Houphouët-Boigny, who would have preferred integration for the material benefits it promised to bring but was determined not to be outwitted by his old rival Senghor, led a demand for independence unrelated to membership of any Community. This, in its turn, was a demand that de Gaulle could not refuse, and thereafter the Community became defunct. Thus slipped away the last chance to preserve a multilaterally structured relationship, albeit with a much reduced set of partners, based, moreover, not on autonomy but on independence.

Fresh Aspirations

If nothing but dreams and nostalgia had animated the notion of *la Francophonie*, it would have remained a mere flight of fancy. Independence need not put a stop to close association, for this can simply take the form of bilateral agreements, and these can be as comprehensive and as intimate as the two contracting parties choose. Indeed, the links that survive the break-up of an empire composed of very diverse elements are perhaps mostly bilateral or, at best, regionally structured. Any overarching association, of which all are members, is more of a symbolic nature, with the additional advantage that it gives to the relationship a rather diffuse character which can be translated with the minimum of formality into whatever joint action is considered appropriate at a particular time. An association of this kind is no substitute for bilateral and regional ties: it is supplementary, not unimportant but not vital to the maintenance of links. If it exists, because in the process of decolonisation and at an early stage favourable circumstances and good judgment made it possible, this can be counted a blessing. Since, however, this was not the case, why strive to bring it about? It can hardly be created in a snow-ball fashion, some setting the example for others to follow. If some have reasons for staying out, this in itself would seem fatal to the whole enterprise. It would give rise to invidious distinctions between those in and those out. Given a history of past miscarriages, what chance is there of the necessary general acceptance? The benefits seem marginal and the costs of failure great: why, then, bother?

The enterprise was made feasible by the coincidence of a variety of situations in different parts of the world, all of which focused attention on the French language and its function as a unifying factor. In the 1960s, in parts of Canada, Europe and Africa, the French language symbolised or expressed the solidarity of groups, for whom an expression of solidarity was of importance. It was relatively easy, in these circumstances, to suggest that all these groups of people, and others making extensive use of the French language, were united by it. This may be questioned, but it was a projection that could be made with some assurance of acceptability.

The French language was a symbol of solidarity in the following situations:

(i) Various francophone minorities in Canada, Belgium, and Switzerland experienced grievances which centred, in one or another, on language.

   (a) Many French Canadians were voicing more and more strongly the view that their language put them at a disadvantage economically and socially compared with English-speaking Canadians. They expressed their resentment at being under very great pressure to make themselves bilingual in order to secure employment even in their own home areas, to the detriment of their own culture and of their separate identity, which they wished to preserve. It was a situation in which they were united by their language, and in defence of it.

   (b) In Belgium, the increasingly rigorous zoning of the country into unilingual areas, with more and more restrictions on the use of French in the areas designated as Flemish-speaking, in public offices, in schools, in offices, in church, after more than a century during which the French lanugage was dominant, had aroused particularly strong protests among the French-speaking population. At a time of economic decline in their own part of the country, these increasing restraints on the use of French in the other parts of the country were particularly galling.

   (c) In the Jura, a district of the largely German-speaking Canton of Bern, a referendum of 1959 had shown a majority of the French-speaking population in the northern part of the district, but not the district as a whole, to be in favour of separation. Agitation for separation has continued ever since, led by the *Rassemblement Jurassien*, with some slight support from other francophone areas of Switzerland.

(ii) In large parts of newly independent Africa, the French language was a factor for unity in a double sense.

   (a) First, it was for each of the former French colonies, and also the former Belgian colonies, the official language, it being the only language common to all who held positions of responsibility. It was the language of wider communication for all the different ethnic/language groups of the country.

(b) Secondly, most of these francophone countries found it expedient, in the 1960s, to work together quite closely in matters of diplomacy, in their association with the EEC, for communications, education, etc. Their reasons for coming together as a group were primarily political and economic but their common use of the French language was itself a contributory factor. It made it easier for ex-Belgian and ex-French colonies to associate together, and indeed it enabled an ex-British colony, Mauritius, to be included.

(iii) The French language, in its role as a language used for international purposes, was losing ground to English in two respects.

(a) International organisations tended, in the immediate post-war period, to rely almost exclusively on English as the working language despite the fact that French was invariably one of the officially recognised working languages.

(b) Much scientific and technological advance was published in English, and the French language was in this respect not keeping up to date.

All these situations, each in its own way, contributed to the idea of an overall francophone solidarity. The francophone minorities counted on a sympathetic hearing throughout *la Francophonie*, and Quebec at least openly and unambiguously identified itself with *la Francophonie* rather than the rest of Canada. The African states sought outside assistance on a grand scale for all sorts of purposes: *la Francophonie* could provide a special relationship between themselves and the richer industrialised francophone countries. The whole of *la Francophonie* had an interest in safeguarding the role of the French language as an international language. In all these situations is found the makings of *la Francophonie*.

La Francophonie and la francité

This combination of circumstances was, however, no more than suggestive. If *la Francophonie* was to take on institutional form and to reach out to all those countries and peoples who might be

classified as francophone, how was this to be done? Can the use
of French, unsupported by any other consideration, provide the
necessary solidarity? One has only to pose the question to realise
that this might not necessarily be sufficient. Might not the
'French-speaking' African countries find it more cogent to discuss
their problems on a Pan-African or Third World basis rather than
in a francophone context? Might not educationalists or journalists
consider their professional interests to be served by international
associations representative of all rather than just francophone
countries? To ask such a question is not to suggest that
'francophone' organisations are necessarily incompatible with
these alternative bases of associations. It is merely to seek
clarification of the term 'francophone' and of the collective nature
of the francophone associations constituting *la Francophonie*.
Reference is made, for this purpose, to yet another term, *la
francité*. It is more abstract, for if *la Francophonie* may be said to
have a spatial connotation – all francophone countries – *la
francité* is, to quote President Senghor, 'a mode of thought and of
action: a certain way of setting out problems and resolving them
... a spiritual community, a *noosphère* encircling the earth'. *La
Francophonie*, Senghor goes on to say, 'is more than the
language, it is French civilisation; more precisely, the spirit of that
civilisation, that is to say, French culture'.[1] Thus conceived *la
Francophonie* has a distinct ethos of its own, with its source in
French culture.

This manner of stating the constituent element or dynamic of *la
Francophonie* calls for some comment. *La Francophonie*
comprises countries and peoples of differing cultures, for whom
la francité can echo all too easily the assimilationist policies or
aspirations of French colonialism – an association of ideas which
turns *la Francophonie* into a form of cultural imperialism, a
surrogate for the old-fashioned Empire. To banish this association
of ideas is not easy. It is the concomitant of the bold claim that
French civilisation and culture has a universal value, from which
all humanity can derive a benefit, not of course by slavish
imitation of French ways, but by creating between French culture
and one's own cultures a symbiotic relationship, in accordance
with the dictum that all civilised peoples have two countries; their
own and France.[2] Let us listen again to Senghor writing about *la
Francophonie*:

It is that integrated humanity which weaves itself round the world; that symbiosis of forces which, lying dormant in all continents and all races, awake to each other's warmth. ... France will have been the leaven producing new life in ancient overseas civilisations, grafted onto the French branch. France will have enabled the Arabs to be more Arab and the Negroes to be more Negro, but their arabism and negritude is, in this second half of the 20th century, opened out.[3]

Horace Walpole has drawn our attention to the poet's awareness of nuance, and one of the politician's arts is the deliberate use of ambiguous language, so we should not be surprised that Senghor ranges freely over the whole range of nuance that unites and divides the twin concepts of *la francité* and *la Francophonie*.[4] There is no clear divide between the one, considered as the expression *par excellence* of universal human values, and the other portrayed as a seed-bed for the symbiotic flowering of diverse cultures. Distinctions only begin to sharpen if *la francité* is limited to the culture of the French-speaking communities of Europe and North America, with its roots in French as a mother tongue or first language, *la Francophonie* being the wider term used to include those of other cultures for whom French is an acquired second language. This is, according to Maurice Peron, a semantic curiosity.[5] Yet it does have the merit of drawing attention to a duality all too easily obscured by the single term *francophone* when it is applied indistinguishably to all who use French either as a first or as a second language. *La Francophonie* cannot adequately be understood except in terms of a state of tension between a core and a periphery.[6] The notion of *la francité* is central and essential to the very conception of *la Francophonie*. But at the periphery it has to contend with alternative cultural identifications such as *africanité* or *arabité*. One's views of *la Francophonie*, and one's degree of identification with it depends upon where one places oneself, at the centre or at the periphery. Those with French as their mother tongue, possibly their sole effective language, will tend to place themselves at the centre. Those who have acquired French as a second language may also be attracted to the centre but they may feel drawn to the periphery by their own cultural antecedents. A convenient shorthand way of referring to this duality is to call the one the central and the other the peripheral point of view.

Organisation

This manner of analysis which allows *la Francophonie* to be seen
in a varying perspective, provides a general context in which to
understand the divergence of views often manifest within *la
Francophonie* on many matters. For example, it helps to explain
the debate which took place in the late 1960s on how *la
Francophonie* should be institutionalised. The spokesmen for the
central point of view were the most ardent advocates of
institutions which would symbolise and promote most effectively
a general sense of solidarity, a shared identity. Those of the
peripheral point of view preferred a more limited and more
selective association of a more strictly functional kind. It was the
former which initially made the running but it was the latter who
easily prevailed. As in a convoy, it was a case of the whole
proceeding at the pace of the slowest.

The initial proposal was made in 1966 in a document
sponsored by the OCAM (Organisation Commune Africaine et
Malgache). The document reveals some of the difficulties.

La Francophonie is defined in ostensive fashion, by reference to
the 'little Francophonie', by which was meant the periodic
meetings that had been taking place at ministerial level between
France and most of the former member states of *La Communauté*.

It was proposed to extend this kind of multilateral organisation
– 'without becoming too juridical' – to all the States making use
of the French language. These are classified in a four-fold fashion:
 (i) States using French and French alone as the national
     language: France and Haiti.
 (ii) States using French as a national language, in addition to
     others: Canada, Belgium, Switzerland and Luxembourg.
 (iii) States using French for official purposes: the 'francophone'
     States of Black Africa and Madagascar.
 (iv) States in which French is in use, although not a national
     language: Lebanon, the Maghreb, Indochina.

Yet the document proposed a three-fold categorisation,
introducing additional criteria such as the historical connection
with France and the undeveloped state of the economy.

Francophonie A would bring together France, the former
territories of French West Africa and French Equatorial Africa
(including Mali, but no mention is made of Guinea), Madagascar,

and, if they so desire, Haiti and the three former Belgian colonies Burundi, Rwanda and the Congo (now Zaire). Their association, on a multilateral basis, would cover 'all aspects of culture' (eg. culture, youth and sport as well as education) and extend to financial and economic matters (eg. training, price stabilisation, industrialisation, trade).

Francophonie B would add Lebanon, the Maghreb and Indochina. (Haiti is also mentioned, despite its inclusion under A.) The reasons given for distinguishing this second category are linguistic and monetary. French is not the national language, nor the official language, and their currencies are not linked with the French franc.

These first two categories are said to be 'very close'. They had shared the same historical experience of coming under French rule. They use the French language in their dealings with each other and are said to react in much the same way in international organisation. They are all economically undeveloped and aware of their common future. They are conceived as overlapping to a very considerable extent, and to require much the same organisation. It is envisaged that this would take the form of:
 (i) regular meetings of:
   (a) Heads of State and of Government.
   (b) Ministers with responsibility for education, youth and culture.
   (c) Ministers of Finance and Economic Affairs.
(ii) a Parliamentary Association.

Francophonie C would add Canada, Belgium, Switzerland and Luxembourg. In this wider arena links would have to be limited to cultural matters, through various specialised organisations.

Bourguiba, Senghor and Diori, the Presidents of Tunisia, Senegal and Niger, were the most prominent advocates of proposals along these lines, and they were backed by spokesmen of a whole variety of francophone associations which mushroomed in the later 1960s to give support. They never made much real headway. The scheme was presented to de Gaulle by Diori but it was never publicly endorsed by the French Government as such, a reticence which no doubt reflected that of other governments and which in turn had its own discouraging effect.

The alternative was to organize on an *ad hoc* joint basis and to build on what already existed in this respect. For example, an *Association des Universités Entièrement ou Partiellement de Langue Française* had been created in 1961, and the *Ministres de l'Education Nationale des Etats d'expression française d'Afrique Noire et de Madagascar* had, since 1961, met in conference twice a year. These two very different bodies demonstrate the advantages of distinguishing the activity and also the level of authority at which the activity takes place (e.g. academic and ministerial). It makes possible the widest possible participation for purposes and at levels which are acceptable, and at the same time allows a limited and indirect identification with *la Francophonie*. It is a manner of organization which can be extended to whatever new activities are thought desirable. For example, an *Association Internationale des Parlementaires de Langue Française* was formed in 1966–67, and a *Conseil Internationale de la Langue Française* in 1967.

The *Agence de Coopération Culturelle et Technique*, established in 1969, is strictly speaking, in this same category of *ad hoc* joint institutions, for its functions are limited and membership is selective in the sense that only two-thirds of the thirty-four countries invited to attend the preparatory conference finally decided to participate. It has, however, symbolic importance, in that it bore special witness to the loftiest of aspirations to be associated with use of the French language, and participation was seen as a test or a measure of a government's identification with *la Francophonie*. This was due to a combination of factors:
  (i) its establishment was the culmination of all the efforts that had been made to rally the 'French-speaking' world in the name of *la Francophonie*;
 (ii) it was established by governments signatory to a convention, amid a great fanfare;
(iii) although its functions are limited, these are in the highly sensitive field of 'cultural and technical co-operation', which would be taken to mean – unless care is taken to state otherwise – the promotion of French culture and French industry.

Thus the statement in the Convention that the signatories recognise in the French language the means whereby peoples of different cultures can arrive at a fuller knowledge of each other's culture and so make a joint contribution to world civilisation (*la civilisation universelle*) – which is an expression of confidence in the French language but not a commitment to French culture – passes muster as a statement of the aims and purposes of *la Francophonie*.

Although the ACCT might be thought thus to epitomise *la Francophonie*, its aims and purposes make it more of an outpost, extending the field of vision in a certain direction, but misleading if taken as the sole or major preoccupation of co-operation among francophone countries.

Even at the level of symbolism, it is questionable whether any particular francophone institution has pre-eminence. The conference of ACCT brings together the largest number of *governments* every two years, but the ministers attending are not the most senior, and delegations are sometimes not even led by ministers. The AUPLF, for its part, brings together the largest number of *participant countries*, around thirty, including parliamentary delegations from Switzerland, Jersey, Monaco, Louisiana and the Seychelles. The highest ranking gathering is that of the French president and some of the African heads of state, who have met twice, in November 1973 and in March 1975. Both meetings could, with some justification, be subsumed under the general rubric of *la Francophonie*, although care was taken, especially at the first, to avoid giving the conference any precise name. The agenda was, on both occasions, primarily concerned with questions of aid and finance. The Middle East was discussed in November 1973 and the conditions of immigrant workers in France in March 1975. The first meeting was attended by ten countries (the heads of state of France, Gabon, Central African Republic, Ivory Coast, Niger, Senegal and Upper Volta; the finance ministers of Congo and Mali; the ministers of foreign affairs of Dahomey and Togo). In 1975, the number had increased to fourteen (Burundi, Gabon, Ivory Coast, Mauritius, Niger, Rwanda, Upper Volta, Senegal, Central African Republic and France, all represented by their heads of state or heads of government; Dahomey, Mali, Togo and Congo by ministers). The prime minister of the Seychelles attended as an observer, and the Somali ambassador to Paris apparently invited himself, but did not stay.

The intention is to hold such meetings annually and to secure wider participation.[6a] President Giscard has since made state visits to both Algeria and Morocco, and it is just possible that on future occasions the Maghreb might be included, but this is doubtful.

Organisationally, *la Francophonie* is a conglomerate of *ad hoc* associations and groupings, heterogeneous both in purpose and in membership. The range and level of participation is variable for each and every country. Some countries, such as Algeria and Vietnam, abstain completely, prefering bilateral relations, which strictly speaking puts them outside *la Francophonie*, this being characteristically multilateral in its conception and organisation. Yet one might question whether they are any less francophone than some other countries present in virtually every francophone organisation. There are certainly more French-speaking Algerians, whatever that may mean in terms of competence in the language and the occasions for its use, than there are, for example, French-speaking inhabitants of Niger. None the less, Algeria does not consider itself part of *la Francophonie* whereas Niger is unquestionably deemed to be so. It is one of the great merits of the manner in which *la Francophonie* is organised that it permits such subtleties. The term itself is a sort of umbrella; a rather indeterminate generic term that can be used to refer, in a collective fashion, to whatever francophone organisations exist, and perhaps even to bilateral links between francophone countries. One might even say that there is a multilateral superstructure underpinned by an infrastructure of bilateral relations.

Education and language policy

A central and peripheral point of view is discernible not only in matters of organisation. It is manifest also on questions of educational and language policy, especially in the francophone states of Africa. They have long been dissatisfied with their inappropriate and ineffective educational systems. There are parellels elsewhere, in anglophone African states, but the problems are held to be particularly acute in the francophone countries, because of the reliance upon French as the sole language of instruction and the exclusion of African languages from the curriculum. This has been criticised on psychological, pedagogical and cultural grounds. The school is seen as an alien institution which divorces the child from the native environment and for no good purpose. The percentage of those finishing primary school is rarely higher than 40 per cent, the percentage entering secondary school is much less, and the number who complete secondary school education with the baccalauréat is invariably less than 5 per cent of those who had once started primary school. The majority are said to leave school frustrated; whatever knowledge they may have acquired tends to be bookish and of little practical use; their minds are often turned to mere mimicry; even their knowledge of language is little advanced because most of them soon revert to illiteracy. The indictment is severe but largely justified by the facts, even if the belief that the key to improvement lies in the use of the mother-tongue as the language of instruction is exaggerated.

These arguments in the field of education have broadened out into advocacy of the use of the African mother-tongues for a whole range of other purposes and to the suggestion that French should be relegated to being a foreign language, possibly on a par with other foreign languages. Such proposals strike at the very heart of *la Francophonie*. It is one matter to use the mother-tongues in school, for it can quite easily be argued that this facilitates the learning of French – and if the official language and the language of social advancement remains French it will be learnt. It is quite another matter to promote the mother-tongues out of school; in offices, in workshops, in the cinema and on television, in the press and for publishing generally; this would indeed reduce French to a foreign language, necessary only for external communication. This situation, accepted perhaps as inevitable in North Africa and Indochina, is still considered by many as unrealistic, even undesirable, for most of Black Africa. One basic argument is considered as decisive: a selection among the mother-tongues would need to be made if costs, to the individual and to the society at large, were not to be excessive, and any such selection might easily impair both national unity and inter-African communication. None the less it is a policy that finds strong support at the periphery of *la Francophonie*, while the centre manifests considerable scepticism. For the moment, only skirmishing is taking place.[7] The mother-tongues need to be codified and amplified, then their use in written form learnt and encouraged. Moreover, the skirmishing takes place behind a smoke screen conveniently provided by the term 'bilingualism'.

At the periphery bilingualism is taken to mean that virtually the sole function of the French language will be communication and exchange with the external world, in a two way direction; to inform the outside world of the homegrown culture etc. and to receive from the outside world knowledge of other cultures and technologies, etc. The central point of view envisages that French would have, in addition to this role of external communication, an internal function; for instance, it would remain the main language of work in all those spheres of activity in which dependence on inputs from abroad (eg. technological transfer, consultants) is thought likely to continue for a long time ahead. The mother-tongues would be used in all other activities, especially those which express the inner personality and the cultural tradition of the country.[8]

The present pattern of language use is strongly in favour of the centre. Some active steps are being taken here and there to use some of the mother-tongues in the first two or three years of primary school. A few plays and novels are appearing, despite the difficulty of finding publishers. It is the beginning of a change, but whether it will stop at the point of an internal bilingualism, or proceed beyond that point to a radical revision of the functions of the French language in these African countries, is pure speculation and is scarcely anywhere a practical issue at the present moment.

Conclusion

Let it be emphasised in conclusion, that the central and peripheral aspects of *la Francophonie* are inseparable, like the positive and negative poles of a battery. Without the centre nothing holds; without the periphery nothing flows. Nor is it possible to label particular countries or sociological groups as wholly central or wholly peripheral in their attitudes. It is a matter of degree. For example, there are important nuances in the policies of 'arabisation' practised in the Maghreb. Each country has its own policy and it is subject to revision from time to time. In Madagascar also there are diverse tendencies; the policy of 'malgachisation' has had its ebbs and flows and has still to prove itself. One cannot take as a guide a country's presence or absence on some *francophone* occasion, as this may be a temporary expedient or passing humour. There are also difficulties in taking a country's leaders as authorities in this matter: their pronouncements may be special pleading, and they may be of an older generation that is no longer strictly representative. The parameters of *la Francophonie* are like shifting sands. They cannot be mapped with any great assurance. But the sand is there and it stretches quite a long way both in space and time.

NOTES

1. Speech at Laval University, Quebec, September 1966. See *Études Littéraires* (Presses de l'Université de Laval) 1968 p. 131.
2. A doctrine recently quoted with approval by Mr Michael Foot, despite his dislike of the European Community (*The Times*, March 30, 1976). Could there be any better refutation of cultural imperialism?
3. *Culture Française* No. 2, 1964.
4. Their usage and its evolution have been examined by Maurice Peron in a communication to the Bruxelles Académie Royale de Langue et de Littérature Françaises. Séance extraordinaire du 21 Octobre 1970.
5. *Op. cit.* p. 15 footnote.
6. I am indebted for this terminology to I. Wallerstein's analysis of Panafricanism. See his *Africa: the politics of unity*, New York. Random House 1967.
6a. This has come about. Regular annual meetings have come to be attended by as many as twenty countries, including ex-Portuguese colonies (and, in 1979, even Liberia). At what point does *la Francophonie* burst the seams? When simultaneous translation begins to be required?
7. Except in Madagascar, which is blessed with a single language (albeit several dialects of it) which is in use in primary school, in the press, in church and in the administration to some extent, especially since the change of regime in 1972. In this respect it is more akin to Indochina and North Africa.
8. For a fuller analysis of 'bilingualism' in North Africa and its relation to social class, see Christiane Souriau's contribution to this volume.

IV

INTERNATIONAL RELATIONS

15

Bilateral relations and world diplomacy: Franco-African relations on trial at the UN

Marie-Claude Smouts

One of the results of the independence treaties and co-operation agreements signed by France and its former colonies in Africa and Madagascar between 1958 and 1963 was that relations between the ex-colonial power and the new states evolved along basically bilateral lines. By means of such bilateral agreements, a very close-knit network of contractual ties was built up between France and each of these states, ranging over wide areas of public life and in places over areas of governmental activity as vastly different as the Post Office and defence. As regards foreign policy, the agreements signed in 1960 with the six member states of the 'revived' Community[1] stipulated that all parties to the agreements should hold regular consultations in order to 'compare points of view and endeavour to align positions and activities before taking any major decision'. The agreements concluded with the Entente states[2] and with Cameroun, Mauritania and Togo, although worded in less exacting terms, were also intended to promote agreement and close co-operation in diplomatic affairs.

Once the Community had gone out of existence, co-operative activities between the French government and the Francophone African leaders no longer had an institutional framework within which to operate, no system of regular meetings providing a forum for exchanges of information and opinions was organised. Although the Africans, in particular Senegal, often expressed regret that a 'Commonwealth à la française' had never actually been developed, on the whole the parties concerned did not seem until recently, to resent this lack of formal machinery.[3] Information exchanges and foreign policy consultations were based solely on bilateral negotiation and took place through the usual diplomatic channels – embassies, missions and visits by heads of state; and the personal tone of these consultations was reinforced by the relations that the Elysée and the General Secretariat for African Affairs maintained with the cabinets of African heads of state.

In addition to direct bilateral contacts of this kind, a permanent framework for multilateral discussions was provided by the United Nations. Probably the UN's most important function is to provide a forum for all its members. Conference diplomacy at the UN goes hand in hand with the tactic of relying on delegations with whom one is on friendly terms to obtain information or influence decisions. The communications system at the UN between France and the Francophone African states has the reputation of being very good: although France declined to participate in the Decolonisation Committee, it was very well aware of what went on there, just as it knew what took place in discussions among the African delegations. Through its network of friendly relations with delegations and with French-speaking African officials at the Secretariat, the French permanent mission is able to keep abreast of all major developments among the Third World delegations which now constitute a majority at the UN. France is very anxious not to be branded as neo-colonialist and for this reason has not tried to create any institutional framework to express the sympathies arising from Francophonie, the common cultural background or the shared history. Rather, it has chosen more subtle, yet well considered, methods. France's permanent representatives at the UN personally attend to relations with their African counterparts. One member of the permanent mission is a specialist in matters connected with the IVth Committee[4] and has the special responsibility of maintaining relations with the African delegations. Other members of the mission whose function it is to maintain contacts with the UN Secretariat or press attachés can also contribute towards maintaining the very intimate consultations characteristic of Franco-African relations in the Organisation.

In this way the Francophone African states are able to gain

access to information on and elucidation of French policy, on the making of which they themselves, despite the 1960 agreements, are scarcely consulted. France in its turn has access to information enabling it to estimate how much support it commands and what the consequences of taking a particular course of action will be. The main role of contacts between states at UN level, however, relates to the day-to-day business of UN debates and votes; these contacts can hardly achieve any real change in policies, nor can they counterbalance the centrifugal effects of developments on the international scene.

Conflicting Loyalties

Several factors have been responsible for changes in France's political and economic relations with its former African colonies (including Madagascar). The association of these countries with the EEC and the aid and co-operation given by other Western countries have cut into the direct bilateral relationship established in the early plans of French co-operation. Aspirations towards national independence, together with internal unrest (in Madagascar, Chad, Dahomey etc.), have also altered this relationship to a certain extent and attitudes and behaviour at the UN cannot help being affected by these developments. But the UN also imposes particular constraints and conditions of its own, in that it forces states to make choices between loyalties that are sometimes incompatible and also forces imprecise aspirations and pipe-dreams to be reformulated as explicit policies or goals.

Early studies investigating the behaviour of the new states at the UN draw attention to the distinctive features of the 'Brazzaville group',[5] a dynamic, influential group of states which, although not blindly Francophile as they were unfairly labelled by the 'progressive' states, nevertheless adopted positions very close to those held by the French, even in matters as crucial to the Third World as the Algerian conflict or events in the Congo. Consequently there were times in the immediate post-colonial years when this solidarity almost caused the Francophone states of the Sub-Sahara and the former North African protectorates to come to blows. In October 1961, for example, the Francophone states refused to associate themselves with a resolution acclaiming the success of an initiative taken by Morocco in 1959 and supported by Tunisia, which proposed that Africa should be regarded as a 'denuclearised zone' and that France should be censored for conducting nuclear tests in the Sahara.[6]

Shortly before, in July 1961, the Bizerte crisis illustrated the difficult position that pro-French African states could find themselves in when they were forced to choose between conflicting loyalties. After French parachutists were sent to the French base at Bizerte on 19 July 1961 (the French government's response to Bourguiba's speech of 5 July and his attempts to paralyze the base by staging popular demonstrations), there was an outbreak of incidents involving bloodshed. Tunisia broke off diplomatic relations with France and referred the matter to the Security Council. France refused to participate in the vote taken on 22 July to demand a cease-fire, and later on declined to have anything to do with the Council discussions. The countries of the Brazzaville group were aware of France's concern not to introduce a multilateral dimension into the issue which it wished to resolve bilaterally with Tunisia and therefore they supported France at first. Mr. Senghor and Mr. Houphouët-Boigny tried to convince the Afro-Asian states that this crisis would be better resolved by bilateral negotiations than if it were brought before the UN. When Tunisia tried to convene a special General Assembly meeting, the only Brazzaville group states among the total of thirty-eight that supported this initiative were Upper Volta and Togo, and it was only thanks to Latin American votes that enough supporting votes were cast to form a quorum. Although this constituted a diplomatic victory for Tunisia, it was a very narrow one without support from the Francophone Africans who resisted the many pressures imposed on them and demonstrated their allegiance to France. When the question came to be discussed in greater depth, however, the Brazzaville group associated themselves with a resolution declaring 'Tunisia's sovereign right to demand the withdrawal of all armed forces present on its territory without its consent'[7] and supported Tunisia's demands.[8] The Ivory Coast and Niger were absent.

On this occasion it was obvious that there was a limit to the extent to which the African states and Madagascar were prepared to support France. On the one hand, these states are willing to give their support to France whenever it is trying to avoid diplomatic defeat and UN intervention, by making behind-the-scenes efforts to prevent a particular question coming up for discussion. But once any problem concerning decolonisation has been brought before the UN despite their efforts, then considerations such as the wish to assert their independence, African solidarity and actual basic policy differences with France all lead them to align themselves with the majority vote. If pressure from France is too great and the choice to be made is potentially too costly, then absenteeism is always a possible expedient.

This behaviour pattern could be witnessed when the case of the last French colonies, i.e. the Comoro Islands and the French Somali Coast, came before the UN. Thanks to support from within the UN Secretariat and the activities of Ivory Coast and Madagascar in the Decolonisation Committee, France was able, until 1972, to block the addition of the Comoro Islands to the list of territories falling within the scope of the Declaration on the granting of independence to colonial countries and peoples. On 16 August 1973, in the absence of Ivory Coast and without taking the matter to the vote, the Special Committee adopted a draft resolution in which it reaffirmed 'the inalienable right of the people of the Comoro Archipelago to self-determination and independence', requested France to take all measures necessary to this end and emphatically asserted 'the national unity and territorial integrity of the Archipelago'.[9] Ivory Coast subsequently stated that, had it been present, its delegation would have abstained on account of 'serious reservations', but the file had been badly presented and it was too late. When the draft was submitted to the General Assembly, all the African states voted in support of the resolution except for Gabon which abstained, as did the United States, Japan, South Africa and Western Europe.[10]

Likewise in 1975 France was no longer able to use delaying tactics to prevent the question of the French Somali Coast from coming under scrutiny at the General Assembly. Since 1968 the delegations of Francophone Africa had managed to maintain some degree of consensus among the Afro-Asians not to obstruct France's path and to make the General Assembly adopt a resolution every year postponing any discussion of the question until the following session. The composition of the group of African countries which were parties to the resolution adopted by the IVth Commission on 5 December 1975 is an indication of the precarious position of French attitudes and the dwindling number of African delegations in a position to support them. Of the eleven African states that proposed the resolution, seven were former French colonies and three had long been considered as belonging to the groups of 'friendly delegations'. Benin, Madagascar and Togo joined Algeria, the Congo, Guinea and the Comoros in demanding the withdrawal of all military forces from the 'so-called French Somali Coast' and in criticizing French administration in this territory.[11] Although this resolution was also a criticism of Ethiopia, the only state which voted against it, it was first and foremost an indictment of France. It was carried by ninety-four votes to one with twenty-seven abstentions which included Gabon and Malawi, the only African states at the IVth Commission who disassociated themselves from the motion. At the Plenary Assembly, on the other hand, the resolution demanding that France grant immediate and unconditional independence to the territory of the Affars and Issars was adopted by 109 votes to nil with twenty abstentions. All the African states declared themselves in favour.[12]

If one takes only numbers of votes and quantitative results into account, one is forced to admit to France's growing isolation and dwindling influence at the UN. Feelings of solidarity with Africa, the non-aligned nations and the Third World usually win the day over links or sympathies with the ex-colonial power. For example, when France opposed the 'Declaration proposing to make a peace zone of the Indian Ocean'[13] and abstained from voting on resolutions on this issue, a large proportion of the Francophone African states and Madagascar initially adopted this position too. In 1971 Ivory Coast, Dahomey, Upper Volta, the Central African Republic and Senegal, and Zaire, Lesotho and Rwanda were conspicuous by being the only African states not to support the draft. By 1973 only the Central African Republic and Malawi were left. In 1974 all the African states voted in favour of the Declaration.[14] Thus we can see that even on an issue of no immediate interest to them, states which initially took notice of French arguments ended up by giving way to pressure from non-aligned states in spite of these arguments.

As these few examples show, states linked with France by co-operative agreements are now proving their autonomy at the UN. More often than not they cast their votes differently from France and whenever they define their positions on particular issues they also take account of other loyalties which compete with their friendship with France. This lack of convergence with France is evident in the vote taken on the resolution of 10 November 1975 branding Zionism 'a form of racism and racial discrimination'. On this question – so serious, not only in its political and moral implications but also with regard to its possible repercussions on the life of the UN – only two ex-French African states voted with France against the Resolution. Three abstained and all the others showed solidarity with the Arab nations.[15]

These few observations, however, cannot give a true or complete picture of diplomatic life at the UN, nor of the realities of foreign policy-making. First and foremost, it must be emphasized that the pattern of voting at the UN does not necessarily reflect actual foreign policy directly, for the UN imposes its own unique code of conduct. Thus the great powers are very familiar with the situation where states which are their allies often cast their vote differently from them at the UN, explaining that they could not do otherwise. Consequently the climate of feeling preceding and surrounding a vote may be just as important as the vote itself in determining the strength of alliances. Thus we find that the Francophone African states seem to show their support for France by creating and fostering friendly feelings towards her at the UN. At least, this must be the case, for how else can one explain France's rather paradoxical position at the UN, namely, its growing isolation on the one hand, and its great prestige (as reported by observers) on the other?

Test of Allegiance

There are a number of influential delegations at the UN which take it upon themselves to rally round France whenever it finds itself in difficulty. Thanks to this support France was able to escape outright condemnation in 1972 for the nuclear tests which it was conducting. The matter was taken to the vote in a very sensitive situation indeed. The seventh French nuclear testing campaign had caused a major rift in France's relations with Australia and New Zealand and also resulted in the breaking-off of diplomatic relations with Peru. The matter was brought to the attention of the International Court of Justice in May of that year and the Court announced that France had been violating a number of conservation measures. Public opinion was awakened and alarmed in many countries, and France's position in the South Pacific was called into question. It should be mentioned here that this was the year in which the General Assembly for the first time affirmed the right of the New Hebrides to independence, in a resolution combining the problems of decolonisation with the problems connected with nuclear tests.[16] In spite of the very tense atmosphere, the feverish efforts made by the French permanent mission to avoid a crushing defeat were successful, in the sense that the resolutions adopted on 6 December 1973 were passed by a smaller margin than those adopted on the same issue the previous year. One resolution consisted of a renewed condemnation of all nuclear tests,[17] and another, which was aimed at France in particular, urged that states possessing nuclear arms and conducting tests in the atmosphere should put a stop to all such tests at once.[18] This text was adopted with only sixty-five votes for, seven against and fifty-seven abstentions. This large percentage of abstentions, which included all the Arab and African states, constituted a real victory for France. It is more than likely than the back-stage activities of certain African delegations were largely responsible for the fact that France did not suffer an altogether negative vote; for hitherto, although resolutions condemning nuclear testing had become increasingly denunciatory, containing vehement demands for the cessation of tests in the atmosphere, the African states had not come to France's support. They had simply not attended discussions on the subject, though this was more out of a lack of interest than because of any embarrassment. In 1972 when France, which had hitherto abstained, voted against resolutions directly attacking its activities,[19] the pattern of voting was the same as in previous sessions (i.e. Senegal and Ivory Coast voting in support of the resolution, Dahomey and Gabon absent). At the XXVIIIth session the pattern changed so that France would not suffer too great a diplomatic defeat – for the first time African countries voted on France's side, against resolutions on the subject of nuclear tests. Gabon voted against the first resolution and Gabon and Senegal voted against the second one. At the second session, when the crisis was already past its critical point, the African states fell back into their old ways, i.e. a mixture of absenteeism and voting in favour of resolutions framed in the most general of terms.[20]

A contributory factor in France's success in minimising its diplomatic losses on this occasion was undoubtedly the fact that its nuclear tests did not affect the African and Arab states directly and that they did not present a threat to the two principles which are the cement of African unity: decolonisation and anti-apartheid feeling.

By protesting its hostility in principle to the policy of apartheid, though without respecting the UN embargo on arms to South Africa, and by giving priority to the principle of non-interference in domestic affairs over the principle of self-determination in the Portuguese colonies, France was very sorely trying the patience and friendship of the African delegations.

The African delegations unanimously supported the General Assembly and Security Council resolutions providing for measures to compel South Africa to give up its apartheid policy – except for Ivory Coast which openly advocated a policy of negotiations and called for the initiation of a dialogue with South Africa.[21] It questioned the efficacy of measures adopted by the UN, pointing out on the one hand that the proposed sanctions were not practicable because 'the considerable arsenal in the possession of the minority racist regime makes it impossible to take up arms against South Africa', and on the other that the futility of the UN's threats were proof that a more fruitful policy would be to use more tolerant language and attempt to initiate a dialogue.[22] It would be a mistake to view this policy, which ran completely against the grain of the Organisation of African Unity and was supported only by Ivory Coast and Gabon, as simply the result of pressure from the French government.[23] However, this call for talks from such an influential African government came just in the nick of time for France, whose arms sales to South Africa were coming under heavy criticism just then; for France was finding them difficult to justify, since the Africans were totally unconvinced by the distinction made by the French delegation between 'arms intended for use in external defence and arms likely to be used in the implementation of the apartheid policy'.[24]

The fact that French and Ivory Coast interests coincided at this point did not stop Ivory Coast from often proposing, and always voting, with all the other Francophone African states, in favour of General Assembly resolutions 'condemning the situation created by the breaking of the arms embargo imposed by Security Council resolutions'. With the exception of Lesotho and Malawi, all the African states voted in favour of resolutions condemning the actions of states 'which continue to collaborate with the South African régime in the political, military, economic and other spheres'[25] even when explicit reference was made to France and Great Britain.[26]

In August 1975 Valéry Giscard d'Estaing attempted to allay the ever-growing criticism of the African states incurred by French policy in South Africa. He delivered a rather dramatic speech in Zaire to the effect that France had decided to cut down its arms sales to South Africa. This tactical move was interpreted as a gesture of goodwill but of little significance. Even Mr. Sauvagnargues referred to it only fleetingly in his speech at the XXIXth session of the General Assembly: in the fifteen-odd lines devoted to that 'major problem area', Southern Africa, it took him only two lines to say, 'France's categorical condemnation of racial discrimination has recently led the President of the French Republic to define France's policy on arms sales to South Africa in the most restrictive of terms'.[27]

The sharpest critics of France were the English-speaking African states rather than France's own former colonies, who only made a general criticism of all states collaborating with South Africa and refrained from singling out France in particular. France was condemned along with the United States, Great Britain and West Germany, but none of the Francophone states of Guinea, Algeria, or Mali passed such a severe judgment as Zambia which stated 'France has blatantly defied the Council resolutions', or Sierre Leone, which said 'certain members of the Council are guilty and of all these France is the guiltiest'.[28] Although one would need to carry out a very detailed anal, is to be quite sure of the facts, it does seem that French policy on arms sales was not as heavily criticized as British or American policies, which is an indication of the respect France enjoys at the UN. The agreements linking it with its former colonies and the economic pressure that France is capable of bringing to bear on them, however, cannot fully explain why France enjoys such a position of prestige among the Third World nations. The links that were established in 1960 now exist only with a small number of states, and the nature of these links has changed in the wake of domestic developments, e.g. in Mauritania, Congo, Madagascar and ex-Dahomey. These countries are now giving modest evidence of their independence at the UN in foreign policy-making. The Claustre affair caused a short-lived, though serious, crisis with Chad, and in October 1975 France only just succeeded in preventing the submission of an African resolution condemning French interference in Chad's internal affairs.[29]

From a quantitative point of view, France can now rely on a mere six or seven states.[30] It must be borne in mind, however, that these states belong traditionally to the group of 'moderate' states which are often in the majority at the OAU, and that they also were part of the group of 'twenty-two' at the extraordinary summit of the OAU which refused to recognise the People's Republic of Angola. This prompted criticism such as that 'France has pulled neo-colonial strings in its client states'.[31] It also means, however, that Francophone African states are not in isolation, but are part of an important group of states whose foreign policy is similar to France's in certain ways.

Viewed from another angle, the warm feelings shown towards France by a number of African states are echoed by the Afro-Asian group in areas where French co-operation fits into a wider policy framework. Ever since 1973 Arab influence over the non-aligned group has been on the increase, and France's pro-Arab policy, followed since 1967, has been consolidated under the presidency of Giscard d'Estaing and is still regarded as fruitful despite the fact that it sometimes runs contrary to the basic principles of the new nations. This was evident in the general mood created by the speeches in the Security Council on the Mayotte affair or the Loyada incidents, on which occasion the Comoro representative was heard to say that France had 'spread its democratic ideals' and the Benin representative described how he had sought to find a good justification for France's behaviour, for France was otherwise well-known as a champion of decolonisation.[32] Surprisingly, given the fact that Tanzania was France's chief opponent in the Decolonisation Committee, the Tanzanian representative requested that the Loyada incidents should not be used to trigger off any Council discussions on the decolonisation problems of the Somali Coast.[33]

The fact that the talks could be held in a relatively disaster-free atmosphere was largely due to the skill of the French representative and the good relations which Mr. de Guiringaud succeeded in maintaining with Third World delegations. These good relations, however, could only be maintained because France is still living off capital which it amassed in the 1960s. There is still quite a strong current of sympathy with France which feeds off old memories and factors such as decolonisation in Africa, the memory of General de Gaulle, attitudes adopted during the Vietnam War and demands for national independence tinged with anti-American feeling – all providing nourishment for this sympathetic tide of feeling which could easily be given new impetus if France were to foster attitudes in favour of the 'new world economic order'.

A Second Independence

Membership of multilateral organizations has greatly helped the previously colonised countries to give a definite shape to their pipe-dreams and hopes for 'a second independence' in the economic sphere, and questions raised on a multilateral level have given a boost to bilateral co-operation.

When the first major resolution on permanent sovereignty over natural resources was adopted in 1962, the Francophone African countries played a contributory part in the rejection of a Soviet amendment which laid down that 'the Assembly give its full support to any measures that peoples and states may take to establish or consolidate their sovereignty over natural riches and resources and deem inadmissable any acts aimed at impeding the practice, protection and consolidation of such sovereignty'.[34]

In 1974, however, they voted overwhelmingly in favour of the Charter of Economic Rights and Duties of States and adopted the Declaration and Programme of Action setting forth in equally emphatic terms the principles of a new international economic order.[35] For a number of years now, the positions which the African countries have adopted in discussions on economic and financial questions between themselves and France have been strikingly close to those held on the multilateral level by the Group of 77.[36] In their speeches at the UN they adopt the same tone and address themselves to the same questions as this group, to which they belong and with which they are in complete solidarity. For instance, the Ivory Coast representative talked about 'scandalous conditions in the pricing of our natural resources',[37] and the Senegal delegate expressed his opinion that 'the rapid industrialisation of the developed countries was achieved only by the exploitation at very low cost of raw materials which were and still are in the hands of the Third World'.[38] The Gabon delegate, too, made a speech which was very critical of the industrialized powers. All the Africans demand security for the revenue accruing from the export of primary products, agreements on basic products and provisions on technical and financial matters. They all feel that the assistance given is 'inadequate' and 'misdirected' and that the problem of technical co-operation needs to be thoroughly reexamined.

Mention is seldom made of the two initiatives taken by France: in 1974 it convened a conference on energy and in 1975 one between producers and consumers. As regards the former, Dahomey declared 'We as a Third World nation find our bearings more easily with the lead from the Algerian head of state who preferred an international meeting on a more general topic'[39] and as regards the second initiative, Senegal was the only country to express satisfaction that 'the President of the French Republic took the wise step of convening a conference which brought producer and consumer countries together for the purpose of jointly examining these problems'.[40]

The French government's policy of equilibrium, which keeps a few steps ahead of its European counterparts and lags a few steps behind the demands of the developing countries, is clearly reflected in Mr. de Guiringaud's speech at the sixth extraordinary meeting.[41] On the subjects of nationalisation and producers' associations he spoke more comprehensively than his German counterpart who was representing the EEC, whereas he was more restrained than some of the Third World delegations. Feelings among the Francophone African states were divided on these two subjects – Dahomey (and Madagascar) praised the organisation of producer countries, while Senegal, Gabon and Ivory Coast had little to say on the matter.

The Abelin report, which was presented in September 1975, discusses what conclusions may be drawn from this development which has led to the incorporation of problems of co-operation with African states within a more 'general policy framework of relations between industrialised nations and developing countries'. Whereas close ties with Francophone Africa were usually a sufficient basis for the implementation of a general Third World policy in the 1960s, this is no longer the case. Now it is only by seeking to foster new kinds of relationships between industrialised and developing countries that France will be able to consolidate the economic and cultural sphere of influence which it has managed to retain in Africa south of the Sahara.

NOTES

1. Central African Republic, Congo, Gabon, Madagascar, Senegal, Chad.
2. Ivory Coast, Dahomey, Upper Volta, Niger.
3. The communiqué published on 8 March 1975 at the close of the Franco-African 'summit' in Bangui laid down the following: 'the heads of state and delegation leaders have decided to give the Franco-African conference the status of a permanent institution. The principle of an annual conference meeting has been adopted'. The principle was put into practice and the participants in the Franco-African conference held in May 1976 in Paris decided to meet in 1977 in Dakar.
4. I.e., The Fourth Committee (on Trusteeship, including non-selfgoverning territories) which deals with all matters relating to decolonisation.
5. Born of 'the united nature of the group's attitudes on major issues such as the Algerian war and the Congo crisis, positions defined during a conference held in Congo-Brazzaville in December 1960'. Mirlande Hippolyte, *Les Etats du groupe de Brazzaville aux Nations Unies*, Paris, Armand Colin, 1970, p. 9. The group consists of the following states: Congo-Brazzaville, Cameroun, Ivory Coast, Dahomey, Gabon, Upper Volta, Madagascar, Niger, Central African Republic, Senegal, Chad, Mauritania. Togo joined in 1963.
6. Res. 1652 (XVI) adopted by 55 votes to nil with 44 abstentions. The draft had been submitted by 14 African states including Morocco, Tunisia and Togo. At the time Togo had not yet concluded the co-operation agreements with France and did not belong to the Brazzaville group. All members of the group abstained, Dahomey was absent, and France did not vote.
7. Res. 1622 (S-III) of 25 August 1961 adopted by 66 votes to nil with 30 abstentions. France did not cast her vote. Among the countries that voted in favour of the resolution were: Cameroun, Central African Republic, Chad, Congo-Brazzaville, Dahomey, Gabon, Madagascar, Senegal, Togo and Upper Volta. Niger was absent, but later made it known that it wished to be included with the countries that abstained.
8. Cf Senegal's intervention, A/PV, 997th meeting, 21 August 1961, requesting the initiation of negotiations concerning the drawing up of a

timetable for France's withdrawal from Bizerte in accordance with the wishes of the Tunisian people.

9. Official Documents of the General Assembly, XVIII session, supplement 23. A/9023 Rev. 1, Ch. XI.

10. Res. 3161 (XXVIII), 14 December 1973, adopted by 110 votes to nil with 18 abstentions. France did not vote.

11. The four other states were: Equatorial Guinea, Guinea Bissau, Tanzania and Sierra Leone.

12. A/PV, 2437th meeting. France did not take part in the voting.

13. Draft put on the agenda of the XXVIth meeting at the request of Ceylon and Tanzania. Resolution presented on 30 November 1971 by Ceylon, Iraq, Iran, Kenya, Uganda, Tanzania, Somalia, Yemen, Zambia, India and Yugoslavia.

14. Development of voting pattern on the issue: Res. 2832 (XXVI), 16 December 1971: 61 votes to nil and 55 abstentions; Res. 3080 (XXVIII), 6 December 1973: 95 votes to nil and 35 abstentions; Res. 3259 (XXIX), 9 December 1974: 103 votes to nil and 26 abstentions (the NATO countries, Austria, Israel, Cuba, Eastern Europe excluding Rumania).

15. Resolution passed by 72 votes to 35, with 32 abstentions. African states that voted against were the Central African Republic, Ivory Coast, Liberia, Malawi and Swaziland. African states that abstained: Gabon, Upper Volta, Togo, Botswana, Ethiopia, Ghana, Kenya, Lesotho, Sierra Leone, Zaire, Zambia.

16. Res. 3156 (XXVII), 14 December 1973. The resolution simultaneously confirms the right of the New Hebrides and seven other territories to independence and self-determination and, in paragraph II, requests the governing powers to 'refrain from carrying out any more atmospheric nuclear tests in the South Pacific zone.' All the African countries, except for the Central African Republic which abstained, voted in favour of this resolution, carried by 106 votes to 4 (France, Portugal, S. Africa and Great Britain) with 18 abstentions.

17. Res. 3078 A (XXVIII), 6 December 1973: 89 votes for, 5 against (China, Albania, France, Gabon, Portugal), 33 abstentions including the Central African Republic.

18. Res. 3078 B, 6 December 1973.

19. Res. 2934 (XXVII), 29 November 1972. The Assembly once again emphasizes the urgency of putting an end to all nuclear tests 'in the Pacific and everywhere in the world' (105 votes to 4, 9 abstentions). Res. 2934 C (XXVII) fixed a deadline (5 August 1973) for the cessation of all tests (80 votes to 4, 29 abstentions including Madagascar and Togo).

20. Res. 3257, 9 December 1974, condemning all nuclear tests, regardless of where they are carried out, was adopted by 95 votes to 3 (France, China, Albania) with 33 abstentions (including Madagascar, the Central African Republic and the Congo, the last probably out of solidarity with China rather than with France).

21. Special Political Committee, 662nd meeting, 24th session, 13 November 1969.

22. Idem, 820th meeting, 23 October 1972; 828th meeting, 1 November 1972.

23. Cf the analysis by Tatiana Yannopoulos and Denis Martin, 'L'unité africaine face au pouvoir blanc', *L'Univers politique*, 1971, pp. 267–295.
24. Cf Mr. Claude Chayet's statements to the Security Council, 21 July 1970 – S/PV 1547.
25. Res. 3151 G (XXVIII), 14 December 1973, adopted by 88 votes to 7 with 28 abstentions, was particularly 'hard line'.
26. Cf Res. 3324 E (XXIX), 16 December 1974, condemning 'the activities of states and foreign economic interests which persist in collaborating with the South African regime, appeals to the French and British governments to put a stop to all military collaboration with South Africa'.
27. A/PV 2364, p. 21, 26 September 1975.
28. Security Council, 17 July 1970, S/PV 1542.
29. Mr. Sauvagnargues' statement to France-Inter on 13 October 1975 – programme '13–14'.
30. Cameroun, Ivory Coast, Gabon, Upper Volta, Central African Republic, Senegal, Togo.
31. *Afrique–Asie* 26 January – 8 February 1976, p. 10.
32. 5 February 1976, S/PV 1887.
33. 18 February 1976, S/PV 1889. 'I request the Somali representative not to make use of the Council to go into the details of the conditions that prevail in the French Somali Coast, for we do not intend to discuss the decolonization of the Somali Coast in the Council.'
34. Para. 5 of Res. 1803 (XVII) of 14 December 1962, rejected by 41 votes to 38 with 15 abstentions, 6 of which were French-speaking African countries.
35. The Charter of Economic Rights and Duties (Res. 3281-XXIX) was adopted by 120 votes to 6 with 10 abstentions (including France). The Declaration and Programme of Action were adopted without a vote.
36. Cf Amadou Seydou, 'For a critique of co-operation', *Revue française d'études politiques africaines*, No. 48, December 1969, pp. 64–72.
37. Sixth extraordinary meeting of the General Assembly, A/PV 2212.
38. Idem. A/PV 2211.
39. Idem. A/PV 2214.
40. Seventh extraordinary meeting of the General Assembly, A/PV 2339.
41. Sixth extraordinary meeting of the General Assembly, A/PV 2229.

Index